Performance Solutions

The Addison-Wesley Object Technology Series

Grady Booch, Ivar Jacobson, and James Rumbaugh, Series Editors
For more information, check out the series Web site [http://www.awl.com/cseng/otseries/].

Armour/Miller, *Advanced Use Case Modeling: Software Systems*

Binder, *Testing Object-Oriented Systems: Models, Patterns, and Tools*

Blakley, *CORBA Security: An Introduction to Safe Computing with Objects*

Booch, *Object Solutions: Managing the Object-Oriented Project*

Booch, *Object-Oriented Analysis and Design with Applications, Second Edition*

Booch/Rumbaugh/Jacobson, *The Unified Modeling Language User Guide*

Box/Brown/Ewald/Sells, *Effective COM: 50 Ways to Improve Your COM and MTS-based Applications*

Carlson, *Modeling XML Applications with UML: Practical e-Business Applications*

Cockburn, *Surviving Object-Oriented Projects: A Manager's Guide*

Collins, *Designing Object-Oriented User Interfaces*

Conallen, *Building Web Applications with UML*

D'Souza/Wills, *Objects, Components, and Frameworks with UML: The Catalysis Approach*

Douglass, *Doing Hard Time: Developing Real-Time Systems with UML, Objects, Frameworks, and Patterns*

Douglass, *Real-Time UML, Second Edition: Developing Efficient Objects for Embedded Systems*

Fowler, *Analysis Patterns: Reusable Object Models*

Fowler/Beck/Brant/Opdyke/Roberts, *Refactoring: Improving the Design of Existing Code*

Fowler/Scott, *UML Distilled, Second Edition: A Brief Guide to the Standard Object Modeling Language*

Gomaa, *Designing Concurrent, Distributed, and Real-Time Applications with UML*

Gorton, *Enterprise Transaction Processing Systems: Putting the CORBA OTS, Encina++ and Orbix OTM to Work*

Graham, *Object-Oriented Methods, Third Edition: Principles and Practice*

Heinckiens, *Building Scalable Database Applications: Object-Oriented Design, Architectures, and Implementations*

Hofmeister/Nord/Dilip, *Applied Software Architecture*

Jacobson/Booch/Rumbaugh, *The Unified Software Development Process*

Jacobson/Christerson/Jonsson/Overgaard, *Object-Oriented Software Engineering: A Use Case Driven Approach*

Jacobson/Ericsson/Jacobson, *The Object Advantage: Business Process Reengineering with Object Technology*

Jacobson/Griss/Jonsson, *Software Reuse: Architecture, Process and Organization for Business Success*

Jordan, *C++ Object Databases: Programming with the ODMG Standard*

Kruchten, *The Rational Unified Process, An Introduction, Second Edition*

Lau, *The Art of Objects: Object-Oriented Design and Architecture*

Leffingwell/Widrig, *Managing Software Requirements: A Unified Approach*

Marshall, *Enterprise Modeling with UML: Designing Successful Software through Business Analysis*

McGregor/Sykes, *A Practical Guide to Testing Object-Oriented Software*

Mowbray/Ruh, *Inside CORBA: Distributed Object Standards and Applications*

Naiburg/Maksimchuk, *UML for Database Design*

Oestereich, *Developing Software with UML: Object-Oriented Analysis and Design in Practice*

Page-Jones, *Fundamentals of Object-Oriented Design in UML*

Pohl, *Object-Oriented Programming Using C++, Second Edition*

Pooley/Stevens, *Using UML: Software Engineering with Objects and Components*

Quatrani, *Visual Modeling with Rational Rose 2000 and UML*

Rector/Sells, *ATL Internals*

Reed, *Developing Applications with Visual Basic and UML*

Rosenberg/Scott, *Applying Use Case Driven Object Modeling with UML: An Annotated e-Commerce Example*

Rosenberg/Scott, *Use Case Driven Object Modeling with UML: A Practical Approach*

Royce, *Software Project Management: A Unified Framework*

Ruh/Herron/Klinker, *IIOP Complete: Understanding CORBA and Middleware Interoperability*

Rumbaugh/Jacobson/Booch, *The Unified Modeling Language Reference Manual*

Schneider/Winters, *Applying Use Cases, Second Edition: A Practical Guide*

Shan/Earle, *Enterprise Computing with Objects: From Client/Server Environments to the Internet*

Smith/Williams, *Performance Solutions: A Practical Guide to Creating Responsive, Scalable Software*

Warmer/Kleppe, *The Object Constraint Language: Precise Modeling with UML*

White, *Software Configuration Management Strategies and Rational ClearCase®: A Practical Introduction*

The Component Software Series

Clemens Szyperski, Series Editor
For more information, check out the series Web site [http://www.awl.com/cseng/csseries/].

Allen, *Realizing eBusiness with Components*

Cheesman/Daniels, *UML Components: A Simple Process for Specifying Component-Based Software*

Performance Solutions

A Practical Guide to Creating Responsive, Scalable Software

Connie U. Smith

Lloyd G. Williams

ADDISON–WESLEY

Boston • San Francisco • New York • Toronto • Montreal
London • Munich • Paris • Madrid
Capetown • Sydney • Tokyo • Singapore • Mexico City

The publisher offers discounts on this book when ordered in quantity for special sales. For more information, please contact:

Pearson Education Corporate Sales Division
201 W. 103rd Street
Indianapolis, IN 46290
(800) 428-5331
corpsales@pearsoned.com

Visit AW on the Web: www.aw.com/cseng/

Library of Congress Cataloging-in-Publication Data
Smith, Connie U.
   Performance solutions : a practical guide to creating responsive, scalable software / Connie Smith, Lloyd Williams.
      p. cm.—(The Addison-Wesley object technology series)
   Includes bibliographical references and index.
   ISBN 0-201-72229-1
   1. Computer software—Development. 2. Computer software—Reliability. I. Williams, Lloyd (Lloyd G.) II. Title. III. Series.
   QA76.76.D47 S57 2001
   005.1'068—dc21   2001022849

ISBN 0-201-72229-1
Text printed on recycled paper
1 2 3 4 5 6 7 8 9 10—MA—0504030201
First printing, September 2001

Contents

Foreword by Grady Booch xix

Foreword by Paul Clements xxi

Preface xxv

Part I: Introduction and Overview

Chapter 1: Introduction 3
    1.1 Software and Performance. 3
        1.1.1 Responsiveness 4
        1.1.2 Scalability 5
    1.2 The Importance of Performance 6
        1.2.1 Consequences of Performance Failures 9
        1.2.2 Causes of Performance Failures. 9
        1.2.3 Getting It Right 12
    1.3 How Should You Manage Performance?. 14
        1.3.1 Reactive Performance Management. 14
        1.3.2 Proactive Performance Management 15
    1.4 Software Performance Engineering 16
        1.4.1 SPE Modeling Strategies. 18
        1.4.2 SPE Models 20
    1.5 SPE for Object-Oriented Systems 21
        1.5.1 What Does It Cost?. 22
        1.5.2 What Do You Need?. 23
    1.6 Summary 24

Chapter 2: SPE Quick View 27
    2.1 SPE Process for Object-Oriented Systems. 27

2.2 Case Study 32
    2.2.1 Assess Performance Risk (Step 1) 33
    2.2.2 Identify Critical Use Cases (Step 2). 33
    2.2.3 Select Key Performance Scenarios (Step 3) 33
    2.2.4 Establish Performance Objectives (Step 4) 35
    2.2.5 Construct Performance Models (Step 5) 35
    2.2.6 Determine Software Resource Requirements (Step 6) 36
    2.2.7 Add Computer Resource Requirements (Step 7). 37
    2.2.8 Evaluate the Models (Step 8). 39
    2.2.9 Verify and Validate the Models (Step 9) 39
2.3 SPE in the Unified Software Process 40
2.4 Performance Solutions 41
    2.4.1 Performance Principles 42
    2.4.2 Performance Patterns 42
    2.4.3 Performance Antipatterns 42
    2.4.4 Implementation Solutions. 43
2.5 Summary 44

Chapter 3: SPE and the UML **47**
3.1 Overview. 47
3.2 Extending the UML 48
    3.2.1 Stereotypes 48
    3.2.2 Tagged Values. 49
    3.2.3 Constraints 49
3.3 Use Cases and Scenarios 50
    3.3.1 Use Cases 50
    3.3.2 Scenarios. 52
3.4 Extensions to Sequence Diagram Notation 55
    3.4.1 Instance Decomposition 55
    3.4.2 Looping, Alternation, and References 56
3.5 Specifying Time 59
    3.5.1 Timing Marks. 60
    3.5.2 Time Expressions 60
    3.5.3 Timing Constraints. 60
    3.5.4 Time in Sequence Diagrams 60
3.6 Concurrency 62
    3.6.1 Threads and Processes. 62
    3.6.2 Coregions 63

    3.6.3 Parallel Composition. 64
    3.6.4 Synchronization 65
  3.7 Summary 67

Part II: SPE Models

Chapter 4: Software Execution Models. 71
  4.1 Purpose. 71
  4.2 Representing Software Execution Models 72
    4.2.1 Execution Graphs 73
    4.2.2 Execution Graph Restrictions 77
  4.3 Model Solutions 79
    4.3.1 Basic Solution Algorithms. 80
    4.3.2 More Advanced Solution Techniques 83
  4.4 Analysis Procedures. 83
  4.5 Execution Graphs from Sequence Diagrams 88
  4.6 ICAD Case Study 89
    4.6.1 Architecture 1 90
    4.6.2 Architecture 2 96
    4.6.3 Analysis of Results. 98
    4.6.4 Architecture 3 98
  4.7 Modeling Hints 102
  4.8 Summary 103

Chapter 5: Web Applications and Other Distributed Systems 105
  5.1 Introduction 105
  5.2 Web Applications 106
  5.3 Distributed Object Technology. 109
    5.3.1 Middleware. 110
    5.3.2 Limitations of Distributed Object Technology 111
    5.3.3 Effective Development with Distributed Object Technology . 114
  5.4 Modeling Distributed System Interactions 115
    5.4.1 Types of System Interactions. 115
    5.4.2 Software Execution Model Representation 118
    5.4.3 Representing Middleware Overhead 120
    5.4.4 Software Model Solution Approximations. 121
  5.5 Example: Web e-Commerce Application. 123
    5.5.1 Database Scenario 129
    5.5.2 Order Process Scenario 129

5.5.3 Example Summary 130

5.6 Modeling Hints 130

5.7 Summary 131

Chapter 6: System Execution Models **133**

6.1 Introduction 133

6.2 System Model Basics 135

6.2.1 Performance Metrics 136

6.2.2 Solving the Queueing Model 139

6.2.3 Networks of Queues 141

6.3 Deriving System Model Parameters from Software Model Results . . . 146

6.4 Using the System Model for SPE 150

6.4.1 Advanced System Models 151

6.4.2 Alternate Solution Methods 152

6.4.3 Schedulability 153

6.5 Distributed System Case Study 153

6.5.1 Synchronization Model 160

6.6 Modeling Hints 165

6.7 Summary 166

Part III: Data Collection

Chapter 7: SPE Data Collection **169**

7.1 Introduction 169

7.2 SPE Data Requirements 170

7.2.1 Key Performance Scenarios 170

7.2.2 Performance Objectives 172

7.2.3 Execution Environment 174

7.2.4 Software Resource Requirements 174

7.2.5 Computer Resource Requirements 176

7.2.6 Data Gathering Issues 178

7.3 Performance Walkthrough 179

7.3.1 Topics 180

7.3.2 When to Conduct Performance Walkthroughs 182

7.3.3 Example 183

7.3.4 Tips for a Successful Performance Walkthrough 193

7.4 Resource Estimation Techniques 195

7.4.1 Use Measurements 195

7.4.2 Study Measurements 196

7.4.3 Use a Mentor 196
7.4.4 Best-Worst Case Estimates 197
7.4.5 What to Estimate 197
7.4.6 Estimating I/O Requirements 197
7.4.7 Estimating Network Messages. 200
7.4.8 Obtaining Computer Resource Requirements. 201
7.5 Summary 201

Chapter 8: Software Measurement and Instrumentation 203

8.1 Introduction 203
8.2 What Should You Measure? 204
8.2.1 Workload Data and Data Characteristics 207
8.2.2 Path Characteristics. 207
8.2.3 Software Resources and Processing Overhead 207
8.2.4 Computer Resource Usage 208
8.3 Planning for Performance Measurement 208
8.3.1 Key Considerations. 208
8.3.2 Performance Benchmarks 210
8.3.3 Designing and Conducting Measurement Studies. 210
8.4 Performance Measurement Concepts 214
8.4.1 Terminology. 215
8.4.2 Factors That May Affect Measurements 218
8.5 Data Collection Techniques and Tools. 221
8.5.1 Data Collection Techniques 222
8.5.2 Measuring SPE Data. 224
8.6 Instrumentation 227
8.6.1 Instrumentation Design Considerations 230
8.6.2 Implementation Alternatives. 231
8.6.3 Data Reporting. 233
8.7 Application Resource Measurement 233
8.8 Summary 236

Part IV: Performance Solutions

Chapter 9: Performance-Oriented Design 241

9.1 Principles for Performance-Oriented Design. 241
9.2 Performance Control Principles 242
9.2.1 Performance Objectives Principle 242
9.2.2 Instrumenting Principle 243

9.3 Independent Principles 245
    9.3.1 Centering Principle 245
    9.3.2 Fixing-Point Principle 247
    9.3.3 Locality Principle 249
    9.3.4 Processing Versus Frequency Principle 251
9.4 Synergistic Principles 252
    9.4.1 Shared Resources Principle 253
    9.4.2 Parallel Processing Principle 254
    9.4.3 Spread-the-Load Principle 256
9.5 Using the Principles 257
9.6 Summary 259

Chapter 10: Performance Patterns 261

10.1 Overview 261
10.2 Fast Path 263
    10.2.1 Problem 264
    10.2.2 Solution 264
    10.2.3 Benefits 266
    10.2.4 Consequences 266
10.3 First Things First 267
    10.3.1 Problem 267
    10.3.2 Solution 268
    10.3.3 Benefits 269
    10.3.4 Consequences 269
10.4 Coupling 269
    10.4.1 Problem 270
    10.4.2 Solution 271
    10.4.3 Benefits 272
    10.4.4 Consequences 272
10.5 Batching 272
    10.5.1 Problem 272
    10.5.2 Solution 274
    10.5.3 Benefits 275
    10.5.4 Consequences 275
10.6 Alternate Routes 276
    10.6.1 Problem 276
    10.6.2 Solution 277
    10.6.3 Benefits 278

10.6.4 Consequences 279
10.7 Flex Time 279
    10.7.1 Problem 279
    10.7.2 Solution 280
    10.7.3 Benefits 281
    10.7.4 Consequences 281
10.8 Slender Cyclic Functions 282
    10.8.1 Problem 282
    10.8.2 Solution 283
    10.8.3 Benefits 283
    10.8.4 Consequences 284
10.9 Summary 284

Chapter 11: Performance Antipatterns 287

11.1 Overview 287
11.2 The "god" Class 288
    11.2.1 Problem 289
    11.2.2 Solution 292
11.3 Excessive Dynamic Allocation 293
    11.3.1 Problem 293
    11.3.2 Solution 295
11.4 Circuitous Treasure Hunt 296
    11.4.1 Problem 297
    11.4.2 Solution 299
11.5 The One-Lane Bridge 301
    11.5.1 Problem 301
    11.5.2 Solution 302
11.6 Traffic Jam 304
    11.6.1 Problem 305
    11.6.2 Solution 305
11.7 Summary 306

Chapter 12: Implementation Solutions 309

12.1 Overview 309
12.2 Performance Tuning 311
12.3 General Performance Solutions 316
    12.3.1 Fast Path Speed-Up 316
    12.3.2 Improving Scalability 318
    12.3.3 Algorithm and Data Structure Choices 322

12.3.4 Time Versus Space Trade-Offs 323
12.3.5 Hardware/Software Platform Dependencies 326
12.4 Performance Solutions for Object-Oriented Software 327
12.4.1 Language-Independent Solutions 327
12.4.2 C++ Solutions 331
12.4.3 Java Solutions 333
12.5 Summary 337

Part V: Applications

Chapter 13: Web Applications **341**
13.1 Introduction 341
13.2 Performance Issues 343
13.3 SPE Models for Web Applications 345
13.4 Case Study: Nachtfliegen.com 349
13.4.1 Plan Itinerary Scenario 350
13.4.2 Software Model 356
13.4.3 Hardware/Software Environment 356
13.4.4 Resource Requirements 358
13.4.5 Software Model Solution 360
13.4.6 Performance Improvements 362
13.4.7 System Execution Model 363
13.4.8 Sensitivity and Scalability Analysis 366
13.5 Typical Performance Problems 366
13.6 Summary 371

Chapter 14: Embedded Real-Time Systems **373**
14.1 Introduction 373
14.2 Embedded Real-Time Systems Background 374
14.2.1 Timing Requirements 375
14.2.2 Hardware Constraints 378
14.2.3 Real-Time Operating Systems 378
14.2.4 Distributed Systems 379
14.2.5 Database 379
14.3 Performance Issues 379
14.3.1 Response Time and Throughput 380
14.3.2 Schedulability 381
14.4 SPE Models for Embedded Real-Time Systems 384
14.5 Case Study: Telephony Switching 385

14.5.1 Overview. 385
14.5.2 Architecture and Design 388
14.6 Typical Performance Problems 396
14.7 Summary 402

Part VI: Making SPE Happen

Chapter 15: The SPE Process 407

15.1 Introduction 407
15.2 The SPE Process 408
15.2.1 Assess Performance Risk 410
15.2.2 Identify Critical Use Cases 411
15.2.3 Select Key Performance Scenarios 412
15.2.4 Establish Performance Objectives 412
15.2.5 Construct Performance Models. 413
15.2.6 Determine Software Resource Requirements. 415
15.2.7 Add Computer Resource Requirements 415
15.2.8 Evaluate the Models 416
15.2.9 Verify and Validate Models. 418
15.3 Late Life Cycle SPE Activities 419
15.3.1 More Detailed Models 420
15.3.2 More Precise Data. 421
15.3.3 Performance Testing. 421
15.3.4 Baseline Models 422
15.4 Post-Deployment Performance Management 423
15.4.1 Evolutionary Changes. 423
15.4.2 Capacity Management 423
15.5 SPE Artifacts. 424
15.5.1 Performance Management Plans 425
15.5.2 Performance V&V Plan 427
15.5.3 SPE Configuration Management Plan. 427
15.5.4 Performance Drivers 428
15.5.5 Performance Scenarios 428
15.5.6 Performance Objectives. 428
15.5.7 Execution Environment Specifications 428
15.5.8 Performance Models 429
15.5.9 Model Results. 429
15.5.10 Performance Instrumentation 429
15.5.11 Performance V&V Reports. 429

15.5.12 Performance Test Plans 430
15.5.13 Performance Test Results 431
15.6 Integrating SPE Into Your Software Process 431
15.6.1 The Waterfall Model 432
15.6.2 The Spiral Model 432
15.6.3 SPE in the Unified Process 433
15.7 Summary 436

Chapter 16: Implementing SPE 439

16.1 Introduction 439
16.2 Tools 440
16.2.1 Modeling Tools 440
16.2.2 Development Tools 442
16.3 SPE Adoption and Use 444
16.3.1 Experience 444
16.3.2 Key Considerations 448
16.3.3 Pilot Projects 451
16.3.4 Critical Success Factors for Adoption and Use 452
16.4 SPE Implementation Strategies 455
16.4.1 Organizational Issues 455
16.4.2 Who Pays for SPE? 457
16.4.3 Costs 458
16.4.4 Risks 458
16.5 Critical Factors for Successful Projects 459
16.6 SPE Future 461
16.7 Summary 462

Part VII: Appendixes

Appendix A: UML Notation 467

A.1 Use Case Diagrams 468
A.2 Sequence Diagrams 469
A.2.1 Basic Sequence Diagrams 469
A.2.2 Augmented Sequence Diagrams 469
A.3 Deployment Diagrams 471
A.4 Stereotypes, Tagged Values, and Constraints 472
A.4.1 Stereotypes 472
A.4.2 Tagged Values 472
A.4.3 Constraints 472

Appendix B: SPE Modeling Notations. 475
   B.1 Execution Graph Notation 476
      B.1.1 Basic Nodes 476
      B.1.2 Synchronization Nodes 477
   B.2 Information Processing Graph Notation 478

Bibliography 479

Index 489

Foreword
by Grady Booch

A multitude of pressures weigh upon the members of the software development team. First and foremost, there are the demands of functionality, cost, schedule, and compatibility with legacy systems. Technology "churn" and the need for resilience, especially in the presence of continuous change found in most Web-centric systems, add to the pile. Security, fail-safe/fault tolerance, and reliability/availability all play a role, depending on the domain. Finally (these are often considered last, unfortunately), there are the pressures of capacity, responsiveness, scalability, and, ultimately, performance.

Even if your team crafts the most perfectly functional system under budget and under schedule, you have failed if it doesn't perform in the manner that its users require. Although conventional wisdom may suggest that responsiveness and scalability are things that can always be added later, Connie and Lloyd point out that's just not so: Performance is an intrinsic element of building a system. You can't simply tack on quality to an ugly system, just as you can't apply a quick fix to make an under-performing system better—the causes are generally deep, and they're rooted in the system's architecture.

I think a better title for the book you hold in your hands would have been *Everything You Wanted to Know About Performance But Didn't Have the Time or Resources to Ask*.[1]   Connie and Lloyd have written a

---

1. You can see why I need good editors when I write. That might be a great title for charades, but it's terribly unwieldy for a book.

delightfully approachable and pragmatic book on the practice and problems of performance. Not only is this book eminently readable, but it also covers every aspect of building responsible and scalable software, from architectural issues to modeling, metrics, and process.

Connie and Lloyd speak from deep experience in this field, and they share that experience in this book. I learned a number of things from them, and I'm sure you will as well.

Grady Booch
Chief Scientist, Rational Software
April 2001

Foreword
by Paul Clements

Software performance engineering has for decades been an art practiced by wizards. And for good reasons: It's tricky stuff. Until now most treatments of the subject were hopelessly bogged down in the details of queueing theory, Markov analysis, and esoteric scheduling algorithms. The field resembled, more than anything else, an old seafarer's chart with one big corner labeled "Here there be monsters." Only the brave of heart ventured forth, and an organization's performance engineers—in the unlikely case it even had performance engineers—were self-trained and underutilized; their potential contributions were poorly understood; and they tended to eat by themselves in the cafeteria, mumbling something sounding suspiciously like a Fibonacci sequence.

No more. As our field has matured, forces have come into play to banish the monsters.

First, the need is clear. All safety-critical software—and there's a staggering amount of that these days—is performance-critical. No one would dream of fielding a system on which the health and safety of humans or the environment depended without first making certain it would meet its performance constraints. Ask the people who build antilock braking systems, medical X-ray controllers, or avionics software if performance matters. They'll tell you it's the *only* thing that matters. But we are also coming to the obvious realization, if belatedly, that all software has performance constraints. If you don't believe this, revisit the issue the next time your workstation's operating system decides to show you the little hourglass symbol for no apparent reason, and you're tapping the mouse button, waiting to open a file and counting to ten under your breath. If you make it to ten, or eight, or even two, you're the victim of a performance problem.

Second, the performance engineering field itself is growing up and establishing a body of best practices that non-experts can emulate with repeatable success. Connie Smith and Lloyd Williams have been at the vanguard of this maturation movement, and they have established themselves as world-renowned experts on not just performance engineering theory, but also on performance engineering practice. If you believe that those who can, do, and those who can't, teach, then you don't know Connie and Lloyd. They can, they do, and, lucky for us, they teach. Their combined decades of experience in helping organizations avoid (or climb out of) performance engineering pits serve as the foundation on which they have been able to make performance engineering live up to its name. The techniques are easy to grasp and can be used right away.

And third, in concert with the emerging discipline of software architecture, we are learning the importance of understanding all we can about systems before they are built and all of the bad decisions are cast into code where they are prohibitively expensive to correct.

In short, the "supply" of performance engineering is finally (thanks in no small measure to the authors) meeting the new-found "demand" for it from real organizations building real systems and facing real challenges.

So the time was right for a book, but that only tells half the story. This isn't just any book. As I read through it, I was impressed (and grateful) that Connie and Lloyd never forgot whom they were writing for. Every page is full of guidance that speaks directly to the practitioner. Useful (as opposed to merely entertaining) books tend to be read once, but referenced dozens or hundreds of times, and it is a prudent author who recognizes that. These authors were thoughtful about adopting stylistic conventions that make using the book easier to use and more productive. Where information is used, the location of its defining text is cited for a quick look-up to refresh the reader's memory. Examples are clearly identified separately from the main exposition. Important principles are boldly presented. Notes and asides that amplify the information are generously sprinkled throughout, but they are visually distinguished so as not to interrupt the main flow. Some technical books make you feel like an apprentice sky diver whose instructor just nonchalantly ordered you to "Jump!" Not this one. They're with you every step of the way.

The result is a book that utterly demystifies the job (no longer the art) of performance engineering. Monsters, begone! Wizards, away! It leaves you feeling that you could really do this on your own. And, thanks to Connie and Lloyd, you can.

Paul Clements
Software Engineering Institute
May 2001

Preface

I love it when a plan comes together.

—Col. John "Hannibal" Smith
"The A-Team"

In our roles as consultants, teachers, and mentors to software developers, we see too many software products that fail to meet their performance objectives when they are initially constructed. Fixing these problems is costly and causes schedule delays, cost overruns, lost productivity, damaged customer relations, missed market windows, lost revenues, and a host of other difficulties. In extreme cases, it may not be possible to fix performance problems without extensive redesign and re-implementation. In those cases, the project either becomes an infinite sink for time and money, or it is, mercifully, canceled.

These problems can be prevented by the systematic application of a few simple performance analysis and prediction techniques. Over the years, we have helped many clients produce software that meets performance objectives and is delivered on time and within budget. This book was produced in response to requests from our clients and students to provide a reference to the techniques that we have used and taught so successfully.

Objectives

By applying the material in this book you will be able to answer questions such as:

- Will your users be able to complete their tasks in the allotted time?
- Are your hardware and network capable of handling the load?
- Will your system scale up to meet the future demand?

More importantly, you will be able to answer these questions *before* you have committed a lot of time and money to an implementation, only to find that the answers are an emphatic (and expensive) *no*!

You will learn enough from this book to begin to apply these techniques immediately to manage the performance of your software systems. You will sharpen your skills as you use them on a variety of projects that include Web-based applications, distributed systems, real-time systems, traditional database applications, and others.

Software Performance

Performance is any characteristic of a software product that you could, in principle, measure by sitting at the computer with a stopwatch in your hand. The dimensions of performance include responsiveness (response time or throughput) and scalability.

How do projects get in trouble with performance? The problem is often due to a fundamental misunderstanding of how to achieve performance objectives. The approach is frequently "First, let's make it run; then, we'll make it run fast." The idea is to get the functionality right, and then tune for performance. Unfortunately, by the time the architecture and design are selected, it may already be too late to achieve adequate performance by tuning. It is a mistake to treat a potential performance problem as if it were of the same complexity as a coding error. Coding errors are relatively easy to fix, whereas performance problems may require extensive changes to code.

The proper way to manage software performance is to systematically plan for and predict the performance of the emerging software throughout the development process. This book presents a set of simple techniques that you can use to manage the performance of your software. These techniques do not require an advanced degree in mathematics, nor do they take significant amounts of time away from development activities. By applying them, you will be able to make informed choices among architectural and design alternatives, and proceed with confidence, knowing that your software will meet its performance objectives.

The approach to managing performance presented here is unique. It has grown out of more than 10 years of collaboration between the authors that combines knowledge and experience in both software performance engineering and architectural analysis. Other authors have proposed elaborate modeling techniques that either aren't useful for real systems or require a Ph.D. in mathematics to apply. Our approach is practical, useful by non-specialists, and rigorous.

Software Performance Engineering

The techniques presented in this book are collectively known as software performance engineering (SPE). SPE is a comprehensive way of managing performance that includes principles for creating responsive software, performance patterns and antipatterns for performance-oriented design, techniques for eliciting performance objectives, techniques for gathering the data needed for evaluation, and guidelines for the types of evaluation to be performed at each stage of the development process.

SPE is model-based. Modeling is central to both SPE and object-oriented development. By building and analyzing models of the proposed software, we can explore its characteristics to determine if it will meet its requirements before we actually commit to building it. SPE uses models to quantitatively assess the performance of the emerging software. This book discusses how to quickly and easily create those quantitative models from the architecture and design models that you produce as part of the object-oriented development process. It also describes how to integrate SPE seamlessly into the overall object-oriented development process.

Finally, these techniques are neither new nor revolutionary. They have evolved from a relatively long history of proven quantitative disciplines. Nor are they a silver bullet. They must be used to be effective, and it will take some time to learn to apply them, particularly on your initial project. The amount of time required, however, is not excessive and is appropriate for most projects in their early stages. We have found that when problems are inevitable, your choice is "pay a little now (for the scalability and performance that you need) or pay much more later." Software metrics show that it costs up to 100 times more to fix problems in code than it does to fix problems in the architecture before code is written. The only way to determine whether problems are inevitable is to use the quantitative techniques described in this book early.

Who Should Read This Book

This book is primarily intended for experienced software developers who have used object-oriented techniques on one or more development projects and who are ready for the next step: to learn how to create software systems with built-in scalability and performance. The emphasis is on *how* to apply the techniques.

Other readers will also find information that they can use:

- Project managers will find techniques that they can bring to their projects immediately to improve the way performance is managed. They will also learn how to implement SPE.
- Developers who are new to object-oriented techniques will discover how it is possible to manage performance for object-oriented systems, and find guidelines for creating responsive software that will augment their study of object-oriented development.
- Performance engineers will learn how to adapt their skills to object-oriented systems, as well as discover new approaches that are applicable to other development technologies.
- Students will learn about performance issues that arise in realistic, large-scale software systems and how to solve them.

Familiarity with object-oriented concepts is helpful, but it is not essential. We explain the portions of the Unified Modeling Language (UML) notation useful for performance assessments. If you find you would like more background, refer to other books in the Object Technology Series.[1]

---

1. For object-oriented concepts, see: G. Booch, *Object-Oriented Analysis and Design with Applications*, Redwood City, CA, Benjamin/Cummings, 1994. For UML, see G. Booch, J. Rumbaugh, and I. Jacobson, *The Unified Modeling Language User Guide*, Reading, MA, Addison-Wesley, 1999.

Familiarity with performance modeling techniques is helpful but it is not essential. We assume that you will use an SPE tool, such as *SPE·ED,* to evaluate your systems. We explain enough of the modeling fundamentals for you to become familiar with how such tools work. References are included with the material in case you would like to learn more about the modeling technology.

Organization of This Book

This book is organized into the following seven parts:
- **Part I: Introduction and Overview** provides an introduction to SPE and an overview of the modeling techniques
- **Part II: SPE Models** describes details of the models used in SPE and their solutions
- **Part III: Data Collection** discusses how to obtain SPE data, and provides some background on performance measurement techniques.
- **Part IV: Performance Solutions** presents techniques for designing performance into software systems, and maintaining performance throughout the life cycle
- **Part V: Applications** illustrates the application of SPE techniques to some important types of application domains
- **Part VI: Making SPE Happen** discusses how to implement SPE in your development organization
- **Part VII: Appendixes** summarize the notation used throughout the book.

How You Should Read This Book

Different people will have different reasons for reading this book and different needs for the information in it. The table below offers a suggested road map for reading the material that is keyed to several types of reader interests. The types of readers represented in the table are
- **Developer**—You are responsible for software development and need to make sure that your code meets performance objectives. You need to know it all: what SPE is, what it can do for you, how to construct and evaluate the models, how to design

performance into your software, and how to fit SPE into the development process.

- **Manager**—As a manager, you need to know what SPE is, what it can do for you, and how it fits into the software development process. The modeling details are less important.
- **Performance Engineer**—You are responsible for working with developers to assist with the quantitative analysis of their systems. You also need to know it all: how to explain the SPE and what it can do for developers, how to construct and evaluate the models, how to identify and explain performance solutions and performance problems, and how SPE fits into the development process.
- **Firefighter**—You have a system that has performance problems and need help to get out of trouble. Later, when things calm down, you can go back and apply the SPE techniques to prevent these problems in future systems.
- **Academic**—The material in this book can be used as the basis for a graduate-level course in software performance engineering. The sections on integrating SPE into the software process and implementing SPE are probably less important, however.

The entries show the priority or importance of each part of the book for the various reader interests with letters (A is vital, B is important, C is some value). The numbers indicate the order in which the parts should be read (1 is first, 2 next, and so on).

Reader's Guide

	Part I	**Part II**	**Part III**	**Part IV**	**Part V**	**Part VI**
Developer	A1	A2	A3	A4	A5	A6
Manager	A1	C1	B1	B2	B3	A2
Performance Engineer	A1	A2	A3	A4	A5	A6
Firefighter	A1	A4	A2	A3	A5	B1
Academic	A1	A2	A3	A4	A5	B1

Formatting Conventions

Points, observations, and guidelines that are especially important are italicized and highlighted by a pointing hand in the margin, as shown below:

Software execution models are generally sufficient for identifying serious performance problems at the architectural and early design phases.

Software execution models are discussed in Chapter 4.

Presentation of one topic often includes a reference to another that is discussed elsewhere. To help in making the connection, cross-references are provided in the left margin.

Asides, parenthetical comments, and general guidelines are set apart as notes, as illustrated in the following example.

Note: Execution graphs are similar to program flowcharts, but they are not the same. Execution graphs show the frequency of path execution, and model only those paths that are key to performance.

Example 1-1: Performance Failures

Call Processing A re-implementation of a call-processing system for a telecommunication switch also did not consider performance early in development. The initial object-oriented design required several hundred times the allotted time to complete a call.

Examples and other portions of the text that are important but might interrupt the general flow are set apart, as in the following illustration.

SPE on the Web

The models in this book and a demonstration version of the *SPE-ED* tool are on the Web at http://www.perfeng.com/PerfSolutions/models. Other information about SPE is at http://www.perfeng.com. There is an online discussion group on SPE at http://www.egroups.com/group/softwareperfeng/.

If you discover errors in this book, please email them to perfSolu-tions@perfeng.com. We will periodically post them to http://www.per-feng.com/PerfSolutions/errata.

Acknowledgments

This book was extensively reviewed and even "field tested" before its publication. Thad Jennings and Brent Reeves reviewed early drafts of each chapter. Their comments helped keep the presentation focused on out target audience and provided many useful suggestions. Rob Sartin, after a careful review of Chapter 12, suggested several useful additions.

Inkeri Verkamo (University of Helsinki, Finland) and Ken Sevcik (University of Toronto) used drafts of Chapters 1-9 as a text for their graduate courses on software performance engineering. Their feedback helped identify topics that needed further explanation, and demonstrated the usefulness of this book as an introductory text for SPE.

We would also like to thank the "official" Addison-Wesley reviewers: Paul Clements, Sholom Cohen, Bob Glass, and Jerry Rolia. Their diverse points of view improved the contents of this book and ensured that our discussions focused on what you need to know.

Finally, we would like to express our appreciation to Paul Becker and the rest of the editorial and production team at Addison-Wesley, as well as Janet Butler, for their assistance in getting this book into print.

Connie U. Smith	Lloyd G. Williams
Santa Fe, NM	Boulder, CO
May 2001	May 2001

Part I

Introduction and Overview

Chapter 1

Introduction

Knowledge of what is possible is the beginning of happiness.
—George Santayana

In This Chapter:

- Performance failures and their consequences
- Managing performance
- Performance successes
- What is software performance engineering?
- SPE models and modeling strategies

1.1 Software and Performance

This book is about developing software systems that meet performance objectives. Performance is an indicator of how well a software system or component meets its requirements for timeliness. Timeliness is measured in terms of response time or throughput. The *response time* is the time required to respond to a request. It may be the time required for a single transaction, or the end-to-end time for a user task. For example, we may require that an online system provide a result within one-half second after the user presses the "enter" key. For embedded systems, it is the time required to respond to events, or the number of events processed in a time interval. The *throughput* of a system is the number of requests that can be processed in some specified time interval. For example, a telephony switch may be required to process 100,000 calls per hour.

> *Performance is the degree to which a software system or component meets its objectives for timeliness.*

Thus, performance is any characteristic of a software product that you could, in principle, measure by sitting at the computer with a stopwatch in your hand.

Note: Other definitions of performance include additional characteristics such as footprint or memory usage. In this book, however, we are concerned primarily with issues of timeliness.

There are two important dimensions to software performance timeliness: *responsiveness* and *scalability*.

1.1.1 Responsiveness

Responsiveness is the ability of a system to meet its objectives for response time or throughput. In end-user systems, responsiveness is typically defined from a user perspective. For example, responsiveness might refer to the amount of time it takes to complete a user task, or the number of transactions that can be processed in a given amount of time. In real-time systems, responsiveness is a measure of how fast the system responds to an event, or the number of events that can be processed in a given time.

In end-user applications, responsiveness has both an objective and a subjective component. For example, we may require that the end-to-end time for a withdrawal transaction at an ATM be one minute. However, that minute may feel very different to different users. For a user in Santa Fe in the summer, it may seem quite reasonable. To a user in Minneapolis in January, a minute may seem excessively long. Both objective and user-perceived (subjective) responsiveness must be addressed when performance objectives are specified. For example, you can improve the *perceived* responsiveness of a Web application by presenting user-writable fields first. Then, build the rest of the page (e.g., the fancy graphics) while the user is filling in those fields.

Responsiveness is the ability of a system to meet its objectives for response time or throughput.

1.1.2 Scalability

Scalability is the ability of a system to continue to meet its response time or throughput objectives as the demand for the software functions increases. The graph in Figure 1-1 illustrates how increasing use of a system affects its response time.

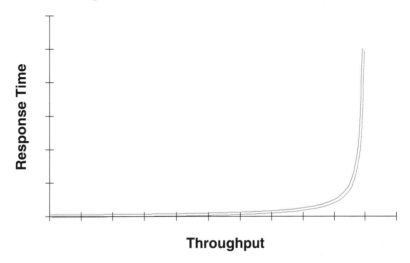

Figure 1-1: Scalability Curve

In Figure 1-1, we've plotted response time against the load on the system, as measured by the number of requests per unit time. As you can see from the curve, as long as you are below a certain threshold, increasing the load does not have a great effect on response time. In this region, the response time increases linearly with the load. At some point, however, a small increase in load begins to have a great effect on response time. In this region (at the right of the curve), the response time increases exponentially with the load. This change from a linear to an exponential increase in response time is usually due to some resource in the system (e.g., the CPU, a disk, the network, sockets, or threads) nearing one hundred percent utilization. This resource is known as the "bottleneck" resource. The region where the curve changes from linear to exponential is known as the "knee" because of its resemblance to a bent knee.

Scalability is the ability of a system to continue to meet its response time or throughput objectives as the demand for the software functions increases.

Web applications are discussed in Chapters 5, 7, and 13.

Scalability is an increasingly important aspect of today's software systems. Web applications are a case in point. It is important to maintain the responsiveness of a Web application as more and more users converge on a site. In today's competitive environment, users will go elsewhere rather than endure slow response times.

In order to build scalability into your system, you must know where the "knee" of the scalability curve falls for your hardware/software environment. If the "knee" occurs before your target load requirements, you must either reduce the utilization of the bottleneck resource by streamlining the processing, or add additional hardware (e.g., a faster CPU or an extra disk) to remove the bottleneck.

This book presents an integrated set of solutions that you can use to build responsiveness and scalability into your software systems. These solutions include a combination of modeling, measurement, and other techniques, as well as a systematic process for applying them. They also include principles, patterns, and antipatterns that help you design responsiveness and scalability into your software. These techniques focus primarily on early life cycle phases to maximize your ability to economically build performance into your software. However, we also present solutions for systems that already exhibit performance problems.

1.2 The Importance of Performance

It's fair to ask at the outset: "Why is performance important?" The following anecdotes illustrate the answer:

NASA was forced to delay the launch of a satellite for at least eight months. The satellite and the Flight Operations Segment (FOS) software running it are a key component of the multibillion-dollar Earth Science Enterprise, an international research effort to study the interdependence of the Earth's ecosystems. The delay was caused because the FOS software had unacceptable response times for developing satellite schedules, and poor performance in analyzing satellite status and telemetry data. There were also problems with the implementation of a control language used to automate operations. The cost of this rework and the resulting delay has not yet been determined. Nevertheless it is clearly significant, and the high visibility and bad press is potentially damaging to the overall mission. Members of Congress also questioned NASA's ability to manage the program. [Harreld 1998a], [Harreld 1998b]

And, on a lighter note:

> The lingerie retailer Victoria's Secret used its new Web site to broadcast its spring fashion show over the Internet. To make sure that there would be a large number of viewers, the company announced the show in a 30-second advertisement during the Super Bowl. A total of 1.5 million people logged on to the Web site to view the broadcast, which used concurrent video streams. Despite extensive pre-planning and the addition of more servers and load-balancing software, viewers experienced jerky video and interrupted audio. At least five percent of those trying to view the show were unable to access it. [Trott 1999]

Both of these anecdotes illustrate performance failures—the inability of a software product to meet its overall objectives due to inadequate performance. Additional instances of performance failures appear in Example 1-1.

Example 1-1: Performance Failures

Distributed Order Management System One Fortune 100 company attempted to implement a new distributed order management system that would integrate several legacy systems with new software to track the status of orders and trigger actions in the other systems at the proper time. Performance problems in the initial version prevented its timely deployment. After three significant schedule delays, a comprehensive study of the end-to-end performance of critical use cases identified significant architectural problems that could not be corrected with either tuning or additional hardware. An attempt was made to deploy the system to meet schedule requirements. Users were disgruntled, and did not use features intended to improve order management because of performance problems. The system was ineffective because of a failure to meet its performance requirements.

Accounting System Another large company attempted a reimplementation of its accounting system. The original schedule estimated a two-year completion. After seven years, the system had been reimplemented three times; none of these implementations met the performance objectives. The third attempt used 60 times the CPU time of the original attempt.

Dynamic Reporting with COTS A large bank attempted to avoid risks by using a commercial off-the-shelf (COTS) package that provided most of the functions it required. The interactive portion of the system performed acceptably, but the bank experienced serious problems with a desired dynamic reporting function. The internal database organization of the COTS package was not in the order desired in the reports, and the processing required to produce the "roll-ups" for desired totals was excessive. The bank was forced to create a new reporting function that would run at night, thus losing the benefit of producing the reports at the time they were desired.

Call Processing A re-implementation of a call processing system for a telecommunication switch also did not consider performance early in development. The initial object-oriented design required several hundred times the allotted time to complete a call.

Automated Teller Machine An object-oriented design for teller machines focused on reuse to streamline the customization required for each bank that purchased the machines. Developers were not worried about performance because the hardware speeds were far greater than typically required for user interactions, and they had never had performance problems with previous implementations. The first implementation was unusable due to performance problems, and required substantial re-work to correct problems.

Electronic Trading Several online brokerage houses experienced unusually large numbers of hits on their Web sites following a stock market dip on October 27, 1997. The Web sites could not scale to meet the demand, so customers experienced long delays in using the sites, if they could get in at all. The result was that investors lost hundreds of thousands of dollars. At least one lawsuit has been filed alleging that online capacity was insufficient to meet users' needs.

Performance is an essential quality attribute of every software system. Many software systems, however, both object-oriented and non-object-oriented, cannot be used as they are initially implemented due to performance problems. For example, if the system is an end-user application, it may not respond rapidly enough to user actions, or handle the number of transactions that occur during peak load conditions. Or, if it is an embedded system, it may not respond rapidly enough to an external stimulus, or be able to process events that occur with a high frequency.

1.2.1 Consequences of Performance Failures

As the anecdotes above and in Example 1-1 illustrate, performance failures can have a variety of negative consequences. These include:

- *Damaged customer relations*: Your organization's image suffers because of poor performance. Even if the problem is fixed later, users will continue to associate poor performance with the product.
- *Business failures*: Poor performance means that your staff needs more time to complete key tasks, or that you need more staff to complete these tasks in the same amount of time. This may mean that you are unable to operate on a peak business day, to respond to customer inquiries, or to generate bills or payments in a timely fashion.
- *Lost income*: You lose revenue due to late delivery. In some cases, you may find yourself paying penalties for late delivery or failure to meet performance objectives.
- *Additional project resources*: Project costs rise as additional resources are allocated for "tuning" or redesign.
- *Reduced competitiveness*: "Tuning" or redesign results in late delivery that can mean missed market windows.
- *Project failure*: In some cases it will be impossible to meet performance objectives by tuning, and too expensive to redesign the system late in the process. These projects will be canceled.

1.2.2 Causes of Performance Failures

How and why does this happen? Our experience is that performance problems are most often due to fundamental architecture or design factors rather than inefficient coding. As Clements and Northrup point out:

> Whether or not a system will be able to exhibit its desired (or required) quality attributes is largely determined by the time the architecture is chosen. [Clements and Northrup 1996]

This means that performance problems are introduced early in the development process. However, most organizations ignore performance until integration testing or later. With pressure to deliver finished software in shorter and shorter times, their attitude is: "Let's get it done. If there is a performance problem, we'll fix it later." Thus, performance problems are not discovered until late in the development process, when they are more difficult (and more expensive) to fix.

This "fix-it-later" attitude is actually encouraged by many in the object-oriented community. The following quote from Auer and Beck illustrates this misinformation:

Fix-It-Later Attitude

> Ignore efficiency through most of the development cycle. Tune performance once the program is running correctly and the design reflects your best understanding of how the code should be structured. The needed changes will be limited in scope or will illuminate opportunities for better design. [Auer and Beck 1996]

Reliance on "fix-it-later" has its origins in two performance myths.

Performance Myth #1 This myth is based on the assumption that you need something to measure before you can begin to manage performance:

Performance Myth

> *It is not possible to do anything about performance until you have something executing to measure.*

The following quote from Jacobson et al. is typical of this misconception:

> Changes in the system architecture to improve performance should as a rule be postponed until the system is being (partly) built. Experience shows that one frequently makes the wrong guesses, at least in large and complex systems, when it comes to the location of the bottlenecks critical to performance. To make correct assessments regarding necessary performance optimization, in most cases, we need something to measure ... [Jacobson et al. 1999]

Performance Reality

The reality is that you don't need to wait to address performance until you have some running code to measure. Performance models can predict performance during the architectural and early design phases of the project. Performance estimation and uncertainty-management techniques can compensate for the lack of precise measurements. The models are sufficient to allow evaluation of architectural or design alternatives. It is not necessary to "guess" the location of bottlenecks or to wait until measurements are available to begin the modeling.

In fact, waiting until there is sufficient code to make detailed measurements can be dangerous. As Clements notes:

> Performance is largely a function of the frequency and nature of intercompo-
> nent communication, in addition to the performance characteristics of the
> components themselves, and hence can be predicted by studying the architec-
> ture of a system. [Clements 1996]

As we noted earlier, the architectural decisions, those that have the greatest impact on performance, are made early in the project. Waiting until
there is running code to evaluate the performance impact of these decisions means that you don't find problems until much later—when the
architectural decisions are more difficult and expensive to change, if they
can be changed at all.

Performance Myth #2 This myth is based on the fear that adding performance management to the software process will delay project completion:

*Performance
Myth*

Managing performance takes too much time.

*Performance
Reality*

The reality is that performance management efforts do not automatically require significant amounts of time. The level of effort devoted to
performance management depends on the level of risk. If there is little
or no risk of a performance failure, then there is no need for an elaborate
performance management program. If the risk of performance failure is
high, then a higher level of effort is needed. In these cases, however,
managing performance from the beginning of the software development
process can actually reduce the overall project time by eliminating the
need for time-consuming redesign and tuning.

Performance Myth #3 This myth is based on the fear that performance
modeling will take too much time and consume too many project
resources:

*Performance
Myth*

Performance models are complex and expensive to construct.

*Performance
Reality*

The reality is that simple models can provide the information required
to identify performance problems and evaluate alternatives for correcting them. These models are inexpensive to construct and evaluate. It is
no longer necessary to build a complex simulation model that is as difficult to write as the software itself. Numerous examples throughout this
book illustrate these models and the results they provide. Using simple
models in conjunction with the modeling principles discussed later in

this chapter ensures that you get the information that you need to make software architectural and design decisions when you need to, and in a cost-effective manner.

1.2.3 Getting It Right

Managing performance throughout the development process can reduce the risk of performance failure and lead to performance successes such as these:

> An airline reservation service bureau revised its airfare quote system to improve the accuracy of the "lowest fare" quotes. Performance engineers worked closely with developers throughout the project. The result was a system with 100 percent accurate quotes and *improved* performance.

> A major insurance company designed a system to provide Web access for its own agents as well as independent agents. The first version of the design called for a large amount of code (in the form of ActiveX agents) to be downloaded to client machines. Performance models of this approach showed that, if the downloaded code underwent a significant upgrade, it would take approximately three days at full bandwidth to download the changes to all of the client machines. The design was changed to rely less on downloaded code, and the system was deployed successfully.

These anecdotes illustrate that managing performance from the initial stages of the project can pay off in systems that meet performance objectives. Additional performance success stories appear in Example 1-2.

Example 1-2: Performance Successes

Event Update Performance engineers conducted a study of a new system early in the requirements analysis phase. Initial requirements called for events to be posted to an online relational database within three minutes of occurrence. The analysts estimated the size of the hardware required to support the requirement (assuming a streamlined software system) to be 20 mainframes!

Three minutes appeared to be a reasonable goal, but the tremendous data volume had dramatic consequences on hardware capacity. The performance engineering analysis allowed a quantitative assessment of the impact of this requirement, and made it possible to redefine the requirements to meet the underlying business goal with a more reasonable hardware configuration.

Distributed Data Access In another study, performance engineers studied the architecture for a new distributed system to provide customers with data about their telecommunication usage. The analysis showed that three of the use cases would meet their performance objectives, but one would require significant configuration upgrades to handle the stated workload intensity.

Developers evaluated trade-offs in the frequency of requests, the hardware and network configuration, and the software architecture and design. They selected a software architecture alternative that handled the required workload without hardware upgrades. It was easy to make the required changes before code was written.

This example shows the power of addressing performance early in development. Without the early performance analysis, the problems would have been discovered much later in the development process. Many of the software alternatives would no longer have been cost-effective, and customer pricing would have been fixed, so configuration upgrades would adversely affect the bottom line. It was easy to prevent these problems with early performance management.

Data Acquisition and Reporting In this case, performance analysis helped prevent a bad situation from becoming worse. An existing system failed to meet performance objectives because it did not scale up to support the number of users specified in the contract. As a result, the organization incurred substantial monetary penalties for failure to meet contract terms. After failing to correct problems through tuning, developers proposed replacing key portions of the system with a new object-oriented subsystem. In the process of constructing performance models of the original system (for model calibration, verification, and validation), two key problems were detected in the process synchronization strategy and in the system's technical architecture. Correcting these problems resolved the contract performance failure and provided time to address scalability in a more systematic manner. The proposed new subsystem would not have met performance requirements; in fact, the performance models predicted worse performance than with the original system!

Airline Reservations An airline reservation system included a component to recover and restore the state of the reservations data after a major outage. The project employed good performance management techniques throughout the development process. While the developers could do partial performance tests on the recovery component, the only way to determine actual success or failure was to experience an outage. It was not possible to run an end-to-end test. The performance models predicted that the system could handle the recovery in the required time, and, the first time that a recovery was needed, the performance goals were met.

Two significant morals emerge from these success stories.

 If you intend to rely on hardware to solve performance problems, use performance models early (before other options are closed) to verify that this is a cost-effective solution.

There may be other, more cost-effective solutions than hardware upgrades. As the "distributed data access" anecdote in Example 1-2 shows, there are typically more alternatives early in the process. As more and more architecture and design decisions are made, some options may become prohibitively expensive or simply unavailable.

For its part, the "airline reservations" system story in Example 1-2 shows that

 In some cases, end-to-end performance testing is not possible, so performance models are the only option.

1.3 How Should You Manage Performance?

Are you managing software performance reactively or proactively?

1.3.1 Reactive Performance Management

Do any of these sound familiar?

- "Let's just build it and see what it can do."
- "We'll tune it later; we don't have time to worry about performance now."
- "We can't do anything about performance until we have something running to measure."
- "Don't worry. Our software vendor is sure their product will meet our performance goals."
- "Performance? That's what version 2 is for."
- "We'll just buy a bigger processor."
- "Problems? We don't have performance problems."

If so, you're probably managing software performance reactively. Reactive performance management waits for performance problems to appear, and then deals with them in an ad hoc way.

Reactive performance management is just the "fix-it-later" approach in another guise. It has the same risks of cost overruns, missed deadlines, and project failure.

1.3.2 Proactive Performance Management

Proactive performance management anticipates potential performance problems and includes techniques for identifying and responding to those problems early in the process. There are several characteristics of proactive performance management:

- The project has a performance engineer responsible for tracking and communicating performance issues.
- Everyone on the project knows the name of the performance engineer.
- There is a process for identifying performance jeopardy (a danger of not meeting performance objectives) and responding to it.
- Team members are trained in performance processes.
- The project has an appropriate performance risk management plan based on shortfall costs and performance engineering activity costs.

With Software Performance Engineering (SPE), proactive performance management identifies and resolves performance problems early, avoiding the negative effects of the "fix-it-later" approach.

Historically, performance was managed either proactively or by relying on the hardware and support software to resolve problems. In the early days of computing, developers had no choice but to manage the space and time required by their software. Later, innovations in hardware and operating systems provided some relief, and developers began to worry less about performance. "Fix-it-later" was first advocated at this time. Software performance engineering techniques were originally proposed when performance failures due to the reactive "fix-it-later" approach first emerged.

As new technologies appeared, the learning curve for those technologies again required careful management to prevent performance problems. Once the performance aspects of the new technology were understood and the hardware and support software provided new features to accommodate the technology, developers could again rely more on the hardware and support software. This process repeats as other new technologies are introduced, and the hardware and support software solutions catch up with them.

The use of new software technology requires careful attention to performance until the performance aspects of the new technology are understood.

Note that the "new" technology is not necessarily "bleeding edge" technology—it might just be new to you. If you don't have experience with the technology and the performance intuition that comes with it, the result is the same.

Distributed systems challenge performance intuition. Constructing them involves a complex combination of choices about processing and data location, platform sizes, network configuration, middleware implementation, and so on. Managing the performance of these distributed software systems will likely always call for quantitative assessment of these alternatives.

Intuition about performance problems is not sufficient; quantitative assessments are necessary to assess performance risks.

We have been seeing a phenomenon more and more frequently: as organizations adopt technologies with which they have little experience, such as Web applications, Common Object Request Broker Architecture (CORBA), or Enterprise JavaBeans, they have more performance failures. When using an unfamiliar technology, you are in a situation that requires proactive performance management.

If you are managing performance reactively on systems that use unfamiliar technology, your probability of experiencing a performance failure is much higher.

1.4 Software Performance Engineering

Software performance engineering is a systematic, quantitative approach to constructing software systems that meet performance objectives. SPE is an engineering approach to performance, avoiding the extremes of performance-driven development and "fix-it-later." SPE uses model predictions to evaluate trade-offs in software functions, hardware size, quality of results, and resource requirements.

The "performance balance" in Figure 1-2 depicts a system that fails to meet performance objectives because its resource requirements exceed computer and network capacity. With SPE, you detect these problems early in development, and use quantitative methods to support cost-benefit analysis of hardware solutions versus software requirements or design solutions, versus a combination of the two. You implement software solutions before problems are manifested in code; organizations implement hardware solutions before testing begins. The quantitative assessment identifies trade-offs in software functions, hardware size, quality of results, and resource requirements.

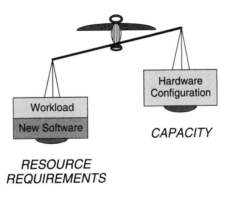

Figure 1-2: Performance Balance

SPE is a software-oriented approach: it focuses on architecture, design, and implementation choices. The models assist developers in controlling resource requirements by enabling them to select architecture and design alternatives with acceptable performance characteristics. The models aid in tracking performance throughout the development process and prevent problems from surfacing late in the life cycle (typically during final testing).

SPE also prescribes principles for creating responsive software, performance patterns and antipatterns for performance-oriented design, the data required for evaluation, procedures for obtaining performance specifications, and guidelines for the types of evaluation to be conducted at each development stage. It incorporates models for representing and predicting performance as well as a set of analysis methods [Smith 1990].

SPE is neither a new nor a revolutionary approach. It applies proven techniques to predict the performance of emerging software and respond to problems while they can be fixed with a minimum of time and expense.

We have found that, with SPE, it is possible to cost-effectively engineer new software systems that meet performance goals. By carefully applying the techniques of SPE throughout the development and integration process, it is possible to produce new systems that have adequate performance and exhibit the other qualities that have made object-oriented techniques so effective, such as reusability, relatively rapid deployment, and usability.

With SPE, you should be able to answer the following questions early in development:
- Will your users be able to complete tasks in the allotted time?
- Are your hardware and network capable of supporting the load?
- What response time is expected for key tasks?
- Will the system scale up to meet your future needs?

1.4.1 SPE Modeling Strategies

The use of these strategies is illustrated in Part II.

SPE uses several modeling strategies to obtain results quickly, to cope with uncertainty in estimates of software and hardware resource usage, and to control costs.

The Simple-Model Strategy The simple-model strategy leverages the SPE effort to provide rapid feedback on the performance of the proposed software.

Start with the simplest possible model that identifies problems with the system architecture, design, or implementation plans.

The early SPE models are easily constructed and solved to provide feedback on whether the proposed software is likely to meet performance goals. These simple models are sufficient to identify problems in the architecture or early design phases of the project. You can easily use them to evaluate many alternatives because they are easy to construct and evaluate. Later, as more details of the software are known, you can construct and solve more realistic (and complex) models.

The Best- and Worst-Case Strategy The models rely upon estimates of resource requirements for the software execution. The precision of the model results depends on the quality of these estimates. Early in the software process, however, your knowledge of the details of the software is sketchy, and it is difficult to precisely estimate resource requirements. Because of this, SPE uses adaptive strategies, such as the best- and worst-case strategy

> *Use best- and worst-case estimates of resource requirements to establish bounds on expected performance and manage uncertainty in estimates.*

For example, when there is high uncertainty about resource requirements, you use estimates of the upper and lower bounds of these quantities. Using these estimates, you produce predictions of the best-case and worst-case performance. If the predicted best-case performance is unsatisfactory, you look for feasible alternatives. If the worst-case prediction is satisfactory, you proceed to the next step of the development process with confidence. If the results are somewhere in between, the model analyses identify critical components whose resource estimates have the greatest effect, and you can focus on obtaining more precise data for them.

A variety of techniques can also provide more precise resource estimates, including: further refining the design and constructing more detailed models, or constructing a prototype or implementation of key components and measuring resource requirements.

The Adapt-to-Precision Strategy As the simple-model strategy states, simple models are appropriate for early life cycle studies. Later in the development process, SPE uses the adapt-to-precision strategy.

> *Match the details represented in the models to your knowledge of the software processing details.*

As the design and implementation proceed and more details are known, you expand the SPE models to include additional information in areas that are critical to performance.

1.4.2 SPE Models

The SPE models are similar to those used for conventional performance evaluation studies. In conventional studies (of existing systems), capacity planners model systems to predict the effect of workload or configuration changes. The conventional modeling procedure is as follows:

- Study the computer system.
- Construct a system execution model (usually a queueing network model).
- Measure current execution patterns.
- Characterize workloads.
- Develop model input parameters.
- Validate the model by solving it and comparing the model results to observed and measured data for the computer system.
- Calibrate the model until its results match the measurement data.

Planners then use the model to evaluate changes to the computer system by modifying the corresponding workload parameters, the computer system configuration parameters, or both. Capacity planners rely on these models for planning future acquisitions. The model precision is sufficient to predict future configuration requirements; models are widely used, and they work, so we use them as the basis for SPE.

SPE performance modeling is similar. However, because the software does not yet exist, and we do not want to wait for measurements of the software, we first model the software explicitly. Figure 1-3 illustrates the difference between conventional models and SPE models. With conventional models, we are concerned with modeling workloads that already exist. The system execution model quantifies the effects of contention for computer resources by different types of existing work. With SPE, we want to include software that does not yet exist. To do this, we introduce a new type of model: the software execution model. The software execution model represents key facets of the envisioned software execution behavior. Its solution yields workload parameters for the system execution model that closely resemble the conventional models.

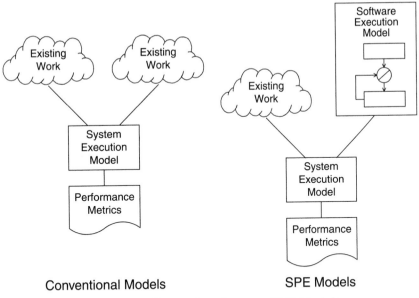

Conventional Models   SPE Models

Figure 1-3: Conventional versus SPE Models

1.5 SPE for Object-Oriented Systems

The bad news is that object-oriented (OO) systems present special problems for SPE. The functionality of object-oriented systems is decentralized. Performing a given function is likely to require collaboration
among many different objects from several classes. These interactions
can be numerous and complex and are often obscured by polymorphism, making them difficult to trace. Distributing objects over a network compounds the problem.

The good news is that object-oriented modeling notations (such as the
Unified Modeling Language [UML]) and methods actually help to
reduce the impact of these problems. Much of the information needed
to perform SPE can be captured as part of the object-oriented analysis
and design process with a minimum of disruption. Use cases, which are
identified as part of the requirements definition, are a natural link
between software development activities and SPE. The scenarios that
describe the use cases provide a starting point for constructing the performance models.

Our approach to SPE is tightly integrated with object-oriented notations, such as the UML. It does not require that you become an expert in performance modeling. To do SPE, you construct analysis and design models as you have always done. When you want to evaluate the emerging software's performance, you use your object-oriented analysis or design models to derive a performance model. Solving the model gives you feedback on the performance and suggests ways of revising the design.

SPE is also language independent. The models are constructed from architectural and design-level information. Thus, SPE works with C++ and Java as well as with other object-oriented and non-object-oriented languages. The execution behavior of the software will be different with different languages. Nevertheless, this is reflected in the resource requirement specifications, not the model structure.

This integration is addressed in Chapter 15.
SPE can be easily integrated into the software development process. It has been used with traditional process models, such as the waterfall model. It works especially well with iterative, incremental processes such as the Spiral Model [Boehm 1988] or the Unified Process [Kruchten 1999], [Jacobson et al. 1999]. With an iterative, incremental process, you can use SPE techniques to assess and reduce the risk of performance failure at the project outset, and at each subsequent iteration.

1.5.1 What Does It Cost?

The cost of SPE is usually a minor component of the overall project cost. Lucent Technologies has reported that the cost of SPE for performance-critical projects is about two to three percent of the total project budget. For other, less critical, projects, SPE typically costs less than one percent of the total project budget. For projects where the performance risk is very high, the SPE expenditure may be as much as ten percent of the project budget.

SPE efforts can save far more than they cost by detecting and preventing performance problems. Bank One reported that, on one project, SPE costs over a five-month period were $147,000. During this time, the team analyzed three applications and identified modifications that resulted in a projected annual savings of $1,300,000 [Manhardt 1998]. Similarly, the performance engineering group at MCI reported a $20,000,000 savings in one year with SPE due to reduced resource requirements that resulted in deferred configuration upgrades [CMG 1991].

1.5.2 What Do You Need?

To perform SPE studies, you need two essential skills:

- Estimation techniques for specifying best- and worst-case resource requirements
- Enough modeling background to understand the translation of OO models into performance models, and to understand the results

This book provides the information you need to develop these skills.

Other factors will make your SPE efforts easier. The following list starts with factors that are easy to find and progresses to those that require more effort but provide substantial benefits.

1. Performance specialists in your computer systems department (capacity planners, system programmers, and so on.) can assist with measurement studies and modeling techniques.

2. SPE tools make it easier for you to create and evaluate the models.

3. Management commitment provides sufficient time and resources to evaluate the risk of performance failures early in the project, and take appropriate steps based on the results. Management commitment provides the incentive and the ability to conduct SPE tasks.

4. Formal integration of SPE into the software development process with specific SPE milestones and deliverables makes SPE less people-dependent and ensures that it will be uniformly applied across projects.

5. An official SPE organization can provide a team of specialists to assist many projects with the SPE modeling and analysis steps. This organization is not the same as the computer system performance specialists in item 1. This team is more closely allied with the development organization, and provides software-specific performance engineering support.

These topics and others are also addressed in this book.

SPE is not a silver bullet—you cannot buy one book or one tool and expect that it alone will resolve performance problems.

SPE takes thought, effort, and analysis to produce the desired results. However, the return on investment for SPE more than justifies its use.

1.6 Summary

Performance is an essential quality attribute of every software system. Many object-oriented and non-object-oriented software systems, however, cannot be used as they are initially implemented due to performance problems. Systems delivered with poor performance result in damaged customer relations, lost productivity for users, lost revenue, cost overruns due to tuning or redesign, and missed market windows.

It is possible to cost-effectively design performance into new software systems. Doing this requires careful attention to performance goals throughout the life cycle. Software performance engineering (SPE) provides a systematic, quantitative approach to managing performance throughout the development process.

SPE uses deliberately simple models of software processing with the goal of using the simplest possible model that identifies problems with the system architecture, design, or implementation plans. It is relatively easy to construct and solve these models to determine whether the proposed software is likely to meet performance goals. As the software development process proceeds, we refine the models to more closely represent the performance of the emerging software and re-evaluate performance.

This book discusses SPE for object-oriented systems. Object-oriented systems present special problems for SPE because their functionality is decentralized, and performing a given function is likely to require collaboration among many different objects from several classes. This makes the processing flow for object-oriented systems difficult to know a priori. Distributing objects over a network compounds the problem. In the following chapters, we illustrate how to use SPE techniques and the UML to overcome these problems.

SPE is not a silver bullet or a cure-all for performance problems. SPE takes thought, effort, and analysis to produce the desired results.

However, SPE efforts can save far more than they cost by detecting and preventing performance problems. The return on investment for SPE more than justifies its use.

Chapter 2

SPE Quick View

> *The aim of science is not to open the door to infinite wisdom, but to set a limit to infinite error.*
>
> —Bertolt Brecht

In This Chapter:

- The SPE process
- Example illustrating the process
- SPE in the Unified Software Process
- Creating software with good performance characteristics

2.1 SPE Process for Object-Oriented Systems

For object-oriented systems, we adapt the general SPE techniques to the process typically followed for object-oriented development, and to the artifacts that it produces.

The SPE process focuses on the system's use cases and the scenarios that describe them. In a use-case-driven process such as the Unified Process ([Kruchten 1999], [Jacobson et al. 1999]), use cases are defined as part of requirements definition (or earlier) and are refined throughout the design process. From a development perspective, use cases and their scenarios provide a means of understanding and documenting the system's requirements, architecture, and design. From a performance perspective, use cases allow you to identify the *workloads* that are significant from a performance point of view, that is, the collections of requests made by the users of the system. The scenarios allow you to derive the processing steps involved in each workload.

Chapter 15 describes these steps in more detail.

The SPE process includes the following steps. The activity diagram in Figure 2-1 captures the overall process.

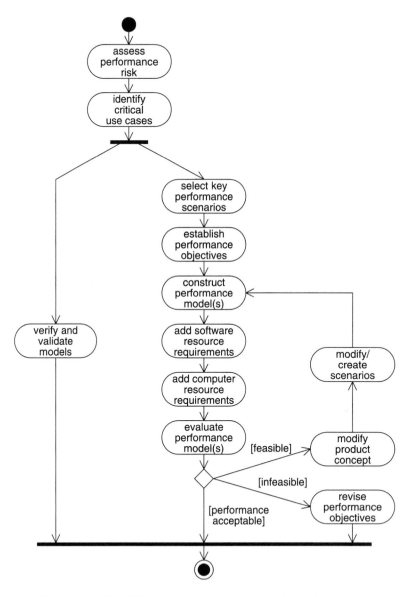

Figure 2-1: The SPE Process for Object-Oriented Systems

1. *Assess performance risk*: Assessing the performance risk at the outset of the project tells you how much effort to put into SPE activities. If the project is similar to others that you have built before, is not critical to your mission or economic survival, and has minimal computer and network usage, then the SPE effort can be minimal. If not, then a more significant SPE effort is needed.

Use cases are discussed in Chapter 3.

2. *Identify critical use cases*: The critical use cases are those that are important to the operation of the system, or that are important to responsiveness as seen by the user. The selection of critical use cases is also risk driven. You look for use cases where there is a risk that, if performance goals are not met, the system will fail or be less than successful.

   Typically, the critical use cases are only a subset of the use cases that are identified during object-oriented analysis. In the UML, use cases are represented by use case diagrams.

Sequence diagrams and their extensions are discussed in Chapter 3.

3. *Select key performance scenarios*: It is unlikely that all of the scenarios for each critical use case will be important from a performance perspective. For each critical use case, the key performance scenarios are those that are executed frequently, or those that are critical to the perceived performance of the system. Each performance scenario corresponds to a workload. We represent scenarios by using sequence diagrams augmented with some useful extensions.

Performance objectives are discussed in Chapter 7.

4. *Establish performance objectives*: You should identify and define *performance objectives* and *workload intensities* for each scenario selected in step 2. Performance objectives specify the quantitative criteria for evaluating the performance characteristics of the system under development. These objectives may be expressed in three primary ways by response time, throughput, or constraints on resource usage. For information systems, response time is typically described from a user perspective, that is, the number of seconds required to respond to a user request. For real-time systems, response time is the amount of time required to respond to a given external event. Throughput requirements are specified as the number of transactions or events to be processed per unit of time.

   Workload intensities specify the level of usage for the scenario. They are specified as an arrival rate (e.g., number of Web site hits per hour) or number of concurrent users.

Repeat steps 5 through 8 until there are no outstanding performance problems.

Chapter 4 discusses execution graphs.

5. *Construct performance models*: We use execution graphs to represent software processing steps in the performance model. The sequence-diagram representations of the key performance scenarios are translated to execution graphs.

Gathering data on software and computer resource requirements is discussed in Chapter 7 and Part III.

6. *Determine software resource requirements:* The processing steps in an execution graph are typically described in terms of the software resources that they use. Software resource requirements capture computational needs that are meaningful from a software perspective. For example, we might specify the number of messages sent or the number of database accesses required in a processing step.

    You base estimates of the amount of processing required for each step in the execution graph on the operation specifications for each object involved. This information is part of the class definition in the class diagram. As described in Chapter 4, when done early in the development process, these may be simple best- and worst-case estimates. Later, as each class is elaborated, the estimates become more precise.

Resource requirements are discussed in Chapter 7.

7. *Add computer resource requirements:* Computer resource requirements map the software resource requirements from step 6 onto the amount of service they require from key devices in the execution environment. Computer resource requirements depend on the environment in which the software executes. Information about the environment is obtained from the UML deployment diagram and other documentation. An example of a computer resource requirement would be the number of CPU instructions and disk I/Os required for a database access.

Note: Steps 6 and 7 could be combined, and the amount of service required from key devices estimated directly from the operation specifications for the steps in the scenario. However, this is more difficult than estimating software resources in software-oriented terms and then mapping them onto the execution environment. In addition, this separation makes it easier to explore different execution environments in "what if" studies.

Performance models and their solutions are discussed in Chapters 4, 5 and 6.

8. *Evaluate the models:* Solving the execution graph characterizes the resource requirements of the proposed software alone. If this solution indicates that there are no problems, you can proceed to solve the system execution model. This characterizes the software's performance in the presence of factors that could cause contention for resources, such as other workloads or multiple users.

   If the model solution indicates that there are problems, there are two alternatives:
   - *Modify the product concept:* Modifying the product concept involves looking for feasible, cost-effective alternatives for satisfying this use case instance. If one is found, we modify the scenario(s) or create new ones and solve the model again to evaluate the effect of the changes on performance.
   - *Revise performance objectives:* If no feasible, cost-effective alternative exists, then we modify the performance goals to reflect this new reality.

   It may seem unfair to revise the performance objectives if you can't meet them (if you can't hit the target, redefine the target). It is not wrong if you do it at the outset of the project. Then all of the stakeholders in the system can decide if the new goals are acceptable. On the other hand, if you get to the end of the project, find that you didn't meet your goals, and *then* revise the objectives—*that's* wrong.

Model verification and validation is discussed in Chapter 15.

9. *Verify and validate the models:* Model verification and validation are ongoing activities that proceed in parallel with the construction and evaluation of the models. Model verification is aimed at determining whether the model predictions are an accurate reflection of the software's performance. It answers the question, "Are we building the model right?" For example, are the resource requirements that we have estimated reasonable?

   Model validation is concerned with determining whether the model accurately reflects the execution characteristics of the software. It answers the question [Boehm 1984], "Are we building the right model?" We want to ensure that the model faithfully represents the evolving system. Any model will only contain what we think to include. Therefore, it is particularly important to detect any model omissions as soon as possible.

Both verification and validation require measurement. In cases where performance is critical, it may be necessary to identify critical components, implement or prototype them early in the development process, and measure their performance characteristics. The model solutions help identify which components are critical.

Late life cycle and post deployment SPE activities are discussed in Chapter 15.

These steps describe the SPE process for one phase of the development cycle, and the steps repeat throughout the development process. At each phase, you refine the performance models based on your increased knowledge of details in the design. You may also revise analysis objectives to reflect the concerns that exist for that phase.

2.2 Case Study

To illustrate the process of modeling and evaluating the performance of an object-oriented design, we will use an example based on an automated teller machine (ATM). This example is based on a real-world development project in which one of the authors participated. It has been simplified for this presentation, and some details have been changed to preserve anonymity.

> The ATM accepts a bank card and requests a personal identification number (PIN) for user authentication. Customers can perform any of three transactions at the ATM: deposit cash to an account, withdraw cash from an account, or request the available balance in an account. A customer may perform several transactions during a single ATM session. The ATM communicates with a computer at the host bank, which verifies the customer-account combination and processes the transaction. When the customer is finished using the ATM, a receipt is printed for all transactions, and the customer's card is returned.

The following sections illustrate the application of the SPE process for object-oriented systems to the ATM.

2.2.1 Assess Performance Risk (Step 1)

The performance risk in constructing the ATM itself is small. Only one customer uses the machine at a time, and the available hardware is more than adequate for the task. Consequently, the amount of SPE effort on this project will be small. However, the host software (considered later) must deal with a number of concurrent ATM users, and response time there is important, so a more substantial SPE effort is justified.

2.2.2 Identify Critical Use Cases (Step 2)

We begin with the use case diagram for the ATM shown in Figure 2-2. As the diagram indicates, several use cases have been identified: OperatorTransaction (e.g., reloading a currency cassette), CustomerTransaction (e.g., a withdrawal), and CommandFunctions (e.g., to go off-line). Clearly, CustomerTransaction is the critical use case, the one that will most affect the customer's perception of the ATM's performance.

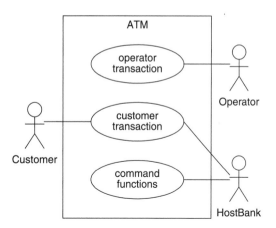

Figure 2-2: ATM Use Cases

2.2.3 Select Key Performance Scenarios (Step 3)

We therefore select the CustomerTransaction as the first performance scenario to consider. This scenario represents typical, error-free customer transactions from the CustomerTransaction use case. Later, after we confirm that the architecture and design are appropriate for this scenario, we will consider additional scenarios. To evaluate the scenario, we need a specification for the *workload intensity*—that is, the number of CustomerTransactions or their arrival rate during the peak period.

Chapter 3 discusses sequence diagrams and their extensions.

Figure 2-3 shows a scenario for customer transactions on the ATM. The notation used is a UML sequence diagram augmented with some additional features. These features allow us to denote repetition and choice. They are indicated by the rectangular areas labeled loop and alt, respectively. This scenario indicates that, after inserting a card and entering a PIN, a customer may repeatedly select transactions which may be deposits, withdrawals, or balance inquiries. The rounded rectangles indicate that the details of these transactions are elaborated in additional sequence diagrams.

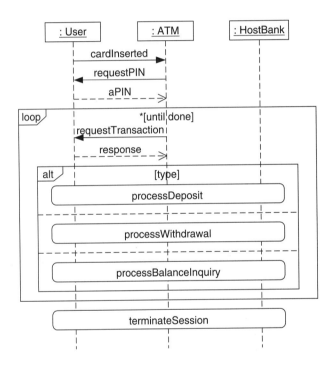

Figure 2-3: Customer Transaction Scenario

The scenario in Figure 2-3 combines the customer transactions of deposit, withdrawal, and balance inquiry. We combine them because we want to model what a customer does during an ATM session, and a customer may request more than one transaction during a single session. While we don't know exactly which transaction(s) a user will request, we can assign probabilities to each type of transaction based on reasonable guesses or actual measurements of customer activities.

Note: We could also represent the information in Figure 2-3 using a UML activity diagram. However, we have found that the extended sequence diagram notation is more familiar to software developers, and is easier to translate to a software execution model.

2.2.4 Establish Performance Objectives (Step 4)

As a bank customer, what response time do you expect from an ATM? Historically, performance objectives have been based on "time in the (black) box," that is, the time from the arrival of the (complete) request to the time the response leaves the host computer. That approach was used to separate things outside the control of the software (e.g., the time for the user to enter information, network congestion, and so on) from those that are more directly influenced by the software itself. If we take this approach for the ATM, a reasonable performance objective would be one second for the portion of the time on the host bank for each of the steps processDeposit, processWithdrawal, and processBalanceInquiry.

However, for SPE we prefer to expand the scope to cover the end-to-end time for a customer to complete a business task (e.g., an ATM session). Then, the results of the analysis will show opportunities to accomplish business tasks more quickly by reducing the number and type of interactions with the system, in addition to reducing the processing "in the box." A reasonable performance objective for this scenario might be 30 seconds or less to complete the (end-to-end) ATM session.

2.2.5 Construct Performance Models (Step 5)

The models for evaluating the performance of the ATM are based on the key scenarios identified earlier in the process. These *performance scenarios* represent the same processing as the sequence diagrams using execution graphs.

Chapter 4 discusses translating scenarios to execution graphs.

Figure 2-4 shows the execution graph that corresponds to the ATM scenario in Figure 2-3. The rectangles indicate processing steps; those with bars indicate that the processing step is expanded in a subgraph. Figure 2-5 shows the expansion of the processTransaction step; the expansion of the other steps is not shown here. The circular node indicates repetition, while the jagged node indicates choice.

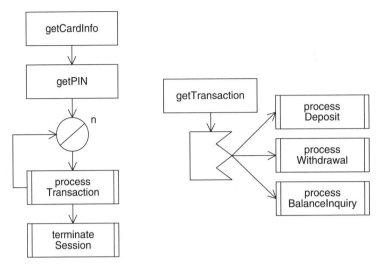

Figure 2-4: ATM Execution
Graph

Figure 2-5: Expansion of
processTransaction

The execution graph in Figure 2-4 expresses the same scenario as the sequence diagram in Figure 2-3: After inserting a card (to provide customer information) and entering a PIN, a customer may repeatedly select transactions, which may be deposits, withdrawals, or balance inquiries. Here, the number of transactions that a customer may perform is indicated by the parameter *n*.

2.2.6 Determine Software Resource Requirements (Step 6)

Software resources are discussed in more detail in Chapters 4 and 7.

The types of software resources will differ depending on the type of application and the operating environment. The types of software resources that are important for the ATM are:

- Screens—the number of screens displayed to the ATM customer
- Host—the number of interactions with the host bank
- Log—the number of log entries on the ATM machine
- Delay—the relative delay in time for other ATM device processing, such as the cash dispenser or receipt printer

---

Note: Software resource requirements are application-technology specific. Different applications will specify requirements for different types of resources. For example, a system with a significant database component might specify a software resource called "DBAccesses" and specify the requirements in terms of the number of accesses. We cover the identification of applicable software resources in Part III.

We specify requirements for each of these resources for each processing step in the execution graph, as well as the probability of each case alternative and the number of loop repetitions. Figure 2-6 shows the software resource requirements for processWithdrawal.

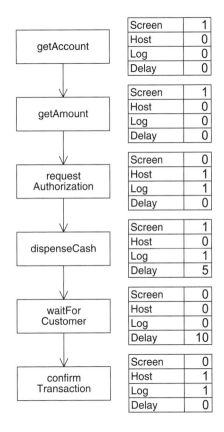

Figure 2-6: Software Resource Requirements for processWithdrawal

2.2.7 Add Computer Resource Requirements (Step 7)

We must also specify the *computer resource requirements* for each software resource request. The values specified for computer resource requirements connect the values for software resource requirements to device usage in the target environment. The computer resource requirements also specify characteristics of the operating environment, such as the types of processors/devices, how many of each, their speed, and so on.

Table 2-1: Example Overhead Matrix

Devices	CPU	Disk	Display	Delay		Net
Quantity	1	1	1	1		1
Service Units	Sec.	Phys. I/O	Screens	Units		Msgs.

	CPU	Disk	Display	Delay		Net
Screen	0.001		1			
Host	0.005			3		2
Log	0.001	1				
Delay				1		

	CPU	Disk	Display	Delay		Net
Service Time	1	0.02	1	1		0.05

Table 2-1 contains the computer resource requirements for the ATM example. The names of the devices in the ATM unit are in the first row, while the second row specifies how many devices of each type are in the facility. The third row is a comment that describes the unit of measure for the values specified for the software processing steps. The next four rows are the names of the software resources specified for each processing step, and the last row specifies the service time for the devices in the computer facility.

The values in the center section of the table define the connection between software resource requests and computer device usage. The Display "device" represents the time to display a screen and for the customer to respond to the prompt. The 1 in the Display column for the Screen row means that each screen specified in the software model causes one visit to the Display delay server. We arbitrarily assume this delay to be one second (in the service time row). Similarly, each Host and Delay specification in the software model results in a delay before processing the next step. We assume the Host delay is 3 seconds; other delays are specified in 1-second increments. Each Host request also sends 1 message via the Net and receives 1 reply message. Each message takes an average of 0.05 second. These values may be measured, or estimates could be obtained by constructing and evaluating more detailed models of the host processing required.

The connection between software resources and processing overhead is discussed in Chapter 4.

Details of the software execution model solution for the ATM are presented in Chapter 4.

Thus, each value specified for a processing step in the software model generates a demand for service from one or more devices in a facility. The computer resource requirements define the devices used and the amount of service needed from each device. The demand is the product of the software model value times the value in the overhead matrix cell times the service time for the column.

2.2.8 Evaluate the Models (Step 8)

We begin by solving the software model. This solution provides a "no contention" result. Here, we find that the total end-to-end time for the scenario is approximately 29 seconds, and most of that is due to the delays at the ATM unit for customer interactions and processing. This is a best-case result and, in this case, confirms that a single ATM will complete in the desired time. Because it is close to exceeding the objective, however, we may want to examine alternatives to reduce the end-to-end time. We should also examine the sensitivity of the results to our estimates. In addition, further studies will examine the host bank performance when there are multiple ATMs whose transactions could produce contention for computer resources. This will affect the time to handle Host requests.

2.2.9 Verify and Validate the Models (Step 9)

Chapter 6 presents details of the system execution model solution for the ATM.

Chapter 8 discusses performance measurement.

We need to confirm that the performance scenarios that we selected to model are critical to performance, and confirm the correctness of the workload intensity specifications, the software resource specifications, the computer resource specifications, and all other values that are input into the model. We also need to make sure that there are no large processing requirements that are omitted from the model. To do this, we will conduct measurement experiments on the operating environment, prototypes, and analogous or legacy systems early in the modeling process. We will measure evolving code as soon as viable. SPE suggests using early models to identify components critical to performance, and implementing them first. Measuring them and updating the model estimates with measured values increases precision in key areas early.

2.3 SPE in the Unified Software Process

To be effective, the SPE steps described in Section 2.2 should be an integral part of the way in which you approach software development. Integrating SPE into your software process avoids two problems that we have seen repeatedly. One is over-reliance on individuals. When you rely on individuals to perform certain tasks instead of making them part of the process, and then those individuals leave the company, their tasks are frequently forgotten. The other problem is that if SPE is not part of the process, it is easy to omit the SPE evaluations when time is tight or the budget is limited.

SPE deliverables are discussed in Chapter 15.

Integrating SPE into the software development process is not difficult. It is compatible with a wide variety of software process models, including the waterfall model [Royce 1970], the spiral model [Boehm 1988], and the Unified Process [Jacobson et al. 1999], [Kruchten 1999]. In each case, integrating SPE into your software process requires that you define the milestones and deliverables that are appropriate to your organization, project, and the level of SPE effort required.

To illustrate the use of SPE in the software process, we will focus on the Unified Process. This process is iterative and incremental, and its features are typical of the process used for many object-oriented projects.

The Unified Process is divided into four phases: inception, elaboration, construction, and transition. One complete pass through these four phases constitutes a cycle that results in a product release. A product evolves over time by repeating the four phases in additional cycles.

The Unified Process is risk-driven. That is, the focus of each iteration is identified, prioritized, and performed based on risks. Risks are anything that might endanger the success of the project, including the use of new technologies, the ability of the architecture to accommodate changes or evolution, market factors, schedule, and others. Because the ability to meet performance objectives is a potentially significant risk, the Unified Process suggests dealing with this and other risks early in the process, when the decisions that you make are the most important and the most difficult to change later. The approach used by the Unified Process is to address important risks, such as performance, in the inception and elaboration phase, and to continue monitoring them during the construction phase. Risks are identified and managed using iterations.

Integrating SPE into the Unified Process is straightforward. When beginning a new project, you assess performance risk by evaluating the extent of use of new technology, the experience of developers, the complexity of the new software and operating environment, the scalability requirements for anticipated volumes of usage, and other factors. When planning another iteration, you evaluate the results of the previous iteration to determine if there is a performance risk. Feasibility models can quantify the achievability of performance goals. If there is a performance risk, you plan and execute the current iteration to reduce that risk.

Note: In cases where performance is critical and the risk is high, you might perform an iteration specifically to address performance concerns. This iteration might involve, for example, implementing or prototyping a critical component to provide measured values for model input, or to demonstrate that the component under consideration can, indeed, be constructed to meet its performance objective.

In the inception and elaboration phases, your knowledge of the details of the system's architecture and design are sketchy. As a result, during these phases, you will focus on best- and worst-case analyses using upper and lower bounds for the resources required in each processing step in the execution graph. Later, as your knowledge of the system's details improves, you can elaborate the model and refine your estimates.

2.4 Performance Solutions

Performance solutions are discussed in Part IV.

The quantitative techniques described in Section 2.2 form the core of the SPE process. SPE is more than models and measurements, however. Other aspects of SPE focus on creating software that has good performance characteristics, as well as on identifying and correcting problems when they arise. They include

- Applying *performance principles* to create architectures and designs with the appropriate performance characteristics for your application
- Applying *performance patterns* to solve common problems

- Identifying *performance antipatterns* (common performance problems) and refactoring them to improve performance
- Using *late life cycle techniques* for tough problems

An overview of each of these aspects of SPE follows.

2.4.1 Performance Principles

Performance Principles are presented in Chapter 9.

Constructing and solving performance models quantifies the performance of your software's architecture and design. After you have modeled a number of different designs, some of which have good performance characteristics and some of which don't, you will begin to develop a feel for what works and what doesn't. You will avoid those design strategies that have repeatedly produced poor performance and, consciously or unconsciously, incorporate those that consistently produce good performance into your standard "bag of tricks."

A set of general principles for creating responsive systems helps shorten that learning process. The performance principles help to identify design alternatives that are likely to meet performance objectives.

The nine performance principles presented in Chapter 9 generalize and abstract the knowledge that experienced performance engineers use in constructing software systems. They help to identify design alternatives that are likely to meet performance objectives.

2.4.2 Performance Patterns

Performance Patterns are presented in Chapter 10.

A pattern is a common solution to a problem that occurs in many different contexts [Gamma et al. 1995]. It provides a general solution that may be specialized for a given context. Performance patterns describe best practices for producing responsive, scalable software. Each performance pattern is a realization of one or more of the performance principles. Chapter 10 presents seven *performance patterns*. These are new patterns that specifically address performance and scalability.

2.4.3 Performance Antipatterns

Performance Antipatterns are presented in Chapter 11.

Antipatterns are conceptually similar to patterns in that they document recurring solutions to common design problems [Brown et al. 1998]. They are known as *anti*patterns because their use (or misuse) produces negative consequences. Antipatterns document common mistakes made during software development. They also document solutions, or *refactorings,* for these mistakes. Thus, antipatterns tell you what to avoid and how to fix problems when you find them.

Performance antipatterns document recurring performance problems and their solutions. They complement the performance patterns by documenting what *not* to do and how to fix a problem when you find one. This approach is particularly useful for performance because good performance is the absence of problems. By illustrating performance problems and their causes, performance antipatterns help build performance intuition.

2.4.4 Implementation Solutions

Implementation solutions are presented in Chapter 12.

If you have a poor architecture or design, it is unlikely that any amount of clever coding will enable you to achieve your performance objectives. This does not mean that later life cycle activities can be ignored, however. In fact, it is necessary to manage performance throughout the software development process to ensure that you will meet your objectives.

In an ideal world, once you have constructed and solved the SPE models to verify that your proposed architecture and design will meet your performance objectives, most of your work would be done. Your primary focus during the later phases of development would be to monitor the evolving software to confirm that the performance is as predicted, or to detect and correct any deviations that arise. For many systems, this may be all that is needed.

The real world is sometimes not so cooperative, however, so it is often necessary to carefully manage performance throughout the software development cycle. For example, some systems have a high risk of performance failure, or have other constraints (e.g., regulatory constraints for safety-critical systems) that require closer monitoring throughout implementation, along with careful attention to detailed design and coding activities.

You may find yourself with a system that has already been implemented and has performance problems. In this case, it is too late to apply the SPE techniques covered in other chapters from scratch. Instead, you must start with what you have and try to make it work.

Our systematic approach to tuning is presented in Chapter 12.

A systematic strategy for tuning poorly performing software that is based on quantitative data helps you to focus on the areas with the highest payoff, rather than expending effort on improvements that have a negligible overall effect.

Once you have identified the causes of the problems, you can correct them by applying the performance principles, using one of the performance patterns. Alternatively, if you have identified a performance anti-pattern, you can apply one of its refactorings. Chapter 12 discusses specific solutions for many common problems, as well as solutions specifically adapted for object-oriented software and the C++ and Java languages.

2.5 Summary

The SPE process focuses on the system's use cases and the scenarios that describe them. This focus allows you to identify the workloads that are most significant to the software's performance, and to focus your efforts where they will do the most good.

SPE begins early in the software development process to model the performance of the proposed architecture and high-level design. The models help to identify potential performance problems when they can be fixed quickly and economically.

Performance modeling begins with the software model. You identify the use cases that are critical from a performance perspective, select the key scenarios for these use cases, and establish performance objectives for each scenario. To construct the software model, you translate the sequence diagram representing a key scenario to an execution graph. This establishes the processing flow for the model. Then, you add software and computer resource requirements and solve the model.

If the software model solution indicates that there are no performance problems, you can proceed to construct and solve the system model to see if adding the effects of contention reveals any problems. If the software model indicates that there are problems, you should deal with these before going any further. If there are feasible, cost-effective alternatives, you can model these to see if they meet the performance goals. If there are no feasible, cost-effective alternatives, you will need to modify your performance objectives, or perhaps reconsider the viability of the project.

To be effective, the SPE steps described in this chapter should be an integral part of the way in which you approach software development. SPE can easily be incorporated into your software process by defining the milestones and deliverables that are appropriate to your organization, the project, and the level of SPE effort required. This chapter presented an overview of how SPE can be integrated into the Unified Software Process.

The quantitative techniques described in Section 2.2 form the core of the SPE process. SPE is more than models and measurements, however. Other aspects of SPE focus on creating software that has good performance characteristics, as well as on identifying and correcting problems when they arise. They include

- Applying *performance principles* to create architectures and designs with the appropriate performance characteristics for your application
- Applying *performance patterns* to solve common problems
- Identifying *performance antipatterns* (common performance problems) and refactoring them to improve performance
- Using *late life cycle techniques* to ensure that the implementation meets performance objectives

By applying these techniques, you will be able to cost-effectively build performance into your software and avoid the kinds of performance failures described in Chapter 1.

Chapter 3

SPE and the UML

The limits of my language mean the limits of my world.
—Ludwig Wittgenstein

In This Chapter:

- Overview of the UML
- Extending the UML to include performance information
- Performance scenarios and their descriptions
- Extensions to the sequence diagram notation
- Specifying time in performance scenarios
- Representing concurrency

3.1 Overview

Applying SPE early in the development process requires that the SPE process be tightly integrated with the software development methods being used. One important aspect of this is to capture performance-related information along with other aspects of the software's architecture and design.

As stated in Chapter 2, we use the Unified Modeling Language (UML) to describe software designs and provide a basis for constructing software performance models. The UML provides a standard object-oriented modeling notation that has gained widespread acceptance. It is compatible with a wide variety of object-oriented methods and, as a result, is ideal for use with SPE.

This chapter reviews the features of the UML that we need for capturing performance-related information. It also describes some extensions to the sequence diagram notation that we have found useful for SPE. These extensions include

- The ability to hierarchically structure sequence diagrams
- The ability to graphically represent repetition (loops) and alternation (choice) in sequence diagrams
- The ability to graphically represent concurrency in sequence diagrams

More information on aspects of the UML other than performance may be found in [Booch et al. 1999] and [Rumbaugh et al. 1999].

3.2 Extending the UML

Our approach is to adhere to the UML standard as much as possible. The UML definition at the time this book was written, however, contained few provisions for capturing performance-related information.[1] Therefore, we extend it to represent this information.

Fortunately, the UML provides built-in extension mechanisms that allow you to tailor the notation for particular purposes. These mechanisms are stereotypes, tagged values, and constraints.

3.2.1 Stereotypes

A stereotype allows you to create new model elements that are derived from existing UML elements, but are specific to a particular problem domain. A stereotype is represented as a string enclosed in guillemets («»). The stereotype appears above the name of the element to which it applies, as shown in Figure 3-1. The cube in Figure 3-1 represents a node that might be used in a UML deployment diagram. The stereotype indicates that this node is a processor.

You can also define graphic elements or icons for stereotypes to give them a distinctive visual representation in a UML model. Figure 3-2 illustrates an icon associated with a stereotype.

---

1. This chapter is based on UML version 1.3.

: Processor

Figure 3-1: Stereotypes   Figure 3-2: Stereotype Icon

3.2.2 Tagged Values

A tagged value is a pair of strings—a tag and a value—that holds information about a model element. Tagged values allow you to include new properties for model elements. The tag is the name of a property, such as processorSpeed, and the value is the value of that property for the model element to which the tagged value is attached (e.g., 500 MHz). These strings are enclosed by braces ({ }) and are attached to a model element, such as a processor node, as shown in Figure 3-3.

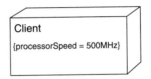

Figure 3-3: Tagged Values

3.2.3 Constraints

A constraint is a condition or restriction that defines additional model semantics. A constraint may be attached to an individual model element or a collection of elements. The constraint is written as a string enclosed in braces ({ }). It is interpreted according to a language, which may be: the UML Object Constraint Language; a programming language, such as C++; a formal notation, such as Z; or a natural language. Figure 3-4 shows an example of a constraint for the ATM.

Account
balance : Currency {balance $\geq$ 0}

Figure 3-4: Constraints

We use stereotypes and tagged values to capture information about the environment in which the software executes (e.g., processor type, processor speed, network speed, and so on). Examples of these uses appeared in Figure 3-1 through Figure 3-3. We use constraints to specify performance objectives (e.g., response time or throughput). This use of constraints is discussed in greater detail in Section 3.5.

3.3 Use Cases and Scenarios

The SPE process focuses on use cases and the scenarios that describe them. By examining the system's use cases, you can identify the functions of the system that are significant to performance. Then, by identifying the scenarios within each use case that have the greatest impact on performance—the *performance scenarios*—you can identify the *processing steps* that execute when these functions are invoked. The processing steps are the operations that are invoked as the result of each interaction (message) in the scenario. This information is contained in UML use case diagrams and interaction diagrams (either sequence diagrams or collaboration diagrams). With it, you can construct the skeleton of the software model.

We'll begin by presenting a quick overview of use cases, and then we'll discuss the representation of scenarios.

3.3.1 Use Cases

Use cases describe the behavior of a system or a portion of it, that is, a subsystem. A use case is "a set of sequences of actions, including variants, that a system performs that yields an observable result of value to an actor" [Booch et al. 1999]. An actor is an entity (e.g., a user or another system) outside the system that interacts directly with the system. A use case does not reveal internal details of these interactions; use cases are specified independently of how they are realized.

Use cases are captured in use case diagrams. A use case diagram shows a set of use cases, as well as the actors that use them, and the relationships between the actors and the use cases. The actors identify the significant stakeholders in the system. Figure 3-5 illustrates a use case diagram for the ATM example introduced in Chapter 2. A use case is represented by an ellipse that contains the name of the use case, while actors are indicated by stick figures or stereotyped icons. The lines between actors and use cases indicate associations between them. The rectangle in Figure 3-5 represents the system boundary.

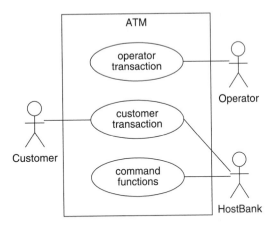

Figure 3-5: Use Case Diagram

Use cases are employed to

- *Model the context of the system*: the system boundary indicates which features are part of (inside) the system, which actors interact with the system, and the meaning of those interactions.
- *Specify the requirements for the system:* use cases describe what the system should do from the point of view of its external actors or clients. By specifying sequences of actions that the system can perform, use cases focus on the intended behavior of the system. Other requirements, such as reliability, safety, security, and, of course, performance, can be specified as annotations to a use case diagram.

From a performance perspective, use case diagrams are a convenient way to identify the functions of the system that are most important to performance. These *critical use cases* are those that

- Are critical to the operation of the system,
- Influence users' perception of responsiveness, or
- Represent a risk that performance goals might not be met

Use case diagrams, however, are limited in their semantic content, thus we focus on the individual scenarios that describe each critical use case. These are described in the next section.

3.3.2 Scenarios

A *scenario* is an instance of a use case. It consists of a sequence of steps describing the interactions between the objects involved in a particular execution of the software. The scenario shows the objects that participate and the messages that flow between them. A message may represent either an event or an invocation of one of the object's methods (operations).

Scenarios are represented in UML *interaction diagrams*—either sequence diagrams or collaboration diagrams.

Note: UML activity diagrams can also be used to document use cases [Schneider and Winters 1998]. We discuss the use of activity diagrams for representing performance scenarios later in this chapter.

Initially, the scenarios that describe use cases will be "black box" representations of interactions between the system and its external actors. As the design of the system evolves, the scenarios are elaborated to include interactions between internal objects as well. Because our performance models are based on these scenarios, they also begin simply and evolve to include more detail as the scenarios are elaborated.

Sequence diagrams and collaboration diagrams represent the same information and are, therefore, semantically equivalent. However, sequence diagrams emphasize the time-ordering of messages, while collaboration diagrams emphasize the structural organization of the collection of interacting objects. We have found that sequence diagrams are more natural to use for constructing performance models.

Note: Many tools that support the UML automatically convert collaboration diagrams to sequence diagrams and vice versa.

Basic Sequence Diagrams Figure 3-6 illustrates a portion of a simple sequence diagram for the ATM application. Each dashed vertical line is known as an *object lifeline*; it represents the existence of an object over time. Interactions between objects are represented by *messages*, the horizontal arrows between lifelines. In the diagram, time increases going down a lifeline. Thus, a message that appears above another occurs before it in time.

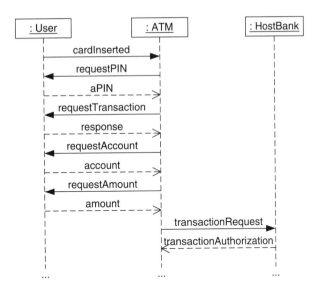

Figure 3-6: Sequence Diagram

Table 3-1: Message Control Flow

——————►	A solid arrowhead indicates procedural flow of control. Any nested operations are completed before the outer-level sequence of actions continues. This models ordinary procedure calls as well as concurrent interactions where the sender waits for a nested sequence of behavior to complete before proceeding.
——————⟶	A stick arrowhead indicates nonprocedural, or flat, flow of control. Each arrow simply indicates the next step in the sequence.
——————⟍	A half-stick arrowhead shows asynchronous communication between two objects.
- - - - -⟶	A dashed arrow with a stick arrowhead shows a return from a procedure call. The return arrow is sometimes omitted because a return is implicit at the end of an activation.

If you want to emphasize that the delivery of a message takes time (e.g., network transmission time), you can draw the arrow with a downward slope. Different types of UML arrows indicate different kinds of message control flow. They are summarized in Table 3-1. Section 3.6 discusses how to represent synchronization.

Activations The thin rectangles attached to the object lifelines in Figure 3-7 represent an *activation*, or focus of control. An activation indicates a period of time when the object is busy performing some action. The object may be performing the action directly by itself or indirectly through a subordinate procedure. The top of the rectangle indicates the initiation of the operation, and the bottom indicates its completion.

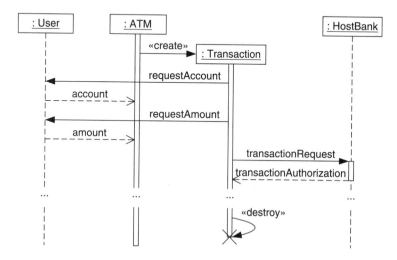

Figure 3-7: Creation and Destruction

An activation shows which operation is performed when a message is received. If the identity of the operation is not clear from the incoming message symbol, you can indicate it by a text label next to the activation.

Note: The activation for the ATM object begins with the cardInserted message and continues throughout the session. This indicates that the ATM object executes concurrently to monitor timing requirements and handles timeouts as appropriate. Although the HostBank object may also execute concurrently, we only show its activation while it is servicing this ATM's requests. Between requests, the object services other ATMs. Similarly, the User is only involved in this scenario when responding to a request from the ATM.

If you want to emphasize the period of time that the ATM is actually computing in response to some request, you can shade that region of the activation rectangle.

Use activations to emphasize the time that an object is responding to a request or to indicate the execution of concurrent objects.

Creation and Destruction Objects may be created and destroyed during a scenario. Object creation and destruction are indicated by the stereotyped messages, «create» and «destroy». Typically, the object lifeline begins at the point of creation and ends when the object is destroyed. A large X is used to mark the end of the object's lifeline. Figure 3-7 illustrates the creation and destruction of a transaction object in the ATM. The transaction destroys itself (by sending itself a «destroy» message) when it has completed its processing.

3.4 Extensions to Sequence Diagram Notation

We have found it useful to augment the UML sequence diagram notation with features from the *message sequence chart* (MSC) standard [ITU 1996]. Message sequence charts are similar to sequence diagrams, and provide similar capabilities for modeling object instances and the messages that flow between them. The MSC features that we add to sequence diagrams make it possible to represent hierarchical structure (instance decomposition and references), looping, alternation, and concurrency.

3.4.1 Instance Decomposition

Consider the sequence diagram in Figure 3-6. This is the sort of sequence diagram that would be produced during requirements analysis. Later, after some preliminary design is done, this scenario would be refined to include some of the objects, such as the card reader and keypad, that are part of the system's design. To indicate this refinement, we use *instance decomposition*.

Instance decomposition makes it possible to attach another sequence diagram to an object lifeline. This allows expansion of a high-level sequence diagram to show lower-level interactions. For the decomposition to be meaningful, the order of messages on the decomposed instance must be preserved. Figure 3-8 illustrates the decomposition of the User axis by showing how the various input/output devices of the ATM user interface (the card reader, keypad, display, and so on) provide

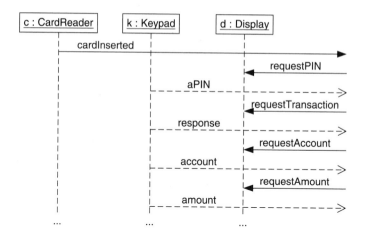

Figure 3-8: Decomposition of :User

the interactions with the user. Using instance decomposition makes it possible to elaborate the sequence diagram as we learn more about the system, without having to re-draw the diagram each time. It also helps ensure that we maintain consistency with the scenario as it was originally described.

Use instance decomposition to elaborate high-level objects as the design evolves.

3.4.2 Looping, Alternation, and References

The scenario in Figure 3-9 combines the customer transactions of deposit, withdrawal, and balance inquiry. We combine these transactions in a single scenario because we want to model what a customer does during an ATM session. A customer may request more than one transaction during a single session. While we don't know exactly what transaction(s) a user may request, we can assign probabilities based on reasonable guesses or measurements of actual customer activities.

The rectangular areas labeled loop and alt in Figure 3-9 are *inline expressions*. They denote repetition and alternation (choice), respectively. An additional label, opt, may be used to designate optional portions of the scenario.

This sequence diagram indicates that the user may repeatedly select transactions, which may be deposits, withdrawals, or balance inquiries.

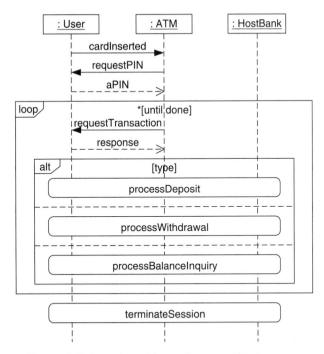

Figure 3-9: Looping, Alternation, and References

The label *[until done] at the top of the loop rectangle is an *iteration clause*. It indicates the condition under which the enclosed section of the sequence diagram is repeated. Here, the section is repeated until the user is done.

The label [type] at the top of the alt rectangle is a *condition clause*. It indicates the condition under which one of the alternative regions of the alt is executed. Here, the selection is determined by the type of transaction chosen by the user.

Note: Iteration and condition clauses are part of the UML notation. They are used to indicate messages that are repeated or conditional. Rumbaugh [Rumbaugh et al. 1999] notes that you can show iteration in a sequence diagram by enclosing a set of messages and marking them with an iteration clause. The means of enclosing the set of messages, however, is undefined. We have chosen to use the MSC loop construct for this purpose.

It is difficult to represent anything other than simple branching (conditional execution) on sequence diagrams using the standard UML notation

[Booch et al. 1999]. The alt and opt constructs used here make representing even complex branching relatively straightforward.

Show repetition and alternation explicitly because the number of times a sequence is repeated or the probability that a given sequence is executed will be parameters for the software execution model.

The rounded rectangles in Figure 3-9 are "references" which refer to other sequence diagrams. The use of references allows another way of hierarchically composing sequence diagrams. The sequence diagram that corresponds to the processWithdrawal reference is shown in Figure 3-10.

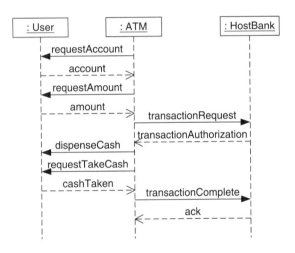

Figure 3-10: Expansion of processWithdrawal

Use references to reduce the complexity of sequence diagrams. Using references also helps in constructing hierarchical software execution models (see Chapter 4).

Inline expressions and references can both be added to the basic UML notation as stereotypes of interaction. Additional extensions to the sequence diagram notation that help express concurrency are described in Section 3.6.

Note: It is also possible to use UML activity diagrams to describe combined scenarios like those in Figure 3-9. The activity diagram in Figure 3-11 describes the same scenario as that in Figure 3-9. The activity diagram in Figure 3-12 shows the expansion of processWithdrawal. The rectangles in Figure 3-12 are "swimlanes" that partition the activity diagram to indicate which object is responsible for each activity.

We prefer sequence diagrams for expressing performance scenarios because they are easier to derive early in the process, when little is known about specific activities. Sequence diagrams with the extensions described here are also more straightforward to translate to execution graphs. However, if you prefer activity diagrams, feel free to use them.

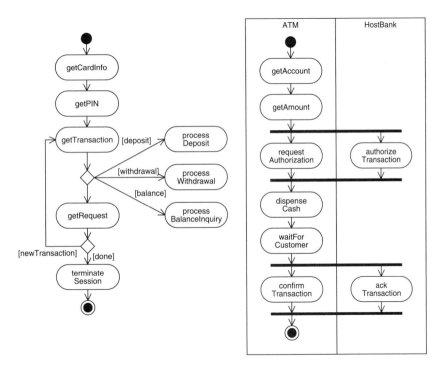

Figure 3-11: Activity Diagram for ATM   Figure 3-12: Expansion of processWithdrawal

3.5 Specifying Time

The UML allows you to specify timing requirements through the use of timing marks, time expressions, and timing constraints.

3.5.1 Timing Marks

Timing marks may be used to denote the time at which a message or an event occurs. A timing mark is an expression formed from the name of the message; for example,

message.sendTime()   The time that the message is sent

message.receiveTime()   The time that the message is received

where message is the name of the message.

3.5.2 Time Expressions

A time expression is an expression that evaluates to an absolute or relative value of time. Time expressions typically express an elapsed time or the occurrence of some particular time; for example,

after(500msec)

when(t = 08:00)

The first expression might be used to indicate the time elapsed after a particular state is entered. The second denotes the occurrence of the time 08:00.

3.5.3 Timing Constraints

A timing constraint (an application of a UML constraint) expresses a constraint based on the absolute or relative value of time. For example, the constraint

{b.sendTime() - a.receiveTime < 10 msec}

indicates that the time between receiving message a and sending message b must be less than 10 milliseconds.

3.5.4 Time in Sequence Diagrams

The UML uses timing constraints to model time in sequence diagrams. You can use timing constraints to model the absolute time of an event, the relative time between events, or the time it takes to perform an action. The most straightforward way to use timing constraints is to name messages, and then use the names in constraint expressions.

Figure 3-13 illustrates a typical use of timing constraints. The constraints on user actions (e.g., b.receiveTime() - a.sendTime() < 60s) are to prevent the ATM from waiting forever for a user who has left without canceling the session. The user has 60 seconds to respond to a prompt (e.g., requestPIN). If a response is not received within that time, the ATM will assume that the user has left and take appropriate action. The 45-second constraint on receiving a response to a transactionRequest is to prevent the ATM from waiting forever for a response from the HostBank in the event of a host computer or network failure. Again, after 45 seconds, the ATM will assume that there is a problem in handling the request and abort the transaction.

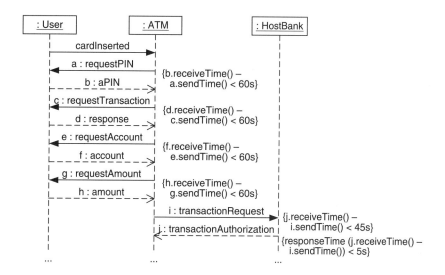

Figure 3-13: Time in Sequence Diagrams

Notice that these timing constraints specify timeout conditions, and are not particularly useful from a performance perspective. At best, they give us a worst-case picture of the end-to-end time for the transaction. When specifying performance, we are more interested in response time than timeouts. A more reasonable approach for the ATM would be to specify a response time using a time expression such as

responseTime (j.receiveTime() - i.sendTime())

to produce a constraint such as

{responseTime (j.receiveTime() - i.sendTime()) < 5s}

This constraint, also included in Figure 3-13, indicates that the performance objective is for the HostBank to respond to a transactionRequest in less than 5 seconds.

 Use time expressions that are meaningful from a performance perspective, such as responseTime(), *to specify performance objectives.*

3.6 Concurrency

For systems that have multiple threads or processes, you will need to specify various additional information about the threads or processes, including which objects are assigned to each thread or process, where the code executes, and the type of communication and synchronization used. It is also useful to represent the parallel composition of messages on a sequence diagram. This section discusses modeling concurrency with the UML. We also present some additional extensions that are useful for modeling concurrency.

3.6.1 Threads and Processes

Processes or threads are modeled in the UML as active classes and objects. A *process* represents a flow of control that executes in parallel with other processes each having its own address space. A *thread* executes concurrently with other threads inside a process. The threads belonging to a process all share the same address space. A thread is a lighter-weight unit of concurrency than a process.

The UML also defines two standard stereotypes that apply to active classes: «process» and «thread». An active class or object is indicated by a thick border on the entity's rectangle. Figure 3-14 shows an active object that is the root of a process.

Figure 3-14: Active Object

The UML allows you to indicate where a component executes by specifying its location. You indicate a component's location in a deployment diagram by nesting the component inside the node upon which it executes, as shown in Figure 3-15. You can also indicate a component's location by drawing a dependency between the component and its node. The bold rectangles with tabs in Figure 3-15 are predefined stereotype icons for executable components [Booch et al. 1999].

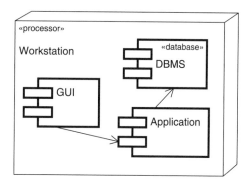

Figure 3-15: Deployment Diagram

In other contexts, such as a sequence diagram, you can show location as a tagged value:

{location = Server}

This is illustrated in Figure 3-17.

3.6.2 Coregions

The messages in a sequence diagram are strictly ordered in time. In some cases, however, this is not appropriate. For example, you may want to specify that messages a and b occur before message c, but that either a or b can come first. With the standard UML sequence diagram notation, the only way to indicate this is with a textual annotation on the diagram.

Coregions allow an exception to total ordering whereby messages within a coregion are *unordered*. A coregion is indicated by a solid line, enclosed by horizontal dividers, overlapping an object's lifeline.

Note: The MSC standard uses a dashed line to indicate the coregion and a solid line for the instance axis (lifeline). Because UML sequence diagrams use dashed lines for lifelines, we have adopted a solid line for the coregion.

Figure 3-16 illustrates the use of coregions. The example here is drawn from the domain of Web applications. When a Web browser requests a Web page, the page may contain one or more images in a graphics format such as Graphics Interchange Format (GIF). If there are multiple images, they may be requested in parallel. Each image may be requested and received over a separate connection to the server. The images may be requested in any order and, once requested, received in any order. Figure 3-16 models the interaction between this type of browser and a Web server.

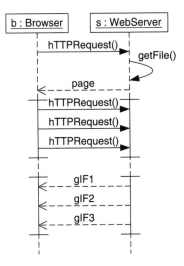

Figure 3-16: Coregions

3.6.3 Parallel Composition

Some objects may be capable of initiating or responding to concurrent requests. One way to show this is by using coregions, as shown in Figure 3-16. Coregions allow you to show some forms of the interleaving of messages that occur in parallel processing, as with downloading graphics to a Web browser. In some circumstances, however, coregions may be too restrictive. For those situations, we use *parallel composition*.

Parallel composition is indicated by an inline expression that encloses a portion of the sequence diagram within a rectangular area, similar to the loop, alt, and opt constructs. The parallel composition is indicated with the label par. The par region is divided into sections by dashed horizontal lines. The sections are executed in parallel, and the order of events within each section is preserved.

Figure 3-17 illustrates an alternative way of expressing the concurrent downloading of graphics to a Web browser. Note the use of tagged values to show the locations of the Browser and WebServer. Figure 3-18 shows the expansion of the getGIF references.

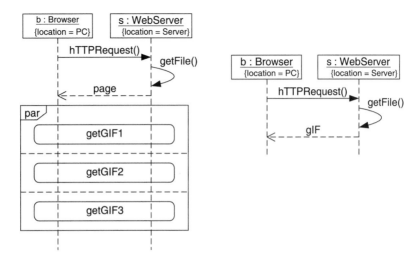

Figure 3-17: Parallel Composition   Figure 3-18: Expansion of getGIF

Note: The behavior described in Figure 3-17 is different from that in Figure 3-16. In Figure 3-16, all of the requests are sent before any response is received. In Figure 3-17, it is possible that a response to one request could be received before another request is sent. Thus, Figure 3-17 allows for interleaving requests and responses, while Figure 3-16 does not.

3.6.4 Synchronization

You can show synchronous and asynchronous messages in the UML by using different types of arrowheads. Figure 3-19 shows a synchronous communication using a filled arrowhead for the message and a return arrow for the reply. Figure 3-20 shows an asynchronous communication using a half stick arrowhead. Both of these examples use standard UML notation.

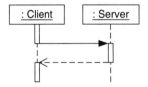   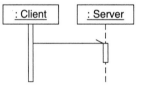

Figure 3-19: Synchronous   Figure 3-20: Asynchronous
Communication   Communication

We have also found it useful to model a situation similar to a synchronous interaction in that the client sends a message to the server and expects a reply. In this case, however, the client sends the message and continues processing. Then the client requests the result later. This type of interaction is shown in Figure 3-21 and Figure 3-22 using an extension to the sequence diagram notation. The extension is the addition of

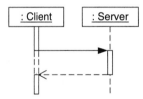   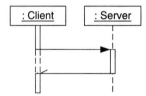

Figure 3-21: Deferred Synchronous   Figure 3-22: Asynchronous
Communication   Callback

a dashed section of the activation bar to show that the client has a potential delay while the server finishes responding to the request. Figure 3-21 represents deferred synchronous communication in distributed systems (e.g., Common Object Request Broker Architecture [CORBA] based systems). With this type of communication, the client issues the call, and (possibly) waits for the reply later. Some systems that do not support the reply-wait function implement this behavior with asynchronous callback, as in Figure 3-22. The client issues an asynchronous call, and receives another asynchronous call containing the reply later.

Contention effects and the system model are discussed in Chapter 6.

Modeling concurrency is important in the later stages of SPE for evaluating contention effects. Early in the development process, you may not know much about the concurrency and synchronization properties of the proposed software. At that point, it is better to focus on using the software model to make sure that there are no problems in the absence of contention. Then, as your knowledge of the software increases, you can add in concurrency and synchronization.

3.7 Summary

Applying SPE early in the development process requires that the SPE process be tightly integrated with the software development methods being used. We have found that the UML, when augmented with a few additional features, provides the level of integration that we need. This chapter has provided an overview of the UML notation for representing use cases and scenarios that are significant to performance.

We also present some extensions to the sequence diagram notation that we have found useful for SPE.

- *Instance decomposition*: Instance decomposition allows a sequence diagram to be attached to an object lifeline.
- *Looping, alternation and optional regions*: The loop construct indicates a portion of the sequence diagram that is repeated. The alt construct indicates sections of the sequence diagram that are executed conditionally. The opt construct indicates a portion of the sequence diagram whose execution is optional.
- *References*: A reference is a pointer to another sequence diagram. Both references and instance decomposition allow hierarchical structuring of sequence diagrams.
- *Coregions*: Coregions allow an exception to the total ordering of messages whereby messages within a coregion are *unordered*.
- *Parallel composition*: Parallel composition indicates sections of the sequence diagram that are executed in parallel.
- *Potential delay for server response*: This extension uses a dashed section of an activation bar to indicate that the sender of a request may have finished processing, and is or may be waiting for the reply.

We will use these extensions throughout this book.

By describing software architectures and designs with this notation, you can capture much of the information needed for SPE studies as part of the development process. The design documents can then serve as input to the SPE process, as illustrated in Chapter 4.

Tool interoperability is discussed in Chapter 16.

It is our hope that the extensions described in this chapter will be adopted as part of the UML standard. Adding these features to the standard will encourage their inclusion in tools that support the UML. This, in turn, will make it easier to capture performance information as part of the software design process, and will make it possible to export performance information from design tools to SPE tools.

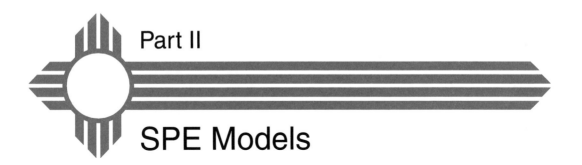

Part II

SPE Models

Chapter 4

Software Execution Models

Make everything as simple as possible, but not simpler.

—Albert Einstein

In This Chapter:

- Execution graph representation of software execution models
- Solving software execution models
- Translating sequence diagrams to execution graphs
- Case study

4.1 Purpose

Early in the development process, our knowledge of the software's design and implementation details is sketchy. The knowledge that we do have is insufficient to model the system's performance precisely. This does not, however, mean that early modeling is not useful. On the contrary, early modeling is essential to ensure that the software architecture is one that will make it possible to meet performance objectives.

The lack of knowledge about the software's design and implementation details means that, at this stage of development, we want to construct the simplest possible models that capture the essential performance characteristics of the software (the *simple-model strategy* from Chapter 1). The models should be easy to solve so as to get rapid feedback on whether the proposed software is likely to meet performance objectives. The software execution model has these characteristics.

Solving the software execution model provides a static analysis of the mean, best- and worst-case response times. It characterizes the resource requirements of the proposed software alone, in the absence of other workloads, multiple users or delays due to contention for resources. Because of this, the software model solution provides optimistic results. However, if the predicted performance in the absence of these additional performance-determining factors is unsatisfactory, then there is no need to construct more sophisticated models—adding delays due to contention will only make matters worse.

Software execution models are generally sufficient for identifying serious performance problems at the architectural and early design phases.

The system execution model is discussed in Chapter 6.

Later, as our knowledge of the software's design and implementation details becomes more complete, we can refine the software execution model in critical areas. We can also use the results from solving the software execution model to provide input parameters for the system execution model. This model represents the software's performance more precisely, and solving it characterizes the software performance in the presence of factors such as other workloads or multiple users, which could cause contention for resources.

The absence of problems in the software model does not mean that there are none.

There may be problems due to contention for system resources. After you rule out serious design problems with software models, use the system execution model to look for contention problems. These problems may be corrected with a different software design or with hardware configuration alternatives.

4.2 Representing Software Execution Models

Activity diagrams are discussed in Chapter 3.

We use *execution graphs* to represent software execution models. Execution graphs provide a visual representation of the software processing steps, and help to confirm that you have correctly interpreted the software execution. They also provide a convenient format for presenting the results of the performance evaluation. Execution graphs are based on elementary graph theory, so it is possible to prove the correctness of the solution algorithms (although we will not subject you to derivations or proofs here). They are similar to UML activity diagrams, so their notation should be familiar.

Note: It is not strictly necessary to use execution graphs—the analysis could be done directly from sequence diagrams or activity diagrams *if* additional information, such as resource requirements, is incorporated into them. We chose to keep the execution graphs because they help to explain the analysis steps and the interpretation of model results. Furthermore, there are currently no tools for analyzing the performance of sequence diagrams or activity diagrams directly. Tool issues are discussed in Chapter 16.

4.2.1 Execution Graphs

You construct an execution graph software model for each *performance scenario*. The graphs consist of nodes and arcs. The nodes represent *processing steps*—a collection of operation invocations and program statements that perform a function in the software system. The arcs represent the order of execution.

Figure 4-6 shows the basic types of nodes in an execution graph

Basic nodes represent processing steps at the lowest level of detail appropriate for the current development stage. Resource requirements are specified for each basic node. Figure 4-1 shows an execution graph for the user interaction with the ATM. The sequence diagram corresponding to this interaction is in Figure 3-6. All of the nodes in the execution graph in Figure 4-1 are basic nodes.

Deriving execution graphs from sequence diagrams is discussed later in this chapter.

Note: The execution graph in Figure 4-1 is a one-to-one correspondence to the sequence diagram in Figure 3-6. For performance assessment, we typically aggregate related steps in the sequence diagram with minimal processing into an abbreviated execution graph such as the one in Figure 4-2.

Software execution models elaborate details of interest for performance. They do not need to represent all of the processing details known about a design. In fact, the simple-model principle recommends that details that are not pertinent to performance should be excluded. Deciding which details are relevant and which should be excluded requires some performance intuition. This comes with experience.

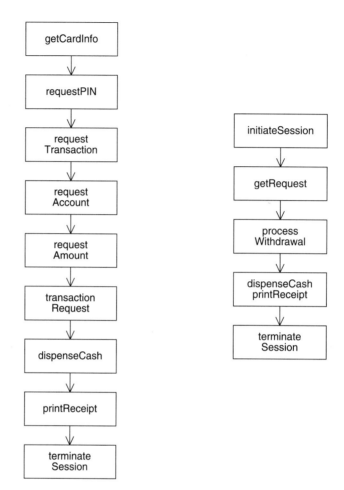

Figure 4-1: Sample Execution
Graph

Figure 4-2: Abbreviated Graph

Figure 4-3 and Figure 4-4 are derived from the sequence diagram in Figure 3-9.

Expanded nodes represent processing steps elaborated in another sub-graph. They show additional processing details that are identified as the design evolves and more information is available about the processing steps. The processTransaction and terminateSession nodes in Figure 4-3 are expanded nodes. The subgraph corresponding to processTransaction appears in Figure 4-4. Similarly, the processDeposit, processWithdrawal, and processBalanceInquiry nodes in Figure 4-4 are also expanded nodes. Their details would appear in additional subgraphs.

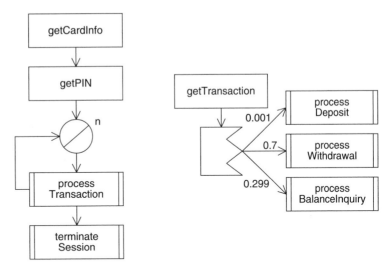

Figure 4-3: Execution Graph for
General ATM Scenario

Figure 4-4: Subgraph for
processTransaction Expanded Node

A *repetition node*, which is a circle with a diagonal line through it, represents one or more nodes that are repeated; the *repetition factor* associated with the node specifies the number of times the processing steps repeat. An arc connects the last node repeated with the repetition node. The graph in Figure 4-3 has one repetition node with one processing step in the loop, processTransaction. If you need to represent additional steps in the loop, it is best to expand the basic node attached to the repetition node, as we have done here.

The irregularly shaped node in Figure 4-4 is a *case node*. It represents conditional execution of processing steps. It has one or more *attached nodes* that represent the steps that may be executed. Each attached node has an *execution probability*. Figure 4-4 has a case node with three attached nodes: processDeposit has a probability of 0.001, processWithdrawal has a probability of 0.7, and processBalanceInquiry has a probability of 0.299. Note that other possible paths, such as a transfer transaction, are omitted from this scenario because they have an insignificant effect on performance. In fact we would typically omit processDeposit for the same reason. It is included here only to match its sequence diagram.

Note: The probabilities of conditional paths need not sum to 1.0. For example, a case node with only one attached node represents an optional step. The step is executed with the specified probability, p; and, with probability 1-p, execution proceeds to the processing step following the case node.

The number of transactions per user session modeled in Figure 4-3 is determined by the value of the repetition factor, n.

Figure 4-2 and Figure 4-3 illustrate two approaches to representing scenarios. Figure 4-2 is a specific scenario for an ATM session that consists of exactly one withdrawal transaction, while Figure 4-3 (with the subgraph in Figure 4-4) is a general sequence that allows one or more transactions in an ATM session, and specifies the probability of each type of transaction. Figure 4-2 is appropriate when the specific sequence (Withdrawal) is one of the most frequent uses and the other alternatives are not. You can always represent the specific case by the more general one (in this case, by setting the repetition factor *n* to 1, the probability of a processWithdrawal to 1, and the other probabilities to 0). The specific case, however, is simpler if it is the only one you need to consider.

Figure 4-5 shows one way to represent parallel execution within a scenario (not from the ATM example). The figure shows a *pardo* node (as in *parallel do*) indicating that executeRemoteQuery and createResultsScreen execute in parallel. Both must complete before the putDataInScreen step may proceed. A *split* node (shown in Figure 4-6) designates processing steps that execute in parallel but need not synchronize upon completion.

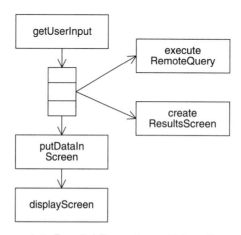

Figure 4-5: Parallel Execution within a Scenario

Note: Execution graphs have additional types of nodes, such as lock-free, that are beyond the scope of this book. For information on them, see [Smith 1990].

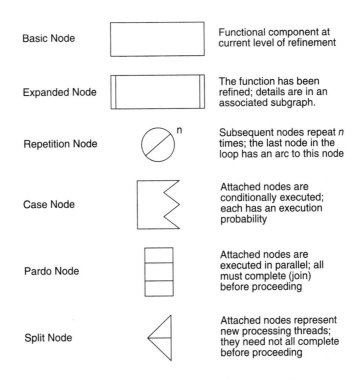

Basic Node	Functional component at current level of refinement
Expanded Node	The function has been refined; details are in an associated subgraph.
Repetition Node	Subsequent nodes repeat n times; the last node in the loop has an arc to this node
Case Node	Attached nodes are conditionally executed; each has an execution probability
Pardo Node	Attached nodes are executed in parallel; all must complete (join) before proceeding
Split Node	Attached nodes represent new processing threads; they need not all complete before proceeding

Figure 4-6: Basic Execution Graph Notation

A complete summary of the execution graph notation appears in Appendix B.

Figure 4-6 summarizes the basic execution graph notation. Basic nodes represent components at their current lowest level of detail. Expanded nodes show elaboration; a subgraph shows the next level of detail. Repetition nodes identify components that are repeatedly executed, and case nodes identify components conditionally executed. Pardo and split nodes show parallel execution within a scenario. Other types of nodes represent details of synchronization among distinct scenarios. They are described in more detail in Chapter 5.

4.2.2 Execution Graph Restrictions

There are two restrictions on the construction of execution graphs:

1. *Initial node restriction*: graphs and subgraphs can have only one initial node

2. *Loop restriction*: all loops in the graph must be repetition loops

An *initial node* is the first processing step executed in the graph. Initial nodes can only be the origin of arcs, not the destination. If you have multiple possible entries to a subgraph, you can use a case node, and show each entry as an attached node with the appropriate probability of each entry. Figure 4-7 shows equivalent graphs: (a) violates the initial node restriction; (b) is equivalent and legal.

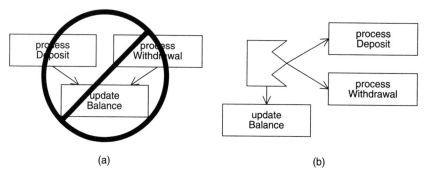

(a)   (b)

Figure 4-7: Initial Node Restriction. The graph in (a) is illegal; the graph in (b) is equivalent and legal.

The loop restriction does not reduce modeling power because, for any graph that violates this restriction, you can find equivalent representations that contain only repetition loops. For example, Figure 4-8 (a) shows an execution graph that violates the loop restriction. The arc from processRequest to getRrequest introduces a loop that is not a repetition loop. The revised graph in (b) represents the same processing with a repetition loop.

The purpose of these restrictions is to simplify the solution algorithms and enable the quick solution of many software alternatives. They do not restrict the modeling power of the graphs because, for every situation that seems to require a violation of these restrictions, there is an equivalent, legal representation. In fact, the restrictions not only facilitate the solution, they also facilitate the interpretation of results. It is convenient to see results for all loop repetitions as well as results for an

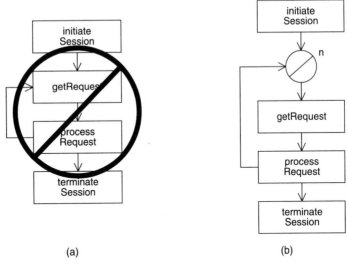

Figure 4-8: Loop Restriction. The graph in (a) has an illegal loop from processRequest to getRequest. The graph in (b) is equivalent and legal.

individual repetition (in its subgraph), and to see the impact of each potential entry to a subgraph.

Note: Execution graphs are similar to program flowcharts, but are not the same. Execution graphs show the frequency of path execution, and model only those paths that are key to performance.

Just as it is possible to construct very different programs that perform identical functions, it is also possible to construct different execution graph models that represent the same software. There is no single "right way." Graphs may differ in their representation of software hierarchy, and in the details they abstract. The selection of the details to model is the "art" of performance modeling.

4.3 Model Solutions

Remember, the primary purposes of the software execution model analysis are

- To make a quick check of the best-case response time in order to ensure the architecture and design will lead to satisfactory performance
- To assess the performance impact of alternatives
- To identify critical parts of the system for performance management

System model parameters are discussed in Chapter 6.

We also use software execution models to derive the parameters for the system execution model for further study.

This section explains the solution algorithms to a depth sufficient for you to understand how the models work. There are commercially available tools that help you create and solve software and system models so you do not have to memorize these algorithms.[1]

Note: You can use spreadsheets to represent and solve software models (we did before other tools were available). The problem with spreadsheets is that you want to be able to quickly study many design alternatives, and spreadsheets are more difficult to change. Also, it is too easy to inadvertently "clobber" the solution formulas. Thus, more work is required for modeling alternatives and validating results with spreadsheets.

4.3.1 Basic Solution Algorithms

Various interpretations of "time" are explained in Section 4.4.

The solution algorithms are intuitively easy to understand: You essentially examine the graphs and identify a basic structure, compute the time for the structure, and replace the structure by a "computed node" whose "time" is the computed time. This is known as a graph reduction step because it "reduces" the structure to a single node. You continue to reduce the structures, one by one, until you have reduced the entire graph to a single computed node whose time is the result of the analysis.

The basic structures are sequences, loops, and cases. When the structure is a sequence, as in Figure 4-9, the computed node time is the sum of the times of the nodes in a sequence.

---

1. The examples in this book were created and solved with the *SPE•ED* software performance engineering tool (www.perfeng.com).

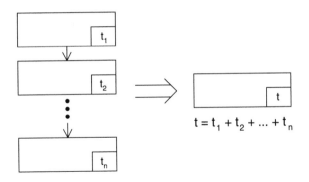

$$t = t_1 + t_2 + \dots + t_n$$

Figure 4-9: Graph Reduction for Sequential Structures

For loop structures, you multiply the node time by the loop repetition factor, as shown in Figure 4-10.

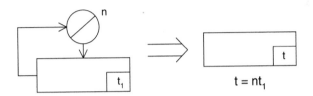

$$t = nt_1$$

Figure 4-10: Graph Reduction for Loop Structures

The computation for case nodes differs for shortest path, longest path, and average analyses. For the shortest path, the time for the case node is the minimum of the times for the conditionally executed nodes. For the longest path, it is the maximum of the times for the conditionally executed nodes. For the average analysis, you multiply each node's time by its execution probability, as shown in Figure 4-11.

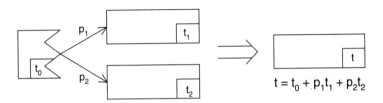

$$t = t_0 + p_1 t_1 + p_2 t_2$$

Figure 4-11: Graph Reduction for Case Nodes

For expanded nodes, you apply these algorithms recursively to the subgraph, and substitute the computed result for the expanded node.

Example 4-1 illustrates the use of these algorithms to calculate the best-case, worst-case, and average times for the ATM example in Figure 4-3 and Figure 4-4.

Example 4-1: Best, Worst, and Average Times for ATM Scenario

To illustrate the basic path reductions, consider the ATM scenario in Figure 4-3 and the subgraph for processTransaction in Figure 4-4. Assume the node "times" in the following table.

Node Times for ATM Calculation

Node	Time
getCardInfo	50
getPIN	20
getTransaction	30
processDeposit	500
processWithdrawal	200
processBalanceInquiry	50
terminateSession	100

First, use the sequential-path and conditional-path reduction rules to compute the time for processTransaction. The shortest path is getTransaction + ALT + processBalanceInquiry. The longest path is getTransaction + ALT + processDeposit.

processTransaction:
   Shortest path: 30 + 50 = 80
   Longest path: 30 + 500 = 530
   Average path: 30 + 0.001(500) + 0.7(200) + 0.299(50) = 185.45

Next, use these calculations to evaluate the graph for the session scenario in Figure 4-3. Combine the repetition-path reduction and sequential-path reduction to get

Session:
   Shortest path: 50 + 20 + 2(80) + 100 = 330
   Longest path: 50 + 20 + 2(530) + 100 = 1,230
   Average path: 50 + 20 + 2(185.45) + 100 = 540.9

These algorithms apply irrespective of the interpretation of "time." Section 4.4 explains various interpretations for "time."

4.3.2 More Advanced Solution Techniques

So far, the algorithms are relatively simple because we have focused on basic structures. The analysis of parallel execution nodes differs depending on the analysis and type of node. At this stage, we analyze simple best and worst cases for parallel execution. Later chapters will cover additional analyses.

The best case assumes that all other parallel paths are complete when the longest of the concurrent paths completes. The simple worst-case analysis assumes that the parallel paths serialize; that is, when one path completes the next begins. Thus, the best case uses the longest of the concurrent paths, and the worst case uses the sum of the concurrent paths. They are simple estimates of best and worst, but the actual performance may have contention effects between the parallel paths, or delays between executions of concurrent paths. This simplification is sufficient, however, for early life cycle approximations.

Note that the algorithms are formulated for evaluating execution graphs. The graphs are the formal basis for the algorithms. Once you understand them, you can apply the algorithms to software models that were constructed using other representations. For example, it is not necessary to draw a case node to compute its execution time. Instead, you can use the algorithms to analyze a spreadsheet representation of the execution structure, as long as you can identify the conditional execution. The graphical representation makes identifying these structures easy.

4.4 Analysis Procedures

After you gather performance specifications and create the software models from the sequence diagrams or activity diagrams, you are ready to evaluate the proposed system. Recall the two crucial analysis strategies presented in Chapter 1: (1) use both the best- and the worst-case estimates of resource requirements, and (2) begin with a simplistic analysis of the best case and introduce more sophisticated analyses of realistic cases as more detailed information becomes available.

The previous section defined the formulas for software model analysis using a generic "time." This section substitutes different data values for time to calculate the metrics of interest. For example, if a scenario consists of one sequential path, as in Figure 4-1, and you use the lower bound for CPU time for each node in the sequential-path reduction rule, the result is the lower bound for the CPU time for the scenario. Alternatively, if you estimate the lower bound elapsed time for each node and use it in the same formula, the result is the lower bound elapsed time for the scenario. The next few paragraphs explain these concepts, and incorporate the analysis of processing overhead to estimate elapsed time.

Note: CPU time is the amount of time a process actually uses the CPU. Elapsed time is the amount of wall-clock time that a process executes. Elapsed time includes the time a process executes on each device in the hardware and network configuration, such as CPU, I/O, and network time, plus delays waiting in a queue for a device, plus delays such as synchronization or communication.

For each basic node you specify the best- and worst-case values for the amount of service required from each software resource. Consider the hypothetical processing for authorizing a transaction (authorizeTransaction) on the host bank shown in Figure 4-12. It consists of three processing steps—validateUser, validateTransaction, and sendResult—that are sequentially executed. The template to the right of each step shows the names of the software resources and the best-case value for service units required for each component. For example, the software resources are WorkUnits, Database accesses (DB), and network messages (Msgs). Step sendResult requires 1 WorkUnit, 1 DB access, and 1 Msg. The values for each of the steps are in the figure.

Note: WorkUnits are a convenient way to specify relative CPU consumption of tasks. This example uses a range of values from 1 to 5; 1 being a simple task, and 5 being the most complex task for this application. The processing overhead then specifies an approximate number of machine instructions for the simple task. The number of instructions for the complex task is then five times that of the simple task. Chapter 7 describes this estimation convention in more detail.

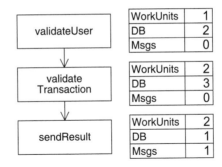

Figure 4-12: authorizeTransaction Software Resource Requirements

Table 4-1 shows the *processing overhead*, which is a chart of the computer resource requirements for each of the software resource requests. The names of the devices in the ATM unit are in the first row, while the second row specifies how many devices of each type are in the facility. The third row describes the unit of service for the values specified for the software processing steps. The next three rows are the names of the software resources specified for each processing step, and the last row specifies the service time for the devices in the computer facility.

Table 4-1: Processing Overhead

Device	CPU	Disk		Network
Quantity	1	1		1
Service Unit	KInstr.	Phys. I/O		Msgs.

WorkUnit	20	0		0
DB	500	2		0
Msgs	10	2		1

Service time	0.00001	0.02		0.01

The values in the center section of the table define the connection between software resource requests and computer device usage. For example, the row for DB specifies that each DB request requires 500K CPU instructions and 2 physical I/Os (no network messages). Msgs requires 10K CPU instructions, 2 I/Os (for logging), and 1 (outbound) Network message. Similarly, each WorkUnit requires 20K CPU instructions.

Note: We use the convention of specifying outbound messages, whereby the process sending the reply will specify the reply as its outbound message.

Note that the value in the CPU column specifies that each WorkUnit specified in the software model maps into 20K machine instructions. It is usually easier to estimate the number of lines of application code that will be executed, and then estimate how they map onto the chosen processor. The 20K estimate includes all the processing that occurs for operation invocations, system calls, code expansion from source to compiled lines of code, and so on.

The numbers in the table are hypothetical (and are probably unrealistically low, since a typical DB query may take one million instructions). We chose numbers that make it easy to demonstrate the calculations. Your SPE models will use values derived from measurement data for your computer environment, or from estimates of processing overhead. This shows more specifically what data you need for the *computer resource requirements* introduced in Chapter 2.

Step 1 uses the processing overhead matrix to calculate the total computer resources required per software resource for each node in the graph. Example 4-2 shows the calculation for the sendResult step.

Step 2 computes the total computer resource requirements for the graph. Table 4-2 shows the total for the host authorizeTransaction scenario graph in Figure 4-12. It is a simple graph that only requires the sequential-path reduction rule. You compute the results for each row using the algorithm in step 1, and then apply the reduction rules (in this case, it is a sequential path, so add the columns) to get the total computer resource requirements for the graph. More complex graphs use the

Table 4-2: Total Computer Resource Requirements for authorizeTransaction

Processing Step	CPU Kinstr	Physical I/O	Network Messages
validateUser	1,020	4	0
validateTransaction	1,540	6	0
sendResult	550	4	1
Total: authorizeTransaction	3,110	14	1

Example 4-2: Total Computer Resource Requirements for sendResult

The left section of the table below shows the best-case values for service units requested by each software resource. The right section of the table shows the processing overhead for each software resource request. The **Total:** sendResult at the bottom of the table is calculated by multiplying the service units requested times the corresponding value in the processing overhead column, and then adding the results for each column (type of computer resource).

Total Computer Resource Requirements for sendResult

Software Resource Requests		Processing Overhead		
Name	Service Units	CPU Kinstr	Physical I/O	Network Messages
WorkUnit	2	20	0	0
DB	1	500	2	0
Msgs	1	10	2	1
Total: sendResult		550	4	1

For example, the total physical I/O computer resource type is (2 WorkUnits *x* 0 I/O per request) + (1 DB *x* 2 I/O per request) + (1 Msgs *x* 2 I/O per request) = 4.

Check your understanding by computing the total CPU instructions for sendResult. Then, compute the computer resource totals for the validate-Transaction processing step. Check your results against Table 4-2.

other reduction rules to calculate the total computer resource requirements.

Queueing delays are discussed in Chapter 6.

Step 3 computes an estimate of the best-case elapsed time. It is a best case because it excludes queueing delays when multiple scenarios want to use the same computer resources at the same time. You compute the best-case elapsed time by multiplying the total resource requirements for each computer resource by the service time for that resource (from the bottom row of the processing overhead specification), and summing the result for each computer resource. For example, using the service times in Table 4-1, and the total computer resource requirements for authorize Transaction from Table 4-2, the best-case elapsed time for the host authorizeTransaction step is

$$(3,110 \times 0.00001) + (14 \times 0.02) + (1 \times 0.01) = 0.3211 \text{ second}$$

Even though these computations are relatively simple, you need an SPE tool to automate the analysis. Then, you don't have to worry about making arithmetic errors. You can also modify the graphs and get results quickly so you can feasibly study many alternatives.

4.5 Execution Graphs from Sequence Diagrams

For single-threaded scenarios or scenarios with sequential flow of control, going from a sequence diagram to an execution graph is straightforward. For scenarios that involve multiple threads of control or distributed objects, a little more effort is needed to identify operations that serialize and account for communication and synchronization delays. In either case, the process of translating a sequence diagram to an execution diagram is similar.

Each message received by an object triggers an action, which is either an operation or a state machine transition. The simplest way to construct an execution graph from a sequence diagram is to follow the message arrows through the performance scenario, and make each action a basic node in the execution graph. However, in many cases, individual actions are not interesting from a performance perspective, so several of them may be combined into a single basic node. An example of combined steps appeared in Figure 4-1 versus the summarized nodes in Figure 4-2. Alternatively, you can use an expanded node to summarize a series of actions and provide details of the sequence of actions in its subgraph, as in the expansion of the processTransaction step in Figure 4-3 and Figure 4-4.

If you use the MSC extensions discussed in Section 3.2, repetition and case nodes are easy to identify. If not, you will need to walk through the scenario to identify repetitions. To find alternative processing steps, you will probably need to look at different scenarios from the same use case that represent alternative uses of the system.

A reference is most easily rendered as an expanded node, with the execution graph corresponding to the sequence diagram that it points to in the subgraph.

Following these guidelines, the sequence diagram in Figure 3-9 translates to the execution graphs in Figure 4-3 and Figure 4-4.

> **Note:** This discussion assumes that you will use sequence diagrams to create software execution models. You may choose to use activity diagrams instead. It is a bit more difficult to translate activity diagrams to execution graphs because the branch symbol could describe either repetition or alternation. You might want to define stereotypes for repetition and alternation to overcome this problem.

4.6 ICAD Case Study

This example is based on an interactive system, known as ICAD, that supports computer-aided design (CAD) activities. Engineers will use the application to construct and view drawings that model structures, such as aircraft wings. The system also allows users to store a model in a database, and interactively assess the design's correctness, feasibility, and suitability. The model is stored in a relational database, and several versions of the model may exist within the database.

In this chapter, we begin the example by presenting a preliminary design and illustrating the types of data required to construct and solve the performance models.

An ICAD drawing consists of nodes and elements. Elements may be: beams, which connect two nodes; triangles, which connect three nodes; or plates, which connect four or more nodes. Additional data is associated with each type of element to allow solution of the engineers' model. A node is defined by its position in three-dimensional space (x, y, z), as well as with additional information necessary for solution of the model.

Several different use cases have been identified for ICAD, including Draw (draw a model) and Solve (solve a model). For this example, we focus on the Draw use case and one particular scenario, DrawMod. In the DrawMod scenario, a typical model is drawn on the user's screen. A typical model contains only nodes and beams (no triangles or plates) and consists of 2,000 beams. The performance goal is to draw a typical model in 10 seconds or less.

Figure 4-13 shows a high-level sequence diagram for the DrawMod scenario.

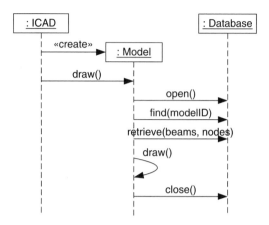

Figure 4-13: The DrawMod Scenario

4.6.1 Architecture 1

Our initial design uses an object to represent each node and beam. This design offers a great deal of flexibility, makes it possible to treat all types of elements in a uniform way, and allows the addition of new types of elements without the need to change any other aspect of the application. The important elements of the class diagram describing this design are illustrated in Figure 4-14.

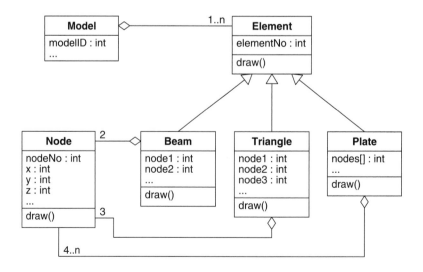

Figure 4-14: Class Diagram for ICAD Design

For this design, we elaborate the DrawMod scenario to represent the processing details as shown in Figure 4-15. The looping construct in Figure 4-15 indicates that the actions of retrieving a beam, retrieving its nodes, and drawing them are repeated for each beam in the model.

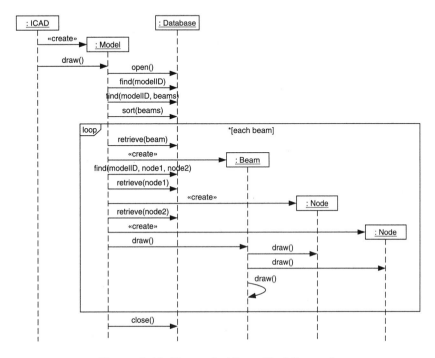

Figure 4-15: Expanded DrawMod Scenario

Figure 4-16 shows another view of the ICAD model. Here we see that the ICAD system is actually made up of three processes: the ICAD GUI, the ICAD application, and the database management system. As indicated in the deployment diagram (Figure 4-17), these components all execute on the same processor.[2]

At this point, we have all of the structural information necessary to define the software execution model's performance scenario and its processing steps. There are three processes (as shown in Figure 4-16), and

---

2. The bold-outlined component icon is a suggested stereotype indicating an executable component [Booch et al. 1999].

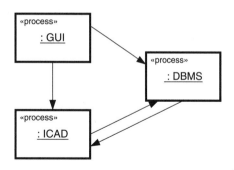

Figure 4-16: ICAD Processes

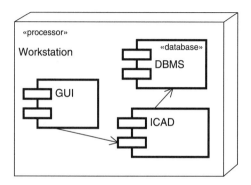

Figure 4-17: ICAD Deployment Diagram

they all execute on the same processor (the Workstation in Figure 4-17). The sequence diagram in Figure 4-15 specifies the steps that occur when DrawMod is invoked.

Figure 4-18 shows the execution graph corresponding to the scenario in Figure 4-15.

Note: In Figure 4-15, the sequence of messages starting with retrieve-Node() to get a node, followed by a «create» to create the node, is executed once for each node. In Figure 4-18, that sequence has been abstracted into a single node, setUpNode, which is used in a repetition loop executed two times.

The processing steps start in (a); the expanded nodes for the initialize processing step are in (b) (i.e., the steps preceding find(modelID) in the sequence diagram); and the expansion of the drawBeam processing step in (c) contains all the steps within the loop in the sequence diagram.

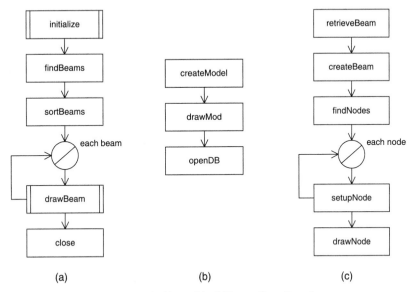

Figure 4-18: DrawMod Execution Graph

The next step is to specify *software resource requirements* for each processing step. The software resources we specify for this example are

- *EDMS*—the number of calls to the ICAD Database process
- *CPU*—an estimate of the number of instructions executed
- *I/O*—the number of disk accesses to obtain data from the database
- *Get/Free*—the number of calls to the memory management operations
- *Screen*—the number of times graphics operations "draw" to the screen

You need values for these requirements for each processing step in the model, as well as the probability of each case alternative and the number of loop repetitions. Part III covers techniques for estimating these resource requirements. This example focuses on using the values to evaluate the proposed architecture for DrawMod. The values we use are in Table 4-3.

Table 4-3: Values for DrawMod Software Resource Requirements

Processing Step	EDMS	CPU	I/O	Get/ Free	Screen
createModel	0	2	0	0	0
drawMod	0	1	3	2	2
openDB	1	2.3	6	1	0
findBeams	1	346	7.08	0	0
sortBeams	1	339	42.28	2	0
finish	1	1.5	2	1	0
retrieveBeam	1	2	4.03	0	0
createBeam	0	2	0	0	0
findNodes	1	4.5	4.1	0	0
setupNode	1	4	4.02	0	0
drawNode	0	0.55	0	0	1

Part III covers techniques for determining processing overhead.

Next, you need the *processing overhead* for each software resource request. It includes a specification of the types of devices in the computer configuration, the quantity of each, their service times, and the amount of processing required from each device for each type of software resource request. Table 4-4 shows the processing overhead for this case study.

Table 4-4: Processing Overhead

Devices	CPU	Disk	Display
Quantity	1	2	1
Service Units	K instr.	Phys. I/O	Units

	CPU	Disk	Display
EDMS	0.253	0.002	
CPU	1		
I/O	0.1	1	
Get/Free	0.1		
Screen	0.05		1

	CPU	Disk	Display
Service Time	0.000005	0.03	0.001

To solve this model manually, you calculate the computer resource requirements per node as in step 1 (see Example 4-2), and then apply the reduction rules to the graph as in step 2 (Table 4-2). Compute the best-case elapsed time as in step 3. We used the SPE tool to automatically produce the results shown in Figure 4-19. Check your understanding by solving the model manually, and comparing your results to those shown in the figure.

Figure 4-19 shows the elapsed time results for the software execution model solution, showing the elapsed time for one user to complete the DrawMod scenario with no contention delays in the computer system. The figure shows that the best-case elapsed time is 969.29 seconds. The time for each processing step is next to the step. The times are also color-coded with relatively high values shown in red, and relatively low values shown in cooler colors. (For publication, the high values are shaded gray and the low values are not shaded.)

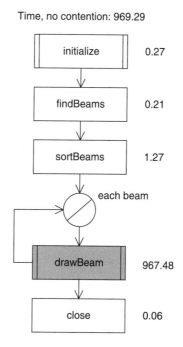

Figure 4-19: Best-case Elapsed Time for DrawMod Architecture 1

The drawBeam processing step requires approximately 967 seconds for all 2,000 iterations. The time per iteration (not shown) is 0.4837 seconds. The results show that Architecture 1 clearly will not meet the performance goal of 10 seconds, so we explore another possibility in the next section.

4.6.2 Architecture 2

Architecture 1 uses an object for each beam and node in the model. While this provides a great deal of flexibility, using an object for each node and beam is potentially expensive in terms of both runtime overhead and memory utilization.

We can reduce this overhead by using the Flyweight pattern [Gamma et al. 1995]. Using the Flyweight pattern in ICAD allows sharing of beam and node objects, and reduces the number of each that must be created in order to display the model. Each model now has exactly one beam and node object. The node and beam objects contain *intrinsic* state information that is independent of a particular beam or node (such as coordinates). These objects also know how to draw themselves. *Extrinsic* state is stored separately; that is, coordinates and other information needed to store the model. This information is passed to the beam and node flyweights when it is needed.

The Flyweight pattern is applicable when
- The number of objects used by the application is large;
- The cost of using objects is high;
- Most object state can be made extrinsic;
- Many objects can be replaced by fewer, shared objects once the extrinsic state is removed; and
- The application does not depend on object identity [Gamma et al. 1995]

The SPE evaluation will determine whether the ICAD application meets all of these criteria.

Instead of using an object for each beam and node, we use a shared object, based on the Flyweight pattern. The state information is removed from the Beam and Node classes and is stored directly in Model. The class diagram for this approach is shown in Figure 4-20.

The principal effect of this change is that constructors for Node and Beam are executed only once, resulting in a savings of many constructor invocations.

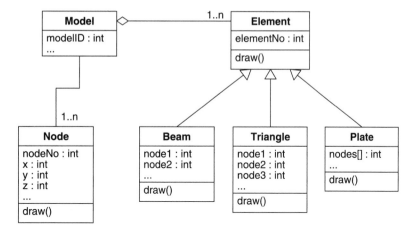

Figure 4-20: Class Diagram for Architecture 2

This architecture change has a minor effect on the process view, and no effect on the physical view. The Beam and Node classes are still part of the DrawMod process, but now there is only one of each. In the physical view, the three processes are still assigned to the same processor.

The changes to the execution graph for this architecture are trivial. The graph nodes corresponding to the «create» processing steps moved from the subgraph that represents the drawBeam processing step to the subgraph corresponding to the initialize processing step. This takes the corresponding resource requirements out of the loop that is executed 2,000 times. After you make these changes, you re-solve the model and compare results.

Note: Even though the arithmetic for solving models is relatively simple, you will want to use a tool. You need to be able to quickly make small changes and see the results, to be able to evaluate many design alternatives rapidly.

The overall response time is reduced from 969.29 to 969.23 seconds! The results of the software execution model for this approach indicate that using the Flyweight pattern did not solve the performance problems with ICAD. Constructor overhead is not a significant factor in the DrawMod scenario.

Note: The amount of constructor overhead used in this case study was derived from a specific performance benchmark and will not generalize to other situations. It is compiler, operating system, and machine dependent; in our case, constructors required no I/O. It is also architecture dependent; in our example, there is no deep inheritance hierarchy. It is also workload dependent; in this case, the number of beams and nodes in the typical problem is relatively small.

The evaluation of Architecture 2 illustrates two important points:

 Modifying performance models to evaluate alternatives is relatively easy.

It is important to quantify the effect of design alternatives rather than blindly follow a "guideline" that may not apply.

4.6.3 Analysis of Results

Actually, a thorough analysis of the solution to the Architecture 1 performance model provides sufficient information to indicate that the primary problem is the excessive time for I/O to the database. Consider the resource demand results in Figure 4-21. Note that the time spent at the Disk devices for drawBeams accounts for 965 of the 969 seconds. Figure 4-22 shows that the I/O is fairly evenly spread in the drawBeam submodel: 0.12 second. for both retrieveBeam and findNodes, 0.24 second. for setUpNode.

The problem in the original design, excessive time for I/O to the database, is not corrected with the Flyweight pattern, so the next architecture focuses on reducing the I/O time due to database access.

Note: The relative value of improvements depends on the order in which they are evaluated. If the database I/O and other problems are corrected first, the relative benefit of using the Flyweight pattern will be greater.

4.6.4 Architecture 3

We choose to retain the Flyweight approach in Architecture 3. It will help with much larger ICAD models, where the overhead of using an object for each beam and node may become significant, making the architecture more scalable.

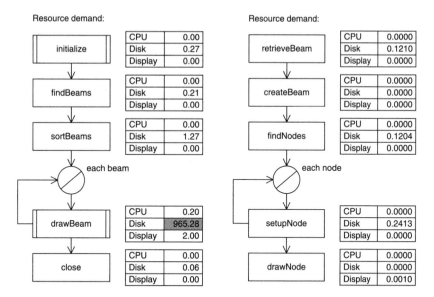

Figure 4-21: Resource Demand Results for Architecture 1

Figure 4-22: Resource Demand for drawBeam Submodel in Architecture 1

This architecture uses an approach similar to Architecture 2 (Figure 4-20) but modifies the database management object with a new operation to retrieve a block of data with one call: retrieveBlock(). Architecture 3 uses this new operation to retrieve the beams and nodes once at the beginning of the scenario, and stores the data values for all beams and nodes with the model object rather than retrieving the value from the database each time it is needed. This new operation makes it possible to retrieve blocks containing 20K of data at a time instead of retrieving individual nodes and beams.[3] A single retrieveBlock can fetch 64 beams or 170 nodes at a time. Thus only 33 database accesses are required to obtain all of the beams, and nine accesses are needed to retrieve the nodes.

---

3. Note: A block size of 20K is used here for illustration. The effect of using different block sizes could be evaluated via modeling to determine the optimal size.

The class diagram for Architecture 3 does not change from Architecture 2. Figure 4-23 shows the sequence diagram that corresponds to the new database access protocol.

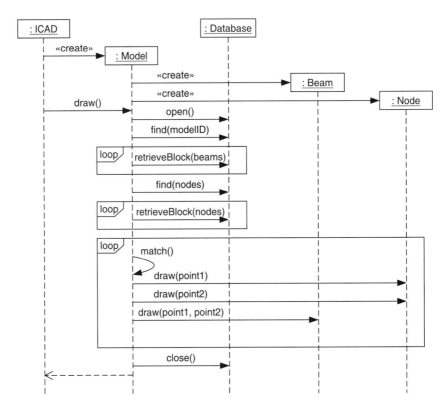

Figure 4-23: DrawMod Scenario for Architecture 3

The logical, process, and physical views are essentially unchanged; the only difference is the new database operation, retrieveBlock().

Figure 4-24 shows the execution graph corresponding to Figure 4-23, along with the results for the best-case solution. The time for Architecture 3 is approximately 8.5 seconds—a substantial reduction.

Other improvements to this architecture are feasible; however, this serves to illustrate the process of creating software execution models from architecture documents and evaluating trade-offs. It shows that it is relatively easy to create the initial models, and the revisions to evaluate alternatives are straightforward. The simple software execution models

Time, no contention: 8.5126

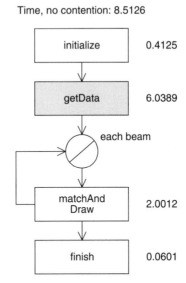

Figure 4-24: Execution Graph and Results for Architecture 3

are sufficient to identify problems and quantify the performance of feasible alternatives. Software execution models also support the evaluation of different process compositions and different assignments of processes to physical processors. Once a suitable architecture is found, SPE studies continue to evaluate design and implementation alternatives.

Chapter 6 explains the next type of study.

Analysts will typically evaluate other aspects of both the software and system execution models to study configuration sizing issues and contention delays due to multiple users of a scenario and other workloads that may compete for computer system resources. In these additional performance studies, the most difficult aspect has been getting reasonable estimates of processing requirements for new software before it is created. The SPE process and the software execution models alleviate this problem. Once this data is in the software performance model, it is relatively easy to conduct the additional studies.

It is important to continue the SPE modeling throughout development.

Chapter 12 discusses life cycle performance management.

Do not get complacent when preliminary results indicate that performance is satisfactory. Early models are more abstract, and model ideal environments. The evolving software may be quite different.

4.7 Modeling Hints

1. It is not necessary to include all of the details of the software's processing flow in the performance model. Remember that the model is not the software—it is an abstraction of the software. The abstraction should include only those details that are relevant; in this case, only those details that are relevant to performance. The difference between Figure 4-1 and Figure 4-2 illustrates the use of abstraction to combine related steps that don't have a significant effect on performance characteristics. In Figure 4-18, related steps were also combined into one processing node in the execution graph.

2. Use hierarchy to help make your models easier to understand and modify. You can use expanded nodes to hide processing details at one level, and elaborate on them in another subgraph.

   Another way to use hierarchy effectively is to expand nodes as your knowledge of the software increases. Early in the process, you may not know much about the processing details. At that point, you can represent an operation at a high level with a single basic node. Later, when you know more about the details of the processing, you can use an expanded node and elaborate the details in a subgraph.

3. Use best- and worst-case estimates of resource requirements to help compensate for uncertainty early in the process. If the best-case results indicate that there is a problem, fix it before proceeding. If the worst-case results indicate that there is no problem, you can proceed to the next step. If the results are in between, look at the processing steps that consume the most resources, and focus on obtaining better resource requirement estimates for them.

4. Study the sensitivity of the performance results to the input parameters. If a small change in resource requirements causes a large change in results, your software is sensitive to those specifications. The sen-

sitivity studies identify critical resources and components whose use of those resources should be monitored. This may occur when

- Devices have high utilization (>90%). In this case, a small increase in resource requirements may cause a very large increase in response time.
- Processing is in loops because a small increase is multiplied by the loop repetition factors.
- You have significant synchronization and resource-sharing delays. Small increases are multiplied by the number of processes that may be delayed.

4.8 Summary

In the early phases of the software development process, we want to construct the simplest possible models that capture the essential performance characteristics of the software. The models should be easy to solve in order to provide rapid feedback on whether the proposed software is likely to meet its performance objectives. The software execution model has these characteristics.

Solving the software execution model provides a static analysis of the mean, as well as the best- and worst-case response times. It characterizes the resource requirements of the proposed software alone, in the absence of other workloads, multiple users, or delays due to contention for resources. Later, as our knowledge of the software's design and implementation details becomes more complete, we can refine the software execution model in critical areas. We can also use the results from solving the software execution model to provide input parameters for the system execution model.

We use *execution graphs* to represent software execution models. The graphs consist of nodes and arcs. The nodes represent *processing steps,* a collection of operation invocations and program statements that perform a function in the software system. The arcs represent the order of execution. Execution graphs can be derived from the sequence diagrams for critical performance scenarios.

The algorithms and formulas for solving software execution models are straightforward for average, as well as best- and worst-case times. You can solve the models by hand or by using a spreadsheet or SPE tool. An SPE tool eliminates errors that can be introduced by hand or spreadsheet solutions and makes it easier to study the performance implications of design alternatives.

This chapter provided several examples of execution graph models and their solutions. A case study illustrated the overall process.

Chapter 5

Web Applications and Other Distributed Systems

Technology...the knack of so arranging the world that we need not experience it.

—Max Frisch, 1957

In This Chapter:

- Web applications
- Distributed object technology
- Avoiding pitfalls of distributed object technology
- Modeling distributed system interactions
- Example

5.1 Introduction

Distributed systems were once the exception, constructed only rarely and with great difficulty by developers who spent significant amounts of time mastering the technology. Now, as modern software technologies have made distributed systems easier to construct, they have become the norm. The explosion of Web applications is just the tip of the distributed systems iceberg.

The ease of constructing today's distributed systems is both a blessing and a curse. The blessing, of course, is that today's distributed systems are easier and faster to construct. The curse is that modern support technology makes it so easy to construct distributed systems, particularly Web applications, that it is easy to ignore good software engineering practices. A related problem is that, as we will see, in order to take advantage of the blessing you have to ignore factors that are crucial to performance, such as object placement and concurrency semantics. The result is that many distributed systems are deployed with less than satisfactory responsiveness and scalability.

The system execution model is presented in Chapter 6.

This chapter begins with an overview of Web applications, distributed object technology, and the important considerations for performance engineering. Then, we describe how to represent and analyze interactions among multiple systems. As usual, we begin with the simple software execution models, add some extensions for distributed systems, and use approximate solution techniques that identify significant problems if they exist. After eliminating problems, we proceed to the system execution model to analyze contention effects.

The issues that we want to address include
- The placement of objects (i.e., their assignment to processes and processors)
- The frequency of communication among objects
- The type of synchronization primitive for each communication
- The amount of data passed during each communication
- The amount of processing done by an object
- The use of multithreaded objects

In this chapter, we focus on how to construct a software performance model that reflects the performance characteristics of a particular combination of choices. Later, we'll consider the assessment of architectural alternatives and how to correct performance problems.

5.2 Web Applications

Web applications are discussed in detail in Chapters 7 and 13.

Web applications provide the functionality of more traditional applications, such as financial transactions, using a Web site as their front end. Those Web-like features, such as shopping carts, that we have come to expect are, in reality, just another way of entering a transaction.

Web applications typically employ multi-tiered architectures that include a "front-end" client tier that hosts a Web browser, a "back-end" data tier that includes data resources, and one or more middle tiers that provide Web server and application functions. Often, they incorporate legacy applications that were never intended for the interactive environment in which they now find themselves.

The extent to which technology has simplified the development of components that interact in distributed systems is nowhere more evident than with Web applications. Today's development environments make it possible to create Web applications with little or no training in distributed systems technology or even in computer science. Couple this with the pressure to develop and evolve applications in "Internet time," and you have a recipe for disaster. Many development organizations find themselves deploying Web applications without the benefit of serious analysis, design, or SPE.

In effect, the development process used for these applications takes "fix-it-later" to an extreme, with an accompanying high risk of performance failure. In many cases, these failures are highly visible, sometimes with embarrassing headlines. (Recall the electronic trading anecdote from Chapter 1 in which several online brokerage houses experienced failures due to large numbers of "hits" on their Web sites, following a large dip in the stock market. The effects included losses by investors, loss of user confidence, and a lawsuit.)

There are two important dimensions to performance for Web applications: responsiveness and scalability. Responsiveness is important because, in today's competitive environment, users will simply go elsewhere rather than endure slow response times. Scalability is important to maintain responsiveness, as more and more users converge on a site.

> *Both responsiveness and scalability are important for Web applications.*

Web applications are deceptively simple. At first glance, all you have is a browser on the user's machine, a Web server, and some HTML. When the user clicks on a link, the browser opens a connection to the server and requests the page. The server parses the request, retrieves the page, and returns it to the browser. When the request has been filled, the connection is closed.

If all you do is serve up static content, it really is that simple. Things start to get interesting, however, when you want to add an additional layer of activity to provide dynamic content, query or update a database, process orders online, or do any of a myriad of other tasks that make a Web site a Web application.

Figure 5-1 shows the class diagram for a generic Web application that provides dynamic content and uses a database. Now, when the user requests a page, the server may use a preprocessor to interpret a scripted page (e.g., a Java Server page), which generates some dynamic content, possibly after accessing the database. Or, the server may run an external executable (e.g., a CGI process or servlet) to accomplish the same purpose.

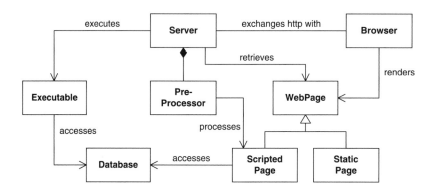

Figure 5-1: Generic Web Application

This additional layer of activity generates some significant software performance concerns, including

- Forecasting the volume of activity
- Choice of mechanism for executables (e.g., CGI programs versus servlets)
- Allocation of executables to processing nodes
- Mechanisms for accessing the database
- Mechanisms for handling persistent data
- Mechanisms for providing access and/or data security
- Instrumentation for characterizing Web application usage
- Location of the database (e.g., on the server node or a separate node)
- Interactions with middleware

- Interfaces to legacy systems
- Impact of downloading applets or other code

and many more.

There are also significant capacity planning concerns for Web applications, such as selection of the number of processing nodes, the number of processors for each node, the speed of the processors, and so on. There are also some significant performance tuning issues that must be addressed. Killelea [Killelea 1998] provides a useful discussion of performance tuning issues for Web applications.

Performance models that provide quantitative data for these alternatives use essentially the same techniques as those for other types of distributed object systems. The next section explains the performance issues that are important for distributed object technology; subsequent sections explain the models and their solutions. The last section illustrates the techniques with a Web application example.

5.3 Distributed Object Technology

Many of the advances in support for constructing Web applications and other distributed systems have been enabled by the merging of object-oriented techniques with distributed systems technology. This combination is often referred to as *distributed object technology* or DOT. With distributed object technology, the object is the unit of computation and distribution in a heterogeneous multi-platform computing environment. This approach exploits two key features of objects: their ability to encapsulate both data and operations in a single computation unit, and their ability to separate their interface from their implementation.

With DOT, applications can be distributed over a heterogeneous network, making it possible to run each component on the most appropriate platform. "Wrappers" can be used to make commercial, off-the-shelf (COTS) products and legacy applications appear as objects. This makes it possible to integrate COTS or legacy software into new systems, such as Web applications, that run on other platforms.

5.3.1 Middleware

Distributed object technology is enabled and supported by "middleware" such as the Object Management Group's (OMG) Object Management Architecture. This architecture provides referential transparency and high-level inter-object communication mechanisms. Middleware provides a layer of services between the application and the underlying platform (operating system and network software). It provides application-independent services that allow different processes running on one or more platforms to interact.

The various types of middleware include
- *Common Object Request Broker Architecture* (CORBA): CORBA specifies a standard architecture for object request brokers (ORBs), a form of middleware that manages communication between objects in a distributed environment. The CORBA standard was developed and is maintained by the Object Management Group. Interfaces between objects are defined using the OMG's Interface Definition Language (IDL). Objects may be implemented in different languages, and may execute on different hardware platforms and operating systems.
- *Component Object Model* (COM) and *Distributed Component Object Model* (DCOM): COM and DCOM both refer to a specification and implementation of ORB technology that was developed by Microsoft Corporation. COM allows components (objects) on the same machine to interact, while DCOM supports component interaction over a network. In order to communicate, the components must conform to the binary structure defined by Microsoft. As long as the components adhere to this binary structure, they may be implemented in different languages.
- *Java 2, Enterprise Edition* (J2EE): J2EE supports a component-based, multi-tier application architecture using three types of Java components: applets, servlets (including JSP), and Enterprise JavaBeans. The J2EE specification defines the Java APIs that must be present in order to implement the J2EE platform. A J2EE application may be deployed to any environment that implements this platform.

- *COM+*: Microsoft's COM+ is an extension of COM that is both an object-oriented programming architecture and a set of operating system services. COM+ combines COM and Microsoft Transaction Server (MTS), and it adds some new features such as message queueing and publish-and-subscribe event handling.

These technologies will evolve, and more middleware technologies are likely to emerge.

Our approach addresses the *software architecture* and *design* decisions that you must make regardless of the implementation or technical architecture (e.g., the specific platforms and middleware packages). We model the software at the architectural level. Details of specific middleware technologies are handled by measurement. These SPE model templates apply to all types of distributed object technology used for the implementation. We will also explain how to represent the specific execution behavior of the middleware that you use in the SPE models.

5.3.2 Limitations of Distributed Object Technology

The holy grail of distributed object technology has been to develop a system without regard to the locations of objects in the network, or the nature of the communication between them. This approach focuses on using a "natural" interface between objects whereby all objects are accessed in the same way (i.e., naming the object and invoking an operation), without regard to where they reside in the distributed system.

This approach theoretically reduces the overall complexity of the programming task. However, it often leads to performance problems due to latency in accessing remote objects and excessive overhead in the middleware [Clements 1996]. For example, referential transparency may require that a local object be accessed by making middleware calls rather than using a more efficient mechanism, such as a static call to a local object. When performance problems arise, the system must be "tuned" by fixing the locations of critical objects (e.g., making remote objects local) and replacing middleware calls with more efficient ones (e.g., statically linking the local objects together).

This development paradigm is based on three fundamental assumptions:

1. There is a single "natural" object-oriented design for an application, regardless of how it is deployed.

2. Performance issues are governed by the implementation of components and are not relevant during early design.

3. The interface of an object (for example, its concurrency semantics) is independent of the context in which it will be used.

All of these assumptions are false! There are four fundamental differences between local and distributed computing [Waldo et al. 1994]:

1. Latency

2. Memory access

3. Partial failure

4. Concurrency

> *Do not ignore latency, memory access, partial failure, and concurrency when designing and implementing distributed systems.*

The following sections explore these four aspects of distributed computation and the consequences of ignoring them.

Latency Latency is the difference in response time between a local and a remote operation invocation. Sources of latency include network speed, middleware (e.g., ORB) overhead, and communication overhead due to objects being in different address spaces. This difference can be as much as four or five orders of magnitude. This situation is not likely to improve significantly, because increases in network speed will be offset by increased traffic and software demands.

Latency is due to the fact that communication is more expensive than computation. The relative difference between communication and computation is likely to increase, since processor speeds are increasing faster than network speeds. Because of this, performance in a distributed system is governed by communication overhead rather than component implementation. Thus, issues of object placement must be considered early in the process to prevent performance problems.

Memory Access Objects are accessed differently depending on whether they are local or remote. Objects in the same memory space can be accessed efficiently using pointers. If they reside in different address spaces, they must be accessed using less efficient object references.

The differences in the way local versus remote objects are accessed requires that either

1. The programmer must be aware of the ultimate location of the object (local or remote) and manage the difference. This makes the programming task more complex.

or,

2. The execution environment must provide a uniform mechanism for accessing objects that hides their location. This requires that programmers learn how to use this new mechanism. It also requires that the mechanism be used for all accesses to avoid errors.

Partial Failure In distributed systems, components can fail independently. The network may fail, leaving individual processors isolated from each other, or a given processor may fail while the others continue to operate and communicate normally. Partial failures can cause problems because, in a distributed system, there is no persistent global state, and thus it is difficult to restore consistency following a failure.

There are two alternatives for coping with partial failures. The first is to treat all objects as if they were local. This solution leads to nondeterministic behavior in the case of partial failure. For example, say you assume the object resides locally and make a call to an operation assuming it will return with a valid result. If the object is remote and you cannot access it, your system may hang or the middleware may return an error condition instead of a valid result. The second alternative is to treat all objects as if they were remote. This solves the problem of nondeterminism, but it adds additional latency for accessing local objects. It also makes objects that will never be remote more complex than they need to be.

Concurrency In a distributed environment, an object's methods may be invoked concurrently. To prevent inconsistencies or data corruption, these objects must define and maintain critical sections to manage concurrent access to their data.

If all objects are to be treated uniformly, one of three possible approaches must be used.

1. Ignore the problem. Unfortunately, this approach also ignores a significant mode of failure in the system when multiple objects attempt to update the same data at the same time.

2. Make all objects single threaded. If performance problems result, however, extensive changes may be required to convert objects to execute correctly in a multithreaded environment.

3. Include concurrency semantics in all objects, regardless of their location. This adds unnecessary complexity and overhead to objects that won't be accessed concurrently.

5.3.3 Effective Development with Distributed Object Technology

While the goal of programming without regard to the location of objects in the network or the nature of the communication between them might be a noble quest, the foregoing discussion of latency, memory access, partial failure, and concurrency demonstrates that this is not a realistic approach to constructing distributed object systems.

A more realistic approach is to fix object locations and concurrency semantics early in the development process. If these decisions are not made at design time, they are difficult to change later. For example, if you know an object will be remote, you will choose a design that minimizes the number of calls to the object, and maximizes the value of the results obtained. (This and other performance design principles are covered in Part IV.)

 Use SPE techniques to fix object locations and concurrency semantics early in development.

These design decisions involve trade-offs. From a performance perspective, the only rational way to make these trade-offs is to base them on quantitative information. This requires constructing and evaluating performance models for the various alternatives.

5.4 Modeling Distributed System Interactions

Chapter 6 discusses system modeling techniques.

Early in development, the SPE process calls for using deliberately simple models of software processing that are easily constructed and solved to provide feedback on whether the proposed software is likely to meet performance goals. Thus, our approach is to first create the software execution models as described in Chapter 4, use them to study the fundamental architecture and design issues, and then later use system execution models to study additional facets of distributed system interactions. This chapter discusses representing distributed system interactions and software modeling techniques.

The essence of the distributed system software architecture is the placement of objects and the communication and synchronization among them. As Clements notes:

> Performance is largely a function of the frequency and nature of inter-component communication, in addition to the performance characteristics of the components themselves, and hence can be predicted by studying the architecture of a system. [Clements 1996]

One aspect of distributed systems that can have a significant impact on performance is the overhead required for communication and synchronization among distributed objects. In keeping with our "keep-it-simple" approach, we first create the software execution models without explicitly representing synchronization—it is represented only as a delay for a client to receive results from a server process. Later, more realistic models add specific synchronization notation to the sequence diagrams and software execution models. These models may be solved using software model approximation techniques (described next) or the system model techniques described in Chapter 6.

5.4.1 Types of System Interactions

Sequence diagram extensions to represent synchronization were introduced in Chapter 3.

To illustrate the construction and solution of software models for distributed-object systems, we will focus on four types of communication and synchronization that are typically supported in middleware:

- Synchronous
- Asynchronous
- Deferred synchronous, and
- Asynchronous callback communication

Each of these is described in the following sections. The descriptions use the terms "client" and "server" processes; however, they apply to more general distributed systems. The roles of "client" and "server" refer to a particular interaction, and may be reversed in subsequent interactions. In addition, the "server" process may interact with other processes, and multiple types of synchronization may be combined.

Synchronous Communication The timing diagram in Figure 5-2 shows what happens when a client makes synchronous requests to a server process. The figure indicates when each processing node (client, server, or network) is active. The absence of activity (i.e., Idle) indicates that the corresponding processing node is not processing this request—shared processing nodes (the network and server) may process other requests at those times. Processing for a request is initiated on the client: The synchronous request is transmitted via the network, the server processes the request and sends a reply, the network transmits the reply, the client receives the reply and begins processing that will make another synchronous request, and so on.

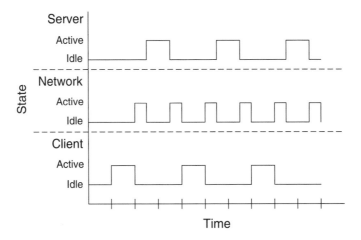

Figure 5-2: Synchronous Communication

Note: In these illustrations, we arbitrarily show the client and server objects on separate processors, and the invocations must be transmitted through the network. If they reside on the same processor, there is no delay for network activity.

We do not explicitly represent middleware (e.g., ORB) processing that occurs for runtime binding of the client and server processes. You could model the role of the middleware explicitly as another row in the timing diagram, or implicitly by adding processing overhead for each middleware request. We will address these strategies later in this chapter.

Asynchronous Communication Figure 5-3 shows the timing diagram for the processing flow when the client invokes an asynchronous request from the server. The client process invokes the request and continues processing. The processing on the network and server processing nodes for transmitting and processing the request is the same as before, but there is no reply.

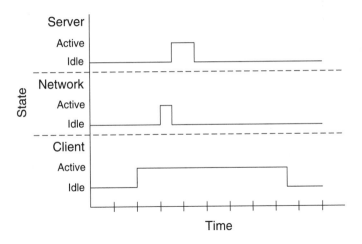

Figure 5-3: Asynchronous Communication

Deferred Synchronous Communication Figure 5-4 shows one possibility for the processing flow when the client invokes a deferred synchronous request from the server. The client process invokes the request and continues processing. The processing on the network and server processing nodes is the same as before. At some point in the processing, the client needs the result from the server before it may proceed. The dashed portion of the line representing the client processing indicates time that the client must wait for the request to be completed and returned.

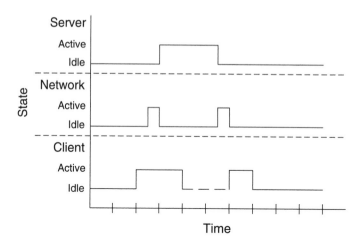

Figure 5-4: Deferred Synchronous Communication

It is also possible that the deferred synchronous request is completed before the client needs the result to proceed. In this case, there is no delay on the client before receiving the result. A timing diagram representing this possibility would omit the dashed line and show a continuous active region for the client.

Asynchronous Callback With this type of synchronization, the client process makes an asynchronous request to the server and continues processing. The request includes the information necessary for the server process to "callback" to the client process with another asynchronous call when the operation is complete.

The timing diagram in Figure 5-4 also represents the behavior of the asynchronous callback. The implementation is slightly different—deferred synchronous calls may be implemented within one client process, whereas asynchronous callback may require two client processes, one for the call and another for the callback. Deferred synchronous calls are easier to implement if your middleware supports them. Asynchronous callback may be used with any type of middleware that supports asynchronous calls.

5.4.2 Software Execution Model Representation

We represent these coordination mechanisms directly in both the design models and the performance models. In Chapter 3, we introduced extensions to the sequence diagram notation to represent synchronous, deferred synchronous, and asynchronous communication.

Note: You can use the deferred synchronous communication notation for asynchronous callback with one process. If the callback involves two processes, show it as two asynchronous calls.

Figure 5-5 shows the execution graph nodes that represent these types of communication and synchronization. The appropriate node from the left column of the figure is inserted in the execution graph for the calling scenario. The called scenario represents the synchronization point with one of the nodes from the right column, depending on whether it sends a reply.

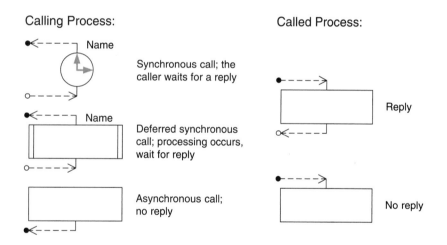

Figure 5-5: Execution Graph Nodes for Software Synchronization

---

Note: The synchronization occurs in the calling process, so the called process need not distinguish between synchronous and deferred synchronous calls.

Any of the rectangular nodes may be expanded to elaborate processing steps that occur between the dashed arrows or in connection with asynchronous calls. The expansion may contain other synchronization steps. The called process may also execute additional processing steps after the reply is sent.

Note: In this notation, the filled dots with arrows leading into them represent a potential delay for the called process to act on the request. Think of it as the request entering a queue. The filled dots with arrows leading out of them represent the request being taken from that queue. The empty dots with arrows leading into them represent the response being sent back to the calling process. Think of it as freeing the calling process to execute. Note that the asynchronous call has the arrow and filled dot after the node rather than before it like the other calling nodes. This is because there is typically some processing required to set up parameters and make the call (represented by the node), but there may not be any action required after making the call.

5.4.3 Representing Middleware Overhead

The middleware that supports the DOT is responsible for managing communication between objects without regard to: object location, implementation and state, or inter-object communication mechanisms. We illustrate this overhead with the CORBA Object Request Broker and its Object Adaptor, but the techniques also apply to the other types of middleware.

Aspects of the ORB that enable object interaction are:

- *The interface definition language:* declares the interfaces and types of operations and parameters (e.g., float, string, struct, etc.)
- *Language mappings:* specify how the interface definition language features are mapped to various programming languages
- *Client stubs and server skeletons:* provide mechanisms for interacting with the ORB to convert (static) request invocations from the programming language into a form for transmission to the server object, and to similarly handle the response
- *Dynamic invocation and dispatch:* a generic mechanism for dynamic request invocations without compile-time knowledge of object interfaces
- *Protocols for inter-ORB communication:* the mechanism for ORB-to-ORB handling of request invocations

The Object Adapter is the component of the ORB that actually connects objects to other objects. Functions that it provides are: registration of objects and interfaces, object reference generation, server process activation, object activation, static and dynamic invocations, communication overhead for transmitting request invocations, and processing overhead for converting requests across languages, operating systems, and hardware.

Techniques for conducting measurement studies are discussed in Chapter 8.

While these features affect the overall performance of a distributed system that includes an ORB, they are modeled implicitly by measuring their resource requirements and including it as "processing overhead" for each invocation of a server object. For example, the use cases describe the operating conditions for the remote object calls, such as whether the server process and the object are active, whether we make a static or a dynamic call, and so on. We will conduct a performance benchmark that measures the resource requirements of the ORB (or other types of middleware) for each type of call in our use cases. We then use the measured resource requirements for our processing overhead. Finally, the software execution models specify the number of calls of each type for the processing steps that require ORB calls.

5.4.4 Software Model Solution Approximations

The solution of detailed models of complex synchronization behavior can require hours of simulation time. We prefer approximate solutions that can be solved quickly to identify serious problems, and to permit the analysis of many alternatives. Once we choose one of the alternatives and have more concrete data, we refine the models and use system execution models to evaluate additional levels of detail.

Use approximate solutions of software models to easily identify serious problems and to permit quick analysis of many architectural and design alternatives.

We begin by identifying the *facilities* that are likely to have the greatest effect on performance. A facility is the location where the processing executes. It consists of one or more computer resources and, in a distributed system, it includes the network. The identified facilities will be those with the greatest demand—either because they are relatively slow, or because they have much more work to do. Create a separate performance scenario for each key facility on which the software executes. For each scenario, we specify resource requirements corresponding to the active regions (regions of an object's lifeline that have an activation), and estimate the delay between active regions. Later, if needed, we can model scenarios for individual processes on each facility. In the early stages of modeling, however, this level of detail is not necessary.

Begin by creating separate performance scenarios for each key facility. Specify resource requirements for active regions and estimate delays between active regions. Later, if necessary, model individual processes on each facility.

When the coordination uses either deferred synchronous or asynchronous callback, and the called process is expected to complete before the client requests the response, the delay estimate is zero. With asynchronous calls, there is no delay.

In summary, the distributed system models consist of a set of performance scenarios, one for each key facility, that represent the objects that interact. You insert synchronization nodes at appropriate points in the processing steps. To solve the models, you specify

- Resource requirements for the processing nodes,
- The estimated delay for synchronization nodes,
- The number of messages sent via the network, and
- The processing overhead for middleware that handles remote calls.

We use the model solutions for each scenario to refine the delay estimates in other scenarios in subsequent model solutions. For example, we solve the software models for the client and server separately by using the initial delay estimates. The solution for the server scenario gives the estimated elapsed time for the server process and the reply. If this result differs from the initial delay estimate in the client scenario, we replace the estimate with the software model elapsed time. We also adjust the server delay and re-solve the model. We repeat this process until the delay estimate stabilizes. It usually requires only a few iterations.

Note: The server delay is also affected by the number of client processes that call it. Clients may experience delays for the server's computer resources because other client requests are ahead of them, and they may have to wait for an available server "thread." These effects will be studied with the system execution model. We will continue the evaluation of distributed systems in Chapter 6 after we have covered these additional analysis techniques.

The solutions to these approximate models provide quantitative data for the combination of choices you make for the following:

- The placement of objects (i.e., their assignment to processes and processors)
- The frequency of communication among objects
- The type of synchronization primitive for each communication
- The amount of data passed during each communication
- The amount of processing done by an object

Note: Another important choice is whether you require multiple threads for objects. We will use the system execution model for this analysis.

You evaluate architectural alternatives to correct any performance problems you detect. To evaluate the alternatives, modify the performance models to reflect alternative placement, fewer communications among objects (perhaps with more data per communication), different synchronization primitives, and/or revised object processing. By comparing the solutions of multiple alternatives, you can identify the best combination of choices.

5.5 Example: Web e-Commerce Application

To illustrate the construction and solution of software execution models for distributed systems, we use a simple e-commerce application in which users may purchase items via the Web. With the browser, the user selects items for purchase. Once all selections have been made, the user "checks out," and the order is processed. When order processing is complete, the user receives an acknowledgement. This application has been assembled from legacy components that were part of a telephone agent order entry system.

This is a simple example that illustrates how to construct the set of performance scenarios for distributed objects that interact, and create and solve their software execution models. In actual system evaluations, it is difficult to cleanly separate the software model analysis from the system model analysis of contention because they flow together. So this chapter illustrates the software model creation with a simple example.

An extensive case study of a distributed system is provided in Chapter 6 after the system execution model analysis is explained.

Note: To keep the example simple, we omit several details, such as the Web server processing that occurs before the application is called, firewalls, encrypting and decrypting requests for security, and so on. Also, because we're primarily interested in the "time in the box" (the time between when the checkOut request is received and the ack is sent), we omit the time required to transmit and render the Web page and its included graphics.

Consider the sequence diagram in Figure 5-6. We begin by modeling the performance scenario corresponding to the processing represented in anOrderTaker column. The timing diagram corresponding to this sequence diagram is in Figure 5-7. Note that all of the messages are synchronous except checkOut and triggerOrderProcess.

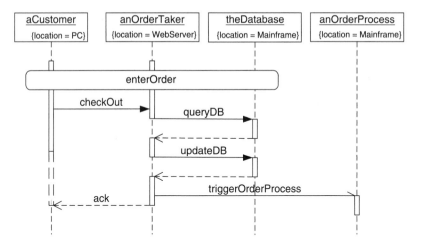

Figure 5-6: checkOut Scenario

The software execution model for this scenario is in Figure 5-8. It begins with enterOrder, followed by the node representing the called process with a reply checkOut. The checkOut processing is expanded in Figure 5-9. The initial startCheckOut node in Figure 5-9 is followed by the queryDB call to the mainframe. This is represented in the figure with a synchronous call node. The processing that occurs on the client after completion of the query and before the update is represented in the

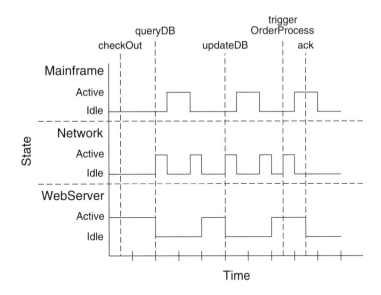

Figure 5-7: Timing Diagram for newOrder Scenario

graph with the initiateOrder node. This is followed by the synchronous call to updateDB on the mainframe. The last processing step is triggerOrderProcess represented by the asynchronous call node.

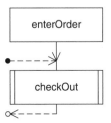

Figure 5-8: checkOut Execution Graph

Note: For simplicity, the enterOrder step is summarized in this model with a single execution graph node. A more detailed model would represent this node with an expanded node, and represent its details in a subgraph. We represent aCustomer's checkOut with a deferred synchronous node because customers may do other processing while waiting for the acknowledgement.

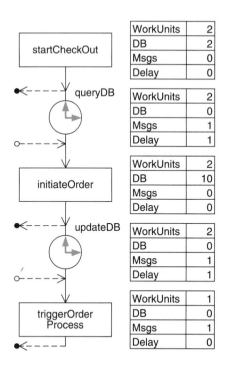

startCheckOut	
WorkUnits	2
DB	2
Msgs	0
Delay	0

queryDB	
WorkUnits	2
DB	0
Msgs	1
Delay	1

initiateOrder	
WorkUnits	2
DB	10
Msgs	0
Delay	0

updateDB	
WorkUnits	2
DB	0
Msgs	1
Delay	1

triggerOrder Process	
WorkUnits	1
DB	0
Msgs	1
Delay	0

Figure 5-9: Expansion of checkOut

The next step is to specify software resource requirements for each processing step. This model focuses on the checkOut processing represented in the subgraph in Figure 5-9. The key resources that we are concerned with in this model are: the WorkUnits for the CPU processing, the number of requests to the local database (DB), the number of messages sent among processors (Msgs), and the estimated Delay in seconds for the work on other processors before the response is received. These values also appear in Figure 5-9.

Note: The WorkUnits for the two synchronous nodes represent the processing required to build and invoke the synchronous database calls.

The overhead matrix was introduced in Section 4.4.

Table 5-1 shows the computer resource requirements for this case study. The contents of the processing overhead matrix were described in Chapter 4; they should be familiar by now. The far right column represents the shared network "device" GlNet. It is shared by all computer processing facilities in the model.

Table 5-1: Web Server Computer Resource Requirements

Devices	CPU	Disk	Delay	GINet
Quantity	1	1	1	1
Service Units	K Instr.	I/Os	Visits	Msgs.
WorkUnits	25			
DB	500	4		
Msgs	25	1		1
Delay			1	
Service Time (sec.)	.000001	0.05	0.5	0.1

Note: The GINet column is separated from the other devices. This highlights the difference between this device and the others in the table—the other devices in the table will only be used by scenarios executing on this facility (the Web server). The GINet, on the other hand, is a global "device" that may be used by all scenarios in the model.

For example, the table specifies that each Msg in the software model causes one visit to the network device. Its service time per message is 0.1 seconds. Each Msg in the software model also causes 25K instructions to be executed on the CPU and 1 Disk I/O (for logging). The Delay in the software model is specified in visits; each visit represents a delay of 0.5 seconds. Techniques for deriving these values are discussed in Part III. They are derived once and reused for all studies of performance scenarios that execute in that environment.

Note: The middleware resource requirements do not appear in Table 5-1 because the ORB is on another processor which is not part of this model. The CPU processing overhead for Msgs includes overhead for communicating with the ORB.

In the client scenario, we estimate a 0.5-second delay for each synchronous call to the database process, and specify that one message is sent via the GINet device. There is no delay for the asynchronous triggerOrderProcess, and one message is sent via the GINet device.

Note: The software model values for DB for the queryDB and updateDB steps are zero because the update occurs on the database server, and, in this model, DB represents processing on the local database. The software model for the database server processing described later will specify its resource requirements for the query and the update.

The model solution in Figure 5-10 shows that the elapsed time for the client process with no contention is 3.86 seconds, most of which is for disk I/O for local database processing in the shaded initiateOrder node. The synchronization with other processes requires 0.65 second for each synchronous call. The "Total Resource Usage" table in Figure 5-10 shows that the total time for sending messages via the network is 0.3 second with an estimated 1-second delay for the two synchronous calls. The software model solution indicates that there are no particular response time problems. Scalability will be addressed when we discuss the system execution model in Chapter 6.

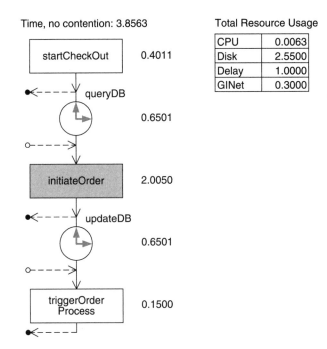

Figure 5-10: checkOut Software Model Results

5.5.1 Database Scenario

Figure 5-11 shows the processing steps for the second performance scenario derived from theDatabase column in Figure 5-6. The top-level model has a single node for a called process with a reply. Its basic node is expanded to represent three types of calls shown in the subgraph: query, update, and write. In this scenario, the probability of a query is 0.5, an update is 0.5, and a write is 0.

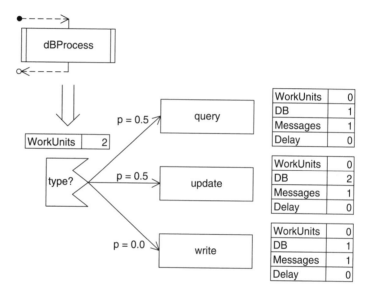

Figure 5-11: Server Processing Steps

The software execution model solution (not shown) results in an elapsed time of 0.24 seconds. The results indicate that this example has no particular performance problem at this point. The next step is to evaluate the contention solution for this scenario.

5.5.2 Order Process Scenario

The scenario in Figure 5-12 represents the column in Figure 5-6 for anOrderProcess. It executes as a result of the triggerOrderProcess asynchronous call in the anOrderTaker process. This example summarizes the scenario with a single called process node, which sends no results. The scenario also executes on the Mainframe facility. The no-contention

WorkUnits	200
DB	20
Messages	0
Delay	0

Figure 5-12: processOrder Scenario

solution results in an elapsed time of 1.6 seconds. Again, there are no particular performance problems.

5.5.3 Example Summary

This example has illustrated the construction and solution of software execution models for distributed systems. The modeling strategy that we use is to model scenarios individually, using estimates for delays introduced by communication and synchronization with objects on other processors. The models can be solved iteratively to refine these estimates, if necessary. If the software execution model indicates that there are problems, they should be fixed before moving on. If there are no problems, we proceed to construct and solve the system execution model as described in the next chapter. The solution to the software execution model provides the parameters that are necessary to solve the system execution model.

5.6 Modeling Hints

Performance Scenarios Begin by creating separate performance scenarios for each key facility. Specify resource requirements for active regions, and estimate delays between active regions. Later, if necessary, model individual processes on each facility.

Early Models Early in development, you may not know the type of synchronization primitive to use. For very early models, you don't have to use the synchronization nodes. Instead, you can create a software resource for "delay" (in the overhead matrix), and specify a delay for the (basic) nodes that will interact with other facilities. You will get the same solution data for evaluating placement, frequency, and amount of data for communication, and so on; and the models will appear much simpler. Simplicity is important for early studies to help you identify problems and focus on alternatives. You can replace the simple nodes with synchronization nodes later.

The list of alternatives is in Section 5.3. **Synchronization** For early models, use synchronous communication when you need the reply, and asynchronous when you do not. The model solution will identify cases that have excessive delays for the reply; then you can explore alternatives to reduce the delay. If placement, revised communication patterns, and so on cannot correct the problems, you can evaluate deferred synchronous or asynchronous callback as alternatives. It is generally better to stay with the simpler synchronization primitives, if possible, because software implementation and testing will be easier. It is possible to reduce delays when you can find other alternatives.

 Stay with synchronous and asynchronous communication when possible to simplify software implementation and testing.

5.7 Summary

Distributed systems, once rare, have become commonplace. Modern software technologies have made distributed systems easier to construct. These technologies have also made it easier to omit important performance considerations. As a result, performance failures in distributed systems are all too frequent and, in the case of Web applications, often very public.

Early in development, the SPE process calls for using deliberately simple models of software processing that are easily constructed and solved, to provide feedback on whether the proposed software is likely to meet performance goals. Thus, our approach is to first create the software execution models, and use them to study the fundamental architecture and design issues. Then, later, we use system execution models to study additional facets of distributed system interactions.

The software execution models for distributed systems consist of a set of performance scenarios; one for each key facility. Special execution graph nodes are inserted to represent synchronization between the scenarios. To solve the models, you specify
- Resource requirements for processing nodes,
- The estimated delay for synchronization nodes,

- The number of messages sent via the network, and
- The (measured) processing overhead for middleware that handles remote calls.

The solutions to these approximate models provide quantitative data for the combination of choices you make for the following:

- The placement of objects (i.e., their assignment to processes and processors)
- The frequency of communication among objects
- The type of synchronization primitive for each communication
- The amount of data passed during each communication
- The amount of processing done by an object

The next step is to use the system execution model to quantify the effects on elapsed time of computer and network contention delays, and thus the system's scalability. These results also help us determine if we need multithreaded objects. The next chapter will explain these additional analysis techniques. It will then present a more comprehensive distributed system case study, and illustrate how to identify problems with both the software and system execution models, and how to evaluate potential solutions to problems.

System Execution Models

A little inaccuracy sometimes saves tons of explanation.

—H. H. Munro

In This Chapter:

- System execution model basics
- Performance metrics
- Solving the system execution model
- Advanced system execution models
- Case study—modeling distributed systems

6.1 Introduction

The software execution model is presented in Chapter 4.

The software execution model provides a static analysis of the mean, best- and worst-case response times for your software. It characterizes the resource requirements of the proposed software alone, in the absence of other workloads or multiple users that could cause delays due to competition for resources. If the predicted performance in the absence of these additional performance-determining factors is unsatisfactory, then there is no need to construct more sophisticated models.

Problems revealed by solving the software execution model should be fixed before proceeding to construct and solve the system execution model.

Clearly, the software execution model is an optimistic one. Most software systems do not execute in isolation. They operate in an environment where there is competition for system resources. This competition for resources leads to *contention delays* when the software is ready to use a resource, such as the CPU, that is busy serving another request. In a system where there are significant contention effects, the software execution model will provide a result that is an overly optimistic reflection of the system's performance.

> *If the software execution model indicates that there are no problems, then you are ready to construct and solve the system execution model to account for contention effects.*

The system execution model is a dynamic model; it characterizes the software's performance in the presence of factors, such as other workloads or multiple users, that could cause contention for resources. Solving the system execution model provides the following additional information that we cannot get from the software execution model:

- More precise metrics that account for resource contention
- Sensitivity of performance metrics to variations in workload composition
- Scalability of the hardware and software to meet future demands
- The effect of new software on service level objectives of other systems that execute on the same facility
- Identification of bottleneck resources
- Comparative data on options for improving performance via: workload changes, software changes, hardware upgrades, and various combinations of each

The simple model strategy was introduced in Chapter 1.

Notice that we are following the simple-model strategy here. We use the simplest possible model that will uncover potential problems with the software's architecture, design or implementation plans. If that model uncovers problems, we address them before proceeding. If not, we can proceed to construct and solve a more realistic model.

The software execution model is easily constructed and solved to provide rapid feedback on the software's performance at minimum cost. If the software execution model indicates that there are no problems, we proceed to construct and solve the system execution model. We haven't lost anything, since the results of solving the software execution model are needed as input parameters for the system execution model.

Note: This chapter provides insight into how the models work and, in some cases, shows the solution formulas. You don't need to actually do the calculations by hand; there are performance modeling tools that will compute the solutions for you. Knowing something about how the model is solved, however, will help you to quickly check the result produced by the tool, so that you know whether to trust what the tool is telling you and where you may have errors in the model specifications. Performance modeling tools are discussed in Chapter 16.

6.2 System Model Basics

There are several possible sources of contention for resources in a computer system:

- There may be multiple users of the system. For example, several customers at different ATM machines may request transactions at about the same time.
- There may be other applications or systems executing on the same hardware resources. For example, at the bank, the application that handles ATM transactions may execute on the same facility as the application that handles teller transactions, a reporting application, a payroll system, and others.
- The application may itself consist of several concurrent processes or threads. This is often the case in embedded, real-time systems.

Note: We use the term *process* to represent a flow of control that executes in parallel with other processes, each having its own address space. A *thread* is a lightweight unit of concurrency that executes in parallel with other threads inside a process. The threads belonging to a process all share the same address space.

The system execution model represents the key computer system resources as queues and servers. A *server* represents a component of the environment that provides some service to the software, such as a processor, a disk, or a network element. The *queue* represents jobs waiting for service: When a request arrives, if the server is busy, the job making the request must wait until the server is free. For example, when a job enters the system, it requires CPU processing to begin execution. If the

CPU is busy, the job must wait in the CPU's queue. When its turn to use the CPU comes up, it is removed from the queue and receives the required amount of service.[1] The job then leaves the server. This flow repeats at each of the other servers that the job must use. When all service requests are filled, the job leaves the system.

Note: We use the term *job* generically to indicate a computation that enters the system, makes requests of one or more computer system resources, and leaves the system upon completion. A job could be a transactionAuthorize request, a teller transaction, a batch report program, a database stored procedure, and so on.

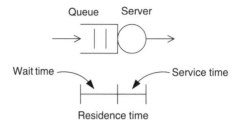

Figure 6-1: Queue-Server Representation of a Single
Computer System Resource

Figure 6-1 depicts a simple queue and server. The open rectangle represents the queue, and the circle represents the server. The figure illustrates the execution behavior of a single computer system resource, such as the CPU or a disk. Jobs or requests arrive at the resource, wait in the queue if necessary, receive service, and leave upon completion. The time spent in the queue is known as the *wait time*. The time spent receiving service from the resource is the *service time*. The total time spent at the resource (wait time plus service time) is the *residence time*.

6.2.1 Performance Metrics

The important performance metrics for each server are

---

1. It is also possible to model other scheduling policies, such as time slicing, preemption, priorities, and so on. Many of these policies, however, cannot be solved with the simple formulas in this chapter.

- *Residence time*: the average amount of time that jobs spend at the server (this includes both time receiving service and time waiting)
- *Utilization*: the average percent of time that the server is busy providing service
- *Throughput*: the average rate at which jobs complete service
- *Queue length*: the average number of jobs at the server (this includes both those receiving service and those waiting)

The values of these metrics depend on
- The number of jobs,
- The amount of service they need,
- The time required for the server to process individual jobs, and
- The policy used to select the next job from the queue (e.g., first-come-first-served or priority scheduling).

Performance modeling tools are discussed in Chapter 16.

Note: These metrics are averages for the observation period. The metrics for an individual job may differ from the average. The difference depends on the *distribution* of arrivals and service requirements. Averages are usually sufficient at early development stages. If absolutely necessary, you can get additional metrics such as minimum, maximum, variance, and so on from some performance modeling tools.

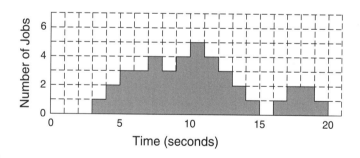

Figure 6-2: Hypothetical Execution Profile

Figure 6-2 shows a hypothetical execution profile for the resource in Figure 6-1. In Figure 6-2, each step up in the graph represents an arrival; each step down represents a completion. Simultaneous arrivals and completions are not allowed. Note that the last job leaves the server at the end of the 20-second observation period.

Performance measurement is discussed in Chapter 8.

The execution profile is based on system measurements. You observe the resource and measure the arrivals, completions, the length of the observation period, and the busy time for the resource during the observation period.

Example 6-1 illustrates the calculation of the important performance metrics for the execution profile in Figure 6-2. The derivation of these equations is not shown here.

Example 6-1: Calculation of Performance Metrics

From the execution profile in Figure 6-2, we obtain the following data:

Measurement period, T	20 sec
Number of arrivals, A	8 jobs
Number of completions, C	8 jobs
Busy time, B	16 sec

From these values, we can immediately calculate the *utilization* and *throughput*:

$$\text{Utilization, } U = \frac{B}{T} \qquad \frac{16}{20} = 0.80$$

$$\text{Throughput, } X = \frac{C}{T} \qquad \frac{8}{20} = 0.4 \text{ jobs per sec}$$

We can also calculate the *mean service time* for these jobs. This is the average amount of time that a job spends receiving service from the resource:

$$\text{Mean service time, } S = \frac{B}{C} \qquad \frac{16}{8} = 2 \text{ sec}$$

To calculate the residence time and queue length, we first need the area under the graph. This is calculated by adding the number of jobs at the server for each time interval.

$$\text{Area under graph, } W = \sum_{\text{time}} (\# \text{ of jobs})$$

$$W = 0 + 0 + 0 + 1 + 2 + 3 + 3 + 4 + 3 + 4 + 5 + 4$$
$$+ 3 + 2 + 1 + 0 + 1 + 2 + 2 + 1 = 41 \text{ job-sec}$$

With the area under the graph, we can now calculate the residence time and queue length:

$$\text{Residence time, } RT = \frac{W}{C} \qquad \frac{41}{8} = 5.125 \text{ sec}$$

$$\text{Queue length, } N = \frac{W}{T} \qquad \frac{41}{20} = 2.05 \text{ jobs}$$

Remember that the queue length (N) includes the jobs receiving service as well as those waiting.

6.2.2 Solving the Queueing Model

When we are in the early phases of a development project, we can't make measurements of the software to derive an execution profile. To estimate the software's performance, we use calculations similar to those in Example 6-1 that are based on predicted *workload intensity* and *service requirements*. The workload intensity is a measure of the number of requests made by a workload in a given time interval. Service requirements are the amount of time that the workload requires from each of the devices in the processing facility.

We make the assumption that the system is fast enough to handle the arrivals, and thus *the completion rate or throughput equals the arrival rate*. This property is known as *job flow balance*.

Note: The arrival rate you will use depends on your performance objective for the period you are evaluating. For example, you may use the maximum value or an average value. At early stages, a scalar value is usually good enough, and it simplifies the analysis. Later, advanced models can examine different arrival rate distributions.

Example 6-2 illustrates the calculation of the performance metrics from a predicted arrival rate and average service time. Again, the derivation of the formulas is not shown here.

The software execution model solution is discussed in Chapter 4.

In Example 6-2, we specified the arrival rate and mean service time. The obvious question is, "Where do these numbers come from?" You may estimate the arrival rate based on anticipated uses of the system. Alternatively, you may measure it by observing a similar (manual or automated) system. For example, ATM arrival rates may be estimated

Example 6-2: Performance Metrics from Predicted Execution
             Characteristics

For this example we specify the *arrival rate* and *average service time* as
follows:

Arrival rate, λ 0.4 jobs per sec

Mean service time, S 2 sec

We then calculate the following average values:

Throughput, $X = \lambda$ 0.4 jobs per sec

Utilization, $U = XS$ $0.4 \times 2 = 0.8$

Residence time, $RT = \dfrac{S}{1-U}$ $\dfrac{2}{1-0.8} = 10$ sec

Queue length, $N = X \times RT$ $0.4 \times 10 = 4$ jobs

from marketing projections, empirical data from a previous model of the
ATM, or observations of customer arrivals for transactions with human
tellers. The service times are obtained from the solution to the software
execution model.

The formula for queue length in Example 6-2 is fundamental to the system execution model analysis. It is known as *Little's Formula,* after its
author, J.D.C. Little [Little 1961]. It establishes the relationship among
queue length, throughput, and residence time. Example 6-2 uses Little's
Formula to calculate queue length from throughput and residence time,
but any time you know the values of two of these metrics, you can use it
to calculate the third.

Check out Little's Formula the next time you're waiting in line at a ticket
office, the bank or some similar place. Use the throughput (or arrival
rate) and the number of customers ahead of you to compute your
expected "residence" time. For example, if a customer leaves every 2
minutes and there are 10 people ahead of you, how long should you
expect to wait? How does your calculated residence time compare with
your actual wait?

Remember that the specifications and calculated results are average values. If different customers have widely varying service times, your individual results may differ from the average. For example, if you wait in line to buy movie tickets, the time it takes to buy a ticket (the service time) doesn't vary much from customer to customer, so your calculated time should be close to the actual time. On the other hand, if you wait in line at an airline ticket counter, the service time will be short for passengers who only check luggage, but long for passengers changing their entire itinerary. So, in a mixed queue, your calculated time may not be close to the "average."

6.2.3 Networks of Queues

The calculations in Example 6-1 and Example 6-2 were for a single computer system resource. Most software, however, requests service from several resources (e.g., the CPU, one or more disks, the network, and so on). Thus, to adequately model real systems, we need to extend the model to encompass a network of queues and servers. A model that includes several queue-servers connected in a network is known as a *queueing network model* (QNM).

Figure 6-3 shows a simple QNM. The topology of this model indicates that jobs arrive at Enter and then visit the CPU. When they leave the CPU, they either request service from the Disk or proceed to the Exit node, thus leaving the system. (The "dot" between the CPU and Disk is a branch point.) The bottom arrow indicates that, after completing processing at the Disk, jobs always return to the CPU. This process repeats for each job that arrives. This is Information Processing Graph notation as described in [Neuse and Browne 1983], [Smith 1990].

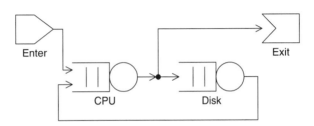

Figure 6-3: A Simple QNM

Note: Jobs do not actually "move" in the system; their *locus of execution* moves. That is, at one point the job's locus of execution may be the CPU and, at another, the disk.

There are two types of QNM: closed models and open models. They have different characteristics and different solution procedures. The following sections discuss these two types of models.

Open Queueing Network Models Figure 6-4 illustrates an *open* QNM. The topology of this model indicates that the flow is similar to the previous example: Jobs enter the system (Enter) and proceed to the CPU. When they leave the CPU, they request service from either of the two Disk devices or, if all processing is complete, they leave the system (Exit).

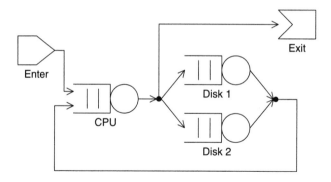

Figure 6-4: Open QNM

This type of model is appropriate for systems with external arrivals and departures, such as an automated teller machine. The number of jobs in the system varies with time. To solve an open QNM, specify the *workload intensity* and *service requirements*. For an open QNM, the workload intensity is the arrival rate, the rate at which jobs arrive for service. The service requirements are either the *number of visits* for each device and the *average service time* per visit, or the total *demand* for that device.

Note: Whether you specify the number of visits and average service time per visit or the total demand will depend on the type of solution technique or tool that you use. The demand is just the number of visits times the average service time per visit.

Example 6-3 shows the solution formulas.

Remember, these formulas illustrate how the models work; you will use tools that solve the models for you.

Example 6-4 illustrates the computation for the open QNM in Figure 6-4 for a particular set of parameters.

Example 6-3: Open QNM Computation

We specify the following parameters:

λ System arrival rate

V_i Number of visits to device

S_i Mean service time at device

Any units may be used for arrival rate and service time as long as they are consistent. For example, if the arrival rate is jobs per second, the service time must be in seconds. The results you calculate will also be in seconds.

Next, we calculate the performance metrics from the following formulas:

1. The *system throughput* equals the system arrival rate because we assume job flow balance:

    System throughput, X_0 $X_0 = \lambda$

2. *Device throughput* is the system throughput times the number of visits to the device:

    Throughput of device *i*, X_i $X_i = X_0 \times V_i$

3. *Device utilization* is device throughput multiplied by mean service time:

    Utilization of device *i*, U_i $U_i = X_i \times S_i$

4. The *device residence time* for each visit to the device is:

Residence time per visit at device i, RT_i $\qquad RT_i = \dfrac{S_i}{1 - U_i}$

5. The device residence time and throughput yield the *device queue length*:

Queue length for device i, N_i $\qquad\qquad N_i = X_i \times RT_i$

6. The *average number of jobs* in the entire QNM is the sum of the mean device queue lengths:

System queue length, N $\qquad\qquad N = \sum_i N_i$

7. The *system response time* uses Little's Formula:

System response time, RT $\qquad\qquad RT = \dfrac{N}{X_0}$

Example 6-4: Open QNM Solution

Sample parameters:

System arrival rate, $\lambda = 5$ jobs per second

Number of visits, V		Mean service time, S	
CPU	5	CPU	0.01
Disk1	3	Disk1	0.03
Disk2	1	Disk2	0.02

First, use the formulas in steps 1 and 2 of Example 6-3 to compute the throughput for each device. The device throughput (line 1 in the following table) is the system throughput (5 jobs per second) multiplied by the number of visits to that device.

The mean service time for each device (line 2 of the table) is simply the value of the parameter given above. The metrics for each device appear in lines 3 through 5 of the table. They are calculated using the formulas in steps 3 through 5 of Example 6-3.

The average number of jobs in the system is the sum of the mean device queue lengths from line 5. In this example, the average number of jobs in

Calculated Performance Metrics

Metrics	CPU	Disk1	Disk2
1. X, throughput	25	15	5
2. S, mean service time	0.01	0.03	0.02
3. U, utilization	0.25	0.45	0.10
4. RT, residence time	0.013	0.055	0.022
5. N, queue length	0.325	0.825	0.111
Total jobs in system $= 0.335 + 0.825 + 0.110 = 1.26$			
System response time $= 1.26/5 = 0.252$ sec			

the system is 1.26, and the system throughput equals the arrival rate, 5 jobs/second, so the system response time is 0.252 second.

Closed Queueing Network Models This type of model has no external arrivals or departures. A fixed number of jobs keep circulating among queues. Figure 6-5 illustrates this type of system. In closed QNMs, a delay node replaces the source (Enter) and sink (Exit) nodes. Here, the user enters a request at the delay node (User) and transmits it to the system. The request moves through the QNM as usual. When the request is complete, the response goes to User, the user enters another request, and the process repeats.

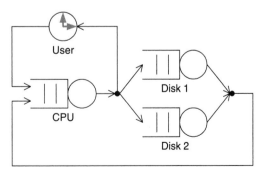

Figure 6-5: Closed QNM

Note: The delay at the User node typically includes the time to transmit the results, evaluate them, enter the next request, and transmit it to the CPU. In system execution models, this delay is typically called "think time."

To solve a closed QNM, you again specify the workload intensity. This time, however, the workload intensity is the *number of users* (or number of simultaneous jobs) and the *think time* (the average delay between the receipt of a response and the submission of the next request). You also need to specify the number of visits and service times or total demand for each device. The model solution is more complex than that of an open model because the system throughput depends on the response time. Looking at the topology of the model in Figure 6-5, you can see that, if it takes longer to produce a result, it will be longer before the next request arrives. Because of this, the solution algorithm must use throughput to calculate response time. Typically, tools use a "mean value analysis" algorithm derived from Little's Formula. Because the details of this solution are beyond the scope of our discussion, we do not present them here. Jain [Jain 1990] provides additional details regarding the solution of closed QNMs.

6.3 Deriving System Model Parameters from Software Model Results

Modeling tools are described in Chapter 16.

The types of system model parameters you need and how you specify them depend on the performance modeling tool that you use. Your job will be easiest if you use an SPE tool, such as *SPE·ED*, which automatically calculates the system model parameters from the software model. This section gives an overview of how such tools derive the model parameters. If you use a system modeling tool as opposed to an SPE tool, you will need to compute these parameters yourself. Then you will likely want the additional information about the computation provided by Smith [Smith, 1990].

Performance walkthroughs are discussed in Chapter 7.

To construct and solve the system execution model, begin by using queue-servers to represent the key computer resources or devices that you specified in the software execution model. Then, add the connections between queues to complete a model *topology* such as that in Figure 6-4. This step requires knowledge of both the operating environment and the software execution characteristics. If necessary, you can get this information from a performance specialist during a walk-through.

Note: Whether or not you need to draw the model topology depends on the type of tool you use. Some use queue symbols; others use icons that look like processors, disks, and so on to represent devices. *SPE▪ED* does not require the topology. It uses the devices specified in the overhead matrix.

The next step is to decide whether the system is best modeled as an open or closed QNM. Recall that open QNMs are best for situations, such as transaction processing systems, where jobs arrive, receive some service, and leave the system. The rate at which jobs arrive does not depend on the time required to respond to a request. Closed QNMs are more appropriate for interactive systems where users enter a request, receive the results, and enter another request. Here, the rate at which requests arrive depends on the response time to the previous request. If you model the workload as an open QNM, add a source and a sink node. If you model it as a closed QNM, add a delay node to represent the user.

Note: Another important property in QNMs is the queue scheduling discipline: the strategy used to select the next job for service from the waiting jobs. Performance modeling tools support a variety of queue scheduling disciplines, some of which produce models that cannot be solved by the formulas given in this chapter. We'll assume, however, that the queue scheduling discipline is one that supports the formulas presented here. You can find more information about scheduling disciplines in [Jain 1990].

Techniques for determining workload intensity are discussed in Chapter 7.

Next, determine the workload intensities for each scenario that will execute on the facility. For open workloads, this is the arrival rate. For closed workloads, it is the number of users and the think time. These numbers can be difficult to obtain. Possible sources include marketing projections, measurements of usage on similar systems (perhaps a previous version), or observation of the manual system that the software is intended to replace.

The solution to the software model is discussed in Chapter 4.

The final step is to specify the service requirements. The device characteristics (processor speed, average time to complete an I/O, and so on) come from the execution environment specifications. For I/O devices (e.g., a disk or network), the number of visits is the number of physical I/Os. The visits, service time, and demand for devices comes from the software model. Example 6-5 illustrates this calculation.

Example 6-5: Calculation of System Model Parameters from the Software Performance Model

To illustrate how to obtain system model parameters from the software model, we'll continue the ATM example from Chapter 4, focusing on the authorizeTransaction scenario. This example illustrates the computation with a simple example, and lets us start with the results calculated in Chapter 4. The figure below shows the software model for this scenario along with the software resource requirements for each node.

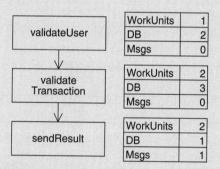

Software Model for authorizeTransaction

The following figure shows the queueing network model for this example. The host bank has a CPU and a single disk for storing account information. Each of these is represented by a queue and server. The network is also represented by a queue and server. This is an open QNM, so we need to specify the rate at which requests for transaction authorizations arrive (the arrival rate), and, for each device, either the total demand or the number of visits and the average service time per visit.

We solved this authorizeTransaction software model in Chapter 4 using analysis steps 1 and 2, and produced the results in the following table.

First, consider the disk and the network. The software model result produces the number of visits to the disk device: 14. The service time for the disk comes from the overhead matrix: 0.02 second in this example. Similarly, the number of visits to the network is 1 (from the previous table),

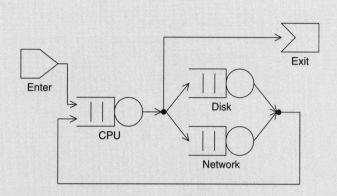

Host Bank Computer Facility

Processing step	CPU Kinstr.	Disk	Network Messages
validateUser	1,020	4	0
validateTransaction	1,540	6	0
sendResult	550	4	1
Total: authorizeTransaction	3,110	14	1

and the service time from the overhead matrix is 0.01 second. If your tool requires the total demand for these devices, multiply the number of visits by the service time.

Calculating the number of visits and average service time for the CPU is more complex since the CPU executes multiple instructions per visit. This calculation is discussed by Smith [Smith 1990]. Fortunately, many tools use the total demand for the CPU, rather than visits and service times. The demand is equal to the service time for that device times the number of visits. This is the result calculated from the software model in the table above: 3,110 multiplied by the service time of the CPU, 0.00001, for a total demand of 0.0311 second. The total demand for the disk and network are 0.28 and 0.01 second, respectively.

Note: The units for the service times and arrival rates also depend on the type of tool you are using. Here, we assume that everything is specified in seconds. Other tools may use transactions per hour, milliseconds for device specifications, and so on, but internally the tools must convert units to the same common denominator if they use the simple formulas like those in Example 6-3.

The following table summarizes the visit and service time parameters for each device in the host bank facility. The parameter specifications assume that you are using a tool such as *SPE▪ED*, which uses total demand for the CPU and visits and service times for the other devices.

Device	Visits, *V*	Device Service Time, *S*
CPU	all	.0311
Disk	14	.02
Network	1	.01

Other types of tools, such as simulation-based tools, may need the number of visits and the prorated service time for the CPU as well. As noted previously, that calculation is discussed by Smith [Smith 1990].

We complete the parameter specifications with the arrival rate for authorizeTransaction. The arrival rate is derived from a performance walkthrough. A reasonable value for this example is 1 transaction per second. Check your understanding of these topics by using these values and computing system model results similar to those in Example 6-4.

This discussion explains how to derive the system model parameters for one performance scenario. If you have multiple scenarios, repeat the calculation of parameters for each scenario independent of the other performance scenarios. Modeling tools solve these *multi-class* models by adapting the QNM formulas to compute results for each workload (or by simulating multiple workloads). This makes it easy to vary the workload intensity to study the performance effects of variations in the workload mix.

6.4 Using the System Model for SPE

The system execution model results provide quantitative data on the following effects of resource contention:
- *More precise metrics that account for resource contention:* quantify the elongation of the response time due to waiting in queues for

busy devices, and show the utilization of devices by all types of jobs using the devices.

- *Sensitivity of performance metrics to variations in workload composition:* vary the workload intensity of each job to study various combinations of jobs and compare results.

- *Scalability of the hardware and software to meet future demands:* solve the model with projections of future workload intensity.

Performance measurements are discussed in Chapter 8.

- *Effect of new software on service level objectives of other systems:* include other systems as separate additional workloads in the model, using measured resource usage and intensity values of the other systems.

- *Identification of bottleneck resources:* identify the resource that will saturate first. It is the resource with the highest demand (visits *x* service time). Calculate its maximum throughput at saturation by dividing the number of devices of that type by the calculated demand.

- *Comparative data on options for improving performance:* consider workload changes, software changes, hardware upgrades, and various combinations of each. Modify the workload intensity, software model, processing overhead, and/or hardware configuration to quantify the effect.

6.4.1 Advanced System Models

So far, we have used very simple SPE models. Perhaps you are skeptical about their usefulness for "real" systems assessment. Experience shows that these simple models can detect serious performance problems very early in the development process. The simple models isolate problems and focus attention on their resolution. After they serve this primary purpose, though, we need to augment them to make more realistic performance predictions as the software evolves.

Advanced system models are usually appropriate when the software reaches the detailed-design life cycle stage. Even when it is easy to incorporate the additional execution characteristics earlier, it is better to defer them to the advanced system execution model. It is seldom easy, however, and the extra time required to construct and evaluate the advanced models is usually not justified because the data available to you early in the life cycle is imprecise. Thus, constructing and solving these more complex models does not necessarily improve your predictions.

Facets of performance that require more advanced models include
- Intricate details of computer system devices, such as networks, I/O channels, and so on, and their queue scheduling disciplines
- Use of passive resources—resources that are required for processing but do no work themselves; for example, the lock-free mechanism that protects bank accounts from multiple simultaneous updates, and the communication and synchronization among concurrent processes or threads
- Additional metrics, such as minimum, maximum, and variance; arrival distributions, and so on

These factors are seldom important early in the development process because the design is not sufficiently elaborated to include this level of detail. Later, when more details are known, these factors can be modeled using the advanced techniques if they are important.

6.4.2 Alternate Solution Methods

The basic system execution models that we discussed in Section 6.3 can be solved efficiently using exact analytic methods (i.e., the formulas). The advanced system models must be solved either by using approximate solution techniques or using simulation. The advanced models can take much longer to solve since the quality of the result that you get from a simulation solution depends on how long the simulation runs. Some tools use a hybrid approach, using the formulas for portions of the model where an analytic approach is appropriate, and combining these results with a simulation solution for other parts of the model. These hybrid solutions can be faster than a pure simulation solution.

Remember that the formulas give you *average* values for the metrics. There are times when you might want to look at more detailed behavior. In these cases, a simulation solution can yield additional metrics such as minimum and maximum queue lengths.

Modeling techniques appropriate for distributed systems are covered in the case study in the next section. Procedures for formulating and solving the other types of advanced models are beyond the scope of this book (however, they are covered in [Smith 1990]). When you reach this stage in development, you will want to either learn more about advanced system models, or join forces with a performance modeling expert who can assist you with advanced modeling techniques.

6.4.3 Schedulability

An example of Rate Monotonic Scheduling is presented in Chapter 14.

Schedulability is concerned with determining whether certain critical tasks in a multi-tasking system will meet their deadlines, even under conditions where the software is temporarily overloaded. SPE does not directly address issues of schedulability. There are several techniques for scheduling a set of tasks. The best known of these is Rate Monotonic Scheduling [Liu and Layland 1973].

While SPE does not directly address schedulability, it does provide support for using schedulability techniques such as Rate Monotonic Scheduling. These techniques use the execution times of the tasks as an input parameter. Typically, these times are measured after the tasks have been implemented (late in the development process). The SPE techniques we have discussed allow you to estimate these execution times early in the development process. With this information, you can use the scheduling techniques to determine whether the tasks are schedulable, before you have implemented them. If you find a problem, you can take corrective action early, when changes are easier to make.

6.5 Distributed System Case Study

This case study is from an actual project; however, application details have been changed to preserve anonymity. The software supports an electronic virtual storefront, wasteBucks.com.[2] We saw the takeCustomerOrder portion of the system in Chapter 5. This case study focuses on the heart of the system: the Customer Service component that collects completed orders, initiates tasks in the other components, and tracks the status of orders in progress.

The use case we consider is processing a new order illustrated by the sequence diagram in Figure 6-6. We will first consider the best-case model. It begins with takeCustomerOrder, a reference to another, more

---

2. wasteBucks.com is a fictional Web site. At the time this case study was originally written, no such site existed.

detailed sequence diagram (covered in Chapter 5). When the order is complete, an ACK is sent to the customer and the order processing begins. For this case study, we assume that a typical customer order consists of 50 individual items. The unit of work for both the takeCustomerOrder and closeCustomerOrder components is the entire order; the other order processing components handle each item in the order separately; the sequence diagram shows this repetition with a loop symbol. The similar symbol labeled "opt" represents an optional step that may occur when wasteBucks.com must order the item from a supplier.

Each column in Figure 6-6 represents an independent process, so the columns are modeled separately. At this stage, we assume that the first

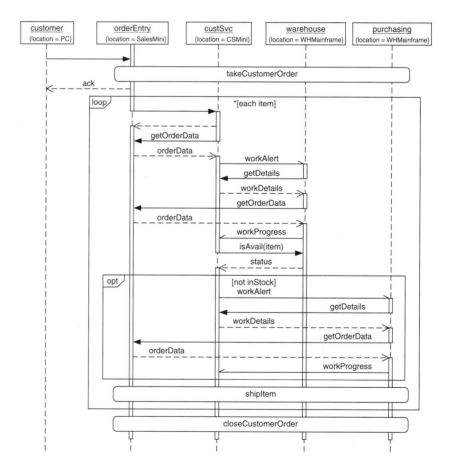

Figure 6-6: New Order Scenario

three columns each execute on their own facility; the warehouse and purchasing processes share a facility.

Figure 6-7 shows the execution graph for the custSvc column in Figure 6-6. Everything inside the loop is in the expanded node, process-ItemOrder. Its details are in Figure 6-8. The two workAlert processing steps are also expanded. Their details are not shown here—we will discuss them later. This software model depicts only the Customer Service facility; we approximate the delay time to communicate with the other facilities.

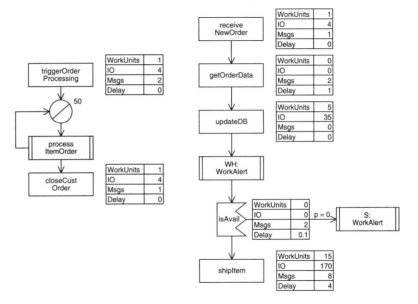

Figure 6-7: Execution Graph
custServ:NewOrder

Figure 6-8: Expansion of
processItemOrder

Note: This model does not explicitly represent the synchronization. At early architecture stages, you probably haven't decided whether calls will be synchronous, asynchronous, or something else. We just represent the primary facility and its scenarios, and estimate the delay for interacting with other facilities. Later, we will add the synchronization.

The next step is to specify resource requirements for each processing step. The key resources in this model are the CPU WorkUnits for database and other processing, the number of I/Os for database and logging activities, the number of messages sent among processors (and the associated overhead for the middleware), and the estimated delay in seconds until the message-reply is received. These values are also in Figure 6-7 and Figure 6-8. They are best-case estimates derived from performance measurement experiments. They may also be estimated in a performance walkthrough. Techniques for deriving these software resource requirements are covered in Part III.

Note: The probability of taking the path from the case node Avail in Figure 6-8 is set to 0 because the best case model assumes the items are available.

Processing overhead is discussed in Chapter 4.

The processing overhead:

- Represents each of the hardware devices in each of the distributed processors
- Connects the software model resource requests to hardware device requirements
- Incorporates any processing requirements due to operating system or network overhead

Table 6-1: Processing Overhead

Devices	CPU	Disk	Delay		LAN
Quantity	6	3	1		1
Service Units	Sec.	Phys I/O	Units		Msgs.

WorkUnits	0.01				
DB		1			
Msgs	0.0005	1			1
Delay			1		

Service Time	1	0.003	1		0.05

Table 6-1 shows the processing overhead for the Customer Service facility for this case study. There are 6 processors, 3 disks, a Delay node, and a LAN with the service times shown in the last row.

Note: The WorkUnits were derived from measurements that include the processing time for the database, so the DB row has no CPU requirement.

The models also assume that the disk visits are equally spread over the three Disk devices.

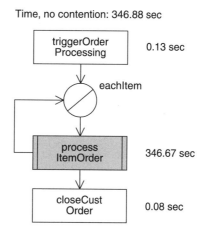

Time, no contention: 346.88 sec

Figure 6-9: Best-Case Elapsed Time for newOrder Scenario

Figure 6-9 shows the best-case solution with one user and thus no contention for computer devices. The solution is computed using the techniques in Chapter 4. Details for this computation and solutions presented later are not shown here. The end-to-end time is 347 seconds; most of it is in processItemOrder (the value shown is for all 50 items). Results for the processItemOrder subgraph in Figure 6-10 indicate that each item requires approximately 6.9 seconds; most of that is in the ship-Item processing step. Other results (not shown) indicate that 5.1 seconds of the 6.9 seconds is due to estimated delay for processing on the other facilities. The results also show that network congestion prevents the system from achieving a satisfactory response time with one user. It will be far worse for the desired throughput of 0.1 orders per second.

You can evaluate potential solutions by modifying the software execution model to reflect architecture alternatives. We select an alternative that processes orders as a group, rather than individual items in an order. The changes to the software execution model for this alternative are relatively minor—the number of loop repetitions is reduced to two (one for orders ready to ship, the other for orders requiring back-ordered items), and the resource requirements for steps in the loop change slightly to

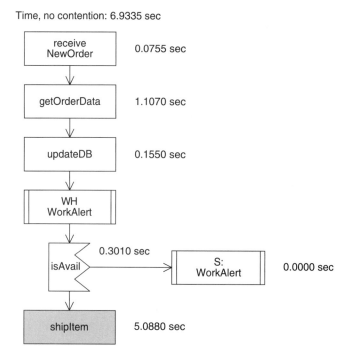

Figure 6-10: Best-case Elapsed Time for Each processItemOrder

reflect requirements to process a group of items. This alternative yields a response time of approximately 15 seconds with the desired throughput.

Note: There are many different ways to model this alternative. We chose a simple one that doesn't change the model structure; this model only changes the values for resource usage. This assumes that customer orders include some items that are shipped immediately, and (with a specified probability) other back-ordered items that are shipped when they arrive. You might instead create separate scenarios for ready orders versus back orders, if you want to evaluate their response time explicitly. You could also perform the availability check once at the beginning of the processItemOrder loop, rather than each time through the loop. Other improvements are possible but are not covered here.

The next step is to construct and evaluate the system execution model. We use the *SPE▪ED* software performance engineering tool, which automatically generates a queueing network model and calculates its parameters from the software execution model. Figure 6-11 shows the topology

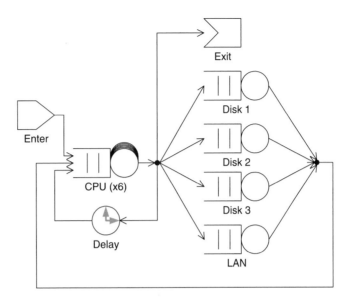

Figure 6-11: QNM for the Customer Service Facility

of the QNM generated by *SPE•ED* for the Customer Service (CS) facility. As shown in Table 6-1, there are 6 CPUs, 3 Disks, a Delay node, and a LAN. The six CPUs are indicated by the replicated circle for the server. Note that there is a single queue for all six CPUs. Jobs wait in this queue and are serviced by the next available CPU. This situation is similar to waiting for service at the post office where there is a single line served by all clerks.

To solve the model, we add the specified arrival rate of newOrders of 0.1 orders per second, and the tool produces the results in Figure 6-12 (using the techniques covered in Section 6.2). The response time, including the resource contention due to multiple orders, increases to 14.9 seconds. Further results (not shown) indicate that the expected utilization of the devices of the Customer Service facility are 2% for the CPU, 5% for the disks, and 17% for the LAN. Thus, the models indicate that we have corrected the earlier performance problems.

According to the models, the overhead and delays due to process coordination were a significant portion of the total end-to-end time to process a new order. Improvements resulted from processing batches of items

Residence time: 14.906 sec

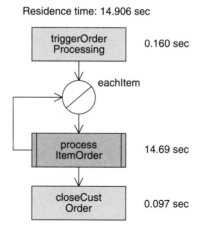

Figure 6-12: System Model Results for Grouped Items

rather than individual items. These simple models provide sufficient information to identify problems in the architecture before proceeding to more advanced system execution models. It is easy and important to resolve key performance problems with simple models before proceeding to the advanced models described next. The next step is to include the synchronization among processors in the models.

6.5.1 Synchronization Model

This section illustrates the creation and evaluation of the detailed models of synchronization. Figure 6-6 shows that all the synchronization steps are either asynchronous or synchronous.

Note: Deferred synchronous calls and asynchronous callback are only useful when the results are not needed for the next processing steps. They may also be more complex to implement. Thus, it is sensible to plan synchronous calls unless the models indicate that other calls result in significant improvements.

Figure 6-13 shows the synchronization nodes in the processItemOrder step. It first receives the NewOrder message and immediately replies with the acknowledgement message, thus freeing the calling process. Next, it

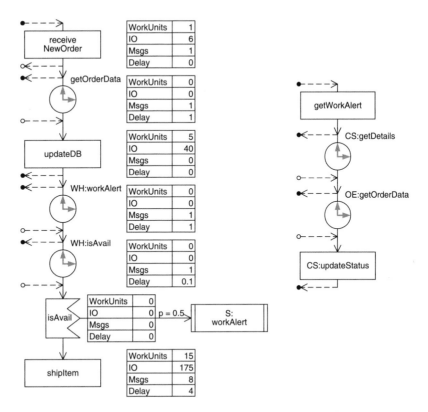

Figure 6-13: Synchronization in processItemOrder

Figure 6-14: WH:work Alert Processing

makes a synchronous call to OE:getOrderData and waits for the reply. The availability check is now explicitly modeled with a synchronous call to WH:isAvail?. The processing steps here are similar to those in the approximate model.

We still need to check to see if the item is available, even though the entire order is explicitly either ready to ship or is back ordered. The Order Entry (OE) portion of the processing checks an availability database that is cached on the OE facility with the inventory status as of beginning of business. Processing in this scenario verifies the status of each item and handles the flow accordingly.

Figure 6-14 shows the processing that occurs on the Warehouse facility. It receives the asynchronous request from the CS facility, acknowledges its receipt, makes a synchronous call to CS:getDetails, makes a synchronous

Example 6-6: Model Evolution

Examine the processing steps that occur on the Customer Service (CS) facility for invoking WH:workAlert in the figure on the left below. First, we invoke the workAlert on the Warehouse (WH) facility. The WH facility will then invoke the getDetails process on the CS facility. We will expect to

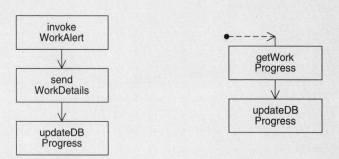

Approximate Software Processing for workAlert on the Customer Service facility.

Synchronization Software Processing for sendWorkDetails on the Customer Service facility

receive this request and do the processing required to send the response. Sometime later, the WH facility will invoke updateDBProgress to report its status in processing the order. In the earlier approximate model we knew to expect this processing, but did not yet know whether calls would be synchronous, asynchronous, and so on; nor did we know how many separate processes would be involved on the CS facility.

When we move to the synchronization model, however, we represent each of these synchronization points to determine whether we will have excessive delays for server processes to handle each request. So the processing in Figure 6-14 shows the separate calls and whether they are synchronous or asynchronous. Note that CS:statusUpdate (progress) is an asynchronous call. The figure on the right shows the scenario on the CS facility that will receive this asynchronous request and perform the processing. Similarly, we also model the scenario to receive the synchronous request to sendWorkDetails. It is not shown here.

call to OE:getOrderData, and then (after the order is shipped) makes an asynchronous call to CS:updateStatus.

Table 6-2 shows the advanced system model results produced by *SPE•ED's* performance simulator. The first column shows the name of each process, while the next four columns show the response time for each process. The sixth column shows the number of times the process executes per second (TPut), and the last three columns show the number of jobs in the queue waiting for the process to handle its request. The CS:NewOrder(NA) row shows results when the items are not available in the warehouse; the CS:NewOrder row shows results when the items are available.

Table 6-2: Advanced System Model Results

	Response Time (sec)				TPut	Queue		
	Mean	Min	Max	Variance		Mean	Max	Time
CS:NewOrder	8.2	0.1	64.5	50.2	0.2			
CS:NewOrder(NA)	8.6	0.1	72.8	51.4	0.2			
OE:OrderData	0.2	0	4.0	0.1	1.0	0.304	8	0.31
CS:WorkDetails	0.2	0	4.3	0.1	0.6	0.160	2	0.27
CS:updateStatus	0.2	0	4.7	0.1	0.6	0.014	4	0.02
WH:WorkAlert	1.8	0.1	11.6	1.6	0.4	1.741	28	4.40
S:WorkAlert	2.0	0.1	13.1	1.8	0.2	0.217	9	1.10

Note: These results are more difficult to interpret than the system execution model results in Figure 6-12. If you have ever tried to debug systems with extensive synchronization, you know that the interactions among synchronous and asynchronous processes can be quite complex. Thus the analysis of this behavior is also difficult. This is the reason that we recommend that you first use the software execution models and the system execution models described earlier to rule out performance problems, before you move to these advanced system models.

The maximum queue length and the queue time for WH:WorkAlert suggests that more concurrent threads are needed for scalability. OE:Order-Data and S:WorkAlert may also need multiple threads. These are important results: If you do not create software to be multithreaded, it may be impossible to make those modifications later.

> *Use SPE models to identify processes, before they are implemented, that will likely require multithreading to meet performance and scalability requirements.*

The simulation results also reflect problems due to "lock-step" execution of concurrent processes. Lock-step behavior occurs when one or more processes follow another process around through the queues (like a caravan). Note that the mean response time for S:WorkAlert is slightly higher than for WH:WorkAlert, even though they execute the same processing steps and S:WorkAlert executes less frequently (see throughput values). This is because the asynchronous calls to WH:WorkAlert and to S:Work-Alert occur very close to the same time, and cause both processes to execute concurrently on the same facility. This introduces slight contention delays for the process that arrives second (S:WorkAlert). In this case study, the performance effect is not serious, but it illustrates the types of performance analysis relevant for this life cycle stage and the models that permit the analysis.

Note: In this model, we were able to identify lock-step behavior because the software models are identical for the two processes involved. So, while we would expect the performance results to be almost the same, they were not. In general, you can find these problems by comparing the software model time without contention to the advanced system model response time and look for processes that have a greater relative increase in response time than other processes that execute with comparable workload intensity (arrival rate or number of users).

Note that most of the useful results in early life cycle stages come from the software execution model. For example, you can use the simpler model to evaluate the amount of communication and the synchronization points in the architecture and design, the assignment of methods to processes, the assignment of processes to processors, and so on. It is difficult to validate models of systems that are still under development. Many changes occur before the software executes and may be measured, and the early life cycle models are best-case models that omit many processing complexities that occur in the ultimate implementation. Nevertheless, the results are sufficiently accurate to identify problems in the software plans, and quantify the relative benefit of improvements. In this study, the models successfully predicted potential problems in the original architecture due to network activity.

6.6 Modeling Hints

Multiple Users and Workloads The system models account for multiple users by specifying the workload intensity, either an arrival rate, or the number of users and think time. To model multiple workloads on a facility, you assign all of the relevant workloads to the same facility. The model parameters for each workload come from the solution to its software execution model.

Average versus Peak Performance Remember that, for basic QNMs, the tools calculate average values. Make sure that you are averaging over the right period of time. For example, the behavior in a peak hour is not likely to be the same as the overall average for 24 hours. If you are interested in the peak hour, make sure the workload intensity and the model specifications are all for peak-hour behavior.

Sensitivity You can determine the sensitivity of the system model results to parameters such as the workload intensity, number of devices, or device service times by changing one of these parameters and re-solving the model. If a small change in one of these causes a large change in the computed metrics, the model is sensitive to that quantity. This may give you a clue about how to improve performance (e.g., use a faster disk) or indicate the need to improve your estimate of the value of a parameter (e.g., workload intensity).

Scalability You can determine the scalability of your system by solving the model using projected future workload intensities. The model solutions will tell you which devices limit scalability (i.e., those with the highest demand or highest utilization). If the response times for your anticipated future loads are not acceptable, you can explore making changes to the software, using faster devices, or adding more devices (e.g., additional CPUs or disks) to improve the situation.

Bottlenecks The "bottleneck" device is the one with the highest utilization [Jain 1990]. This is the device that will limit your scalability. Again, you can use the models to explore the effects of: changes to the software, using a faster device, or adding more devices.

6.7 Summary

After the solution to the software execution model indicates that there are no performance problems, we construct and solve the system execution model. The system execution model characterizes the software's performance in the presence of factors, such as other workloads or multiple users, that could cause contention for resources.

The system execution model is represented as a network of queues and servers, whereby a queue represents jobs waiting for service, and a server represents a component of the execution environment that provides some service to the software. Solving the queueing network model provides metrics for the average amount of time that jobs spend at a server (waiting and in service), the percent of time that the server is busy providing service, the average rate at which jobs complete service, and the average number of jobs at the server.

The basic system models presented here can be solved quickly using tools that implement the formulas given in this chapter. More advanced system models provide additional details on devices and their queue scheduling disciplines, as well as information on the use of passive resources. These advanced models must be solved using analytic approximations or simulation techniques, however. Simulations can take much longer to solve, because the quality of the result that you get from a simulation solution depends on how long the simulation runs.

The case study demonstrated that most of the useful results in early life cycle stages come from the software execution model. It also illustrated how the advanced system execution model can uncover some subtle effects, such as processes that should be multithreaded, or "lock-step" behavior.

Part III

Data Collection

Chapter 7

SPE Data Collection

All solid facts were originally mist.

—Henry S. Haskins

In This Chapter:

- *What* data do you need and *how* can you collect it?
- Who can provide the information?
- How do you conduct a performance walkthrough?
- How do you estimate resource requirements?

7.1 Introduction

The chapters in Part II covered the modeling techniques for SPE. We assumed that we had the necessary data, and used it to create and solve the software and system performance models. The hardest part of the SPE process is getting the data you need to create the models. Once you have the data, it is relatively easy to perform SPE studies.

This chapter focuses on techniques for collecting data early in the life cycle, when precise information about the architecture, design and implementation is not yet available. We begin by explaining the five types of data you need. We then introduce the performance walkthrough, a mechanism for collecting SPE data, and illustrate what transpires in a walkthrough with a detailed example. Finally, we provide advice on how to estimate resource requirements. Chapter 8 continues with techniques for measuring resource requirements.

7.2 SPE Data Requirements

SPE data requirements were introduced in Chapter 2.

We need the following five types of data for SPE:

1. *Key performance scenarios:* the important use cases and the scenarios that will be the focus of the SPE efforts, their processing steps, and their intensity

2. *Performance objectives:* the criteria for evaluating the software system plans and the performance of the completed software

3. *Execution environment:* this includes the hardware configuration upon which the system will execute, the operating system and other support software routines that interface between the software and the hardware, and any middleware that connects software components

4. *Software resource requirements:* computational needs for each processing step that are meaningful from a software perspective

5. *Computer resource requirements:* the mapping of the software resource requirements onto the amount of service they require from key devices in the execution environment

Each of these is elaborated in the following sections.

7.2.1 Key Performance Scenarios

Scenarios make it possible to isolate and extract the processing steps that are associated with a particular execution of a use case. Each scenario is a sequence of actions describing the interactions between the system and its environment (including the user) or between the internal objects involved in a particular execution of the system. The scenario shows the objects that participate and the messages that flow between them. A message may represent either an event or an invocation of one of the object's operations. Activations identify the processing associated with the event or operation invocation.

To identify the scenarios that are important for performance, we begin by identifying the critical use cases: those that are important to the operation of the system or are important to responsiveness as seen by the users. Not all of the scenarios for a critical use case will be significant from a performance perspective, however. There is usually a small subset (<20%) of all of the functions provided by a system that are used most (>80%) of the time. Think about your use of text editors, spreadsheets, automated teller machines, and other systems. Does the rule hold? The performance of a system is dominated by these functions, so our first performance assessment focuses on these use cases and scenarios.

Performance is also affected by large tasks (i.e., "heavy hitters") even though they execute less frequently. For example, if displaying a Web page takes an excessive amount of time, users may abandon the site. Scenarios that have high resource usage demands can also make other, more frequent scenarios perform poorly because of queueing delays. Finally, critical scenarios such as recovery after an outage must complete within the allotted time for the system to meet its functional requirements. All of these are candidates for performance scenarios.

The scenarios we select for performance engineering will be called *performance scenarios*. It's best to begin with typical uses. Later, you can add error handling, infrequent uses that are "heavy-hitters," and so on.

We usually begin with the identification of one or a few of the most important performance scenarios and conduct the performance studies for them. It is easy to add additional performance scenarios to the models later.

> *Identify one or a few of the most important performance scenarios for initial studies. Add additional performance scenarios later.*

In addition to the performance scenario description, we need an estimate of the *workload intensity:* the arrival rate of requests, or the number of concurrent users along with the time between successive user requests. Each performance scenario may have a different workload intensity. You may want to specify a set of intensities for different situations, such as peak hour, average hour, peak day, and so on. We elaborate on these situations in the following section.

The system architect, in collaboration with marketing representatives and/or a user representative and a performance engineer, should be able to provide this information.

7.2.2 Performance Objectives

Performance objectives specify quantitative criteria for evaluating the performance characteristics of the scenarios in the system you are developing. Without well-defined, quantitative performance objectives, it is difficult to know where you are going. It's even harder to know when you have gotten there.

> The cat only grinned as Alice approached... "Cheshire-Puss," she began, rather timidly... "Would you tell me, please, which way I ought to go from here?"
>
> "That depends a good deal on where you want to go to," said the Cat.
>
> —*Alice's Adventures in Wonderland,* by Lewis Carroll

Quantitative performance objectives have the following benefits:
- They provide a basis for selecting appropriate architecture and design alternatives.
- They help you confirm that individual design choices are globally compatible and consistent with end-to-end objectives.
- They improve development effectiveness by focusing attention on the operations that have significant performance impact and by avoiding excessive work on those with negligible impact.
- They enable you to select the necessary hardware configuration well in advance.
- They provide early warning when planned configurations are inadequate.

In each case, if you quantify the objectives, having model results for proposed alternatives will help you select the appropriate one.

A performance objective is not just a number; it is typically a set of numbers describing a combination of the input-processing-output for a particular situation. With SPE, this combination is characterized by the scenario definition. The scenario combined with a specification of workload mixes and intensities (to describe the situation) is typically associated with a performance objective. Each member of the set of situations and scenarios may have a different number. For example, we may specify a peak load situation and the arrival rate of each scenario in that time frame, and specify the response time for each scenario in that situation. Another member of the set may describe the situation at the end of month, and so on.

You can express performance objectives in several different ways, including response time, throughput, constraints on resource usage, or bounds on hardware utilization. For information systems, you will typically describe response time for a performance scenario from a user perspective, that is, the number of seconds required to respond to a user action or request. For real-time systems, response time is the amount of time required to respond to a given external event. Throughput requirements specify the number of transactions or events to be processed per unit of time.

Constraints on resource usage are limitations on the amounts of various resources used by a scenario or a portion of it. For example, you may specify that a portion of a scenario use no more than 200 msec of CPU time, and no more than 10 I/Os. Constraints on resource usage are typically used in well-understood systems where there is historical knowledge about both how the software should be implemented and what are reasonable bounds on resource requirements for that type of implementation.

Constraints on hardware utilization are frequently used in real-time systems. For example, you may require that CPU utilization be less than 50%, or that memory usage be limited to 4 kilobytes.

You may specify response time objectives as times for individual transactions or end-to-end times for complete user tasks (i.e., a complete scenario). Complete tasks may include multiple transactions and may execute on multiple processors. While the focus has traditionally been on individual transaction times because they are easier to model and to measure, if you use end-to-end times, you can often find opportunities to improve system effectiveness as well as system responsiveness. For example, each individual screen in an order entry process may have acceptable response time, but the end-to-end time to complete all order entry screens may be too long. Improvements would minimize the number of screens required, and streamline their content.

Regardless of the type of objective you select, it must be *specific* and *measurable*. Vague statements such as "the system must be efficient" or "the system shall be fast" are not reasonable performance objectives. A better statement is, "the end-to-end time for completion of a 'typical,' correct order entry performance scenario must be less than 2 minutes, and each user interaction in the performance scenario must complete in less than 5 seconds." The performance scenario defines the average number of items and so on contained in a "typical" order.

The system architect, in collaboration with marketing representatives (and/or a user representative) and a performance engineer, should be able to provide this information.

7.2.3 Execution Environment

The execution environment consists of:

- The hardware and network configuration upon which the software will execute—the devices and their processing speed
- The operating system, middleware, and other support software routines that interface between the new software and the hardware—the routines or APIs that have large processing demands, and the amount of processing they require from each device
- Database usage—the tables and their size, keys, and order
- Other software that shares the computer system and thus competes for computer resources—other significant workloads and their processing demands

Scenario performance clearly depends on the execution environment. For example, the response times for Web applications depend on the number and speed of CPUs, the number and speed of I/O devices, the number of users making "simultaneous" requests, and the amount of other work that executes on the computer system such as other Web applications, or internal operational software systems.

The characteristics of the execution environment help to determine the next two types of data: the types of software resources to be specified, and the types of computer resource requirements and their values (such as number of CPUs).

The system architect or a developer will know how the system is to be deployed.

7.2.4 Software Resource Requirements

The processing steps in a scenario are described in terms of the software resources used. The specific types of software resources applicable to your system depend on your execution environment and the type of software that you are constructing and interfacing with.

Table 7-1 illustrates several types of software resources and how they are specified. The particular resources that you choose will depend on the type of application you are building.

Table 7-1: Types of Software Resources

Software Resource Types	Description
CPU usage	specified in work units, estimated number of instructions executed, or CPU time (when measurements of similar systems are available)
SQL	specified as the number and type of SQL statements (read, write, update, etc.) executed when the software accesses a database
File I/O	specified as the number of logical or physical I/Os
Messages	specified as the number or size in Kbytes of messages sent via a local LAN or other type of network, and the number or size of those sent via an external network such as a WAN, Internet connection, and so on
Logging to files or databases	specified as the number of log events that execute
Calls to middleware functions	specified as the number and type of call (e.g., connectionOpen, queueGet, requestSend, and so on) when applicable
Calls to software in a different process, thread, or processor	specified as the number, type, and target of the call. (Note that some software interactions may be modeled explicitly when the interacting software is also under study, as in the examples in Chapter 5.)
Delay for remote processing	specified as the estimated elapsed time for each request

One of the most difficult resources to estimate early in the development process is CPU usage. How do you decide how many CPU instructions will be needed to perform an operation which has only been roughly designed? One way to approach this is to use *work units*. Work units focus on the relative amount of work performed in a processing step. We often use a five-level scale with 1 representing a light-weight operation and 5 representing a heavy-weight one. The scale is linear. That is, a level 5 operation is estimated to require five times as much work as a level 1 operation. You can use either measurements or your experience to estimate the order of magnitude of CPU resources required for a work unit. For example, one work unit might correspond to 10,000 instructions. Five work units would then be 50,000 instructions.

Note: Some of the software resources, such as file I/O, messages, and delay, could also be types of hardware usage. You may actually directly specify the hardware usage in the software model (e.g., CPU time or number of physical I/Os). Alternatively, you may think of the software resource as a *service*, such as a file I/O service or message passing service. Then the computer resource requirements specify the processing overhead for each of the software services provided, such as the CPU time and physical I/Os for each file I/O service requested.

Early in development, models typically will use two to five types of software resource specifications. Later, you may include more software resource types and additional kinds of requests such as synchronization, lock requests, and so on. The selection of software resources that are applicable to your project is addressed later in this chapter.

This information is best obtained through collaboration among the developers and a performance engineer.

7.2.5 Computer Resource Requirements

Computer resource requirement specifications map software resource requirements onto the amount of service they require from key devices in the hardware configuration. The types of computer resources applicable to your system depend on your execution environment.

The types of computer resource requirements include
- CPU time—for work units or instructions, as well as the number of processors and their processing speed
- I/O—the number of physical I/Os as well as the number of devices and their service times
- Messages—the size of each message and the network bandwidth, or the time to transmit a typical message

- Processing overhead (CPU, I/O, messages) for SQL queries, creation and transport of messages, logging, middleware calls, remote software calls, and so on

The computer resource requirements are represented in the processing overhead matrix. Table 7-2 shows a sample overhead matrix. It shows four software resource requirements in the first column: WorkUnits, I/O, Msgs, and Delay. These resource requirements are related to four types of computer resources in the next four columns: CPU, Disk, Delay, and GINet. The first row shows the names of the devices, the second row shows the quantity of each device that is available in this facility, and the third row is a comment that describes the specification units for each software resource request.

Table 7-2: Sample Processing Overhead Matrix

Devices	CPU	Disk	Delay		GINet
Quantity	6	3	1		1
Service units	Sec.	PhysI/O	Sec.		Msgs

	CPU	Disk	Delay		GINet
WorkUnits	0.01				
I/O	0.0005	1			
Msgs	0.0005	1			1
Delay			1		

	CPU	Disk	Delay		GINet
Service time	1	0.003	1		0.05

The WorkUnits row specifies that each work unit represents 0.01 second (10 ms.) of CPU time. The I/O row specifies that each I/O specified in the software execution model results in one physical I/O to the Disk device. The Msgs row specifies that each message in the software model requires 0.0005 second of CPU time, 1 physical I/O to the Disk (for logging), and one message sent to the GINet shared network. The Delay row specifies that each delay specified in the software model results in 1 visit to the Delay device in the system model.

The bottom row specifies the service time for each device. The number of seconds of CPU time per work unit is specified above, so the service time is 1. The time for a physical I/O is 0.003 second, each unit of delay is 1 second, and the time to transmit one message is 0.05 second.

Note: You create a processing overhead matrix for each set of software resources and processing facilities in your models. Select the software resources to specify from the list in Table 7-1. Select the devices for the facility from the following list of typical devices:

CPU
Disks
User
Delay
Network
Box

Use the "box" device to represent a generic device with queuing delays such as a printer. Use a Delay device if you need to represent a generic device, such as a screen, keyboard, or mouse, that has no queueing delay.

The values in the overhead matrix typically come from measurements. The rest of this chapter discusses techniques for selecting the types of software resources and devices, and estimating values for the software execution model. Chapter 8 discusses measurement techniques for obtaining computer resource requirements.

Computer resource requirements are best obtained from a performance engineer and/or a capacity planner.

7.2.6 Data Gathering Issues

Don't worry if you cannot get precise information for all of these data requirements early in the software life cycle. You can use guesses, approximations, and estimates of upper and lower bounds to begin, and then augment the models as better information becomes available. For example, in the architecture creation stage, you can identify some key database tables but may not know their contents. You can get a very general description of high-use screens, but you may not know all the fields they will ultimately contain.

Start with these approximations. If the models reveal a performance problem using these guesses, you should address it at this stage anyway, before more details on database tables and other processing are added. This approach has the added advantage of focusing attention on key workload elements to minimize their processing. You can easily revise the data later in the life cycle when more precise data is available.

Note: In Chapter 9, we will prescribe these types of improvements with *principles*—this one is called the Centering Principle.

It is a good idea to document the performance specifications as you collect them. The problem is that few current-generation Computer-Aided Software Engineering (CASE) tools provide features to include performance specifications.[1] They will, however, let you enter comments. So, it is a good idea to define standards for including the specifications as comments in your CASE tool.

 Document the performance specifications as you collect them. Define standards for including them in your CASE tool.

7.3 Performance Walkthrough

A *walkthrough* is an informal review in which a member of the development team leads participants through selected details of the system's architecture, design or implementation. Walkthroughs are typically used to identify errors or omissions in the portion of the software under review.

A *performance walkthrough* is similar except that the purpose is to gather the information needed to construct performance models. Because one person seldom has all the information required for the software performance models, we favor using performance walkthroughs to bring together the people who can help you understand the workload, the execution environment, and their interaction with the software and database.

This section presents a list of suggested performance walkthrough topics and illustrates the process. Techniques for estimating resource usage are discussed later in this chapter.

---

1. In fact, most current-generation CASE tools document designs once you have determined what the design is; they do not help you determine what the design should be.

7.3.1 Topics

Table 7-3 provides a list of suggested topics for a performance walk-through that will help you gather the necessary information for an SPE evaluation. The list of topics is in the order that they should be covered. You can adapt the suggested topics to your environment.

The *roles* in Table 7-3 describe roles of various stakeholders who provide the information. A *user representative* provides data on how the system will be used, how often, typical usage conditions (time of day, work dependencies, etc.), performance requirements, and other information. A *system architect* provides the overview of the system and its components, and information about its use cases. A *performance specialist* is someone who is familiar with measurements of the target configuration and who can either provide data for computer resource requirements or conduct measurement studies to gather the data.

Table 7-3: Performance Walkthrough Topics

Topic	Roles
1. Purpose of the walkthrough and identification of performance risks	All
2. System overview (optional)	System Architect
3. System requirements and use cases	System Architect
4. Performance drivers	All
5. Selected performance scenario(s)	System Architect
6. Workload intensity and performance objective	User Representative, System Architect, and Performance Engineer
7. Proposed configuration	System Architect or Software Developer and Capacity Planner
8. Software resource template	Performance Engineer
9. Estimate of software resource requirements	Software Developer and Performance Engineer
10. Computer resource requirements	Performance Specialist
11. (later) Present results	Performance Engineer

A person may have more than one role. For example, as a developer you may also conduct the performance analysis step, thus filling the roles of both *software developer* and *performance engineer*. You may need advice from another experienced *performance engineer* to assist with defining the software resource template, and estimating the software resource requirements.

Topic 1 is a discussion of the purpose of the walkthrough, and the performance questions to be resolved. Make sure that you understand the consequences of performance failures and the types of evaluation to conduct. This will partially determine the level of detail you need. For example, early in the life cycle, you may need to determine whether you can process a login, create and display a user's home page with an acceptable response time, and determine whether the envisioned system will support 10,000 concurrent users. A relatively simple analysis can determine whether it is impossible, or if the risk of failure is high. Thus, it is unlikely that you will need data for detailed synchronization models such as those in Chapters 5 and 6 at this early stage.

Topic 2 is an overview of the features to be implemented. It is optional when everyone has been involved from the outset. You need to understand the overall processing to help identify those parts that are likely to be critical to performance.

Topic 3 is a general overview of the requirements and use cases as they are currently understood. Again, you need to understand the overall requirements to help identify the important use cases for the performance assessment.

Topic 4 covers *performance drivers*; that is, variables inherent in the application domain that affect performance. Examples include: the number of customers, the number of invoices per customer, the number of line items on an invoice, the peak hours, the number of remote transactions, and so on. Performance drivers have a strong influence on the business tasks in an organization, and thus on the computer systems that support these business tasks. They are often forecast and tracked by business analysts. Performance drivers help to identify the important performance scenarios, provide a basis for estimating the workload intensity for the scenarios, and define some values for the software model.

Topics 5 through10 directly address the types of data that you need to construct software performance models. They were covered in detail in Section 7.2.

Once the performance is analyzed, the group reconvenes to discuss Topic 11 to learn the results, set appropriate directions, and, when necessary, to schedule the next walkthrough.

While the topics may be covered in one session, for large, complex systems they may require multiple sessions. You will need to tailor the number of sessions and the division of topics to your project and environment.

7.3.2 When to Conduct Performance Walkthroughs

You should begin your first performance walkthrough as soon as a general idea of system functions is available. An initial performance assessment should be part of an overall feasibility study for the project. Because our goal is to obtain the data before requirements or design documents are created, in order to detect problems while they can still be changed, we want the information directly from the creators. Walkthroughs initially address high-level scenarios; later, we elaborate their execution details. Even this high level can reveal problems such as the number of database tables accessed by a high-frequency transaction.

Conduct your first performance walkthrough and performance assessment as soon as there is a general idea of system functions.

Critical components may not be completely defined until detailed design and implementation culminate. Performance walkthroughs should continue well into implementation, to track the scenarios and their resource usage as they evolve. This practice helps to avert local-but-not-global optimization problems. Users should continue to participate in order to provide workload information that drives resource requirements, such as data characteristics, cardinality, percent of customers affected, and so on.

Once the system implementation begins, much of the walkthrough data can be tabulated in machine readable form for subsequent use. This is crucial to the performance studies in late life cycle stages, because large systems have so much data that manual performance analysis quickly becomes intractable. Automated data collection and SPE data management concepts are discussed in Chapter 8.

Use the level of performance risk to determine the frequency of performance walkthroughs and studies.

Performance risk assessment is discussed in Chapter 15.

The frequency with which you conduct performance walkthroughs will depend on the level of performance risk for the project. If there is a high risk, you should plan for more walkthroughs.

You may also need to iterate the walkthrough steps in order to produce the models that you need. Gathering information in a walkthrough will allow you to construct some initial models. Constructing these models will help you learn more about the software you are modeling. This, in turn, will require that you gather more data, and so on. It is good to plan for this iteration. For example, with a new system you may want to cover the first seven walkthrough topics and construct a software model., which will help you determine the most appropriate software resource template. Then you can gather any additional information that you need in order to solve the model.

7.3.3 Example

To illustrate what transpires during a walkthrough, we will examine a hypothetical application, the Nachtfliegen Airlines Web Site. We will derive information from the walkthrough that is representative of each of the topics. We focus on data gathering here; the results of this exercise will be used to solve models in Chapter 12.

Note: At the time this book was written, there was no Nachtfliegen.com Web site. This example is representative of many airline Web sites, but is not based on any particular airline.

Example 7-1 provides background information on the project that is typical of what you, the software developer and performance engineer, would typically know at this stage in the project.

In this walkthrough, the users of the system are represented by a reservationist who is knowledgeable about the functions to be provided and the characteristics of travelers' patterns of requests for reservations. The other participants are the software architect who will develop the archi-

Example 7-1: Nachtfliegen.com

Nachtfliegen Airlines maintains a modest Web site that provides static content with information about the company, along with some simple dynamic content to advertise upcoming promotions.

In order to be competitive with other major airlines, the marketing department has proposed a major Web site expansion to allow all users to:
- Check the status of today's flights
- Request information on flight schedules, fares, and availability
- Purchase tickets

Members of Nachtfliegen's Frequent Flyer Club (Vielenreisen) will be able to use the above functions and to:
- Get current information about the status of their account (number of miles flown to date this year, number of miles available for award travel, most recent flights taken, etc.)
- Purchase tickets using either frequent flyer miles or a credit card

In order to ensure privacy and prevent unauthorized use of frequent flier miles, access to frequent flier accounts will require that the Vielenreisen user login by entering an account number and a personal identification number (PIN). When Vielenreisen members login, they will see a custom home page tailored to the preferences entered on their Member Profile form (e.g., showing specials on travel to Hawaii) and their flying habits (e.g., most frequent flight segments) as stored in the member history database. Members may update their Member Profiles online.

Management agreed to marketing's proposal with some conditions. In order to save money and get the enhancements in place as soon as possible, management decreed that the Web site would reuse certain existing systems rather than develop new replacements. They are
- The Vielenreisen account management system. This system stores information about member flights, award miles balance, and redemption history. It is currently used in batch mode to generate members' monthly statements.
- The Vielenreisen member profile database. This system stores member profiles (class of service and seat preference, special dietary requests, etc.) and is accessed when a reservation that references a Vielenreisen frequent flyer number is made.
- A marketing database that keeps track of flights taken, fare class, and so on to generate special announcements to include in Vielenreisen members' monthly statements.
- Fare quotes are currently provided by a Nachtfliegen legacy system. Requests for fare quotes will be sent to this application and database.

> - The class of service availability database keeps track of the availability of a seat at the particular fare, and the availability of award travel seats. Itineraries are verified against this database immediately before issuing a ticket, to confirm availability.
>
> In order to attract Web users, the new corporate home page will contain several custom-designed graphic elements, along with an extensive description of the corporation and its mission. Marketing has seen some research that indicates that users will wait no longer than 8 seconds for a Web page, so the performance objective is to display the home page to the user in 8 seconds or less.

tecture for the new features, the software developers who will design and implement the new software system and conduct the initial performance studies, and a performance engineer who will assist in gathering performance data and assist in the modeling when necessary.

End-to-end and transaction response times are discussed in Section 7.2.

Purpose Participants first discuss the SPE purpose. They decide to determine whether the users' response time will be competitive with other reservation sites for peak holiday-season reservations. Some discussions follow in order to quantify the current and future response times of the competition, and to determine whether the target is the end-to-end response time or the individual transaction response time.

They decide that it is most important to minimize the time to display each page, and to address the end-to-end time by minimizing the number of pages required to create an itinerary and purchase the tickets. Specific response time objectives will be associated with each page. In addition to response time, a key performance risk is the scalability of the system to meet future demands, and to respond gracefully to a potential sudden influx of Internet requests. No one is able to specify the maximum number of users that should be supported by the system. Participants decide to use the models to determine the number that can be supported, and to work offline with business specialists to better define the scalability requirements.

These discussions tell us the kind of studies we will need to conduct, and thus the data that we will collect in subsequent topics. For example, if we study end-to-end response times, we need to know approximately how much time it takes for users to enter data.

System Requirements and Use Cases The software architect then describes the plans for the new system, a summary of the pertinent system requirements as represented by the use cases, and scenarios that describe anticipated typical uses. The system architect presents the use case diagram for many of the typical cases such as that in Figure 7-1. It shows that a Customer may purchase tickets, plan an itinerary, and check flight status. Frequent Flyers may do all of those, as well as access or update their profile information and review their frequent flyer account information. A Marketer may access profile information and create promotions. A Business Analyst may study system usage.

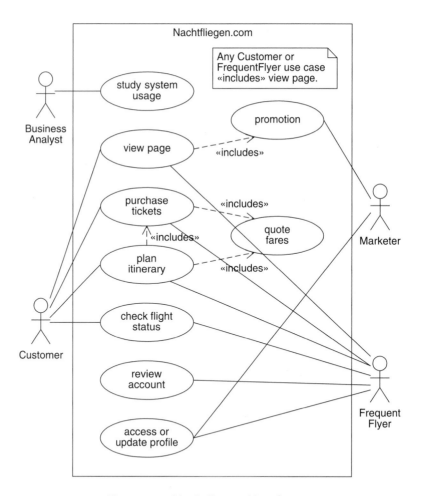

Figure 7-1: Nachtfliegen Use Cases

The participants also address questions such as how many Customers, Frequent Flyers, Marketers, and Business Analysts will use the Web site, the frequency of use of the various scenarios, critical times of day, and so on. This information, combined with the performance drivers (in the next section), will help determine which scenarios to select for performance modeling. In this part of the walkthrough we learn that:

- Typically, there will be three Marketers and two Business Analysts using the Web site.
- No one knows how many Customers and Frequent Flyers will use the Web site. It will depend on the success of the future marketing efforts.
- No one knows what the peak times of day will be; however, after discussions, they decide that new Web-surfer users will likely use the system in the evening. The team makes an action item to get forecasts from marketing predicting the number of new Web users.
- The system architect expects that 80% of users will plan an itinerary. Initially, 20% of users who plan itineraries will also purchase tickets (though they hope the percentage will increase over time), 1% will check flight status, 1% will access or update their profile information, and 2% will review frequent flyer accounts.

Participants question the effect of the promotions on the use of the system. The user representatives (marketers) hope that the promotion information on the home page and all subsequent pages will entice more users to purchase the special fares. They hope that users will bookmark the home page and check it frequently to check the special promotions. The performance engineer asks how often users will access the home page without continuing to another use case. The user representative expects that this might happen frequently in the future, but cannot predict either the number of users who might do this, or how to modify the percentage of the total users of the system who only visit the home page.

Note: We obtained some of the information we need for SPE from this discussion, but we still have some unanswered questions. This happens often on projects in which participants have not used SPE techniques on previous projects. We will deal with these missing items in the analysis steps, where we will study the performance sensitivity over a range of values. The analysis of this case study is in Chapter 12.

Performance Drivers Participants will also identify the performance drivers, such as the number of round trips versus one-way trips versus multiple segment trips, the typical number of segments in an itinerary, the typical fares desired (e.g., business versus discount versus award travel), special requests, and so on. These drivers affect performance by characterizing the number and types of user interactions and thus the resource requirements for scenarios. The following are typical values:

- 75% round trips
- 10% one-way trips
- 15% other (e.g., combined trips, open jaw, etc.)
- An average 3.8 segments in an itinerary
- 83% of users want lowest fare; 17% use other criteria (e.g., direct flights)
- 55% of users are expected to do seat selection online

They record this data and other similar statistics for use in future studies.

Select Scenarios Together, participants identify important performance scenarios. Candidate scenarios are: displaying the home page; checking the status of current-day flights; requesting information on flight schedules, fares, and availability; purchasing tickets, logging on to the site to check frequent flyer accounts, and so on. Participants select scenarios that they expect to represent typical user behavior, and include scenarios that may execute less frequently but have a significant performance impact when they execute.

For the initial study, participants decide to focus on two scenarios: displaying the home page, and planning an itinerary. For a typical itinerary, we will use the following assumptions:

- A simple round trip
- Up to two segments in each direction
- User request for the lowest round-trip fare (rather than selecting each segment and then requesting the fare for the selection)
- No special requests (for meals, assistance, etc.)

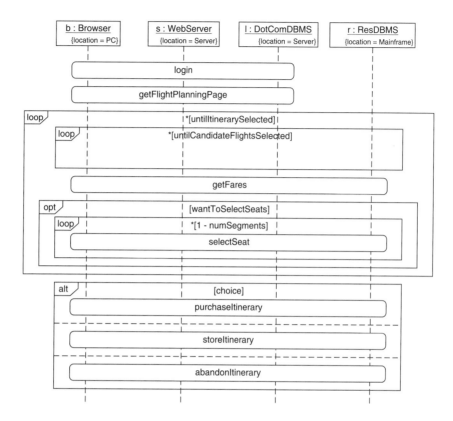

Figure 7-2: Sequence Diagram for Frequent Flyer PlanItinerary Scenario

For each selected scenario, the sequence diagram specifies the processing steps that are expected to execute and, when appropriate, the steps that conditionally execute, loop repetitions, and so on. The sequence diagram in Figure 7-2 shows the performance scenario for a frequent flyer who logs in and plans an itinerary.

When a frequent flyer requests his or her home page, the system presents a login screen. Upon successful login, the home page is displayed. We assume the frequent flyer wishes to book a simple round trip, and thus clicks on the appropriate tab. Each of the rounded rectangles in the sequence diagram corresponds to a page that will be displayed to the user. The processing for the getFlightPlanningPage request is as follows:

- The request is received by the WebServer.
- The WebServer gets the HTML file containing the page and starts to process it.

- The file contains a CGI script that completes the page, returns the result to the WebServer, and returns the page to the user's browser.

The remainder of the scenario contains similar processing for each screen that the user visits to create the itinerary, and then either purchases, stores, or abandons the itinerary. Details of the page creation are in another sequence diagram for each reference (rounded rectangle).

Workload Intensity and Performance Objective For each selected scenario, participants must define the workload intensity and the response time objective. For example, they expect 720 frequent flyers to visit the Web site in a peak hour during the peak holiday travel season. They want to process the login and display the home page in 8 seconds.

Note: The participants were unable to specify the number of users during the discussion of Topic 3. Once the performance scenario was selected, however, it was possible to determine the number of frequent flyers expected to plan an itinerary based on historical information about typical frequent flyer travel behavior. We still need to estimate the workload intensity for other Web customers.

Proposed Configuration In this example, the configuration is already known (although a capacity planner or system specialist may be consulted to resolve configuration questions that arise during the walk-through). For example, there is a LAN connecting the separate processing facilities for: the firewalls, the WebServer, and the Mainframe for Reservation Information and for the Frequent Flyer Club (Vielenreisen) records. The processors that are significant for the frequent flyer PlanItinerary scenario are shown as location constraints in Figure 7-2.

Participants next attempt to answer questions about the LAN and each processing facility, such as the network transfer rate, the number and speed of CPUs, the type and speed of the disk devices, and so on. The following data results:

- LAN speed is 100 megabits per second.
- Each WebServer has 6 CPUs with 500 MIPs processing speed.
- Each WebServer has 3 disk devices with average service time per I/O of 3 milliseconds.

- The speed of the user's network connection is unknown, so we will use 56 kilobits per second as the lowest common denominator.

Software Resource Template The performance engineer suggests the key software resource requirements for each processing facility in the configuration for the selected scenarios. For example, the software resources to be specified for the WebServer are

- The CPU work units
- The number of I/Os
- The number of 2K messages sent across the LAN
- The estimated delay for remote processing

Software Resource Requirements The walkthrough participants estimate the resource usage, taking into consideration the user representative's knowledge about the workload, the software specialist's knowledge of the processing, and the performance engineer's knowledge of the hardware and software configuration. For example, for each processing step in each scenario, we need an estimate of the CPU work units, the number of I/Os, and so on. After much discussion, we estimate that the best case for two of the steps in getFlightPlanningPage, getData(promo), and buildPage(), have the resource requirements shown in Table 7-4. The getData(promo) step has 1 WorkUnit of CPU processing and 20 I/Os to the dotComDBMS to get the promotion data. The buildPage() step has 2 CPU work units and 2 I/Os to get other data for the page. Neither of these steps uses the LAN nor has a delay for remote processing. Techniques for estimating these requirements are in Section 7.4.

Table 7-4: Sample software resource requirements

Software resource	getData(promo)	buildPage()
WorkUnits	1	2
I/O	20	2
Msgs	0	0
Delay	0	0

Performance measure-ment techniques are discussed in Chapter 8.

Note: This discussion assumes that the resource requirements are esti-mated in the walkthrough. When measurements of similar systems can be used, the discussion focuses on what should be measured, who will conduct the studies, and so on.

Computer Resource Requirements   The performance specialist will likely gather the data that translates the software resource requirements into computer resource requirements after the meeting. This discussion will focus on what data is already available, what should be measured, whether measurements must be obtained on a dedicated machine or whether background work is acceptable, and so on. For this example, we need the computer resource requirements for each of the four software resource requirements (CPU, I/O, Msgs, Delay). For messages we need: the CPU processing time to prepare a LAN message, to determine whether there is any I/O for logging or other purposes for each message, and the transfer time on the network. The information we gather leads to the overhead matrix for the WebServer that appeared in Table 7-2.

Meeting Conclusion The meeting concludes with a summary of the data that will be used, pending action items, responsible persons and completion dates, and a schedule for the results presentation and the next walkthrough.

The only action item we have is to collect data on the marketing projec-tions for the number of Web users.

Present Results After the meeting, the performance engineer constructs and analyzes the performance models. He or she then summarizes the models, which results in a subsequent walkthrough review. The purpose of this review is to ensure that the model faithfully represents the planned processing and that no significant processing has been omitted; to confirm that the results are reasonable; and to make decisions on alternatives when predictions indicate that there are significant problems that should be addressed. The results of this case study will be covered in Chapter 12.

 Always reconvene to cover the results so participants get value for the time they invest.

7.3.4 Tips for a Successful Performance Walkthrough

The following tips will increase the likelihood of a successful performance walkthrough.

SPE Familiarity Your first performance walkthrough will be problematic unless all participants are familiar with its purpose, and they understand specifically what information you need and what you will do with it. You can accomplish this by presenting a briefing on Software Performance Engineering and by giving an example of an SPE model, explaining the five types of information used to create the models, and the results the model produces. The briefing should also explain SPE terminology such as performance scenarios, resource requirements, and so on. The five types of information and most of the terminology are explained in Section 7.2. Chapter 2 provides a high-level view of the models.

Before conducting the performance walkthrough, make sure that participants are familiar with SPE and SPE terminology, the five types of information used to create models, and the types of results the model produces.

Managed Meetings The manager of the meeting should be familiar enough with performance walkthroughs to ascertain when discussions are relevant and when they become sidetracked. For example, if a potential performance problem is discovered during the walkthrough, it is easy to get sidetracked by working on alternatives that may solve the problem. The problems should be noted, but it is inappropriate to discuss details of solutions during the walkthrough.

The topics should be covered in the recommended order. For example, unless you have identified processing steps in a scenario, you cannot estimate software resource requirements for those steps. Our experience also shows that it is vital to record the information on a big board (a white board or flip chart) and regulate the flow of the meeting by using the big board to focus the discussions.

Use a white board or flip chart to focus discussions, and appoint a meeting manager familiar with performance walkthroughs to keep discussions relevant to the topics.

Determine What Happens First If you are having difficulty understanding the processing steps in a scenario, start by asking, "what is the first thing that happens when the user makes a request?" and begin to create the sequence diagram on a white board or flip chart. Then ask "what happens next?" and continue to fill in the sequence diagram as participants explain the scenario.

When sequence diagrams are not yet available, start by asking what happens first, and create the sequence diagrams on a big board as participants explain the scenario.

Use Offline, One-On-One Communication for Some Topics Performance walkthroughs have the dual purpose of gathering data and raising awareness of participants on the end-to-end interactions among various systems. The walkthrough meeting is not always the best venue for gathering detailed data. For example, it may be more efficient to meet with network specialists to get preliminary information on transfer rates, connectivity, and so on. You can present the results of these interviews at the next walkthrough.

Gather detailed, specific information in interviews with specialists, and then review the findings in the next walkthrough.

Partition Long Walkthroughs into Multiple Meetings When you are dealing with a large, complex system that is partially implemented, it is likely that there will be too much information to cover in one meeting. Allocate about two hours for each session. In the first session, aim for covering the first five topics (through the selection of performance scenarios). Between meetings, you can determine whether workload intensity data and computer configuration data are available with one-to-one communication. In the subsequent meetings, address one scenario at a time, and make as much progress on the remaining topics as possible. Always begin subsequent meetings with a review and confirmation of the results from the previous meeting.

Partition the performance walkthrough into multiple meetings when there is too much to cover in one meeting.

Minimize Action Items The hardest part of building the SPE models is developing the model of the first scenario. It is very easy to change portions of the model when new information is discovered. Therefore, it is vital to proceed with the development of the first model rather than to wait for everyone to deliver results from his or her action item. When you determine that information is not available in the walkthrough, rather than waiting for it, formulate some best guesses or contingency plans so you can proceed with the initial model development while others are working on action items. If you have to wait long for action item completion, other facets of the model may change, and it will be difficult to gain control of the model creation process.

Minimize action items. Formulate best guesses and contingency plans in order to proceed with initial model development.

Include Solution Alternatives with the Results People want solutions, not more problems. When your model results indicate that there are potential performance problems, analyze and develop quantitative results for alternatives. If alternatives seem feasible, explore other aspects of their cost-effectiveness such as time to implement, potential impact on other aspects of the system, risk factors, and so on. Then a solution alternative can be selected during the results presentation meeting while stakeholders are present (rather than deferring the resolution until a committee examines details of the alternatives).

Prepare quantitative results for alternatives and include cost-effectiveness data for viable alternatives for the presentation of results.

7.4 Resource Estimation Techniques

Resource requirements are the most difficult specifications to estimate. The precision of model results, however, depends on the fidelity of the estimates. You may find this step difficult in your initial SPE studies, but, as you gain experience, it will become much easier. The techniques in this section will increase the precision of your estimates.

7.4.1 Use Measurements

We have found that stakeholders are far more likely to believe initial model results when they are based on measurements of similar software or earlier versions of the modeled software. Even when you begin with estimates, use the model results to study the sensitivity of model results to the estimates. Identify estimates with the greatest sensitivity, and obtain measurements to substitute for the estimates as early as possible.

Once parts of the system are implemented or prototyped, you can measure the resource usage of key components. Some portions of the system may be fully operational and can be measured, while other parts may still be in early or middle stages of design. Mix measurements of implemented components with walkthroughs of others to develop model specifications. Then you can more precisely evaluate the system as it evolves.

Incorporate measurements into models when similar systems can be measured and as the key components are implemented.

7.4.2 Study Measurements

The best way to familiarize yourself with typical resource requirements is to periodically review measurements of software performance and resource usage of similar systems. You will gain an understanding of typical values and the cause and effect of anomalies. You will be better able to estimate values for future studies if you compare estimates and actual measurements for other systems.

Study measurements of similar systems to develop a frame of reference for estimates of resource requirements.

7.4.3 Use a Mentor

The best estimates are provided by someone with previous experience. For your initial performance walkthrough, your estimates will be better if you use a mentor to advise you on the resource estimates. It will greatly reduce your stress if you haven't participated in SPE studies before.

Use a mentor to assist and advise you on resource estimates on your initial walkthroughs and studies.

7.4.4 Best-Worst Case Estimates

The best-worst strategy was introduced in Chapter 1.

When it is infeasible to use measurements and you must begin with estimates, the best-worst strategy is vital in the early model evaluations when uncertainty is greatest. First use the best case estimates. If the best case has performance problems, they must be addressed before you expend time developing more precise estimates. When the worst case is problem-free, it is unnecessary to develop more precise estimates, but it is vital to confirm that the worst case estimates are indeed the worst case.

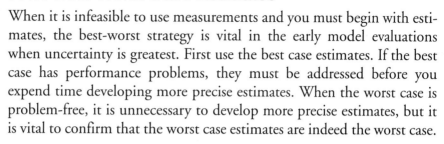

Use best- and worst-case estimates in initial model evaluations to compensate for uncertainty.

7.4.5 What to Estimate

Focus on the *dominant resource usage* for the initial SPE studies. The dominant resources are the ones that account for most of the elapsed time of a scenario, either because they have large service times relative to other resources, or because the cumulative use of the resources causes long queueing delays. For example, on current-generation computers the elapsed time of an application program is likely dominated by disk accesses rather than CPU time. If the application program interacts with a remote processor, the network may also be a dominant resource, depending on the number of interactions and the message size.

In today's systems, most of the dominant resource usage occurs as a result of software resource requests such as database accesses. This is good news because the CPU usage of application programs is more difficult to estimate than other resource requirements. Thus, you may *initially* ignore application CPU usage or use rough estimates such as relative work units required. Later you can update these rough estimates.

The software resources to specify are those that have large resource requirements or those that are used most of the time. Examples of important software resources are illustrated in Table 7-1.

Focus on the dominant resource usage for the initial SPE studies.

7.4.6 Estimating I/O Requirements

You need two types of information to estimate I/O resource requirements:

1. *The number of physical I/Os*: the number of times the I/O device is accessed to read or write data

2. *I/O service times*: the time required to complete a physical I/O on each type of device; for example, for a typical disk device, the service time is the sum of the seek time plus the average rotational delay plus the data transfer time

I/O service time is part of the computer resource requirements discussed in Section 7.4.8. The number of physical I/Os is part of the software resource specification. The remainder of this section focuses on the estimation of the number of physical I/Os.

There are two ways to estimate the number of physical I/Os for a processing step. One is to estimate the *logical I/Os* (the number of times the component requests data from an I/O device) and then estimate or study the sensitivity to various *hit ratios* (the percentage of time the data is found in a buffer or a cache and the physical I/O is bypassed). This technique also works for physical writes: Specify the number of times the data changes and estimate the *write ratio* (the percentage of time the data must be written from a buffer or cache; multiple changes may be handled by one write, or one write may also change an index). This is an indirect method of estimating physical I/O. The second way is to directly estimate which I/O requests are likely to be found in or written from a buffer or a cache as you are estimating logical I/Os, and count only the I/O requests that are likely to result in physical I/Os. For example, because the top level of an index of a heavily used table is likely to always be found in a buffer, and not result in a physical I/O, it would not be counted.

For read requests that randomly access an indexed file or table, the number of logical I/Os is $i + 1$ where i is the number of levels in the file index and 1 is the I/O to read the data record. The number of levels in the file index depends on the number of records in the file and the number of keys that fit in one index record. One typical way to estimate the number of physical I/Os is to assume the top two levels of the index will be found in a buffer, and thus the remainder of the logical I/O will require physical I/O. Another typical estimate is

$$I_p = (i + 1) \times (1 - h)$$

where Ip is the number of physical I/Os, i is the number of levels in the file index, and h is an estimate of the hit ratio on the computer system. The hit ratio is the percentage of attempts where you find the data in a buffer instead of having to do a physical I/O. For writes, the worst case is $(i + 1)$, when a change to a record or row also affects all levels in the index; and the best case is 1 when the index is not affected. You can use a *write ratio* as before to produce an average value between the best and worst.

For read requests that sequentially access a file, the number of physical I/Os is n/b where n is the number of records requested and b is the blocksize or number of records that fit into one physical block of data. For write requests, the number is the same if the physical write occurs for the entire block, and n if the physical write occurs for each change. The choice you use will depend on your operating system settings.

Some I/O devices read one *track* with each physical I/O. The size of a hardware track is device dependent, but it usually holds multiple blocks of data. Requests for subsequent blocks are found in a buffer and do not result in physical I/O. For these types of devices, the number of physical I/Os is n / t where t is the number of tracks to be accessed.

For read requests that access a database, the number of logical I/Os depends on the complexity of the SQL statement. Start with estimates of the simple cases. For example, consider a simple SELECT statement such as

SELECT <fields> from table where key = x

The number of I/Os for the SELECT will typically be the same as the random example above when a small number of rows is selected. It will be the same as the sequential example if a large number of rows is selected and the data is stored in the "key" order. Write requests will be the same as the random access case.

For more complex SQL, your database administrator (DBA) can probably help you with estimates. There are also some software products that report the estimated CPU and I/O based on input specifications of tables and the SQL to be estimated. Your DBA should be familiar with these products. You will typically specify the number of SQL statements of each type for each processing step in the software model. The computer resource requirement will specify the path length for each key type of SQL statement.

Early in the analysis stages, you may not know whether I/O will be random or sequential, or the specific syntax of SQL statements. Start with a simple estimate; you can update it later. For example, if you have a large number of I/Os, the best case will be sequential I/O with the assumption that a block of records can be retrieved with one physical I/O and the records will be used in the same order as they are in the block. The worst case will be random I/O because each access requires physical I/O for the index as well as the data record.

7.4.7 Estimating Network Messages

You can specify either the number of messages transferred or the number of characters transferred. With either specification, you must account for the characters required for message headers in addition to the application messages.

To estimate messages, first consider the amount of data to be transferred in the request (or input). The number of messages for input is

$$M_i = d/(m - h)$$

where d is the amount of input data, m is the message size, and h is the message header size.

Next, estimate the amount of data transferred for the result set. The number of output messages is

$$M_o = (r \times s)/(m - h)$$

where r is the number of rows in the result set, s is the row size, m is the message size, and h is the message header size.

You can easily adapt these formulas to calculate the number of characters transferred if that specification is more appropriate.

Note: Estimating the amount of data transferred in a message is more difficult with Java, where objects may be serialized and sent over the network. This all happens under the covers as part of Java's magic. Using a network trace tool to measure similar systems making similar requests is helpful here. You may be surprised at how many bytes it takes to transmit what appears to be a small amount of information.

7.4.8 Obtaining Computer Resource Requirements

You need the computer resource requirements for each of the software resource requirements you estimated earlier in this section. For example, when you specify the number of messages transferred for each processing step, you also need the overhead for transferring a message. This will include a CPU path length for preparing the message, perhaps a physical I/O for logging the message, and time to transfer both the message and the extra messages required for protocol. For each physical I/O you need the CPU path length for preparing the I/O, and the I/O service time (e.g., seek, rotational delay, and transfer time). For database accesses, you need the CPU path length and the number of I/Os.

You may be able to obtain estimates for computer resource requirements from performance specialists. You may be able to obtain database path lengths from the software products that estimate processing requirements for SQL statements (mentioned earlier). Some performance modeling tools include these overhead requirements in their model libraries. If none of these options work, you will need to conduct a performance measurement study to get estimates to use. Performance measurement for this and other purposes is covered in Chapter 8.

 Once you obtain the computer resource requirements, create a library so that others can use them for future studies.

7.5 Summary

You need the following five types of data for SPE studies:
- Performance objectives
- Key performance scenarios
- Execution environment
- Software resource requirements
- Computer resource requirements

Because one person seldom has all of this information, one of the best ways to obtain SPE data is by performing a performance walkthrough. A performance walkthrough brings together the people who can help you understand the workload, the execution environment, and their interaction with the software and the database.

Performance measurement is discussed in Chapter 8.

Most of the model data is easy to obtain. Some of it will come from measurements. Early in the development process, other data must be estimated. Resource requirements are the most difficult specifications to estimate. You may find it difficult to gather them in your initial SPE studies, but, as you gain experience, it will become much easier. The techniques presented in this chapter will help increase the precision of your estimates.

It may also be difficult to determine the workload intensity for new Web applications because it is difficult to predict how many users you will have initially. Use the best estimates you can obtain, and then use the models to study sensitivity and scalability.

It is important to verify and validate the data and the models. This is the only sure way to confirm that the model predictions are accurate. The next chapter covers the important measurement concepts you need for initial data requirements, and for verification and validation.

Chapter 8

Software Measurement and Instrumentation

It is much easier to make measurements than to know exactly what you are measuring.

—J. W. N. Sullivan (1928)

In This Chapter:

- Performance measurement concepts
- Measurement tools
- Instrumentation techniques
- Application Resource Measurement (ARM)
- Performance experiment design

8.1 Introduction

Measurement is a key part of the SPE process. Measurements provide input data for SPE models, verify and validate models, determine whether performance goals have actually been met, and monitor the performance of systems over their lifetime.

Obtaining the right measurements isn't always easy, however. There are tools for obtaining system-level measurements, such as the percentage of time the CPU is busy. Profilers are also available to provide code-level measurements, such as the number of times that a program calls a particular operation. While these tools can be useful, we need different information for SPE, such as the amount of time required to execute a particular operation. Obtaining this information often requires specialized tools and techniques.

In addition, simply having measurement tools is not enough. We also need a measurement strategy that defines what data we need, how to collect it, and how to design experiments to provide the proper context for the measurements.

This chapter provides an overview of the data you need for SPE, and the techniques and tools used to obtain it. We begin by discussing the uses of measurement in SPE, and the types of data required for these uses. Section 8.3 discusses planning and designing performance measurement studies. Section 8.4 presents basic concepts of performance measurement, while Section 8.5 summarizes the different measurement techniques available and the types of data that they provide. Section 8.6 describes the use of internal instrumentation for collecting performance data, and Section 8.7 presents the Application Resource Measurement (ARM), a platform-independent API that assists in instrumenting code.

8.2 What Should You Measure?

Software measurements serve these five purposes in SPE:

1. *System understanding:* Measurements of existing systems provide performance information about a similar system, or an earlier version of the system being planned.

2. *Model specifications:* Measurements of experiments, prototypes, or similar systems provide workload data and estimates of resource usage.

3. *Model updates:* Measurements of evolving software replace earlier specification estimates to improve model precision.

4. *Model verification and validation:* Measurements provide data for comparing the SPE models to actual performance, and demonstrating performance-objective compliance or specific problems requiring improvement.

5. *Software performance evaluation:* Measurements provide data for monitoring software performance and identifying areas for improvements upon deployment (until it is retired).

Chapter 7 contains more information about each type of data.

These uses require the following four types of measurement data:

1. *Workload data:* the number of requests for each workload function, the rate at which they are requested, and patterns of requests.

2. *Data characteristics:* the amount of data and the size of each data item. If you are redesigning the software for a database application, it is also helpful to measure the frequency of requests for each data item as well as which data items are requested together (locality of references). Having these numbers for the existing system will help guide database design to improve the performance of the replacement.

3. *Execution characteristics*: there are three types of execution characteristics to measure:
   - *Path characteristics*: measure the number of times each significant path is executed to compute the loop repetitions, and the execution probabilities for conditional paths
   - *Software resource usage:* for each software resource requested, measures the number of times it is requested and the average elapsed execution time (e.g., network messages, database SELECTS, and so on)
   - *Processing overhead:* measures the amount of service the software resources require from each of the key computer system resources. Key resources include the CPU, I/O devices, networks, and any other resources that are limited and must be shared among the executing processes.

4. *Computer system usage*: these measurements allow you to compute the following statistics for the complete scenario and for each node in an execution graph—both basic nodes and expanded nodes:
   - *Scenario response time:* the end-to-end elapsed time from the scenario request until its completion (the actual service time and the time spent waiting in queues)
   - *Scenario throughput:* the number of times that the scenario is executed per unit of time (e.g., hour, second, peak hour, and so on)

- *Key computer system resource usage:* the actual service time as well as the wait time of each workload scenario for each of the key computer system resources
- *Resource utilization:* the percentage of time busy
- *Resource throughput:* the rate at which the resource completes service requests
- *Resource queue lengths:* the average number of jobs waiting for service

Table 8-1 illustrates the relationship between the uses of measurements in SPE and the various types of data. The columns in the table correspond to the purposes of the data, and the rows correspond to the types of data. The entries in the table correlate the types of data with their uses. The following paragraphs give examples for each of the applicable cells in the table. Note that because their entries are all the same, the subcategories of computer system usage are represented by a single row in Table 8-1.

Table 8-1: Performance Data of Interest for SPE

Performance Measurements	SPE Uses				
	System Under-standing	Model Specs	Update Models	Model Verifica-tion and Validation	Evaluate Software Perform-ance
Workload Data	yes	some	yes	yes	some
Data Characteristics	yes	some	yes	yes	some
Path Characteristics		yes	yes	yes	some
Software Resources	yes	yes	yes	yes	some
Processing Overhead	yes	yes	yes	yes	yes
Computer System Usage				yes	yes

8.2.1 Workload Data and Data Characteristics

The entries in the table for workload data and data characteristics are the same. This indicates that these measurements have similar uses. Both types of measurement help you understand existing systems and give insights into new systems that will provide similar functions. They provide values for workload-intensity parameters for use in system models of existing systems. For new software, they help you estimate workload intensity and characteristics, and replace estimates with actual values as the software evolves. They also verify that the model parameters agree with measured values.

8.2.2 Path Characteristics

Path characteristics tell you the number of times that the path is executed and the probability of executing each alternative. Measuring path characteristics enables you to determine parameters for models and update them as the software evolves. These measurements also help confirm that the models are correct, and identify performance problems as the software evolves.

8.2.3 Software Resources and Processing Overhead

Measurements of the amount of service each scenario uses from each of the key software resources provide parameters for SPE models. They also provide data to determine whether the measured resource requirements for the scenario match those calculated by the software model. This allows you to validate the software model, and to verify the software model results that you use as input for solving the system model.

Occasionally, you can use this data for evaluating the performance effect of reducing the software resource usage. For example, a measurement might indicate that an excessive amount of time is spent using a particular software resource (e.g., database access). You might then use the models to study alternatives that use less of that resource (as in the ICAD example from Chapter 4).

Note: In addition to measuring the total resource requirements for a scenario, you should measure the resource requirements for each important node in the software model. Note that nodes may be of varying levels of detail. For example, the ATM scenario in Figure 4-3 has a processTransaction expanded node that consists of a subgraph with five basic nodes (in Figure 4-4).

For deriving performance specifications, you need data for nodes at the greatest level of detail (elementary nodes). For the ATM example, this means measuring resource requirements for each of the five subcomponents of processTransaction.

For model verification, validation and performance evaluation, you need to measure both the overall resource usage for the processTransaction component (i.e., the combined usage for each of the subnodes), as well as the resource usage for the entire ATM scenario.

8.2.4 Computer Resource Usage

We use the computer system metrics primarily for validating the system execution model, evaluating performance, and identifying bottlenecks in the processing.

8.3 Planning for Performance Measurement

This section discusses issues in planning and designing performance measurements.

8.3.1 Key Considerations

There are two key considerations in planning performance measurements: They must be *representative* and *reproducible*. To be representative, measurement results must accurately reflect each of the factors that affect performance: workload, software, and computer system environment. The goal is to design your measurement in a way that balances the effort required to construct and execute the measurement against the level of detail in the resultant data. If unimportant details are omitted, both the design effort and the overhead required to collect the data are reduced.

Reproducibility gives you confidence in the results. In order for a measurement to be reproducible, the workload, software, and computer system environment must be controlled so that you can repeat the measurement and get the same (or very similar) results each time.

Workload Workload selection is the most difficult aspect of designing performance measurements. User behavior, the requested functions, and data characteristics must reflect the actual conditions under which the software is used. How you accomplish this will sometimes depend on the type of data that you are collecting. For some SPE studies, such as measuring the requirements for CPU time and I/O counts for a method, it is unnecessary to represent multiple concurrent users of the software. For system evaluations, volume testing, and other SPE studies (such as model validity), it is essential to represent multiple users.

For those studies where you do need to represent multiple users, it is best to avoid employing actual end users—it is too difficult to control the experiment and, therefore, to obtain reproducible results. Most multiple-user measurements rely on *load drivers*—software products that simulate user behavior in a reproducible way. With a load driver, you input one or more workload profiles, and the output is a script that simulates user requests. The workload profile specifies the number of users to simulate, the transaction arrival rate, the frequency of each transaction type, and a distribution of input values to generate. The load driver generates the transactions and measures response times. Once generated, load-driver inputs look like actual user requests, so the software executes normally.

Software The software to be measured can be a set of programs, a representative subset of them, or synthetic programs. Synthetic programs mimic the execution characteristics of the actual programs without doing the processing. For example, consider an edit transaction that receives input data, does some processing to verify that the input is valid, accesses a file to check consistency, and transmits the reply. A synthetic edit transaction might issue the same number of file I/Os and use the same amount of CPU time between each, but not actually check data validity.

Computer System Environment The measurement environment must represent the essential elements of the execution environment. The operating system, the computer system resources, and resource competition must be comparable. Often measurements must be run in isolation, to eliminate the effects of competition and enhance reproducibility. For other studies, average or peak load environments provide more realistic measurements of expected performance, by including the side effects of queuing for resources.

8.3.2 Performance Benchmarks

Performance benchmarks are standardized performance measurements that produce data (primarily) for:

- *Hardware or software system evaluations:* for selecting major systems when comparisons require reliable data that is otherwise unavailable
- *Volume testing:* to analyze the effect of varying the number of users on a system
- *Performance measurement:* to gather performance metrics for SPE

Benchmarks may be established for comparative purposes within an industry, or you may design benchmarks for your own software. An example of an industry-wide standard benchmark is the suite of performance benchmarks developed and published by the Standard Performance Evaluation Corporation (SPEC) [SPEC], [Domanski 2001]. You may design your own benchmarks to measure the performance of competitive middleware products, to measure resource requirements for SPE models, and so on. The discussion in this section applies to designing benchmarks, as well as other measurement studies.

8.3.3 Designing and Conducting Measurement Studies

Use the traditional scientific method to design and conduct performance measurements. The steps in the scientific method are to:

1. Understand the purpose of the measurement—the questions to answer or the hypothesis to test.

2. Identify the data needed to answer those questions, along with the data collection tools and techniques to be used.

3. Identify experimental variables and controls. Ideally, if you are studying the effect of changing these variables, you only allow one variable to change at a time. You may be able to use multivariate techniques to analyze your data when this is not possible.

4. Define the test cases: workload, software, and the environment for each test.

5. Execute the tests and collect the data.

6. Analyze, interpret, and present the results.

All steps in this scientific method apply to SPE measurements. Experience shows that the following are vital to success:
- Careful design of the experimental test cases
- Identification of necessary data
- Collection and coordination of the measurement results

Defining the test cases means selecting the approach for representing the workload, software, and environment; and developing a test plan with priorities for the tests to be run.

Identify the necessary measurements and data gathering tools before beginning the experiment.

Too much data obscures essential results, and may even perturb them because of the data collection overhead. Too little data reduces the experiment's usefulness, and may cause you to repeat an expensive set of measurements.

If the data comes from multiple sources, coordinate the measurements: Match the start and finish of the data collection intervals, and the granularity of the measurements.

For example, you cannot equate CPU utilization collected during an hour-long test of peak volumes with CPU utilization averaged over an eight-hour period.

Murphy should have specific laws for software performance measurement! The potential for problems is astounding:
- The software-hardware-workload combinations are incredibly complex, their performance is influenced by many factors, and the amount of data can be overwhelming (if not controlled).
- The studies are labor intensive and usually time constrained; the setup of the workload generator, the software, and measurement tools encounter never-ending problems.
- Control of the system parameters and environmental factors is problematic; software bugs and hardware failures often stall the experiments.

- The number of measurements is further constrained when they must run in isolation.

It is unlikely that you will have time to run all of the measurements that you would like. Without a prioritized plan that defines the measurements to be performed, you are likely to run out of time, only to discover that you are missing the most important data.

Define a measurement test plan that specifies each experiment to be run, its priority, the setup procedure, the measurement tools to run, and the results to produce.

Example 8-1 illustrates the considerations that might go into the design of performance measurements for the ICAD case study.

Example 8-1: Performance Measurement Design

Within the expanded DrawMod scenario in Figure 4-15, there is a processing step to sort a set of beams, sort(beams). Suppose that we must determine whether the sort should use a routine supplied in a standard library or have its own custom sort routine.

Define Purpose: The purpose of the measurement is to quantify the performance of two alternatives for implementing the ICAD function sort(beams). Using a standard sort routine minimizes implementation and maintenance efforts, but the standard sort may not meet performance goals. For a cost-benefit analysis, we need to know the difference in response times for the custom sort and the standard sort routines.

Data Collection: The ICAD case study performance goal is a 10-second response time for the DrawMod user scenario shown in Figure 4-15. We will measure the resource requirements for each sort alternative, then use the SPE models to quantify the response times for each alternative. It is sufficient to measure the resource requirements for one user, because the SPE models use service times to derive the response times for multiple users. Thus, we do not need a load driver. The resources of interest are CPU time, number of I/Os, and memory requirements. The system-event recorder collects this data for programs, but includes the overhead for measurement program initiation and termination, as well as test-case-setup processing in its totals. We can run some experiments to quantify this overhead and then correct for it later, or use internal instrumentation to tally only the metrics of interest. Alternatively, we can insert sleep timers just before and after the sort algorithm, with the sleep interval greater than at least three intervals of the data collection tool, so we measure the algorithm separately. In any case, we need to include the procedure call overhead for calling the sort.

Experimental Variables: The performance of the sort routine depends on the number and size of the sort keys, the number of items, size of the items, the original data order, and the sort algorithm itself. In this case study, the sort key is the beam number. The designers specify that the key length is one byte, and the item length is 64 bytes. The users estimate that the number of items will be a minimum of 1, a maximum of 1 million, an average of 2,000, and a range (for the typical scenario) of 36 to 8,400. The designers and users agree that it is likely that the beams will already be "almost sorted" because of the expected use of the system and its internal design.

For the custom sort routine, we select a published sort algorithm that is expected to perform best for a problem with these characteristics. This will provide sufficient data for the cost-benefit analysis; further algorithm testing can be done later if deemed appropriate.

We do not want the resource measurements to be perturbed by other work executing on the computer system, but "stand-alone" tests are likewise undesirable. Because system-event recorders filter out most external effects, we will run some tests to compare stand-alone measurements to those collected during "normal" processing times. Unless the differences are significant, we will proceed with testing during normal processing.

Test Cases: We will construct a driver program that generates test cases, and calls both the system and custom routines to sort each test.

The tests include
- Isolation versus normal processing
- Overhead for test program
- List length: 36 items, almost sorted
- List length: 2,000 items, almost sorted
- List length: 8,400 items, almost sorted

We can add other experiments as time permits, such as the effect of allocating different amounts of memory for the sort, different list lengths, random ordering, and so on.

Executing the Tests: We will run each test multiple times to verify that the results are reproducible.

Results: We will produce a table showing the test cases and the resource requirements for each. Because the measurements are intermediate results, we will also use them to produce and report response times for the entire DrawMod user scenario for the two sorts.

Other Considerations: This illustrates the steps in measurement design. Your environment may require other data collection techniques and other test cases.

Load-driver measurements are necessary to simulate user behavior under loading conditions. They must usually run in isolation, and are time consuming and labor intensive; therefore, we prefer to use performance models for most SPE tasks. Performance measurements are not cost effective for design trade-off studies. However, they are useful for deriving performance specifications for the models, for verifying and validating the models, and for confirming SPE conclusions when they have major consequences.

 Use performance measurements to gather data for SPE models and validate their results. Then use SPE models to evaluate architecture and design alternatives.

8.4 Performance Measurement Concepts

The previous sections describe the measurements you need, why you need them, and how to plan and design the experiments. This section begins the description of how to actually get these measurements. We begin by describing the general measurement concepts you need to understand to ensure that you get the right measurements. The following sections describe techniques and tools for obtaining measurements, as well as software instrumentation issues.

Performance measurements may be *static* or *dynamic*. Static measurements are made without executing the software. For example, you can measure the size of a database table or a network message without running the application. Dynamic measurements require that the software be executing during the measurement. Any measurement involving time requires that the software be executing. The measurements needed for SPE are primarily dynamic rather than static.

Note: There are tools that predict execution time of code without actually executing it. However, these are modeling tools—not measurement tools.

Because the phenomena we are trying to measure, such as the amount of time required for a method to execute, occur inside a computer and (potentially) happen very quickly, we sometimes need to measure them indirectly. That is, we measure some related quantity and use that data to infer the metric that we need. For example, making a performance measurement is much like timing a runner in a race. We can either use a stopwatch to measure the time required to complete the course (direct) or we can measure the start and finish times and compute the elapsed time from this data (indirect). The direct approach is difficult if there are many runners because each needs his/her own (concurrent) timer.

This section discusses basic concepts of performance measurement, including some terminology and types of performance measurement tools. Later, we'll discuss specific examples of these types of tools.

8.4.1 Terminology

We can perform two types of measurement on a computer system. We can measure information about *states* of the system's hardware or software or we can observe *events* that occur within the system. A state is a period of time when the computer system is doing something. For example, "idle" or "executing job X" would both be states of the CPU. An event corresponds to a change in the system's state. For example, if the CPU changes state from "executing process X" to "executing process Y" the change would be an event.

Note: A switch from "executing process X" to "executing process Y" where X and Y are both user processes is not a simple change, because several operating system processes (e.g., the scheduler, memory manager, and so on) may execute between those two states. An event causes the change of state, but several other intermediate states would also exist.

There are two fundamental measurement techniques corresponding to states and events: *monitoring* states and *recording* events.

Monitoring States A performance *monitor* observes the activities of a computer system and records performance information about states of interest. To avoid perturbing the measurements, monitors typically do not run continuously. Instead, they sample the system's state by periodically activating and recording the current state along with the appropriate performance data about that state. For example, a monitor may activate every 10 milliseconds and record the process that is currently executing. In addition, it may perhaps record the virtual address of the current instruction, from which we can determine the operation or program statement within that process. Upon completion of the process, the data collected by the monitor allows you to identify "hot spots"—those portions of the code that consume most of the CPU time.

Perturbation of measurements is discussed in Section 8.4.2.

Monitors within a computer system are typically *software monitors*— programs that execute independently from the software being measured. Network and distributed system monitors may also be *hardware monitors*; external devices that are attached to the computer system hardware via external wires or probes. Hardware monitors have the advantage that they perturb the system that they measure less than software monitors. You may also find monitors implemented in firmware, or hybrid monitors that combine software, hardware or firmware.

Note: Computer hardware monitors were more common in the earlier days of computing when it was relatively easy to open the backplane of the computer and attach a probe to a key wire to monitor its signals. With the advent of microelectronic chips, it became difficult if not impossible to connect probes to key hardware elements such as the program counter (to detect hot spots).

Now, probe points must be designed into the chip connectors, or a hardware hot-spot monitor must be built into the chip along with its other functionality. Such hardware monitoring capabilities are possible, but rarely accessible to users in today's computers. Perhaps that will change in the future. Hardware monitors are, however, useful for monitoring today's networks.

Monitors may also measure different levels of detail. For example, a monitor may collect data about the overall computer system or about individual programs. A *system monitor* observes the state of the overall system, while a *program monitor* observes the state of the particular program being measured.

Recording Events Recording events requires that you determine which events are of interest. Then, every time one of them happens, you need to record its occurrence along with the appropriate performance data. For example, if we are interested in the number of accesses to the ATM account database, we record it every time one occurs, along with the process that made the request and other data such as the time of the request, the amount of data returned, the amount of CPU time required to process the request, the number of physical I/Os, and the elapsed time required to complete the access.

As with state monitoring, event recording can occur at different levels. For *program event recording*, the events are pertinent to the program being measured, such as the CPU time for a database access, or the elapsed time to send a message during the execution of an ATM scenario. For *system event recording*, certain events are recorded for all executing programs of interest. For example, we may record the CPU time for database accesses for teller and bank analyst transactions, as well as ATM scenarios.

Internal versus External Both monitors and event recorders may be either integrated into a program (*internal*) or *external* to it. Internal measurement requires that code be inserted into programs to detect events and record the pertinent performance data. While a compiler option or a preprocessor could insert and invoke the data collection code, these measurements most often require that programmers insert their own code. External monitors and event recorders execute independently of the software to be measured.

Note: The Instrumenting Principle presented in Chapter 9 currently requires internal measurement as described in Section 8.6. Future advances in external measurement tools may relieve some of this burden from developers.

Granularity All of the possible combinations offer a range of granularity. For example, we can observe the initiation and completion of processes, individual programs, class methods, or individual statements within methods. Similarly, there are three choices for managing the amount of data collected: (1) record all details, (2) summarize the data as it is collected and record the results periodically, or (3) tally data between events and record it when an event occurs. For example, suppose you want to measure the number of I/Os in a program and use the result as an estimate of the I/Os for new, similar software. You could

- Record each I/O event and later compute the total (option 1).

- Count each I/O operation as the program executes and record the total once at the end of the job (option 2).
- Count the I/Os and write the total once per second, minute, or other time unit (option 2).
- Count the I/Os within each class method and write the total upon each method completion (option 3).

Regardless of the data collection technique, you collect and store the performance data, then later run programs to *analyze the data* and *report results*.

Note: Data analysis and presentation usually occurs after the measurements are collected. In some cases, the measurements may be used for runtime performance tuning. The Java Hot Spot compiler is an example of an environment that uses dynamic data analysis to tune performance at runtime.

A given measurement technique will combine choices from all of the alternatives we have discussed. It may use state monitoring or event recording, be internal or external, and collect system or program level data, at various levels of granularity. Later, we describe the use of these alternatives for collecting the SPE data we need (see Table 8-2).

8.4.2 Factors That May Affect Measurements

Regardless of your measurement techniques (state versus event, internal versus external, and program versus system), the factors in this section help you maximize the usefulness of the data for SPE.

System Perturbation The Heisenberg Uncertainty Principle applies to performance measurement. That is, the measurement process may perturb the system being measured, thereby affecting the results. This usually happens with system measurements more than program measurements (because the program's service time is usually independent of the system load, but the overall residence time is not). Perturbation is usually most significant when the system already has severe performance bottlenecks. In these cases, the overhead associated with the measurements may make a poor-performing system appear even worse than it actually is.

Control the system perturbation caused by measurements by creating selective granularity of measurements, and selective activation and deactivation.

Capture Ratios The *capture ratio* characterizes the percent of time that the measurement technique accounts for, either directly or by inference. There are differences in the capture ratios and the way that resource usage is charged to programs. For example, software sampling monitors work by setting a timer interrupt at specified intervals. At the end of a time interval, however, another higher-priority process (such as an operating system routine) may be executing, which delays the monitor execution slightly. During this delay period, the CPU is busy performing a task that may be unknown to the monitor. Can the time delay be measured to get accurate CPU usage data and, if so, how should it be reported? Sometimes monitors can determine that there was such a delay, as well as how long, and why.

System Overhead A monitor may try to apportion the execution time of operating system routines. Some are clearly caused by the program that made the service request (such as a file I/O); others are not so clear. For example, who should be charged for CPU scheduling overhead? Who should be charged for page faults? They may be caused by the program that needed the page or by another program that holds a large portion of real memory, leaving other programs with too little memory to execute.

Include both program processing and system overhead in the software execution models.

Measurement Timing You must control the timing of measurements if the results are to be meaningful. The duration of the events and states must match the resolution of the *operating system clock* used to time them. This clock is not the hardware clock that drives the processor. The hardware clock may be running at 1GHz (one tick every nanosecond), while the operating system clock may only be updated every 10 milliseconds. If a method executes in 1 millisecond but the operating system clock only "ticks" once every 10 milliseconds, the measurements will show that the method requires no time.

Similarly, the sampling interval for monitors must be short enough to detect the states of interest, but not too short; otherwise, the amount of data collected (thus the measurement overhead) is much greater than necessary, and it may perturb the results. If the duration of events and states is much shorter than clock ticks, you should run a very long experiment. Then the average should show the time consumed for each event and state. For example, you might execute a method 1,000 times and measure the total elapsed time. The average time for executing the method would then be the measured time divided by 1,000.

Match the number of events measured to the resolution of the clock. When the duration of an event is much shorter than a clock tick, measure many events (perhaps in a loop) to obtain more meaningful results.

Reproducible Results Other work that executes on the computer system influences the performance metrics (residence times and computer system usage statistics). Therefore, you may need to exclude the other work during measurement periods, particularly if you need *reproducible* results. For example, if you want to study whether allocating more memory to a process improves its performance, the obvious thing to do is measure its execution before and after increasing the memory allocation, and compare the results. The results are only comparable, though, if you either exclude other work, or compensate by collecting the two measurements when the workload, time of day, and duration of measurements are comparable.

Control the measurement environment, the workload, the time of day, and duration of the measurements to collect reproducible results.

Representative Time Periods Many of the metrics provided by measurement tools are averages over the measurement period. However, averages may not be meaningful if the period is too long. For example, peak loads may be 50% or higher than average loads, so an average for an entire day may not accurately reflect the performance of a two-hour peak load that is responsible for your performance problem.

Collect measurements for representative time periods.

Averages for Typical Behavior Performance of many components varies, depending on the state of the system and the processing required. For example, if you want to measure the typical resource requirements for a database SELECT, you cannot measure one SELECT and assume that it is representative of all others. The time required for an individual SELECT varies. For example, in the typical case, the data may be found in database buffers, while the first execution of the SELECT may always require one or more physical I/Os to load those buffers. Of course, if you want to model start-up conditions when more physical I/Os would be required, you need to conduct a measurement study of a start-up state and run it only long enough to capture the initial behavior of the system.

> *Run measurements long enough to get an average, minimum, and maximum that are representative of the system's typical behavior.*

Load drivers are also discussed in Section 8.6.

Workload Generation Finally, you need to determine how you will produce the workload that you will measure. If the performance of your system is dependent on user interactions, you will want a *load driver* that uses a script to mimic user interactions. Using a load driver allows you to vary the (simulated) arrival rate of requests and, more importantly, to replay the scripts in order to increase the likelihood that you will get reproducible results.

> *To collect reproducible results when measuring performance for user-driven software, use load driver software to generate representative workloads.*

8.5 Data Collection Techniques and Tools

There are five techniques for collecting the data we need for SPE. In this section we first describe these techniques and several representative tools for each. Then, we describe the techniques that work best for each of the types of SPE data presented in Section 8.2.

Many computer system vendors offer performance data collection tools with their systems. There are also many commercially available software products that collect and report performance data. It is impossible to completely enumerate the products currently available and to keep the list current in this book. Therefore, while we mention some representative tools, please do not assume that these are the only tools, or even the best available. Consult with your computer performance specialists to learn which tools are available to you. The Computer Measurement Group (CMG) is a good source of information on current measurement products [CMG]. The group's annual conference has a vendor exhibit where most vendors of performance measurement products participate, so it is a good place to learn what is available and to hear new product announcements.

8.5.1 Data Collection Techniques

Table 8-2 illustrates the dynamic measurement techniques for collecting the performance metrics needed for SPE. The table does not include static measurement techniques such as data analysis programs. The table has columns for the five data collection techniques described in the following sections.

System Monitors System monitors observe system-level states and thus require detailed information on operating-system data structures and algorithms, to identify the states and record the pertinent data. Most of the early commercially available products were software monitors for IBM operating systems: BMC's MainView Explorer and Patrol [BMC], Candle's Omegamon [CAND], Landmark's Performance Works [LAND], and Information Systems Manager's PerfMan [ISM] are based on those products.

Since the introduction of open systems, a wide variety of tools are now available to monitor the network and the system performance of UNIX and Windows operating systems. Examples include: UNIX's sar, Tivoli's Performance Reporter, NetView, and others [TIVO], BMC [BMC], Microsoft's Performance Monitor [MICR], Demand Technology's Performance SeNTry [DEMA], Sun's Net Manager [SUN], Hewlett-Packard's Glance Plus [HP], and WHAM's Distributed Resource Monitor [WHAM].

Program Monitors Program monitors are less dependent on the operating system, but may be programming-language dependent (if they relate performance metrics to language statements). Compuware's Strobe works with several languages and subsystems on IBM MVS systems [COMP] (support for other systems is planned). Numega's TrueTime monitors programs written in most popular languages that run on Windows

Table 8-2: Performance Data Collection Techniques

Performance Metrics	Data Collection Technique				
	System monitor	Program monitor	System event recorder	External program event recorder	Internal event recorder
Workload data:					
Function requests			x		x
Rate and pattern			x		x
Data characteristics:					
Type and number					x
Size					x
Locality					x
Path characteristics:					
Execution probability		x		x	x
Loop repetitions		x		x	x
Software resources:					
Type and requirement	x	x			
Elapsed time		x			x
Processing overhead:					
Scenario usage	x	x	x		x
Component usage		x			x
Resource requirements	x	x	x	x	x
Computer resource usage:					
Response time	x	x	x	x	x
Throughput	x	x	x	x	x
Resource service times and wait times	x	x	x	x	x
Resource utilization and throughput	x	x	x	x	x
Queue lengths	x	x	x	x	x

[NUME]. Compuware's Application Expert monitors distributed application activity [COMP]. Hewlett-Packard's cxperf monitors performance of processes and threads [HP]. The standard prof tool profiles UNIX programs, and pacct provides summary statistics for processes. Most development environments, such as Microsoft's Visual Studio [MICR] and Rational DevelopmentStudio [RAT], include a program profiler. Java profilers include OptimizeIt [INTU] and JProbe [SITR].

System Event Recorders System event recording, if available, is provided as an operating system service. Examples include IBM's SMF; and Unisys' SIP, Flame, and SMFII (these products have both event recording and system monitoring in one package).

Commercial products are also available for storing, analyzing, and reporting the system event data. Some of these packages view the data primarily as accounting data, and their reports are oriented toward charging for services. Others have a more comprehensive view, such as Merrill Consultants' MXG [MERR], and Computer Associates' CA-MICS [CA]. Generic data analysis products, such as SAS [SAS] and Excel [MICR] and are also useful for summarizing and reporting system event data.

External Program Event Recorders External program event recorders *trace* program execution by recording sequences of events. Most programming languages offer an option to record each subroutine execution (usually for debugging purposes rather than performance measurement). Operating systems usually offer a trace option to record system event occurrence. This data is usually too detailed, and may not report the performance metrics of interest for SPE. Nevertheless, system event recording is helpful when you must construct models of low-level event handling, as when hardware and basic operating-system software are to be redesigned. Major subsystems, such as database management systems, transaction processing systems, and so on, usually record internal events. For example, IBM's database product, DB2, and its transaction processing product, CICS, each collects and reports its own performance statistics. Commercially available database, transaction processing, and other products offer varying performance metrics.

Internal Event Recorders Internal recorders require the insertion of code into the software to collect performance data about events of interest. This is currently the most useful technique for collecting SPE data. Section 8.6 covers the design and implementation of instrumentation.

8.5.2 Measuring SPE Data

Each of the rows of Table 8-2 corresponds to the types of SPE data we need to measure. The following paragraphs describe the measurement techniques that are useful for each type of data. Do not be misled by

Table 8-2. It is seldom as easy as the chart implies to collect data: It is rarely in exactly the granularity you want, nor does any one report contain all the data you need. The tools were designed for purposes other than SPE so you find yourself "stretching" the tools, trying to interpret their data, and finding clever ways to report it for your purposes. When you need data from several tools, it is difficult to correlate their results because the data collection intervals or capture ratios may differ. Today, most SPE data items come from internal event recorders.

 Use instrumentation to collect SPE data to facilitate the data collection and provide a convenient format for analysis.

Workload Data System event recorders are useful for measuring workload data (the number of requests for each workload function, the rate at which they are requested, and patterns of requests) *if* the granularity of the data collected by the event recorder can be correlated to the workload. For example, UNIX provides performance data on process execution (e.g., system time, user time, number of times executed, and so on). If the workload you are interested in executes as a UNIX process, the results for the process correspond one-to-one to the workload characteristics.

As another example, suppose you want to measure the number of database SELECTs issued when a customer searches for a Nachtfliegen.com itinerary. The number of database SELECTs is likely to be automatically counted by the database management software, so it would be easy to get an average for all customers. On the other hand, data on the number of round trips versus multi-segment trips may be more difficult to obtain. Unless you can compute scenario characteristics from the number of times a specific program executes (e.g., the number of times the multiple-segment-search page is displayed), you need an event counter internal to the Nachtfliegen.com software to capture detailed scenario characteristics, such as the number of times customers search for round trips versus multiple segments, the specific city pairs, and so on. Current commercially available products do not measure request patterns or locality (such as the number of times a customer visits the seat selection page and then returns to the itinerary specification page to search for a different flight); they must be tallied by internal event counters until more support tools are available.[1]

Note: Sometimes you can design performance measurements so that the granularity of the reports matches the information that you need. For example, you may make an individual class method into a program and run it many times. Then, the reported results for the "program" give you the data that you need for the method.

Data Characteristics You can collect many of the data characteristics and some of the workload data with static analysis tools that examine the data and report the statistics. For example, you can obtain the size of the database statically—the database transactions do not have to be executing. Locality of reference, on the other hand, is a dynamic metric. Until additional support tools are available, locality of reference must be gathered with internal event recorders.

Path Characteristics You can measure path execution characteristics using program monitors or external program event recorders. It may be more convenient to get specific data from internal event recorders, though, because the other tools (such as external event recorders) may mix path data with a lot of other data, making it difficult to isolate what you need. For example, to get loop repetitions, you may have to wade through lists of subroutine calls, and count the number of calls to each.

Software Resources You can usually find the types of software resources and their computer resource requirements in system monitor or program monitor reports. You may need an internal event recorder to collect their elapsed execution times.

Processing Overhead System monitors or system event recorders measure the amount of computer resource usage for scenarios—if you can identify the scenarios on the reports. If not, program monitors may report the desired level of granularity; otherwise you need an internal event recorder. Similarly, system-level tools seldom report component resource usage. So, you need program monitors or internal event recorders. The computer resource requirements consumed by the software resources may be provided by any of the measurement

---

1. New Web site measurement tools are emerging. They were not widely available at the time this was written and are not mentioned here.

techniques. Database and other middleware resource requirements are usually provided by instrumentation internal to the product.

Computer Resource Usage Computer resource usage usually comes from system monitors. You may have to hunt for some of the data from the system event recorders, depending on your tool set.

8.6 Instrumentation

The Instrumentation Principle is discussed in Chapter 9.

As discussed in Section 8.5, you can get many of the performance metrics that you need from standard performance measurement tools. However, as we have seen, the data provided by the standard tools is not always what you really need. Getting the right information often requires that you use the Instrumenting Principle. This performance principle suggests that you "instrument systems as you build them to enable measurement and analysis of workload scenarios, resource requirements, and performance objective compliance."

You instrument software by inserting code (probes) at key points to measure pertinent execution characteristics. For example, you might insert code that records the time at the start and end of a business task to measure the end-to-end time for that task.

There are at least three reasons for supplementing the standard tools with instrumentation: convenience, data granularity, and control.

The first reason for instrumenting is to conveniently gather exactly the data you need. Although standard measurement tools may report SPE data, there are currently no tools that conveniently generate one report containing precisely the SPE data you need. Thus, getting the data is inconvenient at best. Some data, such as locality of reference for user actions or data requests, is practically impossible to gather with standard measurement tools—you must analyze detailed traces and derive these logical events from them. Instrumenting allows you to tally the user requests within the software where they are easily identified, and produce convenient reports with exactly the data you need.

The second reason for instrumenting is that the data granularity from standard measurement tools seldom matches the SPE requirements. For example, suppose we want the response time for a typical ATM session.

Most data collection tools report performance data for online systems by "user interaction," that is, the starting event is the receipt of data or control information from the user, and the ending event is the transmission of a response. Using this definition, there are at least five user interactions in the ATM Withdrawal scenario shown in Figure 4.3 (insert card, enter PIN, request the withdrawal transaction, specify account, and specify amount). To use the standard measurement tools, you must gather data for each user interaction, and then calculate the session total from the individual times. For this scenario that isn't difficult, because we know which interactions to tally. But this is an especially simple case, and it is often more difficult to associate the logical events we wish to measure to their physical execution properties.

Furthermore, you need data that correlates with nodes in an execution graph, if you want to associate resource usage with functional components. These nodes are often at varying levels of detail (e.g., basic versus expanded nodes). However, standard measurement tools only provide metrics for programs. Thus, it is virtually impossible to use them for measurements of operations or individual program statements.

The third reason to instrument code is to control the measurement process. For SPE, we seldom need all of the measurement data all of the time; rather, we periodically need some of the data. Collecting data with standard measurement tools is not just a matter of flipping a switch; measurement requires many execution and data analysis steps. If measurements are infrequent, or if experienced personnel are unavailable, others must recreate the measurement steps. Instrumenting your code allows you to easily turn selected measurements on and off as needed.

Use internal instrumentation to collect SPE data for convenience in gathering and analyzing data, to collect data at the desired level of granularity, and to provide controls for enabling appropriate measurements when they are needed.

So it is important to supplement your standard performance measurement tools with software instrumentation.

Why does the instrumentation principle call for designing probes into the software? Why not just insert them later when you need the measurements? There are two primary reasons for designing in instrumentation. First, it is easiest to define measurement requirements and probe points when designers define the system architecture. Second, collecting and analyzing data tends to incur less processing overhead if the probes are integrated as the design evolves. This allows you to control the processing overhead by balancing the data collection and dynamic data reduction overhead against the overhead for recording and analyzing measurements (Section 8.4.2 provides more information on measurement overhead).

Define performance requirements and thus software instrumentation requirements as part of the software architecture. Design the software instrumentation as you design the software to meet these requirements.

The need for designed-in instrumentation is best explained by relating it to another problem observed by software engineers: requirements traceability. That is, it is often difficult to relate a system's overall functional requirements to the code that implements them (for example, to verify that all requirements have been satisfied, or for maintenance). This is because the implementation of any particular requirement invariably involves collaboration among many different objects. Thus, it is much easier to establish the relationship between requirements and code during the design process. Similarly, because there is a direct correspondence between the user functions that we wish to measure and many of the functional requirements of the software system, it is easier to establish the measurement capabilities during design.

There are other advantages of the resulting instrumentation. The data it collects is useful for:

- System testing (to assess test coverage, ensure that performance goals are met, and so on),
- Diagnosing the cause of problems and possibly assisting with the traceability of requirements, and
- Quantifying the execution cost of each requirement.

Having discussed why and when we need instrumentation, we next examine alternatives for design and implementation of instrumentation. We also cover reporting considerations.

8.6.1 Instrumentation Design Considerations

There are three primary considerations when designing instrumentation:

1. Defining the events to be measured

2. Choosing the granularity of the measurements

3. Dynamically selecting the data to be recorded

First, plan for the events that are important for each scenario. Include the beginning and end of key functions, and the beginning and end of critical processing steps.

There are at least three choices for the second consideration, granularity of the measurements. The finest granularity is to record all events and metrics (such as the process ID, a sequence number, a time stamp, the event, other processing state definitions, and so on), to write them to archival storage, and to analyze the data and compute the desired performance metrics later. This option offers the greatest flexibility but at the greatest cost, because many events are likely, and each event may have a significant amount of data.

A coarser granularity is to use the same recording technique, but to define event hierarchies. Thus, rather than recording every event, we could selectively record the data at varying levels of detail, such as: only major components, major and intermediate-level components, or all components. For example, for Nachtfliegen.com we could record
- Only the number of itineraries planned (major component)
- The number of itineraries and details of each segment (major and intermediate)
- Information about each page the customer visits (all components)

The coarsest of the event-recording techniques is to define types or classes of events, tally the metrics for each, and then compute the averages, variances or distributions of the metrics. For example, when instrumenting Nachtfliegen.com, you might define events corresponding to the beginning and end of a planItinerary scenario, and sum the number of requests, the CPU time, and elapsed time for each invocation. You could then compute and print the average CPU and elapsed time at the end of the measurement period.

The third instrumentation design consideration is dynamically selecting the data to be recorded at runtime. You seldom need all the performance data at a given time, and recording and analyzing unnecessary data incurs unnecessary overhead processing. Instead of collecting all of the data all of the time, it's better to use instrumentation parameters to vary the metrics collected and their granularity.

One way to parameterize the instrumentation is to define hierarchies of events and/or data. Then use the instrumentation parameters to trigger the recording of classes of events or data in the hierarchy. For example, you might define a hierarchy of input events for an application such as that shown in Figure 8-1. Selecting mouse events would record all left- and right-click, double-click, and move events, but not details of how many left-click versus double-click events occurred.

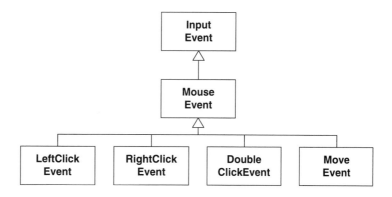

Figure 8-1: Event Hierarchy

8.6.2 Implementation Alternatives

There are three alternatives:

1. Integrate instrumentation into the software products.

2. Use special classes.

3. Use standard system event recording tools.

The first alternative integrates instrumentation specifications into the program and data specifications, thus making instrumentation another product of development. For example, a Nachtfliegen.com software programmer might have a specification to count the number of times that users request the planItinerary scenario.

Note: The code for this instrumentation is pretty simple. It is just a call to increment a counter.

The use of inline directives and other code optimizations is discussed in Chapter 12.

A second alternative is to use special classes to collect and record data. This approach makes use of information hiding to isolate data collection routines that require specific knowledge of the environment, such as the operating system calls that provide resource usage statistics. To collect data, programs will (selectively) call methods belonging to this class. Macro expansion or inline functions could minimize procedure call overhead. This alternative offers the advantage of reusability, if you define an API to the classes that may be used for many software systems.

The Singleton pattern is presented in [Gamma et al. 1995].

For example, we might define a class EventLog that records the time that events occur to a file. Making EventLog a Singleton pattern would mean that every class that uses EventLog would write its events to the same file. The file would be opened in EventLog's constructor, and closed in its destructor. Events would be written using the record() member function:

```
#DEFINE WRITESPEC "%2d%2d%2d%3d$%s\n"

EventLog:: record(char eventName[32]) {
    SysTime time = SysTime::GetCurrentTime();
    fprintf(theFile, WRITESPEC, time.getHour(),
        time.getMinute(), time.getSecond(),
        time.getMSecond(), eventName);
}
```

We could then call the record() operation whenever an event of interest occurs using something like the following:

```
if (instrumentationON)
    theEventLog->record(eventName);
```

Note: SysTime is not the name of a standard clock. You will need to substitute the appropriate system calls for your environment.

ARM is discussed in Section 8.7.

The third alternative uses standard system-event-recording tools. To use them, programs call system routines to record events and performance data on the standard system-event-archive file (for example, on IBM's

SMF file or Windows' registry). A variant of this alternative is to use a standard system extension such as the Application Resource Measurement (ARM) facility.

8.6.3 Data Reporting

When customized, internal instrumentation code collects data, you also need special programs to analyze and report it. Commercially available reporting tools make reporting easy. For example, you could input data to PC spreadsheet or charting packages, or to statistical analysis packages, such as [SAS] or [SPSS]. You could use report generators provided by your database management system to facilitate data presentation. If you integrate data collection into the standard system event recording, you can use its standard reporting capabilities.

Whether you use one of the above reporting tools, or write custom reporting programs, reuse them for other SPE projects. This is best accomplished if you develop and adhere to standards for the data to be collected and its format. Then, use the same conventions for all projects to define and collect the events and metrics. You can then develop and use standard SPE data reporting tools for all SPE projects. For example, define the data contents and format, and use the same specifications for multiple projects.

8.7 Application Resource Measurement

Application Resource Measurement is an application program interface (API) developed by participants from the ARM Working Group member companies [ARM]. The purpose of the ARM API is to

> ...enable applications to provide information to measure business transactions from an end user perspective and the contributing components of response time in distributed applications. This information can be used to support service level agreements and to analyze response time across distributed systems. [Johnson 1999]

ARM is an emerging standard approved by The Open Group [TOG 1998].

ARM provides a platform-independent API for applications. Applications may make calls to the appropriate ARM API function to indicate start and stop events for business activities, or to record application-dependent metrics. The API makes it easy to record events such as specific menu choices, number of bytes sent or received, tables accessed, number of records returned, and so on. Tool vendors provide agents that catch API calls and route the information to a log that may be analyzed later. Thus it is a convenient mechanism for *implementing* the instrumentation that you *design* using the concepts in Section 8.6.

The ARM Working Group provides a system development kit (SDK) that includes

- An ARM shared library, libarm, for testing, and a NULL library to disable actual measurements
- Language header files for supported languages (currently C, C++, and Java) and source code for testing
- Sample programs

The SDK is available through the Web site [ARM]. At the time of this writing, ARM 2.0 was the current standard [Johnson 1999]. A new version of the standard, ARM 3.0, had been proposed and a beta version was available. The following paragraphs describe ARM 2.0; the proposed differences are discussed afterwards.

ARM 2.0 provides the following API calls:

- arm_init()—initializes and returns a unique identifier, registers the application name and optionally the user name
- arm_getid()—returns a unique identifier for each transaction class you wish to track, registers static attributes of a transaction, including its name
- arm_start()—signals the start of an instance of a transaction class, returns a unique handle to be passed to arm_update() and arm_stop()
- arm_update()—records information about the instance. Optionally called any number of times
- arm_stop()—signals the end of a transaction instance, causes the agent to record the response time of the transaction
- arm_end()—signals termination of the application and cleans up the ARM environment

An application usually makes these calls in the above order, first starting ARM, then registering the transaction, and then repeatedly signaling the start, progress, and stop of instances of transactions. The complete signature of arm_update() is

anError = arm_update (start_handle, flags, data, data_size);

where start_handle is returned by arm_start(); the flags parameter is reserved for future use; anError contains a zero if successful, a negative value if an error occurred; and data is application defined.

Note: The EventLog class that we defined in Section 8.6.2 has functionality similar to that provided by ARM. You could use ARM to accomplish the function of EventLog's record() operation by packing the event name and time into "data" and passing it to arm_update().

ARM 2.0 is defined using C language syntax. The Java version has significant proposed changes in ARM 3.0 that may change before the standard is adopted, so it is not shown here.

Note: There are several significant additions in ARM 3.0; however, it will be backward compatible with ARM 2.0. The new features primarily address the generation of the transaction ID to facilitate correlating transactions across platforms. In ARM 2.0, the application provides the application and transaction names, and the agent (provided by a tool vendor) generates a unique transaction ID. In ARM 3.0, the application may statically define a Universal Transaction Identifier (UTID) following a recommended form to ensure that it is unique. A new API call, arm_register_transaction(), replaces the paired arm_init() and arm_getid() when this new capability is desired. Parameters for the API calls also change, so new API calls distinguish ARM 2.0 from ARM 3.0 calls. For example, arm_start_transaction() using the new UTID is the ARM 3.0 version of arm_start() that uses the old-style handle.

ARM 3.0 also provides the arm_complete_transaction() function, an asynchronous call that is made once per transaction instance after the instance terminates instead of having separate start and stop calls. The transaction must measure its own response time and send it as a parameter. This feature is useful for high-performance applications when analysts are worried about a synchronous call to an external library. The new call may be made from a background thread, and may be called long after the transaction completes.

Other ARM 3.0 proposals permit Java applications to make ARM calls using native bindings rather than using the Java Native Interface to load and call programs outside the Java Virtual Machine.

ARM provides a framework for collecting SPE data. To use it, you must define

- A standard format for collecting data
- Standards for which data is to be collected (e.g., business transaction start and stop times when they span multiple individual transactions, such as an ATM session containing multiple individual transactions)
- The specific SPE information to be collected for selected scenarios
- How to select the granularity of measurements (e.g., when flag is set, record details)

You must also address when and how to enable measurements, and which tools to use to analyze and report the SPE data. Thus, you need to do some significant design work to determine what to measure, when to measure it, and how to report it. Once these decisions have been made, ARM provides the platform-independent method for actually recording the data.

For SPE, we need some additional performance data that is not available via the ARM API, such as the CPU time for transactions and portions of transactions, elapsed time for portions of transactions, number of physical I/Os and their elapsed time, and so on. Most systems provide their own API call to obtain CPU time and clock time, but these calls are not platform independent. Perhaps a future version of ARM will provide platform-independent API calls for at least some of this additional performance data.

8.8 Summary

Measurement is a key part of the SPE process. Measurements are used to provide input data for SPE models, verify and validate models, and determine whether performance goals have actually been met. The types of measurement that you need for SPE are workload data, data characteristics, path characteristics, software resource usage, resource requirements, and computer system usage. Table 8-1 matches performance metrics to their SPE uses.

The scientific method is the best way to design and conduct performance measurements to collect SPE data. For SPE, measurements should be used primarily to collect the data for constructing models and validating their results. Measurements are too labor intensive to use for evaluating architecture and design alternatives.

> *To ensure that you get the SPE data you need, carefully plan the tests to run, the execution environment, the tools to use, the data to collect from each tool, the data to collect from instrumentation, and the reporting procedures.*

There are several alternatives for obtaining performance data:
- Monitoring states or recording events
- Making measurements internally or externally
- Using system-level, program-level, and intra-program granularity
- Selectively activating and deactivating various measurements

There are also choices for managing the amount of data collected. You can record all details, summarize the data as it is collected and record the results periodically, or tally data between events and record it when an event occurs.

Different measurement techniques (state versus event, internal versus external, and program versus system) will exhibit different characteristics that may affect the usefulness of the data for SPE. The factors affecting measurement quality are discussed within this chapter.

There are many performance measurement products for monitoring computer systems and programs, and recording system events. Several representative products are described within this chapter. Table 8-2 summarizes the data collection techniques used to obtain each type of SPE data.

Internal instrumentation (i.e., probes inserted at key points to measure pertinent execution characteristics) is currently the best alternative for collecting much of the SPE data. It is more convenient for gathering and analyzing data, collecting data at the desired level of granularity, and providing controls for enabling appropriate measurements when they are needed. Instrumentation requirements and design should be produced along with the architecture, functional requirements, and design. The primary considerations are defining the events to be measured, choosing the granularity of the measurements, and dynamically selecting the data to be recorded.

Application Resource Measurement provides a platform-independent API that allows applications to make calls that record start and stop events for business activities, or to record application-dependent metrics. It is a convenient mechanism for implementing internal instrumentation.

Part IV

Performance Solutions

Chapter 9

Performance-Oriented Design

Few things are harder to put up with than a good example.
—Mark Twain

In This Chapter:

- Principles for performance-oriented design
- Examples of applying performance principles

9.1 Principles for Performance-Oriented Design

You quantify the performance of your software's architecture and design by constructing and solving the SPE models. After you have modeled a number of different designs, some of which have good performance characteristics and some of which don't, you will begin to develop a feel for what works and what doesn't. You will avoid those design strategies that have repeatedly produced poor performance, and, consciously or unconsciously, you will incorporate those that consistently produce good performance into your standard "bag of tricks."

This chapter helps shorten that learning process by presenting a set of general principles for creating responsive systems. These *performance principles* help to identify design alternatives that are likely to meet performance objectives. These principles are neither new nor revolutionary. You will probably recognize some of them as things that you already do. However, they do generalize and abstract the knowledge that performance specialists use in constructing software systems.

These performance principles supplement the quantitative performance assessments that we have seen so far; they do not replace them. Performance improvements involve many trade-offs. For example, a local performance improvement may adversely affect overall system performance. The quantitative techniques provide the data required to evaluate the net effect of a design alternative on performance. You can then weigh the performance improvements of a given alternative against its effects on other quality attributes, such as modifiability, reusability, or cost.

Late life cycle strategies are discussed in Chapter 12.

This chapter presents nine principles for performance-oriented design. They are grouped into three categories:

- *Performance control principles* help you control the performance of an evolving system
- *Independent principles* improve the performance of your software by reducing its resource requirements
- *Synergistic principles* improve the overall performance of a system via cooperation among processes competing for computer resources

These principles are applicable during the early phases of software development. Late life cycle issues (e.g., tuning strategies) are discussed later.

9.2 Performance Control Principles

These two principles help you control the performance of the system as it is being developed and throughout its life cycle.

9.2.1 Performance Objectives Principle

Definition Performance objectives control performance by explicitly stating the required performance rigorously enough so that you can quantitatively determine whether or not the software system meets that objective. If you do not know where you are going, it doesn't matter how you go. But if you can quantify where you need to be, then you can evaluate the alternatives and select the best way of meeting the requirements.

The Performance Objectives Principle states:

Performance Objectives Principle

Define specific, quantitative, measurable performance objectives for performance scenarios.

Performance objectives are discussed in Chapter 7.

Application A well-defined performance objective would be something like: "The end-to-end time for completion of a 'typical' correct ATM withdrawal performance scenario must be less than 1 minute, and a screen result must be presented to the user within 1 second of the user's input." Vague statements such as "The system must be efficient" or "The system shall be fast" are not useful as performance objectives.

Avoid vague or qualitative performance objectives.

Note: Performance objectives may change over a system's lifetime. For example, your current performance objective may be to process 10,000 events per second. However, in two years, you may need to be able to process 30,000 events per second. It is a good idea to consider future uses of your software so that you can anticipate these changes and build in the necessary scalability.

You should define one or more performance objectives for each performance scenario. Throughout the modeling process, you can compare model results to the objective, to determine if there is significant risk of failing to meet the objectives, and take appropriate action early. And, as soon as you can get measurements from a performance test, you can determine whether or not the software meets the objective.

For some types of systems you may define different performance objectives, depending on the intensity of requests. For example, the response time objective for a customer service application may be 1 second with up to 500 users or less, 2 seconds for 500 to 750 users, and 3 seconds for up to 1,000 users.

9.2.2 Instrumenting Principle

Probes are explained in Chapter 8.

Definition Instrumenting software means inserting code (probes) at key points to enable the measurement of pertinent execution characteristics. For example, probes may record the number of times each performance scenario executes, the end-to-end response time, the number of ATM transactions in each session, the average amount of money in a withdrawal, the number of I/Os to update an order, the average size of a network message, and so on.

Note: There is a difference in inserting the probes to enable the measurements, in activating them to actually record the data, and in analyzing and reporting the results. All of these concepts were discussed in Chapter 8.

The Instrumenting Principle does not directly improve performance, but it is essential to improving performance. It has its foundation in the engineering maxim: "If you can't measure it, you can't control it." As Lord Kelvin pointed out over 100 years ago:

> When you can measure what you are speaking about, and express it in numbers, you know something about it; but when you cannot measure it, when you cannot express it in numbers, your knowledge is of a meager and unsatisfactory kind: it may be the beginning of knowledge, but you have scarcely in your thoughts advanced to the stage of science. [Kelvin]

The Instrumenting Principle states:

Instrument systems as you build them to enable measurement and analysis of workload scenarios, resource requirements, and performance objective compliance.

Instrumenting Principle

Instrumenting techniques are discussed in more detail in Chapter 8.

Application It is important to make data collection mechanisms part of the system's requirements and design; it is much more difficult to add them after implementation. You also want to define the data to collect, and a consistent format for collecting it. Then you can develop a set of analysis and reporting tools that can be reused for other systems that you develop.

Even if you have performance measurement tools available, you still need software instrumentation because of limitations in the capabilities of system measurement tools. Most measurement tools that are external to the application itself collect system-level data, such as total program execution time, rather than functional data, such as end-to-end response time (for workflows that span multiple transactions). You need information on resource requirements for critical portions of code, not just the total for the software. To collect this data, you must insert code to call system timing routines, and write key events and relevant data to files for later analysis.

This is particularly true for distributed systems that interact with other applications. If you find performance problems in the end-to-end user tasks, it may be impossible to tell where the problems occurred unless you have measurements within the tasks to determine where the time was spent.

Instrument distributed systems that interact with other applications to measure the time required for the interactions. Then you will be able to easily isolate problems and determine which components are contributing to performance problems.

9.3 Independent Principles

These four principles improve the performance of your system by reducing its computer resource requirements. They are called independent principles because they can be applied independently—they do not conflict.

9.3.1 Centering Principle

Definition Centering leverages performance by focusing attention on the parts of the software that have the greatest impact on performance. This principle is derived from the folkloric "80-20 rule" for the execution of code within a program. This observation states that 20% or less of a program's code accounts for 80% or more of its computer resource usage. We extend the code execution rule to apply to the demand for system functions.

Centering is concerned with identifying the subset (the 20% or less) of the system functions that will be used most (80% or more) of the time. These frequently used functions are the *dominant workload functions*. These dominant workload functions also cause a subset (≤20%) of the operations in a software system to be executed most (≥80%), as well as the code within the operations, and so on. Improvements made in these dominant workload functions thus have a significant impact on the overall performance of the system.

The Centering Principle states:

Centering Principle

Identify the dominant workload functions and minimize their processing.

> **Note:** The criteria for the selection of the dominant workload functions is similar to the criteria for selecting performance scenarios. We are primarily interested in those that have the greatest number of requests, because they dominate the user's perception of performance. In some cases, we will also include those with large resource demands because they may interfere with the performance of functions that execute more frequently. We may also include functions whose performance is critical, even though they execute less frequently. The primary focus of the centering principle, however, is on the functions that execute most frequently.

The SPE process for object-oriented systems is discussed in Chapter 15.

For object-oriented development, centering involves identifying the critical use cases. These are the use cases that are critical to the operation of the system, or that are important to responsiveness as seen by a user. Critical use cases may also include those that relate to risks involving performance. The Centering Principle is so important that identifying critical use cases is the first step in the SPE process.

The Fast Path pattern is discussed in Chapter 10.

To minimize the processing for these dominant workload functions, create special, streamlined execution paths for them using the Fast Path pattern. These Fast Paths include only that processing that is absolutely essential to the function. You can further reduce the processing requirements for a Fast Path by applying the additional principles discussed below, and the additional techniques in Chapter 12.

The dominant workload functions execute frequently, but they may be "trivial transactions," in that they may not require much creative design. Thus there is a tendency to defer working on their design until other, more interesting parts of the system have been specified. In many cases this is a mistake. By the time you are ready to specify these dominant workload functions, their data may be scattered, or other constraints may limit your ability to minimize their processing.

    Design the dominant workload functions first.

ATM use cases are identified in Chapter 2.

Application By far, the most frequently exercised use case for an ATM, and the most important in terms of user satisfaction, is CustomerTransaction. The most frequently executed scenario in the CustomerTransaction use case is Withdrawal. We can streamline this workload function by creating a "Fast Path," which allows the user to press a single key to select a withdrawal of a predetermined amount without having to enter the transaction type, account, and amount (e.g., withdraw $60 from checking). The amounts offered on the menu (e.g., $40, $60, or $100) should be determined by examining historical records for withdrawals (either from the manual system or from a previous incarnation of the ATM). Future systems should permit users to specify preferences for their "usual" session, such as the typical amount for a withdrawal; and perhaps specify a GetBalance, with an option to proceed with the withdrawal or do something else. This improvement reduces the resource requirements and eliminates the overall time required for ATM screen interactions, so it improves the users' end-to-end response time.

9.3.2 Fixing-Point Principle

Definition Fixing connects:

- The desired action to the instructions used to accomplish that action, or
- The desired result to the data used to produce it.

The *fixing point* is a point in time. The latest fixing point is during execution, just before the instructions are to be executed. Dynamic binding in object-oriented languages such as Smalltalk, or polymorphic function calls that cannot be resolved during compilation, exhibit late fixing. Fixing can also establish the connection at several possible earlier times: earlier in the execution, at system initialization, during compilation, or even outside the software.

The Fixing-Point Principle is:

Fixing-Point Principle

For responsiveness, fixing should establish connections at the earliest feasible point in time, such that retaining the connection is cost-effective.

It is cost-effective to retain the connection when the savings realized with it offset the cost of the retention.

Note: In some cases, early fixing may reduce the flexibility of your design. On the other hand, flexibility is often an excuse for not addressing how users need to use the system. You may need to compromise to achieve your performance objectives. For example, the last section suggests creating a special-purpose "quick withdrawal." If that were the only type of withdrawal, flexibility would be sacrificed; however, we can also provide a more general withdrawal that lets the users select the options they prefer.

We would then get the performance improvements (if our design encourages most users to select the quick withdrawal), without sacrificing flexibility for the other users.

Applications Suppose that a bank employee needs summary data of detail records from multiple accounts. The latest possible fixing point would be to summarize the data at the time that the employee requests the summary-data screen. We could establish an earlier fixing point by updating the summary data as the account detail records arrive.

Here, the retention cost is the cost of the storage needed to hold the computed summary data and the operational costs of producing it. If the data is saved for other purposes anyway, the storage cost is essentially zero; otherwise it depends on the quantity of summary data to be stored. To summarize the data on demand, the operational cost is the processing for the software to locate and read each detail record, and then write the summary record. To update the summary as the detail records arrive, the operational cost is the processing for one write for each detail record (however, the write may require additional processing to insert the record in the proper location). Thus, the operational costs are roughly the same for both approaches (performance models would quantify the exact costs). If the data is used for other purposes anyway, early fixing is a good idea because it provides better responsiveness for little or no additional cost.

Note: You must know enough about the anticipated usage patterns of the new system, and the reports that are typically requested, to effectively use these principles. This is why we advocate the participation of users in the performance walkthroughs in Chapter 7.

Another example of early versus late fixing would be the implementation of an OrderedCollection class. The late-fixing solution would be to add items to the collection as the new items arrive, and then perform a sort when it is accessed. Early fixing would insert the item in the proper location, or sort the collection each time an item is added. The best solution here depends on the environment in which the collection is to be used; in particular, how often you need the ordered versus the unordered data. The cost-benefit trade-off would be evaluated in the same way as for the banking example.

Finally, consider an automated telephone directory, such as one for 800 numbers. To improve the responsiveness for frequently requested numbers, we could apply early fixing to cache those that are requested most frequently in memory. This would avoid a database query for those numbers. The cost is the amount of memory used to cache an individual number. If the cache won't hold all numbers, a strategy based on frequency of access could determine which ones would be retained.

9.3.3 Locality Principle

Definition Locality refers to the "closeness" of desired actions, functions, and results to the physical resources used to produce them. For example, if we need to sort a list of names, and that data is in local memory instead of being on a disk on a remote node in the network, the locality is good. This is an example of *spatial* locality.

The types of locality are

1. Spatial,

2. Temporal (i.e., time),

3. Effectual (i.e., purpose or intent), and

4. Degree (i.e., intensity or size).

For the sort example, temporal locality is good if you sort all of the names at the same time, rather than sorting a few names, adding more to the list, and sorting again. It may be possible to execute the sort on different types of processors. Effectual locality is better if the type of processor (its purpose) is matched to the task. A processor with instructions that sort long character strings directly has better effectual locality than one with instructions that only sort smaller units (such as bytes), thus requiring the compiler to break long character strings into smaller units for the sort. Degree locality is good if the entire list of names fits into memory, rather than requiring intermediate storage on disk.

The Locality Principle is:

Locality Principle

Create actions, functions, and results that are close to physical computer resources.

Note: Achieving effectual locality may require that you sacrifice portability of the software. For example, if you write code to exploit special instructions for vector processing, the code may require modifications to run on a general-purpose processor. You need good specifications of both performance and portability objectives to make the appropriate compromise.

Applications In an object-oriented implementation, it is important to keep related data and behavior together. An object should have most of the data that it needs to make a decision or perform an action. Objects that have very frequent interactions should be assigned to the same processor, and should perhaps even be compiled and linked together. Chapter 11 presents a performance antipattern, The "god" Class, which addresses this phenomenon.

As another example, consider how you might locate processing and data in a distributed system. The usual approach is to send queries from a client to a server each time the client needs data. If, however, the client only uses the results of a query to determine which query to send next, there is unnecessary traffic between the client and server. In this case, you can improve locality by having the client send only one request to the server, whereby all subsequent queries and related processing are performed locally on the server. The server then returns the ultimate response to the client. Chapter 11 presents a performance antipattern, the Circuitous Treasure Hunt, which addresses this phenomenon.

A final example considers architectural possibilities for the following two different types of order entry systems:

1. Company A has regional sales forces, the customers are located within each region, accounts receivable are managed regionally, and the inventory is managed and shipped via each region's warehouse.

2. Company B has order-taking phone centers located in several regions, customers call a toll-free number that is routed to any available order taker, accounts receivable are managed nationally, and the inventory is managed and shipped via a central warehouse.

In the first type of system, locality will be best for a distributed architecture with a processing facility located in each region, because most of the system interactions can be handled by the regional facility, and there are few interactions with a central processing facility. In the second type of system, locality will be best for a centralized architecture with one main facility, because few interactions could be handled without consulting the customer data, accounts receivable, and inventory subsystems.

9.3.4 Processing Versus Frequency Principle

Definition This principle is concerned with the amount of work done in processing a request and the number of requests received. It seeks to make a trade-off between the two. It may be possible to reduce the number of requests by doing more work per request, or vice versa.

The Processing Versus Frequency Principle states:

Processing Versus Frequency Principle

> *Minimize the product of processing times frequency.*

Applications When adding many rows to a database, two design alternatives are: (1) to execute the database load commands once per row, or (2) to collect the changes and then execute the database load command once for the entire batch. The Processing Versus Frequency Principle compares the total cost of the alternatives. If the software executes on a client platform and the database resides on a server, the communication overhead processing is part of the total cost.

Consider a system that retrieves results of a query. The choices are to

1. Return all results at once

2. Return one result at a time and wait for a request for the next result

3. Return a "batch" of results (the size of a batch could be set by the system or could be a user-set limit)

The proper choice depends on the number of results typically needed by the user who initiates the query. The first option is best when all results are needed most of the time; the second is best when one result will likely suffice. The third option is a compromise—if the user needs all the results, the processing is lower with option three than with option two, but higher than option one. If the user needs only one result, the opposite is true.

In the call processing application cited as a performance failure in Chapter 1, each time a call was placed, a new Call object was created. When the call ended, the object was destroyed. In this case, the amount of processing required to create a new call object was high, and, at high volumes of switch traffic, the product of processing times frequency was too high. The solution was to pre-allocate a collection of Call objects to reduce the processing time, and thus reduce the product to acceptable limits.

Note: You could also view the call processing example as an application of the Fixing-Point Principle, because with pre-allocation you fix the call objects earlier.

You may find other situations where you make a performance improvement and you are uncertain about which principle it illustrates. This is not unusual because there are often multiple ways to reduce resource requirements. In fact, we often debate about which principle best explains a given improvement. The name of the principle is not important. What is important is that the principles guide you to a solution that reduces resource requirements. You will not find contradictions; one principle will not lead you to a solution that is opposite to that suggested by another principle.

9.4 Synergistic Principles

The following three principles are known as synergistic principles because they improve the overall performance of a system via cooperation among processes competing for computer resources.

The synergistic principles depend on cooperation to reduce delays for resource contention. If all objects do not cooperate, you may not achieve the desired improvement. For example, many highways have blinking permission lights to control the rate at which vehicles enter the highway. This helps traffic on the highway to flow at an even rate. If one entrance ramp's permission light fails to operate and vehicles stream onto the highway, the desired effect may not be achieved. The independent principles do not require this type of cooperation—if you use them in your system, you will benefit regardless of whether or not other systems that execute on the same computer resources use the principles.

9.4.1 Shared Resources Principle

Definition Resources in a computer system are limited, and processes compete for their use. For some resources, sharing is possible, whereby more than one process can use the resource. For example, multiple processes may *read* from the same portion of a database. For other resources, processes require exclusive use and must take turns accessing the resource. For example, only one process may *update* the same portion of a database. The need for exclusive access to a resource can affect performance in two ways. First, additional processing overhead is needed to schedule access to the resource. Second, there is potentially a contention delay as processes wait for their turn to use the resource (i.e., the holding time). This delay depends on how many processes request access to the resource, and how long they hold the resource once they have it.

The Shared Resources Principle is:

Shared Resource Principle

> *Share resources when possible. When exclusive access is required, minimize the sum of the holding time and the scheduling time.*

The Shared Resources Principle improves overall performance through cooperation to reduce contention delays.

Applications Suppose that we need to update bank account records. To avoid corrupting the data, we require exclusive access until the record has been updated. One way to obtain exclusive access for the update is to lock the entire database. This approach minimizes *scheduling time*—it requires less overhead to lock the entire database than it does to lock an individual record because we only need to check the status of one lock indicator. This approach maximizes *holding time*, however, because no other process can access the database until the lock has been released. Another approach is to lock only the individual record. This approach minimizes *holding time* because other processes can access other records, but maximizes *scheduling time* because there is a separate lock status indicator for each record. The best alternative is likely to be a compromise that locks a group of records and thus minimizes the sum of holding and scheduling time. In general, the appropriate solution will depend on the access patterns for the individual application.

Consider an application in which there is a database table of telephone numbers, such as a reverse information directory (i.e., a mapping of numbers to subscribers) for each region. If the table is keyed by telephone number, and the records are also stored in telephone number order, optimal sharing will be difficult because the first six digits of the telephone number (the area code and prefix) are the same for all telephones within a region. Thus, when you add new records, the holding time is likely to be high because processes will have to wait on other additions to the same area code and prefix. You will need to formulate and solve the SPE models to quantify the contention delays. It is likely, however, that you would want an alternate key, such as reversing the order of the digits in the telephone number, so that the first four digits would cause accesses to be more uniformly spread through the database table.

9.4.2 Parallel Processing Principle

Definition Overall processing time can sometimes be reduced by partitioning a computation into multiple concurrent processes. The concurrency may be:

- *Real concurrency*, in which the processes execute simultaneously on different processors. In this case, the processing time is reduced by an amount proportional to the number of processors.
- *Apparent concurrency*, in which the processes are multiplexed on a single processor. Here the situation is more complicated. While some of the processing may be overlapped (one process may use the CPU while another accesses the disk), each process will sometimes experience additional wait time due to contention for the same resource such as the disk.

Both real and apparent concurrency require processing overhead for the communication and coordination among the concurrent processes. If you're not careful, this overhead can equal or even exceed the time saved by partitioning the computation into concurrent processes.

The Parallel Processing Principle is a recognition of this trade-off:

Parallel Processing Principle

Execute processing in parallel (only) when the processing speedup offsets communication overhead and resource contention delays.

The Parallel Processing Principle is another synergistic principle. It addresses trading the additional overhead that accompanies parallel processing for the potential speedup that the parallelism provides. Evaluating the trade-off requires constructing and solving performance models to quantify the speedup, contention delays, and communication delays.

Applications A common use of this principle is found in batch-oriented jobs such as printing statements for a large number of customers. These jobs are usually processed at night to minimize conflicts with daily processing (an example of the Shared Resources Principle), and the jobs must complete within the nightly "batch window." For very large jobs, it is common to partition the jobs and run several jobs in parallel. For example, you can produce the statement for customer Adams in parallel with the statements for Jones and Smith, and thus speed up the processing with no additional communication overhead. Again, you will need to construct and solve the SPE models to quantify resource contention delays in order to select the optimal number of partitioned jobs to run in parallel.

Another example is found in the ICAD system used to illustrate software execution models in Chapter 4. The models in the ICAD system are finite element models that may be solved to provide data for many different types of analyses, such as computing displacements of nodes due to various loading conditions. These models have traditionally been solved using direct solution methods; an alternative is to solve them using an iterative solution method in combination with parallel processing. With the iterative solution method, each node repeatedly:
- Communicates with neighbor nodes to get their current displacement, and then
- Calculates a new displacement based on those values.

The iteration continues until the solution converges to the final displacement values. If each individual node is assigned to a distinct processor, and all the nodes solve for new displacements in parallel, the communication overhead exceeds the speedup due to parallel processing. A better solution is to assign a region of nodes to a processor, so that some of the neighbor node displacement values are found in local memory, and only the boundary nodes require communication with other processors. SPE models quantify the optimal parallelism for the model.

9.4.3 Spread-the-Load Principle

Definition When multiple processes require exclusive use of one or more resources, and must take turns accessing the resource, they will experience resource contention delays. You can reduce these resource contention delays if you can:

- Schedule the processes so that they do not use the resource at the same time, or
- Divide the resource so that the processes use distinct parts of the resource and thus do not need the *same* resource.

The Spread-the-Load Principle is:

Spread the load when possible by processing conflicting loads at different times or in different places.

This principle is similar to the Shared Resources Principle—they both address resource contention delay. The Shared Resources Principle reduces the delay by minimizing scheduling time and holding time. This principle reduces the delay by reducing the number of processes that need the resource at a given time and by reducing the amount of the resource that they need. In some cases there may be some overlap between the two principles. For example, by reducing the amount of the resource that concurrent processes need, we are also reducing the holding time.

Evaluating Spread-the-Load alternatives requires constructing and solving performance models to quantify the resource contention delays for each alternative.

Applications Consider a system that must periodically archive the contents of a memory-resident status table. Now, suppose that there are several processes that periodically update this status table. During the archive, exclusive access is required to the table—status updates must be suspended until the archive action is complete. We can spread the load by partitioning the status table and archiving each partition separately. For example, suppose the archive was planned to save the entire table once per hour. If we could partition the status table into thirds and archive one partition each 20 minutes, we could reduce the resource contention delays. The total work would be the same, but the queueing delays would be shorter, because fewer jobs will arrive during the (shorter) archive and be waiting to update.

9.5 Using the Principles

Constructing and solving the system model is discussed in Chapter 6.

It is possible to quantify the effects of the independent and the synergistic performance principles. For the independent principles (Centering, Fixing Point, Locality, and Processing Versus Frequency), a simple, back-of-the-envelope calculation is usually sufficient. Quantifying the effects of the synergistic principles requires constructing and solving a system model to assess contention delays and other contributing factors.

The existence of the principles is not enough to guarantee that you won't experience performance problems; you must use them effectively. The remainder of this section presents six aspects of effective use of the performance principles.

Components that are difficult to design may or may not be critical to performance. If they are not critical, applying the principles to them will have limited effect on performance.

> *Apply the principles to software components that are critical to performance.*

Principles that are applied to portions of a system without regard to the global performance may have a limited or even detrimental affect. SPE models quantify the net effect of improvements in one part of a system on the overall system performance.

> *Use performance models to quantify the effect of improvements on the overall performance to ensure that improvements are consistent with one another.*

It is almost always possible to further improve performance by applying these principles. However, you eventually reach a point of diminishing returns. Once you have reached your performance objectives, your development efforts are probably best spent in other ways. With well-defined performance objectives, you can stop when you meet the objectives; you do not need to attempt to achieve "optimum performance."

Apply the principles until you comply with well-defined performance objectives.

This example is described in Chapter 1, Example 1-2.

While the principles might suggest performance improvements that will help you reach your objectives, it is important to check that the cost of these improvements is reasonable. One performance engineering team evaluated a proposal that had a performance objective of 3 seconds to record information from a telecommunication switch in a database. They found that it was possible to achieve this objective, but only by using 20 new mainframe computers (which would require four new data centers). Obviously, 3 seconds was not a cost-effective performance objective.

Confirm that performance objectives are realistic and that it is cost effective to achieve them.

You will also find it easier to remember and apply these principles if you create a list of performance improvements that you have made to previous projects, and associate each with the principles. Others in your organization will also be able to understand them better and use them on future projects if you provide examples that are directly relevant to your application area.

Create a customized list of examples of each of the principles that is specific to your application domain. Publicize this list so others in your domain may benefit.

We use these principles to explain improvements that we find in systems we study. It helps others to develop performance intuition and thus apply it to future systems. Otherwise, developers may remember the specific instance of the improvement they use (e.g., increase the block size to 4K) rather than the Processing Versus Frequency Principle. The principle is far more important—you will not always want to use 4K in the future, but you will want to minimize the product of processing times frequency.

Document and explain performance improvements using the principles.

9.6 Summary

The nine performance principles presented in this chapter generalize and abstract the knowledge that experienced performance engineers use in constructing software systems. They help identify design alternatives that are likely to meet performance objectives. The principles are summarized in Table 9-1.

Table 9-1: Summary of the Principles for Performance-Oriented Design

Performance Objectives Principle	Define specific, quantitative, measurable performance objectives for performance scenarios.
Instrumenting Principle	Instrument systems as you build them to enable measurement and analysis of workload scenarios, resource requirements, and performance objective compliance.
Centering Principle	Identify the dominant workload functions and minimize their processing.
Fixing-Point Principle	For responsiveness, fixing should establish connections at the earliest feasible point in time, such that retaining the connection is cost-effective.
Locality Principle	Create actions, functions, and results that are close to physical computer resources.
Processing Versus Frequency Principle	Minimize the product of processing times frequency.
Shared Resources Principle	Share resources when possible. When exclusive access is required, minimize the sum of the holding time plus the scheduling time.
Parallel Processing Principle	Execute processing in parallel (only) when the processing speedup offsets communication overhead and resource contention delays.
Spread-the-Load Principle	Spread the load when possible by processing conflicting loads at different times or in different places.

You can use the SPE performance models to quantify the improvement that you achieve by applying each principle, and to help you select the appropriate alternative for those with trade-offs (such as Processing Versus Frequency).

To use the principles effectively, apply them to portions of the software that

- Are critical to performance
- Result in global improvements
- Attain realistic performance objectives

These are the general principles for performance-oriented design. The next chapters present some patterns that derive from them and some antipatterns that result from failure to properly apply the principles.

Chapter 10

Performance Patterns

Each problem that I solved became a rule which served afterwards to solve other problems.

—René Descartes (1596–1650)
Discours de la Methode

In This Chapter:

- Overview of patterns
- Performance patterns
- Examples

10.1 Overview

A pattern is a common solution to a problem that occurs in many different contexts. It provides a general solution that may be specialized for a particular context. Patterns capture expert knowledge about "best practices" in software design in a form that allows that knowledge to be reused and applied in the design of many different types of software.

Patterns address the problem of "reinventing the wheel." Over the years, software developers have solved essentially the same problem, albeit in different contexts, over and over again. Some of these solutions have stood the test of time, while others have not. Patterns capture these proven solutions and package them in a way that allows software designers to look up and reuse the solution in much the same fashion as engineers in other fields use design handbooks.

The use of patterns in software development has its roots in the work of Christopher Alexander, an architect. Alexander developed a pattern language for planning towns and designing the buildings within them [Alexander 1979]. A pattern language is a collection of patterns that may be combined to solve a range of problems within a given application domain, such as architecture or software development. Alexander's work codified much of what was, until then, implicit in the field of architecture and required years of experience to learn.

Patterns are typically presented by describing a context, a problem, and a solution. The pattern establishes a relationship between these three elements. As Alexander wrote:

> Each pattern describes a problem which occurs over and over again in our environment, and then describes the core of the solution to that problem, in such a way that you can use this solution a million times over, without ever doing it the same way twice. [Alexander et al. 1977]

In the late 1980s, several people in the software development community began to apply Alexander's ideas to software. The first book on patterns, *Design Patterns: Elements of Reusable Object-Oriented Software*, by Erich Gamma, Richard Helm, Ralph Johnson, and John Vlissides (the Gang of Four) was very influential [Gamma et al. 1995]. A number of other books on this topic have appeared since.

The Proxy pattern is described in the next section.

In addition to capturing design expertise and providing solutions to common design problems, patterns are valuable because they identify abstractions that are at a higher level than individual classes and objects. Now, instead of discussing software construction in terms of building blocks such as lines of code or individual objects, we can talk about structuring software using patterns. For example, when we discuss using the Proxy pattern to solve a problem, we are describing a building block that includes several classes as well as the interactions among them.

Patterns have been described for several different categories of software development problems and solutions, including software architecture, design, and the software development process itself.

This chapter explores patterns from a performance perspective. The performance patterns presented here describe best practices for producing responsive, scalable software. We present seven *performance patterns*—new patterns that specifically address performance and scalability. These performance patterns complement and extend the performance principles presented in the previous chapter. Each performance pattern is a realization of one or more of the performance principles.

The Fast Path pattern is discussed in Section 10.2.

Performance patterns are at a higher level of abstraction than design patterns, such as those presented by Gamma [Gamma et al. 1995]. They are, however, closely related. A design pattern may provide an implementation of a performance pattern. For example, our Fast Path performance pattern is a realization of the Centering Principle. The Proxy pattern from Gamma can be used to implement the Fast Path in some contexts [Gamma et al. 1995]. Because these performance patterns are at a higher level of abstraction than design patterns, it is not appropriate to present class diagrams for them. Classes and their interactions can only be determined once a particular implementation of the performance pattern has been selected.

This chapter presents seven performance patterns. Each pattern is defined using a standard template:

- Name: The title of the subsection
- Problem: What is motivating us to apply this pattern?
- Solution: How do we solve the problem?
- Benefits: What are the potential positive outcomes of applying this pattern?
- Consequences: What are the potential shortcomings and consequences of applying this pattern?

10.2 Fast Path

This pattern is concerned with improving response times by reducing the amount of processing required for dominant workloads. Everyone has experienced those annoying automated telephone systems that ask you to press "1" for something that you have absolutely no interest in, "2" for something you never want to pursue, and so on until, finally, after eight or nine steps, you get to what you are really looking for. Then you get to repeat these steps through several more annoying menus. The Fast Path applied to these systems would order the choices by anticipated frequency of use. Then you would be more likely to hear your choice more quickly, and be routed to the appropriate agent without having to go through extra menus.

10.2.1 Problem

Even though an application may implement a large number of functions, we typically find that only a few are used most often. These functions constitute the *dominant workload* for the application, and typically account for most of the resource usage. For example, while an ATM may provide the capability of making deposits, checking your balance, or even buying postage stamps, by far the most frequent use of an ATM is for making a withdrawal from a checking account. These dominant workload functions can have a significant impact on the overall performance of the system.

10.2.2 Solution

The Centering Principle is discussed in Chapter 9.

The Centering Principle tells us to minimize the processing for these dominant workload functions. One way to minimize their processing is to create alternative, streamlined execution paths for them. An alternative path is known as a Fast Path.

A Fast Path in a software application is similar to an express train that stops only at the most important stations along the route. A local train is still available if you need one of the intermediate stations. However, if your stop is a major station, you save time by taking the express train.

In the ATM, it makes sense to provide a Fast Path for withdrawals by allowing a user to press a single key to select a withdrawal of a predetermined amount, without having to enter the transaction type, account, and amount (e.g., withdraw $60 from checking). The amounts offered on the menu (e.g., $40, $60, $100) should be determined by examining historical records for withdrawals (either from the manual system or from a previous incarnation of the ATM). Future systems might permit users to specify preferences such as the typical amount for a withdrawal, and perhaps specify a GetBalance with an option to proceed with the withdrawal or do something else. Then ATM customers could select a "give me the usual" transaction with one selection.

Another example is to minimize the number of screens that you must traverse on a Web site to accomplish your end-to-end task. You have probably visited many Web sites that failed to apply Fast Path. An on-line investment service at one time provided a good example of Fast Path. After logging on, it presented a display of exactly the right combination of data for a portfolio. Unfortunately, the system was subsequently revised, and two key pieces of information (purchase date for each position and cash balance) were removed. To get the other two data items now requires traversing four more pages! We present a similar, more detailed example of improving a Web site with Fast Path in Chapter 13.

Another way to implement Fast Path is to recognize that some data is needed far more frequently than other data, and to minimize the processing required to obtain it. For example, prices for the most frequently traded stocks should be cached to minimize the time required to obtain them.

In their book on design patterns, the Gang of Four [Gamma et al. 1995] use an example for the Proxy pattern that illustrates how this pattern can be used to implement a Fast Path. Suppose that you are building an editor for documents that will include both text and graphic images (which are stored in separate files). Examination of the use cases for the editor shows that all of the critical ones include opening the document. While opening a document isn't necessarily the most frequently used function, if it is too slow, the editor won't be used. Thus, this is a dominant workload and, therefore, a candidate for a Fast Path.

One way to apply the Fast Path pattern to the editor is to load a graphic image only when it first becomes visible. This will save considerable processing since most images will not be visible when the document is first loaded. We will need to know the sizes of all of the images when the document is loaded, however, in order to set pagination and other layout details properly.

The use of collaborations to model design patterns is discussed by Booch [Booch et al. 1999].

The Proxy pattern provides an elegant implementation of the Fast Path pattern in this context. The collaboration in Figure 10-1 illustrates the structure of this solution.

Here, the Editor interacts with an ImageProxy object that serves as a surrogate for the actual Image object. The Editor accesses the Image through the ImageProxy. When the document is initially loaded, the Image is not loaded from its file. The ImageProxy provides the size information (getExtent()) so that the Editor can perform document layout. When the Image appears on screen for the first time, the ImageProxy loads it and forwards the draw() request.

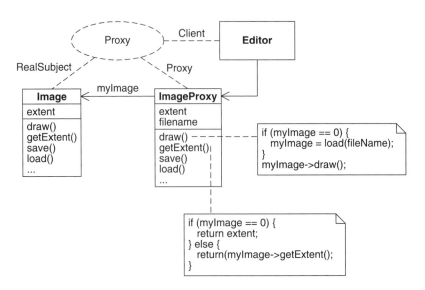

Figure 10-1: Proxy Collaboration

The Fast Path solutions are based on the Centering Principle. The other principles provide ways to streamline the Fast Path. For example, the solution for the excessive Web page problem embodies the Fixing-Point Principle in that it fixes the information on one screen. It also uses the Locality Principle by combining information likely to be needed together. And, it uses the Processing Versus Frequency Principle by minimizing the processing required for the frequent task of displaying key portfolio information.

10.2.3 Benefits

Using a Fast Path reduces the response time for dominant workload functions by reducing the amount of processing required for the most frequent uses of the software. It also reduces the overall load on the system by avoiding some resource consumption. This can, in turn, improve the responsiveness of other functions as well.

10.2.4 Consequences

It is not enough to recognize the need for the Fast Path you must also ensure that it is likely to be used. For example, an ATM that uses a default amount of money for the quick withdrawal that does not match the amount needed by the majority of customers will not be used enough to derive the benefits. That is, if the default amount is $40 and most customers want $100, most customers will not use the quick withdrawal, thereby defeating its purpose.

Of course, usage patterns may change over time. For example, the amount of money requested in an ATM withdrawal may increase over time. Usage patterns may also vary in different environments. For example, the average amount of withdrawals may be lower in a university area than in an expensive shopping area or a casino.

 Use the Instrumenting Principle to monitor usage patterns, and adapt your system to changing patterns.

10.3 First Things First

> Things which matter most should never be at the mercy of things which matter least.
>
> —Goethe

We've all had the experience of being overworked—too many things to do and not enough time to do them. Some of us try to do everything anyway, with the result that nothing gets done well. Others realize that some things are more important and focus on them, letting less important tasks fall by the wayside. Experts in time management advise that you decide what is important and focus on it; in other words, put first things first.

The First Things First pattern uses this strategy to focus on the important processing tasks to ensure that, if everything cannot be completed within the time available, then the least important tasks will be the ones omitted.

10.3.1 Problem

There are many different situations in which a transient overload may temporarily overwhelm the processing capacity of a system. For example, in online trading, high market volatility may generate a burst of activity. Or, in an embedded real-time system, input events may exhibit bursty behavior. In both cases, the temporary overload may cause input data to be lost or response times to be unacceptably slow. In the case of online trading systems, the losses are financial. With embedded real-time systems, the result may be injury, loss of life or property, or damage to the environment.

The problem is illustrated by a radar tracking system [Clark et al. 1999], [Wheeler et al. 1998]. In their original application, tracks were processed in first-in-first-out (FIFO) order. When track processing capacity was exceeded, those at the end of the queue were not processed. Because the tracks in a sensor report usually come in the same order, whole regions of the operator display might not be updated in overload conditions. This was a potentially disastrous situation because there is no correlation between important regions of the sky and the arrival order of sensor reports.

10.3.2 Solution

The solution in software systems is the same as in personal time management: Prioritize tasks and perform the most important ones first. Assign each logical task, such as processing an input event, to a physical task (either a process or a thread). Then assign high priorities to the most important tasks and lower priorities to those that are less important.

Assign priorities to tasks and execute them so that the most important activities receive preference.

Note: Some operating systems use higher numbers to denote higher priority, while others use lower numbers to indicate higher priority. Be sure that you are assigning priorities correctly for your execution environment.

In a financial transaction clearing application, some transactions, such as transactions for billions of dollars, are more important than others. To handle this situation with First Things First, you might assign transactions over a designated amount to a high-priority process that handles the transaction immediately, while others would be assigned to lower-priority processes, depending on their importance.

Priorities may be assigned statically (i.e., at design time) or dynamically (i.e., at run time). In the radar tracking system, the First Things First solution was to compute a value for each track as it was identified, and then use a scheduling algorithm that maximizes the value of work completed to ensure that the most important tracks are up to date.

Rate Monotonic Analysis is discussed briefly in Chapter 14.

When there are multiple tasks that must all be completed, Rate Monotonic Analysis [Klein et al. 1993] will help you determine whether this is possible, given the frequency with which the tasks occur and the amount of processing they require.

First Things First uses the Centering Principle to focus attention on the most important work.

10.3.3 Benefits
First Things First focuses attention on the most important tasks and ensures that they complete. When overloading conditions arise, the system gracefully degrades and gracefully improves as the conditions improve. This maximizes the quality of service of the system and improves scalability.

10.3.4 Consequences
First Things First is only appropriate if the overload is temporary. If there are not periods of lower demand, the system will be unable to catch up, and low-priority tasks may be ignored forever. Even if the scheduler ensures that these low-priority tasks do not starve, processing them will come at the expense of higher-priority activities.

If the system is simply unable to handle the demand, the amount of processing required must be reduced by other means, or the processing environment must be upgraded to handle the load.

If the overload is not temporary, reduce the amount of processing required or upgrade the processing environment.

10.4 Coupling

For performance, we need to match the interface of an object with its most frequent uses. Swiss Army knives come with a large variety of tools in addition to a simple knife blade. One model even comes with a small saw. While this is useful for some tasks, such as tasks on short camping trips, you would probably prefer a chain saw to a Swiss Army knife, if cutting all your firewood for the winter is your task. The Coupling pattern addresses this situation.

10.4.1 Problem

Most classes provide accessor functions for data that may be requested. A customer account class CustAcct may provide getName(), getAddress(), and getZip() accessor functions. If a frequently used task is to create a mailing label, the Coupling pattern suggests a new accessor function such as getMailLabelInfo() to get all the information with one call, and thus reduce the number of interactions required.

The Coupling pattern is particularly important in distributed systems because the cost of remote calls is high. It is also significant for database systems because the cost of remote calls is compounded by the cost of the data access and the network transfer of possibly large result sets.

Many Web applications and other distributed systems query or update a database. In multi-tier architectures, the business logic often resides on one node, while the database resides on another; possibly a mainframe. This approach can provide enhanced flexibility, maintainability, and scalability over two-tier architectures. It can also exhibit poor responsiveness, however, due to latency for frequent remote database accesses. The Coupling pattern addresses that problem.

Consider a distributed application that uses a "back-end" relational database. One way to provide an object-oriented interface to this database is to use a class to represent each table. Each attribute in the table has corresponding accessor functions (getX() and setX() operations) in the class's interface. This produces a class structure that mirrors the physical database schema.

Making the class structure isomorphic (i.e., identical in form and structure) with the physical database schema can lead to performance problems. With an object for each table, the interaction between that application and the database is fine grained and, therefore, frequent. If the database is on a different node, this results in a large number of requests; each for a relatively small amount of data. These remote requests are expensive, degrading both performance and scalability.

Using a class structure that is identical to the physical schema also negatively impacts maintainability. Changes to the database schema require changes to the class structure. Because these objects are accessed remotely, the changes may be quite complex, depending on the type of middleware used.

10.4.2 Solution

The solution is to use more coarse-grained objects to eliminate frequent requests for small amounts of information. These coarse-grained objects are aggregations of the fine-grained objects that mirror the database schema. The best way of constructing the aggregation will depend on the access patterns for the data. Data that is frequently accessed at the same time should be grouped into an aggregation. Often, these aggregate objects will correspond to high-level business objects which have their own identity and life cycle, independent of other objects in the application.

Larman [Larman 2000] presents a version of the Coupling pattern for Enterprise JavaBeans (EJBs). EJBs are Java-based server-side components that provide services to remote clients. In the above example, the equivalent of mirroring the database would be to provide an entity bean (a shared persistent object associated with the underlying database) for each table in the database schema. The application would then access each bean to obtain data.

Communication between JavaBeans is expensive. It is not simple object-to-object communication. Instead, EJB communication takes place via the EJB server, even if the beans are contained in the same Java Virtual Machine (JVM). If the beans are in separate JVMs, then the communication is also a remote access.

Note: EJB servers that provide transaction management capabilities may reduce this communication cost somewhat.

To reduce the communication costs, entity beans are provided only for the aggregate objects. Ordinary Java objects are used for the fine-grained access. Then, the remote operations are coarse-grained while the fine-grained accesses use object-to-object communication within the same JVM.

The Coupling pattern is an example of using the Centering Principle to identify interfaces that should be streamlined. Then it uses the Locality Principle to combine information likely to be needed together. It also uses the Processing Versus Frequency Principle to minimize the total processing required for the interface.

10.4.3 Benefits

The Coupling pattern matches the business tasks to the processing required to accomplish them. The net result is to reduce the total resource requirements of the system, which provides better responsiveness and scalability. Matching the business tasks to the processing should also limit the changes to those that affect the business process. When changes are necessary, their impact should be localized as well.

10.4.4 Consequences

The payoff will be realized when the business processes are stable. If the underlying process is new, finding the right access patterns may require many changes to the interface, which is an undesirable situation.

 Start by identifying information that is stable, and use those objects to reduce the amount of communication overhead required to obtain data.

10.5 Batching

This pattern combines frequent requests for services to save the overhead of initialization, transmission, and termination processing for the request. You find a similar concept in discount warehouse stores. They can sell large packages of products at a lower price than individual packages because the overhead is less for packaging, order processing, inventory tracking, sales, and other costs.

10.5.1 Problem

The problem occurs when requested tasks require considerable overhead processing for initialization (such as constructor overhead, loading initial data, etc.), termination, and, in distributed systems, for transmitting data and requests. For very frequent tasks, the amount of time spent in overhead processing may exceed the amount of real processing on the system.

One frequent instance of the problem occurs when many rows are added to a database. The overhead that must occur is enormous for identifying the location for the new row, identifying indices that must be changed, and all the other database processing. Overhead is exacerbated when the database is on a remote processor, and middleware must execute every time an insert is requested.

The wasteBucks. com case study is discussed in Chapter 6.

We saw another example of this problem in the wasteBucks.com case study. The amount of processing for each item was very high, requiring many calls to remote processes. Another interesting example of this problem is in the back-end processing for wasteBucks.com, when items that are out of stock must be ordered from suppliers. The overhead for ordering each of the out-of-stock items individually would be very high, and the company would not be able to take advantage of volume discounts with individual orders.

Another prominent example occurred in a secure messaging system. Each message required encryption, and involved further overhead to ensure that the security level of the transmission link matched the security level of each message. The security-level check was required at each intermediate link. The amount of work required to transmit a secure message is far greater than that required to send a non-secure message of the same size.

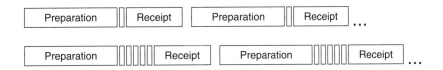

Figure 10-2: Batching Compared to Individual Items

Figure 10-2 illustrates the amounts of work required for overhead processing (preparation and receipt), compared to the amount of work required to transmit a request (the small rectangles) in general. Here, 10 requests can be sent with Batching in less time than three requests without Batching. The amount of processing for preparation and receipt varies, depending on the type of system, communication media, and so on; however, the relative gains will hold for all types of systems.

10.5.2 Solution

The solution to each of these types of problems is to combine the requests into batches so the overhead processing is executed once for the entire batch instead of for each individual item.

Batching can be performed by either the sender or the receiver of the request. With sender-side Batching, the sender collects requests and forwards the collection in one batch. This implementation is appropriate for the database insert problem, when the sender knows that many inserts are to be processed. Rather than sending each row individually, it may send 50 rows at a time. The performance improvement is most dramatic when the rows are to be inserted at the same location. However, even when the rows are sprinkled throughout the database, the overhead for sending the request to the database as well as for subsequent processing will be reduced when batches—rather than individual rows—are processed. Sender-side Batching was also the solution to the wasteBucks.com problem, grouping items into two batches—one for ready orders and another for back orders.

With receiver-side Batching, the receiver collects requests and, when a batch is received, begins the processing for all of them. This implementation would benefit the wasteBucks.com purchasing problem. Here, each request to order an item is added to a list, and when a sufficient number is received, the order for all items in the list is processed. This example may require multiple lists by suppliers, by types of items, and so on.

Receiver-side Batching is also the solution to the secure messaging system. As each message arrives, it is added to a group of messages that has the same security level. When a batch is complete (or when a threshold on delay time is reached), the security processing to match message batches to communication links is done for the entire batch.

Note: You can use the SPE models to determine an appropriate size for a batch. For example, in the wasteBucks.com case study, we modified the execution graph to reflect the processing time for a batch, rather than for individual items. This required decreasing the number of times the corresponding loops were executed, increasing the time required to send the (larger) message, and then solving the model. You would repeat this analysis for each candidate batch size, and select the one with the best overall results.

Be sure to evaluate the candidate batch sizes with the system model. For example, an individual scenario may perform best using a very large batch size, but that may cause excessive delays for other scenarios that must wait on these large messages before they are able to send their message. Therefore, evaluate the system model results to select a batch size that has a global increase in performance.

The Batching pattern uses the Processing Versus Frequency Principle to minimize the product of the processing times the frequency of requests. Batching does slightly more work per execution, but reduces the frequency of execution, thereby yielding a smaller product (than individual requests).

10.5.3 Benefits
The Batching pattern reduces the total amount of processing required for all tasks. Thus, because it reduces the total demand for resources, it improves responsiveness by reducing contention delays. Batching also improves scalability because reducing resource demand frees up resources to handle more requests. With Batching, the effect is that more requests can be processed using the same amount of work as would be required if requests were processed individually.

10.5.4 Consequences
Batching is appropriate for frequent tasks that require a large amount of overhead processing (relative to the processing required for the task itself). You need to understand the rate of requests to determine whether or not Batching is appropriate. For example, if your batch size is five and you discover (later) that an item is only ordered once per year, Batching is clearly inappropriate for that item. Similarly, there is no motivation to batch requests with little overhead, such as an operation invocation that can be in-lined. Batching is most effective when the amount of overhead and the frequency of requests are both high. Batching is also appropriate when the delay due to buffering requests does not cause a responsiveness problem for the requestor.

Use the SPE models to determine the proper batch size for the combination of frequency, overhead, and buffering delay.

10.6 Alternate Routes

This pattern spreads the demand for high-usage objects spatially; that is, to different objects or locations. The net result is to reduce contention delays for the objects. For example, if we learn about a traffic bottleneck on our route, such as a major construction project, we will try to find an alternate route to reach our destination that avoids the problem area.

10.6.1 Problem

This problem occurs frequently in database systems when many processes need exclusive access to the same physical location, usually to execute an update. It happens when new rows are all inserted at the end of the table, when the key is the date-time stamp of the arriving transaction, or when keys are assigned sequentially. When many processes must access the same physical location, the requests must serialize, causing delays for waiting processes. For database updates, the update must also modify the database indices as well as the new data rows, adding additional overhead. A poor choice for the data organization can exacerbate the situation by causing subsequent retrievals to search through overflow areas to find the correct row.

The Traffic Jam and One-Lane Bridge antipatterns are discussed in Chapter 11. The problem also happens when several processes must coordinate with a single concurrent process. In one particular project, we saw incoming processes receiving data, filtering it, and then passing it to another downstream process for further processing. There were many incoming processes, but only one downstream process. Under high loading conditions, the downstream process could not keep up with the load, causing a Traffic Jam.

Note: Another antipattern, the One-Lane Bridge, actually causes the Traffic Jam in these examples. One-Lane Bridge implies that only one process at a time may execute.

A third type of problem occurs when a single dispatching process receives inbound requests and determines which subsequent process is to handle the request. When the arrival rate of inbound requests exceeds a limit, congestion results.

10.6.2 Solution

The solution to these problems is to find an Alternate Route for the processing. There are several strategies for finding Alternate Routes.

In the database access situation, we need to find a way for the accesses to go to different physical locations.

A random selection algorithm is presented in Example 10-1.

- For a date-time stamp, select a hashing algorithm and use it to directly access several different "buckets."
- For sequentially assigned keys, try to use a different key assignment strategy, such as a random selection, from a set of predefined (future) keys. This gives distinct physical areas for the update. If you need to later access the rows in the order they were received, a secondary key or a pointer list can provide this capability.
- Another solution is to access different tables as the updates are executed, and then, at a non-critical time, to restructure the data as needed.

For the process coordination problems, we need to find a way to route requests to different processes. In the multiple-inbound-one-downstream case, we need to find a way to use multi-threaded downstream processes or multiple processes. In the project we mentioned, the reason for the single downstream process was to serialize updates to the RAM data bank. One Alternate Route solution would be to have multiple downstream processes, each one updating its own region of the database.

For the one-inbound dispatcher problem, Alternate Routes suggests using multiple instances of the dispatcher. Some inbound requests are routed to one dispatcher, others to another dispatcher.

On one of our projects, the architecture had such a dispatcher process that routed requests to the appropriate object to handle the request. Over time, the system grew into a distributed system with key objects residing on the primary server, and less important tasks, such as hourly reports, allocated to a "back-end" server. The dispatcher resided on the primary server. The problem with the resulting structure was that less important tasks (the hourly reports) unnecessarily consumed resources

Example 10-1: Random selection algorithm

Most development environments provide a (pseudo) random number generator. In C++ there is a C function rand() that returns an integer value in the range 0-32767. You can use that function to return a value that is uniformly distributed between two values a and b with the following code:

```
double myValue(double a, double b)
{
    double prob, maxval = 32767;
    // generate a probability between 0 and 1
    prob = rand() / maxval;
    return (a + (b - a) * prob);
}
```

You could call a routine similar to this to generate random choices for starting times within a particular time interval. For example, if you want a starting time uniformly distributed over a 15-minute interval, you set a equal to 0 and b equal to 15. This example returns a double precision result for myValue. If you want an integer number of minutes, you will have to modify the code to either truncate or round the result. The system version of the random number generator is probably sufficient for applications such as this. For "industrial strength" mathematical applications, you may want to substitute a better random number generator algorithm from the literature.

on the primary server to determine that the request should be routed to the back-end server, and to transmit the resulting report data from the back-end server to the user requesting the report. An Alternate Route solution is to route the report tasks directly to the back-end server. On this project it was easy to do, because the report-requesting users were a subset of the total users, and they did not need the other functions provided by the primary server. In this case, they could just call a dispatcher process on the back-end server directly.

These solutions all are instances of the Spread-the-Load Principle. They spread the load spatially by routing database accesses to different areas of the database and routing processing tasks to different processes.

10.6.3 Benefits

Alternate Routes reduces delays due to serialization. This improves both responsiveness and scalability. More importantly, Alternate Routes reduces the variability in performance. The perception of quality of service is worse when performance is sometimes fine but at other times unacceptable. This is particularly true when there is no obvious reason for the differences.

10.6.4 Consequences

Alternate Routes has the same problem as the traffic example used at the beginning of this section: If everyone takes the same alternate route, you have the potential to create a new bottleneck on the alternate route. Thus, you must use a strategy that effectively spreads the load spatially.

Make sure that your Alternate Route effectively spreads the load spatially.

10.7 Flex Time

In many cities, the sheer volume of traffic during morning and afternoon rush hours creates traffic jams. The drive to work gets longer and longer as more and more automobiles crowd the highways. To deal with this problem, many companies have introduced a "flex-time" policy for their employees. This policy allows employees to come to work earlier (or later) and leave earlier (or later) to avoid peak times of traffic congestion.

The Flex Time pattern spreads the demand for high-usage objects temporally; that is, to a different period of time. The net result is to reduce contention delays for the objects. For example, if there is a traffic bottleneck on our route, we could try to find a time of day when the traffic is light, rather than taking an alternate route. Thus, this pattern complements the Alternate Routes pattern by spreading the load temporally rather than spatially.

10.7.1 Problem

The Traffic Jam antipattern is discussed in Chapter 11.

This type of problem typically occurs when processing is required at a particular frequency, or at a particular time of day. When many reports are required at approximately the same time of day, the surge in demand results in sluggish responses. For example, stock analysts may wish to see a report on the previous day's market activity when they first arrive in the morning. If all analysts request the report within the same 10-minute interval, they will either experience sluggish performance or you will need to over-size the hardware to support this temporary burst in activity. This is an example of the Traffic Jam antipattern: There is too much work for the available resources.

A variation of this problem occurs when users are allowed to select the time of day when they want the reports, but are all given the same choices for time of day (e.g., every 15 minutes on the hour). This causes processing to occur in bursts every 15 minutes, with no requests between those intervals. This also artificially causes contention delays for processing.

The One-Lane Bridge antipattern is discussed in Chapter 11.

Consider another, similar, example—a system that collects data on activity in a service center and summarizes it in a (RAM) memory data bank. Periodically, the memory data bank is copied into an archival database; in this example it was every half-hour. While this archive cycle executes, the state of the memory data bank must be protected by postponing updates. Thus, the incoming work is temporarily halted. The problem occurs in periods of heavy loads when the queue of incoming work builds, and it takes a long time to clear this backlog and return to normal operating conditions. This is an example of the One-Lane Bridge antipattern because only one job at a time may proceed.

10.7.2 Solution

Identify the functions that execute repeatedly at regular, specific time intervals, and modify the time of their processing.

A Flex Time solution to the time-of-day problem is to move the processing to a different time of day. In the report generation example, we could schedule the reports to run any time after market close, store the report output, and either deliver the report from storage when it is requested, or perhaps direct the report to the analysts' printer during off-hours so it is waiting for them when they arrive.

A Flex Time solution to the processing-time-choice problem is to generate a random number for the selection choices (see Example 10-1). For example, we may still offer the choice for every 15 minutes, but one user may see intervals beginning on the hour, while another user would see intervals beginning at four minutes after the hour. This solution removes the bursts of activity and thus effectively applies the Spread-the-Load Principle.

The Processing versus Frequency Principle is discussed in Chapter 9.

One Flex Time solution to the periodic processing problem is to do less work more often. In the memory archive example, perhaps one-third of the data could be archived every 10 minutes. Of course, this depends on the data characteristics—you have to be able to partition the data so that the state is preserved. For example, if you need to archive an operator ID and the number of calls handled, you could not archive the operator ID in one cycle and the number of calls handled in the next cycle. But you could archive one-third of the operators and their calls in one cycle, and another third of the operators in the next cycle. This is an example of the Processing Versus Frequency trade-off.

All of these solutions apply the Spread-the-Load and the Shared Resources principles.

10.7.3 Benefits

Flex Time works by spreading the load temporally to reduce the congestion. In some cases, it reduces the amount of time that processes are blocked and cannot proceed. In other cases, it reduces the resource demand so that concurrent processes encounter fewer queueing delays for computer resources. Both aspects improve the overall responsiveness of the system.

10.7.4 Consequences

Most of the other patterns reduce the resource requirements of the software. Some of the Flex Time solutions actually require more processing, such as producing reports ahead of schedule and storing them until they are requested. The net effect is to reduce the time that processes wait in queues. Flex Time has the same potential problem as Alternate Routes. That is, if everyone chooses the same alternate time, you have a new bottleneck.

Make sure that not everyone chooses the same alternate time.

10.8 Slender Cyclic Functions

This pattern is concerned with processing that must execute at regular intervals. This type of processing is common in embedded real-time systems. For example, sensor readings occur at regular intervals, they are analyzed, and process control actions may be generated as a result. It also occurs in other systems, such as those that must generate reports at regular intervals or periodically archive data.

10.8.1 Problem

A cyclic or periodic function is characterized by its:

- *Period*: the amount of time between successive executions,
- *Execution time*: the amount of time required for the function to execute, and
- *Slack time*: the amount of time between the completion of execution and the end of the period.

Clearly, the execution time for a cyclic function must be less than its period. For example, if you have processing that must execute once every minute, it must require less than one minute for the processing to complete. If there is only one source of the event that triggers the cyclic function, the event occurs *exactly* once per minute, and there is no other processing to be performed. It does not matter how close to one minute the execution time is, as long as it is less than one minute.

Note: If the event does not occur *exactly* once per minute, things get more complicated. If the cycle time may vary (an aperiodic event), and the processing time is near one minute, you will have performance problems because there is a possibility that new processing may be required before the previous cycle is complete. In technical terms, the period must be deterministic if your execution time is close to the interarrival time.

The problem arises when there are concurrent sources of the event, or when there is other processing to be performed. If the deadline for handling each event is to be met, there must be sufficient slack time to allow the processing of other events, as well as any other work that must be performed. If the execution time is close to one minute, you will have difficulty meeting the deadline when the system becomes congested, or when unforeseen problems arise. The closer the processing requirement is to zero, the more room you have to scale gracefully.

10.8.2 Solution

Identify the functions that execute repeatedly at regular, specific time intervals, and minimize their processing requirements.

The example of archiving data from a RAM memory data bank to a database discussed under Flex Time also has a Slender Cyclic Function solution. The solution is to reduce the amount of time required for the archive. We need to streamline the extensive processing required to copy the memory data bank to the archival database. The processing is extensive because it is not a one-to-one copy; instead, it requires loading the data into multiple database tables and updating keys with each update. One way of reducing the processing is to take a quick snapshot of the real memory contents, copy them to another location in virtual memory, and then allow other work to proceed while you use the copy of the memory contents for the database update. Making a simple one-to-one copy takes far less time than the database update processing. Note that we have increased the overall processing time because we do both the one-to-one copy and the database updates. The net effect, however, is to reduce the time that inbound work must wait so the backlog does not build. This solution uses both the Centering Principle and the Shared Resources Principle.

Howes proposed a similar solution in his work on an Ada design methodology for real-time systems [Howes 1990]. His rule, to "reduce the mean service time of cyclic functions," is for a specific context. Slender Cyclic Functions applies in more general situations.

10.8.3 Benefits

With Slender Cyclic Functions, we reduce the processing requirements so that we have more resources available to share and thus reduce queueing delays. In the archive example, we minimize the time that processes must wait, so the backlog is smaller and takes less time to clear once we resume normal operating conditions. Thus we improve the overall responsiveness of the system and reduce the processing variability.

10.8.4 Consequences

Operating conditions may change over time. The cycle frequency may need to change, or the amount of processing per cycle may change.

 Instrument systems and monitor their performance over time for early warning of potential problems.

10.9 Summary

A pattern is a common solution to a problem that occurs in many different contexts. It provides a general solution that may be specialized for a

Table 10-1: Summary of Performance Patterns

Pattern	Description	Principle(s)
Fast Path	Identify dominant workload functions and streamline the processing to do only what is necessary	Centering
First Things First	Focus on the relative importance of processing tasks to ensure that the least important tasks will be the ones omitted if everything cannot be completed within the time available	Centering
Coupling	Match the interface to objects with their most frequent uses	Centering Locality Processing Versus Frequency
Batching	Combine requests into batches so the overhead processing is executed once for the entire batch instead of for each individual item	Processing Versus Frequency
Alternate Routes	Spread the demand for high-usage objects spatially, that is, to different objects or locations	Spread-the-Load
Flex Time	Spread the demand for high-usage objects temporally, that is, to different periods of time	Spread-the-Load
Slender Cyclic Functions	Minimize the amount of work that must execute at regular intervals	Centering

given context. Patterns capture expert knowledge about "best practices" in software design in a form that allows that knowledge to be reused and applied in the design of many different types of software. Patterns have been described for several different categories of software development problems and solutions, including software architecture, design, and the software development process itself.

This chapter has explored patterns from a performance perspective. The performance patterns presented here describe best practices for producing responsive software.

The seven performance patterns discussed in this chapter are summarized in Table 10-1.

Chapter 11

Performance Antipatterns

Learn from the mistakes of others. You don't have time to make them all yourself.

—Chinese Proverb

In This Chapter:

- Overview of antipatterns
- Performance antipatterns
- Refactoring to improve performance

11.1 Overview

Chapter 10 discussed performance patterns. This chapter discusses the related topic of performance antipatterns. Antipatterns [Brown et al. 1998] are conceptually similar to patterns in that they document recurring solutions to common design problems. They are known as *anti*patterns because their use (or misuse) produces negative consequences. Antipatterns document common mistakes made during software development. They also document solutions for these mistakes. Thus, antipatterns tell you what to avoid and how to fix a problem when you find it.

Performance patterns illustrate "best practice" approaches to achieving responsiveness and scalability. Performance antipatterns provide a complement to performance patterns by illustrating what not to do and how to fix a problem when you find it. A simple analogy from electrical engineering uses examples of series and parallel circuits (i.e., patterns) to illustrate how to build proper circuits, and an example of a short circuit (i.e., an antipattern) to show what to avoid. Both types of examples are needed to build performance intuition.

Antipatterns address software architecture and design, as well as the software development process itself. In many cases, antipatterns may be more useful than patterns. This is because they illustrate how to identify a bad situation *and* provide a way to rectify the problem. This approach is particularly useful for performance, since good performance is the absence of problems. By illustrating performance problems and their causes, performance antipatterns help build performance intuition.

Refactoring is discussed in detail in [Fowler 1999].

Antipatterns are refactored (restructured or reorganized) to overcome their negative consequences. A *refactoring* is a correctness-preserving transformation that improves the quality of the software. For example, a set of classes might be refactored to improve modifiability by moving common properties to an abstract superclass. The transformation does not alter the semantics of the application, but it may improve overall modifiability. Refactoring may be used to enhance many different quality attributes of software, including reusability, maintainability, and, of course, performance.

This chapter explores antipatterns from a performance perspective. We discuss performance problems associated with one well-known design antipattern, and show how to solve them. We also present three new performance antipatterns that occur frequently in software systems. Each of the antipatterns is defined in the following sections using this standard template:

- Name: the section title
- Problem: What is the recurrent situation that causes negative consequences?
- Solution: How can we avoid, minimize or refactor the antipattern?

11.2 The "god" Class

This antipattern is known by various names, including the "god" Class [Riel 1996] and the "blob" [Brown et al. 1998]. Both Riel and Brown et al. discuss the impact of this phenomenon on quality attributes such as modifiability and maintainability. The presence of a "god" Class in a design also has a negative impact on performance.

11.2.1 Problem

A "god" Class is one that performs most of the work of the system, relegating other classes to minor, supporting roles. A design containing a "god" Class is usually easy to recognize. It typically has a single, complex controller class (often with a name containing Controller or Manager) that is surrounded by simple classes that serve only as data containers. These classes typically contain only accessor and mutator operations (operations to get() and set() the data) and perform little or no computation of their own. The "god" Class obtains the information it needs using the get() operations belonging to these data classes, performs some computation, and then updates the data using the classes set() operations.

The following (very) simplified example illustrates the effects of a "god" Class. Consider an industrial process control application in which it is necessary to control the status of a valve (open or closed). Figure 11-1 shows a fragment of the class diagram for a possible design for this application. The Controller class in Figure 11-1 behaves like a "god" Class. The Valve class has no intelligence. It simply reports its status (open or closed) and responds to open() and close() operation invocations. The open() and close() operations in Valve simply set the appropriate value of status.

The Controller does all of the work: It requests information from the Valve, makes decisions, and tells the Valve what to do.

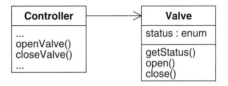

Figure 11-1: A "god" Class

The Controller class is tightly coupled to the Valve class and requires extra messages to perform an operation, as shown by the following code fragment:

```
void openValve() {
  status currentStatus;

  currentStatus = theValve->getStatus();
  if (currentStatus != open)
    theValve->open();
}
```

To open a valve, the controller must first request the valve's status, then check to see that it is not open and, finally, tell the valve to open. This operation requires two messages to open the valve: one to get the status and one to invoke the open() operation. Moreover, if the definition of status is changed in Valve, a corresponding change must be made in all of the applicable operations in Controller.

The solution can be refactored to reduce both the coupling between Controller and Valve and the number of messages required to perform an operation by moving the status check to the Valve class. Figure 11-2 shows the refactored class diagram.

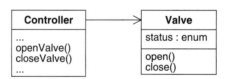

Figure 11-2: Refactored Solution

Now, the status check is in the Valve class (close to the data needed to perform the check). The openValve() operation in Controller is simply

```
void openValve() {
  theValve->open();
}
```

and the open() operation in Valve becomes

```
void open() {
  if (status != open)
    status = open;
}
```

There is also a variant of the "god" Class which, rather than performing all of the work, contains all of the system's data [Riel 1996]. The functions are then assigned to other classes. When one of the function classes needs data to perform an operation, it obtains it from the "god" Class via a get() operation and, if data needs to be updated, the function class updates it using a set() operation. Even though the data is encapsulated by accessor and mutator functions, the data form of the "god" Class is the moral equivalent of global data, or the common block in FORTRAN.

Both forms of the "god" Class are the result of poorly distributed system intelligence. A good rule of thumb when designing object-oriented systems is to keep related data and behavior in the same place. Both types of "god" Class violate this heuristic by assigning behavior to one class and the data needed to provide that behavior to another.

A "god" Class may creep into a design in several different ways. Behavioral "god" Classes are often the result of a procedural design that masquerades as an object-oriented one. "God" Classes are also often introduced while upgrading a legacy system to an object-oriented design. A behavioral "god" Class may be created when developers attempt to capture the central control mechanism in the original, procedural design. On the other hand, if the original system contained a large, global data structure, it is likely to appear as a data "god" Class in the new design.

From a performance perspective, a "god" Class creates problems by causing excessive message traffic. In the behavioral form of the problem, the excessive traffic occurs as the "god" Class requests and updates the data it needs to control the system from subordinate classes. In the data form, the problem is reversed, as subordinates request and update data in the "god" Class. In both cases, the number of messages required to perform a function is larger than it would be in a design that assigned related data and behavior to the same class.

The effect of a "god" Class on message traffic is shown clearly in a case study presented by Sharble and Cohen [Sharble and Cohen 1993]. They present two designs for an "Object-Oriented Brewery." One (Design 1) was produced using a data-driven design technique and contains a behavioral "god" Class. The other (Design 2) was produced using a responsibility-driven technique and corresponds to an appropriately refactored version of Design 1. The difference in the number of messages required by each design for various scenarios is shown in Figure 11-3.

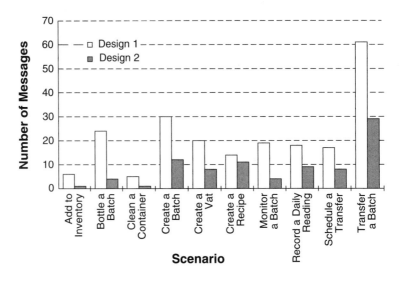

Figure 11-3: Message Counts for Scenarios [Sharble and Cohen 1993].

Sharble and Cohen were concerned with design metrics, such as coupling and cohesion, rather than with performance. They used message counts as a complexity measure. Viewed from a performance perspective, however, their data dramatically illustrates the performance impact of a "god" Class.

As Figure 11-3 shows, the number of messages required to accomplish a function is greater in every case for the design containing the "god" Class—sometimes by a factor of two or more. This excessive message traffic can degrade performance, and is especially problematic in distributed systems where an object of the "god" Class executes on a different processor than objects of its subordinate classes.

11.2.2 Solution

The solution to the "god" Class problem is to refactor the design to distribute intelligence uniformly across the top-level classes in the application. It is important to keep related data and behavior together. An object should have most of the data that it needs to make a decision.

Beware of either: 1) an object that must request lots of data from other objects and then update their states with the results, or 2) a group of objects that must access a common object to get and update the data that it deals with.

The Locality Principle is discussed in Chapter 9.

This solution to the "god" Class problem embodies the Locality Principle because an algorithm and the data that it requires are localized in the same object.

The performance gain for the refactored solution will be

$$T_s = M_s \times O$$

where T_s is the processing time saved, M_s is the number of messages saved, and O is the overhead per message. The amount of overhead for a message will depend on the type of call; for example, a local call will have less overhead than a remote procedure call.

11.3 Excessive Dynamic Allocation

With dynamic allocation, objects are created when they are first accessed (a sort of "just-in-time" approach) and then destroyed when they are no longer needed. This can often be a good approach to structuring a system, providing flexibility in highly dynamic situations. For example, in a graphics editor, it may be a very useful approach to create an instance of a shape (such as a circle or rectangle) when it is drawn, and then destroy the instance when the shape is deleted. Excessive Dynamic Allocation, however, addresses frequent, unnecessary creation and destruction of objects of the same class.

11.3.1 Problem

Dynamic allocation is expensive. Riel [Riel 1996] describes an object-oriented approach to designing a gas station in which, when your car needs gasoline, you pull over to the side of the road, buy a piece of land, build a gas station (which, in turn, builds pumps, and so on), and fill the tank. When you're done, you destroy the gas station and return the land to its original state. Clearly, this approach only works for the wealthy (and patient!). You certainly do not want to use this approach if you need gas frequently.

The situation is similar in object-oriented software systems. When an object is created, the memory to contain it (and any objects that it contains) must be allocated from the heap, and any initialization code for the object and the contained objects must be executed. When the object is no longer needed, necessary clean-up must be performed, and the reclaimed memory must be returned to the heap to avoid "memory leaks." While the overhead for creating and destroying a single object may be small, the performance impact may be significant when a large number of objects are frequently created and then destroyed.

A call processing case study is provided in Chapter 14. This example was one of the performance failures cited in Chapter 1.

The sequence diagram in Figure 11-4 illustrates Excessive Dynamic Allocation. This example is drawn from a call processing application in which, when a customer lifts the telephone handset (an offHook event), the switch creates a Call object to manage the call. When the call is completed (an onHook event), the Call object is destroyed. (Details of the call processing are provided in the sequence diagram referenced by handleCall, which is not shown here.)

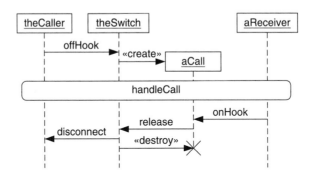

Figure 11-4: Excessive Dynamic Allocation

While constructing a single Call object may not seem excessive, a Call is a complex object that contains several other objects that must also be created. In addition, a switch can receive hundreds of thousands of offHook events each hour. In a case like this, the overhead for dynamically allocating call objects adds substantial delays to the time needed to complete a call.

The cost of dynamic allocation, C, is

$$C = N \times \sum_{depth} (s_c + s_d)$$

where N is the number of calls, *depth* is the number of contained objects that must be created when the class is created, and s_c and s_d are the service time to create and to destroy the object, respectively.

Figure 11-5 shows the cost of Excessive Dynamic Allocation for some typical values of depth and S, the sum of the creation and destruction time. The figure shows how the overhead for dynamic allocation increases as the number of calls increases. Note that the graph shows the total service time for dynamic allocation, regardless of the number of processes handling these calls. Calls are multi-processed, so the response time depends on the number of processes and on contention delays among them. Reducing the service time, however, also reduces the response time.

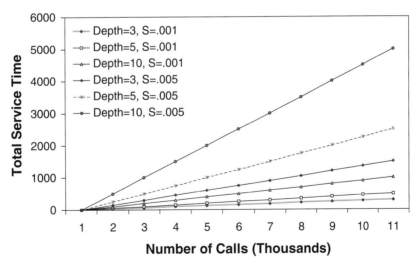

Figure 11-5: Cost of Excessive Dynamic Allocation

11.3.2 Solution

There are two possible solutions to problems introduced by Excessive Dynamic Allocation.

The first is to "recycle" objects rather than to create new ones each time they are needed. This approach pre-allocates a "pool" of objects and stores them in a collection. New instances of the object are requested from the pool, and unneeded instances are returned to it. This approach is useful for systems that continually need many short-lived objects (like the call processing application). You pay for pre-allocating the objects at system initialization but reduce the run-time overhead to simply passing a pointer to the pre-allocated object.

> *Eliminate the need for object creation and destruction by "recycling" objects from a pool.*

The Processing Versus Frequency Principle is discussed in Chapter 9.

This is an application of the Processing Versus Frequency Principle—we minimize the product of the amount of processing times the frequency that it is performed. Returning unused objects to the pool eliminates garbage collection overhead and possible memory leaks.

Another way to refactor the Excessive Dynamic Allocation antipattern is to share objects rather than create new ones.

> *Use sharing to eliminate the need to create new objects.*

An example of this approach is the use of the Flyweight pattern [Gamma et al. 1995] to allow all clients to share a single instance of the object. An application of the Flyweight pattern to alleviate Excessive Dynamic Allocation in the ICAD example appears in Chapter 4.

The first improvement approach affects the cost in Figure 11-5 by reducing the service time, S, to the time to allocate/return an object from the pool, and by changing the depth to 1 because the pre-allocated objects have already created the subordinate objects. The improvement for the second approach is similar.

11.4 Circuitous Treasure Hunt

Do you remember the child's treasure hunt game that starts with a clue that leads to a location where the next clue is hidden, and so on, until the "treasure" is finally located? The antipattern analogy is typically found in database applications. Software retrieves data from a first table, uses those results to search a second table, retrieves data from that table, and so on, until the "ultimate results" are obtained.

11.4.1 Problem

The impact on performance is the large amount of database processing required each time the "ultimate results" are needed. It is especially problematic when the data is on a remote server, and each access requires transmitting all the intermediate queries and their results via a network, and perhaps through middleware and other servers in a multi-tier environment.

The ICAD application is introduced in Chapter 4.

The ICAD application illustrates this antipattern. The application allows engineers to construct and view drawings that model structures, such as aircraft wings. A model is stored in a relational database, and several versions of the model may exist within the database.

Figure 11-6 shows a portion of the ICAD class diagram with the relevant classes. A model consists of elements that may be: beams, which connect two nodes; triangles, which connect three nodes; or plates, which connect four or more nodes. A node is defined by its position in three-dimensional space (x, y, z). Additional data is associated with each type of element to allow solution of the engineer's model.

This example focuses on the DrawMod scenario in which a model is retrieved from the database and drawn on the screen. Figure 11-7 shows a sequence diagram for this scenario. A typical model consists of 2,000 beams and 1,500 nodes (a single node may be connected to as many as four beams). The software first finds the model ID, then uses it to find the beams, and repeats the sequence of steps to retrieve each beam row, using the node number from the beam row to find and then retrieve the node row (which contains the "ultimate results"—the node coordinates). This information is then used to draw the model. For a typical DrawMod scenario, there are 6,001 database calls: 1 for the model, 2,000 for the beams, and 4,000 for the nodes.

A large number of database calls causes the most serious performance problems in systems with remote database accesses due to the cost of the remote access, the processing of the query, and the network transfer of all the intermediate results.

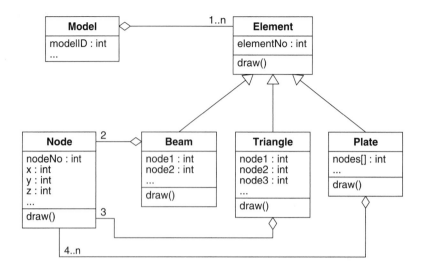

Figure 11-6: ICAD Classes and Associations

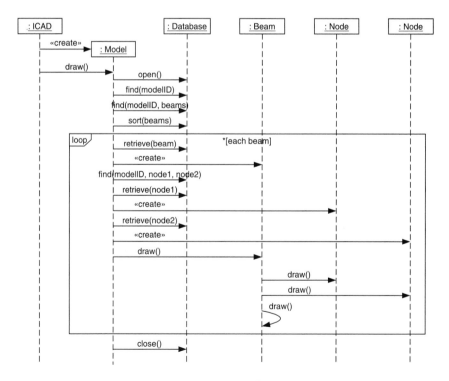

Figure 11-7: DrawMod Example of Circuitous Treasure Hunt

Another instance of the antipattern is also found in object-oriented systems, where operations have large "response sets." In this case, one object invokes an operation in another object, that object then invokes an operation in another object, and so on, until the "ultimate result" is achieved. Then, each operation returns, one by one, to the object that made the original call.

The performance impact is the extra processing required to identify the final operation to be called and invoking it, especially in distributed object systems where objects may reside in other processes and on other processors. When the invocation causes the intermediate objects to be created and destroyed, the performance impact is even greater. This behavior also has poor memory locality because each context switch may cause the working set of the called object to be loaded. The working sets of intermediate objects may need to be reloaded later when the return executes.

The class diagram in Figure 11-6 shows a simple example. Suppose that the model data has been retrieved from the database and is now contained within each object. Then the Model object must determine each Beam object to call (from the association to Beam, probably a table of pointers), and each Beam must determine which Node objects to call (from the association to Nodes). The Model calls the first Beam operation, then the Beam calls two Node operations, and so on.

11.4.2 Solution

If you find the database access problem early in development, you may have the option of selecting a different data organization. For example, the DrawMod database could store the node coordinates (x, y, z) in the beam table. The sequence diagram for the alternative database design appears in Figure 11-8. With the node coordinates in the beam row, the database call to find and retrieve nodes is unnecessary and is omitted. For a typical DrawMod scenario with 2,000 beams, there will be 4,000 fewer database calls.

 Select a data organization that puts the data close to where it will be used.

In general the number of calls saved will be

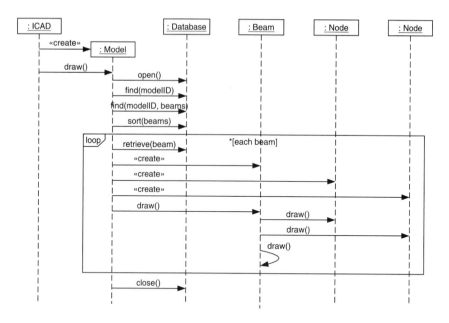

Figure 11-8: Refactored DrawMod Scenario

$$C_s = \prod_{j \,\in\, rootpath} a_j$$

where c_s is the total number of calls saved, a_j is the number of associated objects in the level below for each object in this level—for every object j between the object originally containing the "ultimate result" (the *leaf* class), and the object containing the "first clue" (the *root* class). For example, for the leaf class (Node) a_j is two nodes per beam, and for the intermediate class (Beam) a_j is 2,000 beams per model, so c_s is 4,000.

Note: There are some potential disadvantages to reorganizing the DrawMod data in this way. Optimizing the data organization for one scenario may degrade the performance of other scenarios. To determine the appropriateness of each alternative, the performance engineer will need to analyze the performance impact on other scenarios that use the database. It is unwise to optimize the database organization for a single scenario if it has a detrimental effect on all other scenarios; instead, you want the "globally optimal" solution for the key performance scenarios. To do so, you evaluate the overall performance by revising each scenario that is affected by the change and comparing the model solutions.

For distributed systems, if you cannot change the database organization, you can reduce the number of remote database calls by using the Adapter pattern [Gamma et al. 1995] to provide a more reasonable interface for remote calls. The Adapter would then make all the other (local) database calls required to retrieve the "ultimate result," and return only those results to the remote caller. This reduces the number of remote calls and the amount of data transferred, but it does not reduce the database processing.

For designs with large response sets, an alternative is to create a new association that leads directly to the "ultimate result." For example, in Figure 11-6 we would add an association between the Model class and the Node class. In the DrawMod scenario, this would reduce the number of operations called from 6,000 (2000 Beam calls plus 4,000 Node calls) to 1,500 (the number of Nodes per Model). The performance impact is substantial if these are remote calls that are made via middleware such as CORBA or DCOM.

11.5 The One-Lane Bridge

On the south island of New Zealand, there is a highway with many one-lane bridges; one of them is even shared with a train. This isn't a problem in New Zealand because there is light traffic in that part of the country. It would be a problem, though, if it were in Los Angeles.

11.5.1 Problem

The problem with a One-Lane Bridge is that traffic may only travel in one direction at a time; and, if there are multiple lanes of traffic all moving in parallel, they must merge and proceed across the bridge one vehicle at a time. This increases the time required to get a given number of vehicles across the bridge and can also cause long backups.

The software analogy to the One-Lane Bridge is a point in the execution where one, or only a few, processes may continue to execute concurrently. All other processes must wait. It frequently occurs in applications that access a database. Here, a lock ensures that only one process may update the associated portion of the database at a time. It may also occur when many processes make a synchronous call to another process that is not multi-threaded; all of the processes making synchronous calls must take turns "crossing the bridge."

The sequence diagram in Figure 11-9 illustrates the database variant of the One-Lane Bridge antipattern. Each order requires a database update for each item ordered. The structure selected for the database assigns a new order item number to each item, and inserts all items at the end of the table. If every new update must go to the same physical location, and all new items are "inserted," then the update behaves like a One-Lane Bridge because only one insert may proceed at a time; all others must wait. There is also a second problem in that these inserts are costly because they must update a database index for each key on the table.

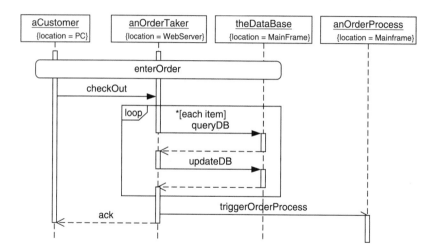

Figure 11-9: Database Contention Problem

Similar problems occur when the database key is a date-time stamp for an entity, or any key that increases monotonically. We have also seen this problem for periodic archives, where processing must halt while state information is transferred to long-term storage.

11.5.2 Solution

With vehicular traffic, you alleviate the congestion caused by a One-Lane Bridge by constructing multiple lanes, constructing additional bridges (or other alternatives), or rerouting traffic.

Provide additional paths to reduce traffic on the One-Lane Bridge.

The analogous solutions in the database update example above would be:

- Use an algorithm for assigning new database keys that results in a "random" location for inserts,
- Use multiple tables that may be consolidated later, or
- Use another alternative such as pre-loading "empty" database rows, and selecting a location to update that minimizes conflicts.

For example, an alternative for assigning date-time keys is to use multiple "buckets" for inserts and a hashing algorithm to assign new inserts to the "buckets."

Reducing the amount of time required to cross the bridge also helps relieve congestion. One way to do this is to find alternatives for performing the update. For example, if the update must change multiple tables, it would be better to select a different data organization in which the update could be processed in a single table.

For the database example above, the magnitude of the improvement depends on the intensity of new item orders and the service time for performing updates. The relationship is:

$$RT = \frac{S}{1 - XS}$$

where RT is the residence time (elapsed time for performing the update), S is the service time for performing updates, and X is the arrival rate.

Figure 11-10 shows a comparison of the residence time for various arrival rates for two different service times. The first curve assumes the service time for the update is 10 milliseconds (thus, the arrival rate of update requests must be less than 100 requests per second), and shows how the residence time increases as the arrival rate approaches the maximum. The second curve shows the improvement if the update service time is reduced by 1 millisecond! The figure illustrates the improvement achievable by reducing the service time (the time required to cross the bridge). If you change the structure of the database so that you update in multiple locations (so fewer processes wait for each update), this is equivalent to reducing the arrival rate—and the figure also shows the relative benefit of this alternative.

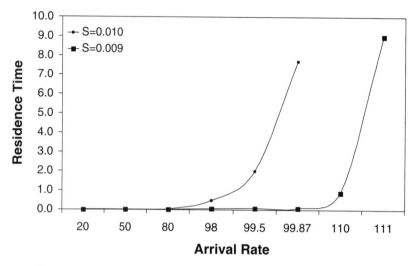

Figure 11-10: Performance Impact of the One-Lane Bridge

Figure 11-10 also illustrates the relative importance of the One-Lane Bridge antipattern: If the intensity of requests for the service is high, it may be a significant barrier to achieving responsiveness and scalability requirements.

The Shared Resources Principle is discussed in Chapter 9.

This solution to the One-Lane Bridge problem embodies the Shared Resources Principle, because responsiveness improves when we minimize the scheduling time plus the holding time. Holding time is reduced by reducing the service time for the One-Lane Bridge, and by rerouting the work.

11.6 Traffic Jam

Have you ever been stuck in a traffic jam on a highway where traffic initially inches along, then goes slightly faster, and then inches along again? Suddenly, you notice that traffic ahead is moving at normal speeds, and there is no sign of the original problem that caused the jam. It is long gone. This same antipattern occurs in software systems. It is often caused by the One-Lane Bridge, but there are other sources as well.

11.6.1 Problem

The performance impact of the Traffic Jam is the transient behavior that produces wide variability in response time. Sometimes it is fine, but at other times, it is unacceptably long. The cause of the problem is seldom visible to users who thus find it even more frustrating.

The problem often occurs when the One-Lane Bridge, or some other cause, produces a large backlog in jobs waiting for service, whereupon it takes a long time to return to "normal" operating conditions. The problem also occurs when a large amount of work is scheduled within a relatively small interval. It occurs, for example, when every user needs a report at approximately the same time, or when stock market activity triggers a sudden surge in trading activity. There are many other, similar circumstances.

11.6.2 Solution

If the problem is caused by the One-Lane Bridge, the solution to that antipattern will reduce the effect of the Traffic Jam.

The Spread-the-Load Principle is discussed in Chapter 9. The Alternative Routes and Flex Time patterns are discussed in Chapter 10.

If the problem is caused by periodic high demand, you should seek alternatives that spread the load, or handle the demand in a different manner. You can accomplish this by using either the Alternative Routes pattern or the Flex Time pattern.

For example, if users select the time for a report to be generated, change the selection options so that they select a time interval rather than selecting a specific time. This gives the software more flexibility in scheduling the reports to reduce contention. If that isn't possible, make sure that the user interface doesn't encourage everyone to select the same default value. You can do this by generating a random number for the default time (e.g., instead of always displaying 7:00 a.m., generate a random time between 6:50 a.m. and 7:10 a.m. and display this as the default value). A random selection algorithm is provided in Example 10-1.

If the problem is caused by external factors such as stock market behavior, there isn't much that you can do in the software other than use SPE techniques to identify the most important workloads, and then streamline their processing as much as possible. Use the models to determine the size of the platforms and network that will be required to support the worst-case workload intensity. For extremely important workloads, you may need to size the execution environment so that it is lightly used under normal conditions.

 Know the limits of scalability of the system before you build it, and plan for handling overload situations smoothly.

11.7 Summary

This chapter has explored antipatterns from a performance perspective. Antipatterns [Brown et al. 1998] are conceptually similar to patterns, in that they document recurring solutions to common design problems. They are known as *anti*patterns because their use (or misuse) produces negative consequences. Antipatterns document common mistakes made during software development. They also document solutions for these mistakes. Thus, antipatterns tell you what to avoid and how to fix a problem when you find it. By illustrating performance problems and their causes, performance antipatterns help build performance intuition.

Antipatterns are refactored (restructured or reorganized) to overcome their negative consequences. A *refactoring* improves one or more characteristics of the software (e.g., performance or reusability) while preserving its original functionality.

The performance antipatterns discussed in this chapter are summarized in Table 11-1. All of the antipatterns may violate the Centering Princi-

Table 11-1: Performance Antipatterns

Antipattern	Problem	Solution	Principle Violated
"god" Class	Occurs when a single class either 1) performs all of the work of an application or 2) holds all of the application's data. Either manifestation results in excessive message traffic that can degrade performance.	Refactor the design to distribute intelligence uniformly over the application's top-level classes, and to keep related data and behavior together.	Locality Processing Versus Frequency

Table 11-1: Performance Antipatterns

Antipattern	Problem	Solution	Principle Violated
Excessive Dynamic Allocation	Occurs when an application unnecessarily creates and destroys large numbers of objects during its execution. The overhead required to create and destroy these objects has a negative impact on performance.	1) "Recycle" objects (via an object "pool") rather than creating new ones each time they are needed. 2) Use the Flyweight pattern to eliminate the need to create new objects.	Fixing-Point Locality Processing Versus Frequency
Circuitous Treasure Hunt	Occurs when an object must look in several places to find the information that it needs. If a large amount of processing is required for each "look," performance will suffer.	Refactor the design to provide alternative access paths that do not require a Circuitous Treasure Hunt (or to reduce the cost of each "look").	Locality Fixing-Point
One-Lane Bridge	Occurs at a point in execution where only one, or a few, processes may continue to execute concurrently (e.g., when accessing a database). Other processes are delayed while they wait for their turn.	To alleviate the congestion, use the Shared Resources Principle to minimize conflicts.	Shared Resources Spread-the-Load
Traffic Jam	Occurs when one problem causes a backlog of jobs that produces wide variability in response time which persists long after the problem has disappeared.	Begin by eliminating the original cause of the backlog. If this is not possible, provide sufficient processing power to handle the worst-case load.	Shared Resources Spread-the-Load

ple if they occur in the dominant workload functions. The Traffic Jam may be caused by violating the principles listed. It may also simply be due to the sheer intensity of the work that must be processed.

Chapter 12

Implementation Solutions

You have not had thirty years' experience...You have had one year's experience thirty times.

—J. L. Carr

In This Chapter:
- Performance tuning strategy
- General and object-oriented performance solutions
- Language-independent solutions
- Java and C++ solutions

12.1 Overview

So far, this book has focused on SPE techniques that are used during the early life cycle phases (e.g., inception and elaboration) to help prevent performance problems. There are two principal reasons for focusing on early life cycle activities.

1. Performance improvements made at the architecture and design stage have a far greater impact on responsiveness and scalability than those made during implementation.

2. Problems introduced at the architecture and design levels are extremely difficult to correct once the software has been implemented.

309

Having a sound, performance-oriented architecture is essential to achieving responsiveness and scalability. If you have a poor architecture or design, it is unlikely that any amount of clever coding will allow you to achieve your performance objectives. In an ideal world, getting the architecture and design right would be all that is necessary. Once you had constructed and solved the SPE models to verify that your proposed architecture and design would meet your performance objectives, most of your work would be done. Your primary focus during the later phases of development would be to monitor the evolving software to confirm that the performance was as predicted, or to detect and correct any deviations that arose.

The real world is seldom so cooperative, however. While having a good architecture and design are essential, having them does not guarantee that you will achieve your performance objectives. For many systems, it is simply not possible to ignore implementation choices and coding details. There are a number of pitfalls that can result in a good architecture and design having poor performance, if you make the wrong implementation or coding choices. Thus, a sound architecture and design are necessary for achieving good performance, but they are not sufficient.

This chapter presents some guidelines for making implementation decisions. It also addresses some coding issues, including both language-neutral suggestions, as well as specific C++ and Java solutions. It will help you go that "last mile" to achieve the responsiveness and scalability that you need.

You may, for a variety of reasons, find yourself needing to tune the performance of your system. Reasons that you might need to do performance tuning include

- Your application was developed without using the SPE techniques described in this book.
- Your choices for data structures or other implementation alternatives were not optimal for your application as it is actually used.
- The language you used contained some "hidden features" that significantly impacted your performance. (Language choice can make a difference.)
- You find yourself needing to meet new, unanticipated performance requirements.

This chapter also presents a strategy for performance tuning that will help you maximize the payoff for your tuning efforts.

It is important to realize that, while the techniques described in this chapter can produce some significant performance improvements, these improvements will not be as large as those that you could achieve at the architectural or design level. Thus, for example, a tuned system will rarely, if ever, exhibit the level of performance that you could have achieved by designing in performance from the beginning. Implementation and code-level performance improvements also have costs. In most cases, they will reduce the reusability of your code, make it harder to maintain, or both. Thus, these "tricks" should only be used where they are absolutely needed—in that 20% of the code that is causing 80% of your problems.

12.2 Performance Tuning

Once code is produced, you can begin to use measurements to identify performance problems. The following performance tuning process guides the isolation of problems and selection of appropriate performance solutions. You can also use this process if you need to make some measurements to identify the best implementation alternative.

Performance tuning is the process of transforming code that fails to meet performance objectives into better-performing code that performs an equivalent function. Tuning is usually conducted late in development (or post-development), when serious problems are discovered and improvements must be made immediately. There is rarely time to redesign the software under those circumstances. Performance may be an order of magnitude worse than required (e.g., a scenario that should take one second or less actually takes 10 seconds). With the limited time available for tuning, and the extent of improvements that are typically necessary, it is vital to identify and focus on those areas that have the highest potential for payoff, rather than to expend efforts on improvements that have a negligible overall effect.

You may also use these tuning techniques to improve performance to meet new responsiveness or scalability objectives. For example, an objective of 1,000 transactions per second was originally specified; now you find that you need to process 5,000 transactions per second.

This section discusses a process for performance tuning that includes strategies and techniques for maximizing the performance and capacity payoff of tuning efforts. The systematic approach begins with measurement studies to quantify the problems and identify their causes. The eight steps, summarized in Table 12-1, are described next.

Measurement studies are discussed in Chapter 8.

1. Prepare test plans that identify the measurements to be taken and the objectives to be achieved. Some of the considerations for the plan are to:

Table 12-1: Performance Tuning Steps

Step	Details
1. Prepare test plans	Objectives to achieve, measurements to make
2. Conduct measurement studies; document results	Mimic desired operational conditions; produce performance reports
3. Identify bottleneck(s)	Hardware device with the highest utilization, software limits on processing such as sockets or threads
4. Evaluate improvements due to tuning the system versus tuning the software	Changes to the overall system do not require code changes but may not yield sufficient improvement
5. Produce a "heavy hitters" list for the bottleneck device(s)	Processes that are the heaviest users of the device during problem periods
6. Profile the heavy hitters to identify "hot spots"	A profile reports the percent of time and resources used in all parts of the program
7. Identify performance remedies and quantify their performance improvement versus impact	Remedies range from low-cost (and usually low-impact) automatic optimization options, to high-cost (and potentially high-payoff) software refactoring or re-creation using the performance principles and patterns
8. Select and implement remedies	Conduct performance stress tests to quantify the results

- Identify the performance problems to be studied. These typically correspond to use case scenarios. If you have not constructed sequence diagrams for these scenarios (whether or not they were explicitly documented), it is a good idea to do this as part of your measurement studies.

- Identify the important workloads for problem scenarios. These will be peak workloads or other operational usage conditions that have been observed to cause problems. Examples include transaction or customer-call volumes, Web application requests, screens displayed, database requests, sensor sampling rates, control signal rates, and so on.

- Characterize the properties of those workloads: arrival rates or number and type of users or, for embedded systems, the sampling interval or the number and types of external events.

- Define the data required and the measurements and reports required to produce it (see item 3 below).

- Identify the measurement tools needed and the specific procedures for their use (e.g., parameter settings, start-up procedures, etc.).

2. Conduct measurement studies under the desired operational conditions, and document the workload characteristics. Your study should produce a comprehensive report that includes computer system usage data such as: CPU utilization; CPU-I/O overlap (the fraction of the measurement period when both the CPU and I/O are busy); I/O rates and average I/O service time by device; communication line utilization, traffic rates, and message sizes.

   You should also collect process-level data such as the number of processes active, process execution time, CPU usage by process (include both system and application processes as well as system and user time), number of file accesses (for primary files), file location, block size and overall file size, the amount of time processes are blocked and why (e.g., locks or semaphores, synchronous calls, etc.), remote procedure calls, memory usage statistics, number of page faults, number of program swaps, and so on.

Bottleneck devices are discussed in Chapters 6 and 8.

3. Identify the bottleneck(s). The device with the highest utilization is the hardware bottleneck. You may also have software bottlenecks, such as limits on threads or sockets that cause jobs to back up, even though hardware resources may be underutilized.

The purpose of the first three steps is to use the *quantitative* data obtained in steps 1 and 2 to identify problems as well as the potential payoff for correcting them. It is always possible to find some aspect of the software whose performance you could improve by tuning. However, tuning a randomly chosen portion of the code will often have little or no impact on overall performance. These steps replace speculation and random improvements with a systematic approach that focuses on vital areas of the code.

 Use quantitative data to identify bottlenecks, and apply a systematic process for reducing or eliminating them.

Once you have identified the bottlenecks, you can apply a systematic process for reducing or eliminating them, as described in the remaining five steps.

4. Evaluate the relative payoff of tuning the overall system versus tuning the software. Changes made to operating system parameters, network configuration, file placements, and so on are usually easier and do not require changes to code and the associated debugging and testing. You can find more information on system tuning in Jain [Jain 1990] and Larman and Guthrie [Larman and Guthrie 2000]. You should also consult with system specialists for tuning options and their expected payoff.

5. Produce a "heavy hitters" list for the bottleneck device(s). These are the processes that are the heaviest users of the device under peak loads or other conditions that cause performance problems.

 In most cases, 20% or fewer of the processes will use 80% or more of the resources.

Profiling is discussed in Chapter 8.

6. To evaluate the benefits of tuning code, profile the heavy hitters to identify the "hot spots" within those processes. A profile is created by running the program under the desired operational conditions and periodically "sampling" the program (e.g., with a program monitor) to determine what it is doing: if it is using the CPU, which

instruction; if it is performing I/O, what are the characteristics of the I/O; if there is a page fault, which page; and so on. If the sampling interval is appropriately set, the results will be representative of the detailed behavior. The 80-20 rule of thumb (from step 5) usually applies within programs as well; that is, in most cases, 20% or fewer of the functions will use 80% or more of the resources.

The overall impact of improvements gained from addressing "hot spots" is far greater than that of making random improvements.

Detailed traces with millisecond (or smaller) timestamps can also identify the source of problems. For example, a problem due to calling a sequence of methods is often too difficult to find with a profiler. Studying a detailed trace, however, will show the entire control flow.

Profiling to identify "heavy hitters" is difficult. To get meaningful results, profiles must be run under operational loading conditions, but the measurement overhead may perturb the system and invalidate the results. One alternative is to collect "trace files" that record operational activity on a "live" system and, later, to use that data to "drive" a laboratory system. This technique facilitates measurement studies and (later) performance testing of improvements.

Note: Not all profilers are sample based. However, sample-based profilers have lower overhead and thus introduce minimal perturbation to the measurements. See Chapter 8 for more details on profilers.

---

7. Identify performance remedies and quantify their performance improvement, development effort, maintenance impact, and other risks. Performance remedies range from low-cost (and, usually, low-payoff) automatic optimization options (e.g., compiler optimizations) to high-cost (and, potentially, high-payoff) software refactoring or re-creation using the performance principles and patterns.

   Intermediate options are to change algorithms and data structures using the rules presented in Section 12.3.3, and/or modify program code to use more efficient constructs, as discussed in Section 12.5 and in Alexander and Bensley [Alexander and Bensley 2000], Knuth [Knuth 1971], and Larman and Guthrie [Larman and Guthrie

2000]. The performance models may help quantify the performance benefits of the candidate improvements.

8. Select appropriate remedies, implement them, and conduct performance stress tests to quantify the results and provide measurements for capacity-planning model studies.

The performance principles are discussed in Chapter 9. Performance antipatterns are discussed in Chapter 11.

This tuning strategy focuses your efforts on those portions of the software that have the greatest potential for improvement. Use the performance principles to identify ways of improving the performance of your software. You may find that the poor performance is caused by one or more performance antipatterns. In that case, use one of the recommended refactorings to eliminate the antipattern.

12.3 General Performance Solutions

This section presents several performance solutions that apply to all types of systems, not just those that are object oriented. They are presented here in the context of improving the performance of an existing system, but they apply equally well to the detailed design and implementation phases of developing new software.

12.3.1 Fast Path Speed-Up

The Centering Principle is presented in Chapter 9. The Fast Path pattern is discussed in Chapter 10.

The Centering Principle and the Fast Path pattern both focus on the dominant workload functions—the 20% or less of the functions that are used at least 80% of the time. This solution focuses on the 20% or less of code that is executed as a result of those dominant workload functions. It trims all extraneous operations and instructions from that path, and leaves only the essential code.

If you began with the early life cycle techniques, you have already identified the Fast Path(s). If you are correcting performance problems late in the development process, you will need to use a profiler to measure the number of times each operation is invoked, and to identify those operations that are called most frequently. This will enable you to determine which workload functions are being processed, and the order in which the operations are executed.

It's also possible that you might not discover an important Fast Path until later in development. An example of a Fast Path that would not become apparent until after implementation and testing on real data is the parsing of the HTTP "Accept:" header, which specifies which document formats a browser will accept.[1] While the HTTP specification allows the "accept" keyword to consist of any combination of upper- and lower-case letters, the vast majority of requests actually contain "Accept:", which is the format sent by both Netscape and Internet Explorer. The Fast Path solution in this situation is to test for the common case first and, if successful, to then process the header. The more expensive case-sensitive comparison is only performed if the common case fails.

The solution for processing "Accept:" headers is an example of the more general technique of ordering the evaluation of conditions by their likely order of occurrence. Additional techniques for speeding up the Fast Path include selecting optimal algorithms and data structures for the typical case, minimizing object creation, removing unnecessary context switches by inlining calls or moving them off the Fast Path, and other solutions discussed later in this chapter. Other extreme techniques include

- Removing unnecessary branching or context switches to eliminate disruptions of the hardware instruction pipeline because the next instruction cannot be determined
- Changing the order in which data is stored in objects to minimize the number of memory cache misses [Bulka and Mayhew 2000]

You should only need to resort to these extreme measures for the Fast Path.

Some profile-based compiler optimizations identify and improve Fast Paths for you by reducing unnecessary branching and cache misses. Their improvements are based on actual measured paths and do not require code changes (but do require recompilation). Examples include compilers by HP [HP] and SGI [SGI].

---

1. This example is taken from Bulka and Mayhew [Bulka and Mayhew 2000].

While general-purpose class methods increase flexibility and reusability, they also provide processing that may not be needed. For the Fast Path and for heavily used routines, you may do better by creating a custom version. For example, you may make use of your knowledge of the size of a data structure to allocate memory from the stack, rather than using the more flexible but costly approach of dynamic memory allocation.

12.3.2 Improving Scalability

One way to scale a software system to handle a heavier load is to add processors (provided, of course, that the CPU is the bottleneck). In order for your software to take advantage of this approach, you will need to carefully design processing steps so that they may execute in parallel. The first step is to select a strategy for a multiprocessing software architecture. Then, you will need to determine the specific mechanisms for communication, coordination, and information exchange among the components. This section discusses these aspects of scalability.

> *It is easier to design in multiprocessing than it is to retrofit it.*
> *Adding parallelism is a difficult and expensive way to tune software.*

Multiprocessing Architecture A *monolithic* software architecture assigns all of the processing steps to one process. The only way to capitalize on multiple processors with this architecture is to run multiple copies of the software concurrently. This is an effective strategy for batch applications that require no interaction among processes (for example, when the processing for "Smith" is completely independent of the processing for "Williams"). In this case, however, the only way to increase the throughput for the individual processes is to upgrade to faster processors.

A *parallel* software architecture partitions the processing steps into *processes* and/or *threads* that may execute concurrently. To do this, you must identify the processing steps that may execute concurrently and determine how they are to be initiated. Identifying concurrent processing steps requires evaluating the algorithm to determine if it can be parallelized, deciding the optimal number of concurrent tasks, and determining whether they should be "heavyweight" (processes) or "lightweight" (threads) tasks. The performance models in Chapters 5 and 6 can help you make these choices.

Typically, processes are initiated when the software is started, and processes initiate threads dynamically during their execution. Depending on the execution environment, both processes and threads may be scheduled independently by the operating system. However, the relative priority of a thread generally depends on the priority of its parent process.

Beyond the models, once you obtain measurements, you may need to fine tune the number of concurrent processes and how they share and exchange information. For example, Larman and Guthrie [Larman and Guthrie 2000] suggest using more threads to exploit idle processor time by anticipating future work and performing the processing in the background.

In general, the more processes and threads that you have, the more context switches you will experience. These context switches cause overhead that reduces performance. In some cases, you may need to reduce the number of threads to improve throughput. One way to reduce the number of threads is to use a single thread to perform background processing [Larman and Guthrie 2000]. The thread maintains a priority queue of command objects that perform various background tasks. Each command object has a polymorphic execute() operation (see the Command pattern in Gamma et al. [Gamma et al. 1995]). This eliminates the need to have a separate thread for each background task.

Note: It is not the number of threads, per se, that causes the problem. It is also possible to have excessive overhead with a small number of processes that make frequent context switches. You are, however, more likely to experience the problem with a large number of threads.

Communication Protocol Conversations between processes on separate processors must use a protocol for communication. Alternatives include remote procedure calls, message queues, operating system messages, TCP/IP, and others.

With the TCP/IP protocol, processes communicate over *sockets,* and there is a limit on the number of sockets that can be active. Allocating a separate socket for each thread may limit the scalability of the software by setting an implicit upper bound on the number of threads that may execute concurrently. You can increase the number of available threads by multiplexing the sockets. That is, use one real socket that is shared (multiplexed) by multiple threads sharing a single "multiplexing connection object" that coordinates messages and responses among the threads. Many middleware packages, such as CORBA, ObjectSpace Voyager, and EJB (Enterprise JavaBean) servers provide APIs that hide the sockets from the application software. Middleware packages that provide multiplexed sockets will allow more concurrent threads to execute. The price you pay is the higher communication overhead to handle the multiplexing, and the contention delay for the socket.

TCP/IP is a connection-oriented protocol that provides reliable delivery of packets. An alternative protocol, User Datagram Protocol (UDP), is connectionless and does not provide reliable delivery. It may be appropriate for some applications. Since it is connectionless, it will not limit the number of concurrent threads. The Java DatagramSocket class provides such a connection.

The Shared Resources Principle is discussed in Chapter 9.

Sharing Strategy Access to shared data may introduce contention among concurrent processes. You can completely eliminate this contention if you can eliminate sharing of the data (as prescribed by the Shared Resources Principle). For example, if you can give each process its own private copy of the data, you can eliminate contention. Note, however, that if you dynamically allocate objects using new and delete, you can inadvertently introduce contention among threads of the same process because the objects are allocated from the same heap, and mutual exclusion code is implicitly executed. The solution is to allocate objects statically (i.e., from the stack) rather than dynamically where possible in each thread. (Note: This works for C++, but not for Java, where all objects are allocated from the heap.)

Some objects can be shared without being thread-safe. Examples include: objects that are immutable (e.g., C++ const instances that are never recast), some core Java classes (i.e., String and container objects for primitives), and objects only modified by one thread.

The Spread-the-Load Principle is discussed in Chapter 9.

If you cannot eliminate sharing, another strategy is to reduce the number of threads competing for each resource by partitioning the resource into *pools,* and assigning threads to resource pools. The mutual exclusion code still executes, but the amount of contention is lower because the number of threads competing for a given resource is reduced. This is an application of the Shared Resource Principle. In order for this strategy to be effective, you need a fast algorithm for assigning threads to pools, and the algorithm must effectively spread the load.

A third strategy applies when data is reused. The initial request requires exclusive access. The data is then cached so that it can be reused without requiring additional exclusive accesses. Note that this strategy works well for read-only data.

Locking Strategy You may be able to reduce the overhead for locking by granting access to multiple resources with one lock. This strategy is effective if all of the resources protected by the lock are always used together, and the lock is held for a short period of time.

There are two strategies for handling requests for locks that cannot be immediately granted. One uses "spin locks" that repeatedly check to see if the resource has become available. This is appropriate when the request is likely to be granted very soon (the lock hold time is very short and the number of contending requests waiting is very small).

The other strategy puts the thread to sleep and awakens it when the resource is available. In this case, if the lock mechanism awakens all processes and they must all try again to obtain the lock, the result is the "Thundering Herd" [Campbell et al. 1991], [Bulka and Mayhew 2000]. All threads except one will "waste a context switch" to find that the resource is busy, thus causing significant CPU degradation that is exacerbated by increasing the number of threads. Some platforms provide a "single-thread wakeup" strategy that eliminates this CPU thrashing. In Java, Object.notifyAll() wakes up all processes, while Object.notify() wakes up only one.

The use of Java notify is potentially risky and a common source of error. Lea recommends isolating uses of notify to concurrency control utility classes that can be heavily optimized, carefully reviewed, and tested [Lea 1997].

Schmidt and Harrison propose the "Double-Checked Locking" pattern [Schmidt and Harrison 1996] to reduce the number of times that locking is required. Rather than making an entire method synchronized, they first check to see if a lock is needed. The synchronized version of the method is called only when it is necessary. This strategy is applicable when the synchronized version is seldom needed—for example, when performing lazy initialization of a Singleton method [Gamma et al. 1995].

Note: The Java language specification has some deficiencies. Double-checked locking may not work in all JVMs [Goetz 2001].

12.3.3 Algorithm and Data Structure Choices

These choices guide the selection and implementation of proper data structures and algorithms for classes that are critical to performance. Algorithms and data structures are the subject of a variety of books (see, for example, [Knuth 1998], [Knuth 1997], [Sedgewick and Flajolet 1996], [Weiss 2001], [Weiss 1999], and others.) These authors discuss the performance characteristics of the algorithms and data structures that they present.

Choices for Collections In C++ and Java, you select the type of data structure when you select the type of collection class to use to hold a set of data elements. For a given circumstance, refer to the data structure texts referenced above to determine whether to use a LinkedList, ArrayList, HashSet, or other collection class. Whatever your choice, specify a realistic size for the collection when you create it. Otherwise, you will pay an expensive performance cost to extend the collection, should you need to increase its size. Increasing the size of the collection will require allocating more space, copying all objects to the new space, and then deleting the original objects. Conversely, making the initial size too large will incur a significant penalty in memory size.

It is particularly important to specify a realistic initial size for hashed collections, because the hash function must produce an even distribution of keys to buckets, to minimize collisions and avoid clustering. Other optimizations for hashed collections include

- Using a prime number for the size of the collection; this helps avoid clustering. Conversely, avoid table sizes that are a power of two—these increase clustering.
- Checking to be sure that the default hashCode() method distributes objects evenly over the collection's buckets. If not, override it to do so. This will minimize collisions.

- Avoiding String keys by using integers as keys, even if this requires a wrapper Key class. Operations such as equality checks are more efficient to perform on base types than on Strings [Larman and Guthrie 2000].

For very large collections, it is not efficient to load the entire collection when it is accessed. In these circumstances, you may want to use a "lazy collection" [Larman and Guthrie 2000]. A lazy collection provides logic for fetching moderate-sized portions of the collection. When a user accesses an element that is not in memory, another portion is loaded. With this approach, there will be a delay as the new portion is loaded. The delay can be reduced by employing additional strategies such as pre-loading portions in the background, or moving frequently accessed elements to the front of the collection.

12.3.4 Time Versus Space Trade-Offs

In his book, Jon Bentley provides specific advice for selecting data structures and algorithms for writing efficient code [Bentley 1982]. He offers two sets of rules. The first set, which contains four rules, saves execution time by using more memory, or "trading space for time." We add a fifth rule derived from the performance principles. The second set of two rules saves memory by executing more code, or "trading time for space." These rules are summarized in the following sections.

Trading Space for Time The first rule stores precomputed results.

Store Precomputed Results Rule

> *Compute the results of expensive functions once, store the results, and satisfy subsequent requests with a table lookup.*

An example of this rule is to eliminate explicit tests (e.g., if, switch) by using polymorphism. To do this, derive specific subclasses from a (possibly abstract) base class, and use virtual function calls to perform the required operation. For example, in a graphics application, you can perform explicit case analysis when drawing a figure, as illustrated by the following code fragment:

```
switch (shape) {
  case 'circle':
    drawCircle(location);
  case 'square':
    drawSquare(location);
  ...
}
```

Alternatively, you can define an abstract Shape class with a pure virtual draw() operation, and derive concrete subclasses such as Circle and Square from it. Each subclass provides its own implementation for the draw() operation. Now the selection is performed polymorphically as

> object->draw(location);

and the explicit case analysis is avoided. Here you are using the stored, precomputed result for the address of the function to be executed (e.g., the vtable entry in C++).

The Store Precomputed Results rule is an example of the Fixing-Point Principle.

The second rule uses caching.

Caching Rule   *Store data that is accessed most often to make it cheapest to access.*

Caching the most frequently accessed data reduces the work needed to retrieve the second and subsequent requests. To implement this strategy, determine what the data access patterns are, and use that information to decide what to cache. For example, if data access patterns are such that the last item retrieved in a query has a high probability of being requested again, it should be cached.

Other strategies include
- Moving each item found in a list closer to the beginning. This puts recently retrieved items near the front of the list where they can be found more quickly [Knuth 1998].
- Caching the timestamp of an HTTP request [Bulka and Mayhew 2000]. This eliminates generating multiple timestamps for a request when they are not needed.
- Caching the most commonly used windows by making them invisible rather than closing them [Larman and Guthrie 2000].
- Using a background thread to generate and cache frequently used Web-page bitmaps [Larman and Guthrie 2000].
- Caching the results of remote communications, database queries or materialized objects (possibly by using a Proxy object [Gamma et al. 1995] to control access) [Larman and Guthrie 2000].

Additional applications of the Caching rule may be found in [Bulka and Mayhew 2000], [Larman and Guthrie 2000] and other texts. The Caching rule embodies the Centering, Fixing-Point, and Processing Versus Frequency Principles.

The third rule postpones processing.

Lazy Evaluation Rule

> *Postpone evaluation until an item is needed.*

Kernighan and Plaugher [Kernighan and Plaugher 1978] illustrate the application of this rule by deferring the calculation of line width in a text editor or word processor until it is required, rather than calculating it after each character is entered. Another application of this rule, lazy instantiation and initialization of objects, is appropriate if the object may not be used.

The Lazy Evaluation rule is an instance of the Processing Versus Frequency Principle.

Bentley's fourth rule simplifies processing.

Data Structure Augmentation Rule

> *Augment data structures with extra information, or change the structure so that it can be accessed more easily.*

The Circuitous Treasure Hunt antipattern is discussed in Chapter 11.

A simple example of using this rule is a doubly linked list which stores pointers to both the next element and the previous one to make forward and backward traversal equally efficient. We saw another example in the ICAD application, where storing the node coordinates with the beams avoided a Circuitous Treasure Hunt.

The Data Structure Augmentation rule is an instance of both the Fixing-Point and Locality Principles.

We add a fifth rule to Bentley's set to reduce processing overhead.

Batching Rule

> *Make fewer calls and process multiple requests with each call.*

The Batching pattern is presented in Chapter 10.

Examples of using the Batching rule include batching remote work, performing multiple operations in one database transaction, and downloading a collection of elements in a JAR file (rather than one file per element) [Larman and Guthrie 2000]. Other examples are described in connection with the Batching pattern.

Trading Time for Space Bentley presents two rules that save space by doing more processing. Their use is appropriate when the actions are needed relatively infrequently.

Packing Rule

Use dense storage representations to decrease storage cost by increasing the time required to store and retrieve data.

File compression techniques use the Packing rule to reduce the amount of disk space required for a file, or the size of messages sent over the network. The amount of time required to access the compressed data is higher than that required to access uncompressed data.

Interpreter Rule

Represent common sequences of operations compactly and interpret as required.

A common example of the Interpreter rule is the implementation of a state machine as a table. Here, the rows represent states and the columns contain events, actions, and new states. When an event occurs, an interpreter uses the table to determine whether a transition can occur. If so, the interpreter calls the indicated action and updates the currentState variable.

Note: The performance principles focus on improving responsiveness; they do not address sacrificing time to save space. Thus, there is no connection of these rules to the performance principles. The packing rule can be used, however, to compress files or data to save *time* for network transfers. That would be an instance of the Processing Versus Frequency Principle. Note that these rules do not address synergistic aspects of performance such as sharing resources, parallel processing, or spreading the load.

Performance tuning is discussed in Section 12.4.

As Bentley points out, each of these rules can be applied inversely to reverse the time and space trade-off. He cites a rich set of examples from the literature for each of the rules, and quantifies the benefits of many of them. He also describes rules for modifying code to be more efficient. Those rules apply to performance tuning in later life cycle stages.

12.3.5 Hardware/Software Platform Dependencies

In general, customizing code to the underlying hardware/software platform is a last resort. In extreme cases, however, you may need to do this to achieve your performance objectives. This section has discussed several examples of the effect of the underlying platform, such as using operating system calls to locking routines, and cache thrashing as a result of inadvertent contention between independent locks. Additional discussion of this topic is beyond the scope of this book. However, you can find more examples in Bulka and Mayhew [Bulka and Mayhew 2000].

12.4 Performance Solutions for Object-Oriented Software

This section presents solutions to performance problems that arise because of the object-oriented nature of software. We begin with solutions to problems that arise regardless of the particular object-oriented language that you use. Then, we discuss some solutions that are specific to the two object-oriented languages that we encounter most frequently: C++ and Java.

The solutions described in this section are at the level of code optimization. Because of this, their potential for performance improvement is limited. In many cases, their use will make the code harder to understand, more difficult to modify or extend, and less reusable. They should be used only as a last resort and then, only on the Fast Path. However, in some situations they may be the only thing you can do.

12.4.1 Language-Independent Solutions

The Excessive Dynamic Allocation antipattern is discussed in Chapter 11.

Reducing Unnecessary Object Creation and Destruction We've already seen that dynamic creation of objects can, in some circumstances, cause performance problems. The Excessive Dynamic Allocation antipattern describes the negative consequences of frequent, unnecessary creation and destruction of objects at runtime. Now that you've been alerted to this antipattern, it's likely that you will recognize and avoid it in your software. If you do find it in your software, the suggested refactorings of recycling or sharing objects will help you solve the problem.

There are, however, other, less obvious situations where object creation and destruction can degrade the performance of your software.

Why is object creation and destruction so expensive? When you create an object, any objects that it contains must also be created. Any objects that those contained objects contain must also be created, and so on. If the object is part of an inheritance hierarchy, its creation will trigger the creation of all of its ancestors. When these objects are created, the memory to hold them must be allocated either from the stack or from the heap. Then, when the object is destroyed, all of the additional objects that were created along with it must also be destroyed, and the memory that they used must be reclaimed.

The amount of work required to create (and destroy) an object thus depends on two factors:

- *The complexity of the object*: the more objects that it contains or the more ancestors that it has, the more costly its construction will be
- *How the memory is allocated*: objects that are created with new use memory from the heap, while those that are declared as local variables use memory from the stack

Heap memory is more expensive to allocate than stack memory because it is allocated dynamically rather than statically. If you want an object to live beyond the scope of its method, however, you can't create it on the stack. A heap is a complex data structure, particularly in multi-threaded environments.

Clearly, one way to reduce object creation (and destruction) overhead is to create simpler objects and allocate them from the stack. For example, you could declare member objects to be of base types rather than other object types (e.g., char or superstring rather than String). Alternatively, you could flatten the inheritance hierarchy to reduce the work required to create (and destroy) ancestors.

The Processing Versus Frequency Principle is discussed in Chapter 9.

Most situations, however, require a more sophisticated approach. One useful approach employs the Processing Versus Frequency Principle. You apply the principle to minimize the product of the number of times an object is created multiplied by the amount of work performed to create it. For example, a given member object may only be needed under certain circumstances. Then, instead of declaring it statically and thereby allocating the member locally every time the parent object is created, you can minimize the product of processing versus frequency by testing to see whether the member object is needed, and then allocate it using new. That way, you only pay for creating the object if and when it is actually needed for the first time.

There are also circumstances where a seemingly innocent operation will cause the "hidden" creation of objects that may not be needed. As an example, consider the following C++ code fragment:

```
String s1, s2, s3, myString;
...
myString = s1 + s2 + s3;
...
```

The creation of the four declared String objects is obvious. What is less obvious is that two temporary String objects are also created (and destroyed) along the way. A String object is created (using the String copy constructor) to hold the return value of each operator+() and is then destroyed when the operator returns. One way to eliminate the use of temporary String objects in this situation is to use String::operator+=() as shown below:

```
String s1, s2, s3, myString
...
myString = s1;
myString += s2;
myString += s3;
...
```

While this code isn't as "clean" or elegant looking as the first example, its performance is better. This sort of optimization is usually only important on the Fast Path.

Note: While the details are different, a similar problem occurs in Java due to the immutability of Java strings.

There are many other situations where temporary objects may be created and destroyed without your realizing it, such as when passing parameters by value, when enlarging a collection, or when performing assignments that have an implicit type conversion. For example, when a Java Vector collection is resized, a new, larger array is created, and all of the objects are copied to the new array. The old array is then available for garbage collection.

Detailed examples of many of these situations and techniques for reducing unnecessary object creation and destruction appear in [Bulka 2000], [Bulka and Mayhew 2000], [Larman and Guthrie 2000], [Shirazi 2000], and [Wilson and Kesselman 2000].

The bottom line is that we can't completely eliminate object creation and destruction. After all, object-oriented systems use objects to get things done. However, it is important to be aware of where and when object creation (and destruction) are performed, and to make sure that you are not paying this cost unnecessarily, particularly on the Fast Path.

Reducing Method Invocation Overhead Overhead for invocation of methods is often a concern in object-oriented software. For example, encapsulation often introduces additional procedure calls, such as accessor functions for an object's attributes. When a method is invoked, several things happen. The arguments to be passed to the called method are pushed onto the stack, along with the address of the instruction to be returned to. The location of the calling method's local variables on the stack is also saved, so that they can be restored when the called method returns. When the called method returns, this process must be reversed to restore the processor state, and to update any arguments that were changed as a result of the invocation.

The exact amount of work required for a method invocation depends on the hardware/software platform, but a good estimate is that a method invocation will consume between 25 and 100 machine instructions [Bulka and Mayhew 2000]. If copies of arguments or return values (or other temporary objects) are created, the overhead will be even higher. In most cases, this overhead is not significant. In others, however, it can determine whether or not you will be able to meet your performance objectives.

One way to reduce overhead for method invocation is to "inline" the called method. Inlining replaces the method call by expanding the body of the called method within the caller. This saves the overhead of saving and restoring the processor state, and saves the cost to load the address of the target instruction. In addition, some compiler optimizations cannot be performed across procedure call boundaries. Inlining, on the other hand, produces large blocks of code that may make these optimizations possible.

To see the effect of inlining, consider a simple accessor method such as

```
int Point::getX()
{
    return x;
}
```

Execution of the method itself should only require three or four cycles while, as we have seen, invoking it can consume many more (by a factor of at least 10). Thus, inlining this method would save considerable overhead. In fact, this situation is such an obvious win that some compilers will inline member functions such as these as an optimization.

Despite its advantages, inlining has several costs. Since the inlined code is substituted everywhere it is called, the size of the code is increased. Inlining large methods that are called from many places can significantly increase the footprint of your software.

C++ and Java handle inlining differently. In C++, you use the keyword inline to indicate a member function that you would like inlined. Java does not have an inline keyword, and all decisions about inlining are made by the compiler. We'll discuss the language-specific aspects of inlining in the sections on C++ and Java solutions.

12.4.2 C++ Solutions

This section discusses some solutions to problems that arise in software coded using C++.

Inlining to Reduce Method Invocation Overhead In C++, you indicate that you would like to have a member function inlined either by using the keyword inline, or by defining the function within the declaration header. While this seems simple enough, the situation is actually quite complex. A request to inline a member function is technically a "hint" that the compiler can either follow or ignore. For example, the problem with simple inlining of a recursive function is obvious. Some compilers will also not inline virtual methods since the target code is not bound until runtime. Others are sophisticated enough to resolve the reference in at least some cases. The details are implementation specific.

As we've seen, inlining methods can dramatically reduce overhead for method invocation. This improvement must be weighed against the accompanying increase in the size of the object code. In addition, any change to an inlined method will require recompilation of every class that uses that method. While this increased time for compilation is not a runtime cost, it can be a significant problem during development. For this reason, inlining in C++ is often deferred until late in the development process.

Profiling is discussed in Chapter 8.

The Fast Path pattern is discussed in Chapter 10.

Bulka and Mayhew recommend profile-based inlining [Bulka and Mayhew 2000]. Profiling your code will show which methods are called frequently and the amount of time that they consume. Small, frequently invoked methods are excellent candidates for inlining. The percentage improvement in performance is high, and the increase in footprint is relatively small. Inlining large methods called from many different places provides less improvement and increases the footprint significantly. It is better to rewrite these methods using the Fast Path performance pattern. Intermediate-sized methods can be selectively inlined. Bulka and Mayhew provide additional guidelines for profile-based inlining.

More Efficient Multithreading C++ (like C) does not provide language-level support for multithreading. Instead, you must use a thread library such as the various POSIX pthreads implementations or the Portable Thread Library (PTL). These libraries provide capabilities for starting and terminating threads as well as for synchronization.

In most cases, it is best to use the standard library calls for managing threads. In extreme cases, however, you may need to make calls to specific operating system routines. For example, suppose you have a multi-threaded environment and need to maintain a count of references to an object. You can use one of the pthread_mutex operations to increment or decrement the reference count, but this will be expensive. If your operating system has specific operations for checking and clearing locks, they may be more efficient than calls to the pthreads library routines. An even better solution would be to make use of an atomic fetch and add instruction, if your platform supports it.

Additional Resources Additional information on performance-oriented coding and tuning for C++ is presented by Bulka and Mayhew [Bulka and Mayhew 2000].

12.4.3 Java Solutions

This section discusses solutions to some problems that arise in software that is coded using Java.

Inlining to Reduce Method Invocation Overhead Java does not have a mechanism such as the inline keyword for requesting that a method be inlined. Instead, these decisions are made by the compiler when an "optimize" option is selected. The types of inlining that are performed depend on the compiler. In general, short methods are more likely to be inlined than long ones. Thus, refactoring frequently called functions to create short methods can improve the chances for inlining.

To inline a method, a static compiler must be able to resolve the reference at compile time. This means that, in general, virtual methods will not be inlined. You can improve the ability of the compiler to resolve these references by declaring methods to be final, static or private, if appropriate. Just-In-Time (JIT) compilers have the additional complication that the compilation takes place in "user-time." Thus, they must trade the performance gain from inlining against the additional compilation time needed to perform the inlining.

Dynamic compilers such as HotSpot can profile the application as it runs, and use this information to inline virtual methods in some cases. Larman and Guthrie point out that if HotSpot identifies a virtual method foo() that has only one implementation loaded, it can inline the method where it is called, for example, in method bar(). Later, if another implementation of foo() is loaded, it can recompile bar() to back out of the inlining [Larman and Guthrie 2000].

Finally, synchronized methods cannot be inlined [Larman and Guthrie 2000].

Reducing Garbage Collection Overhead In C++, you must explicitly destroy objects that you create with new by using the delete keyword after they are no longer needed. Otherwise, their memory remains allocated and is unavailable for reuse by new objects. The failure to destroy objects is known as a "memory leak," and it can severely limit the responsiveness and scalability of your software, as well as its reliability.

In Java, you do not explicitly destroy the objects that you create. The Java runtime environment provides automatic garbage collection; when an object is no longer referenced, the garbage collector automatically removes it. The garbage collector runs on a low-priority thread. In general, this thread executes only when the system is idle. However, if the system is out of memory, the garbage collector will execute when heap memory is requested (e.g., new), causing a noticeable pause in user applications. The amount of work to be done, and therefore the size of the pause, depends on how many objects need to be freed. As Wilson and Kesselman [Wilson and Kesselman 2000] point out, the Java HotSpot garbage collector employs several strategies to improve efficiency and reduce noticeable pauses. Other strategies for improving garbage collection efficiency are discussed by Dimpsey et al [Dimpsey et al. 2000].

Note: The use of automatic garbage collection in Java does not eliminate the possibility of memory leaks. An object is garbage collected when it is no longer reachable; that is, when no other object references it. Objects that are not usable by the program may still be reachable. For example, an object in a collection is technically reachable even though no other object can actually use it. Such objects will not be garbage collected.

Note: Pauses due to garbage collection can also cause erratic results for performance measurements on Java systems.

Destroying an object and reclaiming its memory requires processing. You can't avoid it; this processing is a necessary consequence of having created the object, and the alternative is a memory leak. The real problem is that you don't have control of when the garbage collection is performed. You can request that the garbage collector execute using System.gc(). You might want to do this when you have a natural pause, such as when waiting for a user action, to reduce the likelihood that an important task will be interrupted by garbage collection. Note, however, that calling System.gc() does not guarantee that the garbage collector will actually execute. For a more detailed discussion of garbage collection issues, see Wilson and Kesselman [Wilson and Kesselman 2000].

One good way to reduce garbage collection overhead is to avoid creating unnecessary objects. You can do this by using base types where possible, and by recycling objects as discussed earlier.

Optimizing Serialization Serialization supports the encoding of memory resident objects, and the objects that can be reached from them, as a stream of bytes that can be written to or read from a stream. These objects can then be written to a file or sent over the network and reconstructed from the byte stream. This makes it possible to save the state of a program and restore it later, to transfer objects to other programs, or to store them in non-object-oriented databases.

In order to be serialized, an object must implement the Serializable interface. The Serializable interface is a tagging interface; it doesn't define any methods. Thus, implementing this interface is simply a matter of providing the proper declaration and making sure that all of the class's instance variables are also serializable.

Serialization can be expensive. For example, if objects are transferred via serialization in a remote method invocation (RMI), a significant amount of time can be spent in marshalling and de-marshalling (creating the byte stream and reconstructing the objects). One source of this overhead is that serialization is recursive. When you serialize an object, all of its fields are written to the stream of bytes. If these fields contain other objects, they are also written, and so on.

One way to reduce this overhead is to analyze your application to determine which state information needs to be persistent, and which can be recomputed when the object is reconstructed. Fields that do not need to be persistent can be marked with the transient keyword. These fields will not be written when the object is serialized.

You may also want to consider using the Externalizable interface rather than Serializable. Externalizable extends Serializable with two public methods: readExternal() and writeExternal(). Larman and Guthrie report that providing your own implementation for Externalizable is at least four times faster than Serializable for simple classes. For more complex classes, the savings can be even larger [Larman and Guthrie 2000].

More Efficient Multithreading Java provides language-level support for multithreading. Properly used, multithreading can be a valuable tool for improving both responsiveness and scalability. As with other concurrency strategies, however, it is necessary to trade off the speed-up gained for the overhead required to create and coordinate the threads.

Excessive Dynamic Allocation is discussed in Chapter 11.

The Excessive Dynamic Allocation antipattern applies to threads as well as to ordinary objects. Frequent creation and destruction of threads can add unnecessary overhead to an application both for thread creation and for garbage collection. One way to avoid this in Java is to implement the ThreadPool interface. The thread pool holds a number of threads that are recycled as needed. The pool can also be used to set an upper bound on the number of threads to reduce thrashing and/or avoid exceeding operating system limits (starting a thread in Java causes the allocation of an operating system thread if threads are supported by the operating system).

In a multithreaded application, it is necessary to provide safe access to shared data. Java provides the keyword synchronized, which can be used to prevent the concurrent execution of blocks of code. The block of code may be a portion of a method, an entire method, or even a data member. The use of synchronized prevents more than one thread from accessing the block at a time. Even if your code does not explicitly use synchronized, it is likely that you are implicitly using it via the Java Development Kit (JDK) library. Because of this, it is not unusual for Java applications to execute synchronization operations frequently. This synchronization has a runtime cost.

There are two approaches to reducing the runtime cost of synchronization. The first is to provide more efficient implementations of synchronization locking. The implementations of synchronization in early Java virtual machines (JVMs) were often inefficient, making the use of synchronization a significant performance bottleneck. Newer implementations have become more efficient. For example, the HotSpot compiler provides an implementation that is reported to improve performance substantially [Wilson and Kesselman 2000].

The second approach is to reduce the amount of synchronization that is performed. Many library classes include synchronization to make them thread safe. However, in cases where there is only one thread that can access an instance, the synchronization is not needed, and the synchronization code can be safely removed for those objects. Currently, this is a manual process; however, unneeded synchronization can be removed as a compiler optimization [Bogda and Holzle 1999].

Additional Resources Additional information on performance-oriented coding and tuning for Java is presented in [Larman and Guthrie 2000], [Shirazi 2000], and [Wilson and Kesselman 2000].

12.5 Summary

Most of this book has focused on the early use of SPE techniques to prevent performance problems. In an ideal world, getting the architecture and design right would be all that is necessary. However, while having a good architecture and design are essential, this does not guarantee that you will achieve your performance objectives. For many systems, it is simply not possible to ignore implementation choices and coding details. There are a number of pitfalls that can result in a good architecture and design having poor performance, if you make the wrong implementation or coding choices. This chapter presents some guidelines for making implementation decisions and coding choices that will help you go that "last mile" to achieve the responsiveness and scalability that you need.

Performance tuning is usually conducted late in the development cycle or in post-development, when there are severe time and budget constraints. Because of this, it is necessary to focus on those areas with the highest potential for payoff, rather than expend effort on improvements that have a negligible overall effect. This chapter presents a systematic approach to performance tuning that uses quantitative data to identify problems and the potential payoff for correcting them. It helps you to identify bottlenecks and apply a systematic process for reducing or eliminating them.

Several solutions to specific performance problems are also presented. Some of them are applicable to all types of systems; not just those that are object oriented. These solutions include

- Strategies for speeding up the Fast Path
- Multiprocessing techniques for improving scalability

- Considerations for making algorithm and data structure choices
- Time versus space trade-offs

Other solutions that are specific to object-oriented software include
- Managing object creation and destruction
- Method invocation overhead, including inlining in C++ and Java
- Garbage collection in Java
- Serialization in Java
- Multithreading in C++ and Java

Additional information on performance-oriented coding and tuning for C++ and Java is presented in the references.

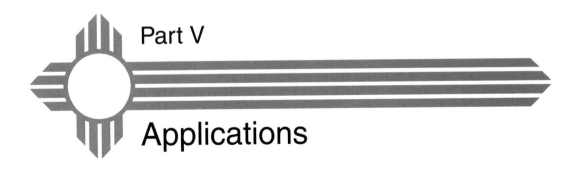

Part V

Applications

Chapter 13

Web Applications

It is as large as life, and twice as natural!

—Lewis Carroll

In This Chapter:

- Overview of Web applications
- Performance issues in Web applications
- Typical performance problems and solutions
- Case study

13.1 Introduction

A Web application is similar to a traditional client/server application that is deployed using a Web site. A Web site allows users to access and view documents using a *browser* running on the client computer. The simplest possible Web site consists of a Web *server* running on a server machine, along with some documents in HyperText Markup Language (HTML) format. The browser sends a document request to the Web server. The Web server then locates the document in the server's file system and sends it to the browser.

Most Web environments are far more complex than that, employing dynamic content rather than static HTML, extensive application (business) logic, and a variety of security techniques, as illustrated in Figure 13-1. The figure shows icons that represent the various hardware devices

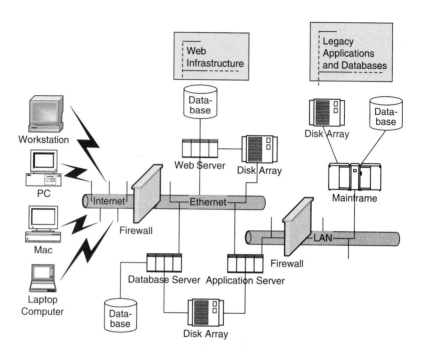

Figure 13-1: Web Applications

and data stores in the Web environment. Lines show how data may flow among them.

A request submitted from a client's browser is transmitted via the Internet or an intranet through a firewall to the Web server for security processing. Intranets may or may not have firewalls. From the Web server, the request goes to the application server, and then to the appropriate Web application. The Web application may interact with another firewall, database servers, a mainframe, external Web sites, and so on. A Web application may also use middleware packages such as J2EE, CORBA or MQSeries to connect the various components of the application. The Web application interprets user input, then queries and/or updates stored business data, and finally returns information to the user that is dependent on these interactions.

From an SPE perspective, we are not particularly interested in Web sites that deliver only static HTML. While their performance is also important, it is usually managed by calculating the amount of data that is likely to be requested and the number of requests expected, and then planning sufficient capacity to handle the requests. We are, however, interested in the Web applications that provide customized processing for user requests. For those applications, SPE is vital to ensure that the architecture and design are appropriate for meeting performance objectives before implementation begins.

This chapter discusses performance concerns that arise during the architecture and design phases of Web application development. Killelea [Killelea 1998] provides a comprehensive discussion of performance tuning for Web applications.

13.2 Performance Issues

Responsiveness and scalability are defined in Chapter 1.

There are two important dimensions to performance for Web applications: *responsiveness* and *scalability*. Responsiveness is the ability of the system to meet its response time objectives. For a Web application, responsiveness applies to both the time to retrieve and display one Web page (and all of its parts), and the end-to-end time to process a business task, which may call for multiple Web pages. Responsiveness is important because, in today's competitive environment, users will go elsewhere rather than endure slow response times. Scalability is the ability of the system to meet response time objectives as the demand for the software functions increases. Scalability is important in order to maintain responsiveness as more and more users converge on a site.

Both responsiveness and scalability are important for Web applications.

Note: Pages can be designed to improve *user-perceived* responsiveness. For example, if the page is designed to display user-writable fields first and then build the rest of the page while the user is filling in those fields, the users will be pleased with responsiveness. If, however, the designers force the users to wait for all the pretty pictures and animated logos to appear before they can enter data, they will be displeased with responsiveness.

We will use SPE models to evaluate the software architecture, the technical architecture, and the implementation choices for the Web application.

The following paragraphs elaborate on the performance issues of each of these.

The Coupling performance pattern is described in Chapter 10.

From the performance perspective, software architecture issues that appear early in development focus on communication among components. For the software architecture we will focus on:

- Decisions about the amount of data sent over the external and internal networks and among processes,
- The number of interactions required to retrieve the data and to accomplish the end-to-end business tasks, and
- How to integrate legacy applications—whether to modify the legacy application to provide a new, customized application program interface (API) based on the Coupling performance pattern; or to use an Adapter [Gamma et al. 1995] that calls existing APIs and reformats data as needed.

The technical architecture choices focus on the hardware and support software platforms. We will use SPE studies to determine the number and size of processors that we need, and to decide which processors the various processing steps should execute on (for example, do we need separate Web server[s], application server[s], and database server[s], or can some functions be consolidated). We may also use SPE models to select among middleware and other COTS packages, and determine how to best configure the environment for redundancy and recovery. There are many other such choices that need to be evaluated.

Web applications have a myriad of implementation options that affect the software architecture. We will also use SPE models to determine the performance effect of implementation options such as:

- How much of the application will execute on the server and which technology is most appropriate (e.g., Common Gateway Interface [CGI] processes, Active Server Pages [ASP], Java [or other language] servlets, or server API applications)
- Whether some of the application will execute on the client and which technology is most appropriate (e.g., scripts, applets, and so on)
- Whether component libraries should be used (e.g., Enterprise JavaBeans [EJB], ActiveX Controls, and so on)
- How to access databases (e.g., remote SQL, stored procedures, midd[leware products, and so on)

The software architecture, technical architecture, and implementation choices affect performance as well as other *quality of service* attributes. Quality of service (QoS) is the degree to which a software product meets its objectives for quality attributes such as performance, availability, reliability, safety, reusability, and so on. In some cases, there are trade-offs to be made among quality attributes. For example, putting the application on a different machine than the Web server may improve availability (because failures in the application will not interfere with the operation of the Web server) but degrade performance (by increasing overhead for communication across machines). If these trade-offs are identified early, the software and technical architecture that address these trade-offs can be selected. If not, it may not be possible to meet some (or all) QoS objectives.

This chapter focuses on using SPE techniques to construct and evaluate performance models of various architectural alternatives early in development. The goal is to select a combination that will meet performance objectives. The evaluation of trade-offs between performance and other quality attributes is beyond the scope of this book. Kazman et al. [Kazman et al. 1998] discuss the analysis of architectural trade-offs.

13.3 SPE Models for Web Applications

The SPE techniques for Web applications follow those that we used in Chapter 5 for distributed systems. Web applications use implementation technologies different from those of other distributed systems, but implementation details do not affect the SPE models during the early life cycle stages. The following paragraphs give a high-level overview of the modeling and evaluation steps; the next section illustrates them with a case study.

The first step in the SPE process is to select a set of use cases that represent the important Web-application interactions. These are usually the most frequent interactions; they also include the important functions that must perform well if the application is to meet its business objectives. Next, we create an end-to-end performance scenario that represents (at a high level) the processing steps for each of the use cases.

After representing the overall flow, we identify the processing steps that have the greatest impact on performance, and add details for them. For example, a database query, particularly on a remote computer, usually has a far greater impact on Web application response time and scalability than firewall processing. We also include specific details for processing steps that correspond to the software architecture alternatives we are evaluating. That is, if we want to compare the performance of two alternatives, such as client versus server processing for form validation, we must represent the processing steps required for form validation in the model.

Next, we convert the performance scenario sequence diagrams into a software execution model, add performance specifications, and solve the software execution model to determine the end-to-end response time (without contention delays). The software execution model often identifies problems with Web applications, particularly when they need to transfer large amounts of data over relatively slow communication lines. After selecting a software architecture alternative that meets performance objectives, we use the system execution model to evaluate technical architecture alternatives, and software scalability and capacity requirements.

The advanced system execution models are discussed in Chapter 6.

The Web execution environment is typically complex. At the architectural level of design, we will use deliberately simple models of software processing that are easily constructed and solved to provide feedback on whether the proposed software is likely to meet performance goals. Thus, our approach is to first create the software execution models that show the interactions among processes, and to estimate the delay to receive results from remote processes. Later in development, more realistic models use advanced system execution model solutions to solve for the delays to interact with distributed processes.

Queueing network models are discussed in Chapter 6.

As discussed in Chapter 5, these simpler, approximate models are more appropriate early in the development process. Now that we've seen the alternative queueing network models, let's revisit the rationale for these "simple" models.

Figure 13-2 shows a highly simplified system execution model for a hypothetical Web application. The symbols on the left show the queue servers in the Web environment (in the IPG notation used in Chapter

6). The lines show the flow of the locus of execution as in Chapter 6. The right side of the diagram is execution graph notation. The simple system execution model consists of N clients connected to a Web server via a network—either an intranet or the Internet (labeled INet in the diagram). Each client is modeled with its own system model, indicated schematically by the CPU and disk at the top of the diagram. User requests are processed on the client's CPU and disk. At some point in the processing, the client makes a request of the server. The request is transmitted via the network (indicated schematically by a delay server, INet), and it is then sent to the server.

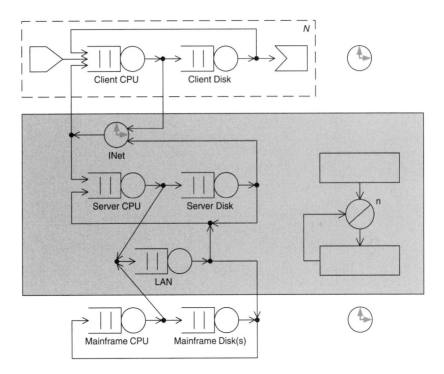

Figure 13-2: "Simple" Web Application Model

Modeling congestion on the Internet is beyond our scope. We use a delay server to estimate the approximate amount of time required to transmit data for a given client connection speed (e.g., 28.8 kbps modem or T1 line). If you want to model your intranet, however, using a single queue to represent the internal network is a reasonable starting point.

The server, in the middle of the diagram, also has a simplified system model consisting of a CPU and a disk. The request is processed on the server's CPU and disk(s) and sent via a LAN (represented by a single queue), to the Mainframe. It is processed on the Mainframe (again simplified to a single CPU and disk) and returned to the Server via the LAN, where it is processed and returned to the INet. When it exits the INet it returns to the Client that made the request.

The middle right side of the diagram illustrates the portion of the overall processing that is explicitly represented in the simple SPE model. The delay symbols on the top and bottom right show the portions of the SPE model that implicitly represent the processing with delays.

The picture in Figure 13-2 is a greatly over-simplified view of a particular interaction. The resulting simulation model is still very complex, however. It contains a large number of queue servers and workloads when all clients are included (there may be thousands of client CPUs and disks). Because of this, the solution time is very long, and it is difficult to compare many alternatives.

Early in development, we are not interested in the intricacies of the interactions between the client, server, and mainframe. We're more concerned with the feasibility and desirability of various architecture and design alternatives. Thus, our goal is to keep the models at this stage simple so we can study as many alternatives as possible.

Suppose that our first concern is the server (the shaded area in Figure 13-2). We first construct a software model for the server processing and estimate the delays for external interactions with the mainframe and client. At this stage, we exclude the other portions of the figure that are not highlighted, and simply treat them as sources of delay. This is the approximation technique that was introduced in Chapter 5. The next section illustrates its application to a particular Web application.

We include the LAN in the Server model because it is easy to do as long as a single queue is an adequate representation. Including it allows us to evaluate the level of congestion on the LAN. Alternatively, we could construct a separate model for the LAN, but this unnecessarily complicates the analysis. Similarly, we include the Internet in the Server model because it lets us estimate the end-to-end response time for the scenario.

The end-to-end time will be the sum of the estimated Client delay, the estimated elapsed time for Internet transmission, the Server processing time, LAN transmission time, and the estimated Mainframe delay.

Initially, we estimate the delays for interaction with the client and mainframe. Later, we construct software execution models for the client and mainframe, and use their solutions to refine the estimated delays. For example, in Figure 13-2 we would create the software execution model for the mainframe processing, and use its solution to adjust the corresponding delay in the server model.

13.4 Case Study: Nachtfliegen.com

This case study was first introduced in Section 7-3.

We will continue with the case study we began in Chapter 7. Nachtfliegen Airlines plans a major expansion to its modest Web site to:
- Expand company information, adding navigation and tabs
- Add promotions and deals to attract customers and encourage purchases
- Add functions for flight inquiry, itinerary planning, and ticket purchase
- Support the frequent flyer club, Vielenreisen, by allowing members to customize their interactions, and purchase tickets with frequent flyer miles as well as with a credit card.

Figure 13-3 contains the use case diagram for Nachtfliegen.com. The most important use cases for Customers and Frequent Flyers are: planItinerary and purchaseTickets. Both of these use cases include promotion and quoteFares. The performance of these use cases is important if the Web site is to meet the marketing goals to generate new revenue. If the performance is poor, users will not use the Web site, and Nachtfliegen will not realize the increased revenues. The other use cases are also important, but they will not be addressed in the initial analysis.

Customers will first see the Nachtfliegen.com home page. From there they may enter any of the use cases (by clicking on a link in the navigation area or selecting the appropriate tab). The Frequent Flyer will start on a login page, after which they will receive a customized version of the home page and select their next action—in this case, planItinerary.

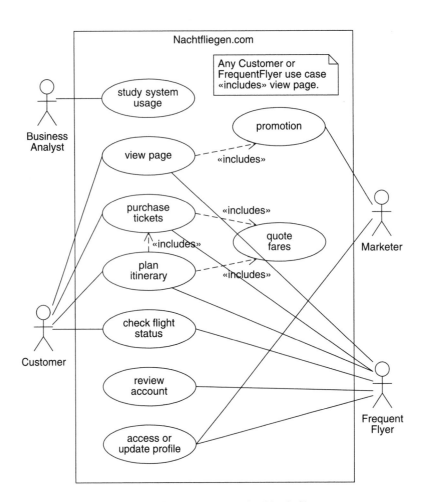

Figure 13-3: Use Case Diagram for Nachtfliegen.com

13.4.1 Plan Itinerary Scenario

The walkthrough to gather data for Nachtfliegen. com is discussed in Chapter 7.

We will first consider the scenario that is expected to be the most important (if the new Web site is to be successful), whereby a frequent flyer logs in, plans an itinerary, and purchases the ticket. We have a performance objective for the login step of 8 seconds (from the walkthrough). We do not have a performance objective for the end-to-end response time to plan an itinerary and purchase the ticket. We will see later how this lack of an objective impedes the performance improvement process.

Note: In Chapter 7 we learned that initially 80% of users are expected to plan an itinerary, and 20% are expected to purchase tickets. Even though ticket purchase is less frequent initially, we chose to include it in the scenario because, if its performance is unsatisfactory, users may abandon the site before purchasing the ticket. This would clearly be a business failure. We represent it in the scenario as a conditional alternative, and then during the model analysis step, we can explore various probabilities for the ticket purchase.

We also learned in the walkthrough that we expect 75% of users to plan a round trip, that the average round trip is 3.8 segments, that 83% will request quotes for the lowest fare, and that we expect 55% of users to do seat selection. Thus, the following scenario and the performance specifications that we use are based on this data.

Figure 13-4 shows a sequence diagram for the planItinerary use case.

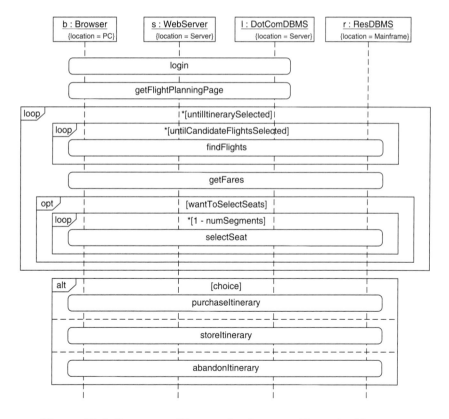

Figure 13-4: Sequence Diagram for Frequent Flyer planItinerary

The sequence of actions for this planItinerary scenario is:

1. The Frequent Flyer login and the customized home page are displayed. The sequence diagram shows this step as a reference; details are in the login sequence diagram (described later).

2. The user requests the flight planning page (another reference).

3. Next, an outer loop will be repeated until a user finds an acceptable itinerary. Within the outer loop is another loop which executes while the Frequent Flyer first explores flights available. (Note the loop symbol and the reference to findFlights.)

4. After selecting a set of flights, the Frequent Flyer requests the fare (getFares reference).

5. Next, an optional loop may execute 0 times if the flight-fare combination is unacceptable; otherwise it executes up to once per segment for the Frequent Flyer to select a seat. At this point, the Frequent Flyer may return to the findFlights page if the flight-fare-seat combination is undesirable, or proceed to the next step if all is well.

6. Finally, the Frequent Flyer either purchases the itinerary, stores it for future reference, or abandons it.

Note: Each step in this sequence diagram is, in itself, a complex sequence of interactions. We represent them in sub-sequence diagrams and show the references here to illustrate the overall interaction more clearly, without distracting details. The software execution model will also have this structure.

Note: This scenario does not represent the firewall. If it were included, each message between the browser and the Web server and between the Web server and the mainframe would be passed through a firewall. We chose to omit it from these models because performance problems with firewall processors are typically corrected with larger processors—the firewall does not directly affect the application design.

Login The first step in the planItinerary scenario for the Frequent Flyer is the login. The account profile, stored in the DotComDBMS on the Web server, is used to create a customized version of the home page, with promotions geared to their special interests.

Figure 13-5 shows the sequence diagram for an error-free login. This diagram corresponds to the login reference in Figure 13-4.

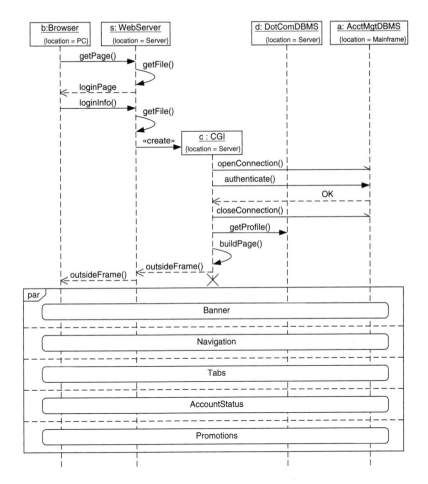

Figure 13-5: Expansion of login

The sequence of actions is the following:

1. The browser sends a request for the login page to the Web server.

2. The Web server gets the file and returns the login page.

3. The user completes the form and sends the request to the Web server.

4. The Web server gets the file and creates a CGI process to handle the login.

5. The CGI process first authenticates the user by opening a connection to the mainframe, sending a request to the AcctMgtDBMS, and closing the connection. We assume the authentication is okay.

6. The CGI process gets the user's profile information from the Dot-ComDBMS.

7. The CGI process then uses the profile information to build the page, and returns the outside frame of the page via the firewall to the browser.

Parallel composition is discussed in Chapter 3.

8. The browser then makes separate requests for the portions of the frame (the banner, navigation, tabs, promotions, and account status). We use parallel composition in the sequence diagram to show that the requests may arrive in any order and may be requested concurrently.

Flight Planning Page The user selects the flight planning page from the navigation area or from the "Plan itinerary" tab on the home page. The sequence diagram in Figure 13-6 depicts the following steps:

1. The browser sends a get(flightInfo) request to the Web server.

2. The Web server gets the corresponding file and creates a CGI process.

3. The CGI process retrieves the data for each promotion that appears on the page (note the loop).

4. The CGI process then builds the page and returns the result to the browser.

Upon completion of these steps, the user sees a page like the one in Figure 13-7. Note that this is a mock-up of the page without the actual graphics that the user would see.

The processing details for the other sequence diagram references are very similar to these. Their details are not shown here.

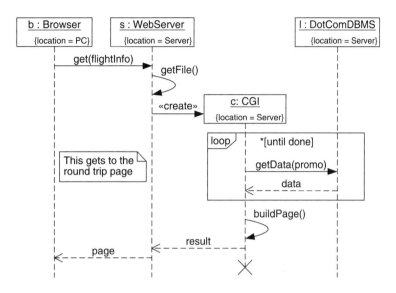

Figure 13-6: Expansion of getFlightPlanningPage

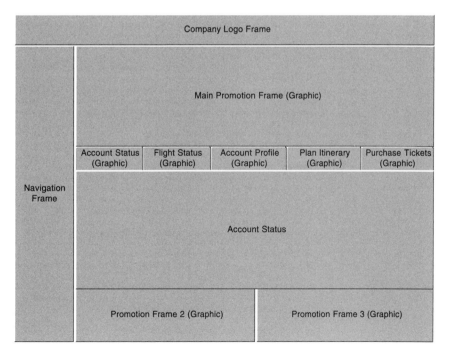

Figure 13-7: Flight Planning Page

13.4.2 Software Model

Figure 13-8 shows the software execution model corresponding to the sequence diagram in Figure 13-4. The login reference in Figure 13-4 becomes an expanded node in the software execution model. Similarly, the getFlightPlanningPage and findFlights references become expanded nodes. The strategy for the choice node and its attached nodes is covered later.

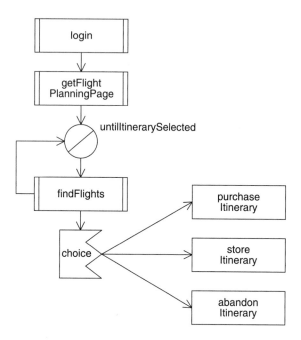

Figure 13-8: planItinerary Software Execution Model

13.4.3 Hardware/Software Environment

In the walkthrough presented in Chapter 7, we learned the LAN speed, the hardware characteristics of the server, and so on. Using this information, and a hypothetical software resource template containing WorkUnit, I/O, Msgs, and Delay, we constructed the processing overhead matrix in Figure 7-2. We used that software resource template because that combination is typical of many types of systems that you will analyze, and thus it better illustrates a general walkthrough (as opposed to a specific Web application walkthrough). For this chapter, however, we will modify the software resource template and the overhead matrix to capitalize on the repetitive nature of Web interactions. Table 13-1 shows the overhead matrix we will now use for the Web server.

Table 13-1: Processing Overhead

Devices	CPU	Disk	INet	Delay		LAN
Quantity	6	3	1	1		1
Service Units	sec	Phys I/O	KBytes	sec		Msgs
Input	0.002		1			
DBAccess	0.0005			0.25		1
LocalDB	0.01	2				
Pagesz	0.0005		1			
Datasz	0.0005		1			1
Service Time	1	0.003	.14222	1		0.000164

Note: The walkthrough in Chapter 7 used a different software resource template and showed some examples of typical values for the resource requirements that would be gathered in the walkthrough. If you had analyzed many Web applications previously, you would have known to use this software resource specification template initially, rather than the more generic one in Chapter 7. This version distinguishes between local I/O to the disk and remote I/O (DBAccess), which includes CPU, LAN, and Delay. This version also allows you to specify the number of Kbytes for pages and data for each processing step. This matrix makes the specification easier, and lets the tool compute the File I/O, Messages, and Delay that were explicitly specified in the previous version.

The steps in the walkthrough and analysis are actually iterative, especially for new types of analyses. For new systems, you would typically cover the first seven topics in the walkthrough, construct the software execution models, and then determine the most appropriate type of software resource template, before proceeding with the subsequent walkthrough topics.

The software resources we will use are the following:
- Input—the number of Kbytes in the input message
- DBAccess—the number of accesses to a mainframe database
- LocalDB—the number of accesses to the DotComDBMS

- Pagesz—the number of Kbytes in the page displayed to the user (including script or code that is downloaded with the page data)
- Datasz—the number of Kbytes of data retrieved from the main-frame that are displayed with the page

The Web server devices in the matrix include the 6 CPUs, 3 Disks, the Internet, the INet, (represented as the delay time to transmit each KByte of the page and data across a 56KB communication link), the Delay to access the mainframe, and the LAN.

In the center of the matrix we see that:
- Each (Kbyte of) Input requires approximately 2 ms. of CPU processing and 1 INet delay
- Each Mainframe DBAccess requires 0.5 ms. of CPU processing, 0.25 sec. Delay, and 1 LAN message
- Each LocalDB requires 10 ms. of CPU processing and 2 I/Os to the Disk device
- Each (KByte of) Pagesz requires 0.5 ms. of CPU processing and 1 INet delay
- Each (KByte of) Datasz requires 0.5 ms. of CPU processing, 1 INet delay, and 1 LAN message

The next step is to use this software resource template to specify the resource requirements for each step in the software execution model.

13.4.4 Resource Requirements

The resource requirements for the steps in login appear in Figure 13-9 and Figure 13-10. For example, the login page takes 1KB of Input, and 1 LocalDB access, and returns a Pagesz of 4KB; while getNavigation takes 1KB of Input and 1 LocalDB, and returns 12 navigation (URL) choices; each represented by 6KB of data (a small gif). None of these steps does a remote DBAccess, thus all Datasz specifications are also 0. We also specify the resource requirements for the other steps in the planItinerary scenario. They are not shown here.

Note: In most cases the Input consists of a small string containing the URL, and perhaps some parameters appended to the end. We arbitrarily specify 1KB for input to compensate for much of the additional protocol required to locate the receiver, successfully transmit the message from the user's browser via his or her ISP, through the Internet, and to Nachtfliegen.com. This is a reasonable approximation. Other options are to ignore this overhead (which gives the best case result), or to measure or estimate the actual time for these steps and include that time as a Delay.

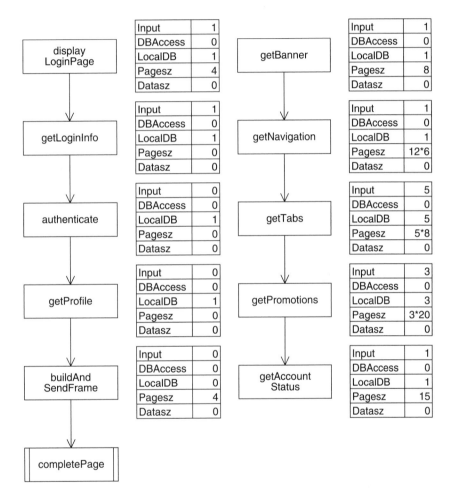

display LoginPage		
Input	1
DBAccess	0
LocalDB	1
Pagesz	4
Datasz	0

getLoginInfo		
Input	1
DBAccess	0
LocalDB	1
Pagesz	0
Datasz	0

authenticate		
Input	0
DBAccess	0
LocalDB	1
Pagesz	0
Datasz	0

getProfile		
Input	0
DBAccess	0
LocalDB	1
Pagesz	0
Datasz	0

buildAnd SendFrame		
Input	0
DBAccess	0
LocalDB	0
Pagesz	4
Datasz	0

completePage

getBanner		
Input	1
DBAccess	0
LocalDB	1
Pagesz	8
Datasz	0

getNavigation		
Input	1
DBAccess	0
LocalDB	1
Pagesz	12*6
Datasz	0

getTabs		
Input	5
DBAccess	0
LocalDB	5
Pagesz	5*8
Datasz	0

getPromotions		
Input	3
DBAccess	0
LocalDB	3
Pagesz	3*20
Datasz	0

getAccount Status		
Input	1
DBAccess	0
LocalDB	1
Pagesz	15
Datasz	0

Figure 13-9: login Software Model   Figure 13-10: completePage

Earlier we noticed that the steps required to retrieve a page, process it, and send it to the browser are repetitious. We elected not to expand each of the nodes, but instead to estimate the total resource requirements for the page and specify the total for each page. So, for example, we did not expand purchaseItinerary, storeItinerary, or abandonItinerary. That is, rather than expanding the steps for storeItinerary as we did for login, we calculate the *total* input, DBAccess, LocalDB, Pagesz, and Datasz for all the pages required for storeItinerary.

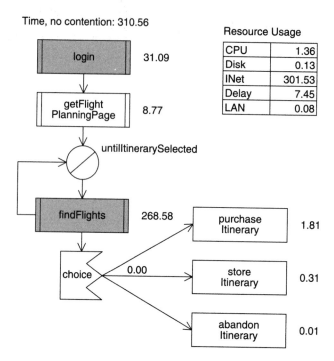

Figure 13-11: planItinerary Software Model Results

13.4.5 Software Model Solution

Figure 13-11 shows the software model results (with no contention) for planItinerary. According to the key results,

- The time to process the login and display the customized home page is 31 sec.
- The end-to-end time for planItinerary is 311 sec.
- Of the total time for planItinerary: 1.4 sec is CPU time, 0.14 sec is Disk time, 302 sec is INet to transmit the pages and data, 7.5 sec is Delay to access the Mainframe, and 0.1 sec is LAN.

The 31 seconds for login (the first node in the execution graph) exceeds the 8-second performance objective obtained in the walkthrough. We didn't have a performance objective for the end-to-end response time for planItinerary so we are not sure if 311 seconds is acceptable. This will be a discussion point when the walkthrough results are presented.

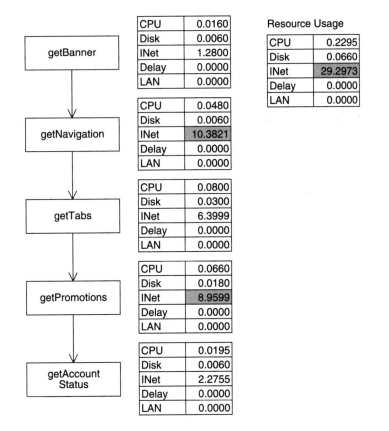

Figure 13-12: login Resource Demand

Figure 13-12 shows the expansion of login along with the resource demand for each step. By viewing the resource demand results for each step in Figure 13-12, we see that the primary problem with the login is that it takes 31 seconds to transmit the pages and data over the Internet. The two biggest contributions to this total come from the getNavigation and getPromotions steps.

13.4.6 Performance Improvements

The performance principles are presented in Chapter 9.

Let's apply some of the performance-oriented design principles to improve the performance

- The *Performance Objectives Principle* calls for a specification of the end-to-end performance goal. Without it we must defer addressing these issues, thus potentially losing some options for reducing the response time. We also need a more precise specification of the performance objective of the findFlights step.

- The *Instrumenting Principle* suggests that we record the typical paths that users take through the scenario. For example, we should collect the end-to-end response time, the number of times through each of the loops in Figure 13-8, the Datasz and Pagesz, the time to retrieve information from the Mainframe, and so on.

- The *Centering Principle* suggests that we minimize the processing for this scenario. We can do this by reducing the size and number of messages sent to the browser. The following principles help us do that.

- The *Fixing-Point Principle* suggests that, rather than using frames that require the browser to make multiple requests to the WebServer, we should combine the frames into a table.

- We can apply the *Locality Principle* by noticing that most of the time the user wants to plan an itinerary rather than view repetitive information on a home page (especially if it takes forever to display) and then have to select getFlightPlanningPage (and wait again). Thus we can improve locality by letting users choose which page they want to see first on the login page (rather than having to load the home page).

- The *Processing Versus Frequency Principle* is the primary way to reduce the problem with the login—by reducing the size of the pages and data. For example, we could use simple text-based URLs in the navigation section, change the promotions to use simpler gifs with catchy phrases, and so on.

We won't consider the synergistic principles yet. They will be more appropriate later in development when it is time to evaluate the contention with the system execution model.

We can evaluate the performance improvement of each of these alternatives and combinations of them by revising the software execution model accordingly and solving the model. Some will have a larger benefit than others, and the relative benefit of each depends on the order in which you apply them.

Figure 13-13 shows the results for a refactored solution that includes a combination of the above improvements. The time for the login and display of the flightPlanningPage is reduced to 3.6 seconds. The time for the findFlights loop is still long, but we have deferred considering further improvements to this section of the scenario because of the lack of a performance objective. Example 13-1 illustrates how that portion of the scenario can be streamlined by considering improvements at this stage. It demonstrates the value of using performance objectives to guide the improvement process.

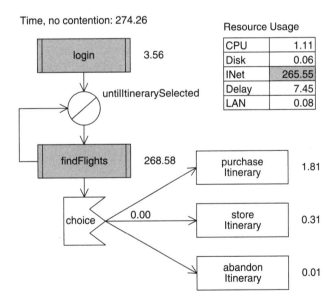

Figure 13-13: Refactored Solution for planItinerary

13.4.7 System Execution Model

Figure 13-14 shows the results of solving the system execution model for 720 users per hour. These results were produced with the *SPE•ED* tool, which uses the algorithms in Chapter 6. The end-to-end time is still

Example 13-1: Improvements to findFlights

The findFlights processing step is in a loop that executes three times in this scenario. It is an expanded node; its processing steps are shown, along with their resource requirements, in the following figure. The results for the findFlights submodel that is the expansion of the steps in the loop are in the adjacent figure. The results show two problems: the selectSegments and the selectSeat steps.

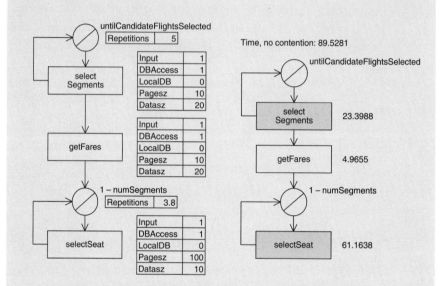

findFlights Resource Requirements   findFlights Results

The selectSegments step presents one page per segment for the user to select the desired flight. The loop repetition factor, 5, is an average number of pages visited in the segment selection process. The first improvement is to present all the segments on one (longer) page and let the user scroll through all segments on one page. The page will be larger, but the number of requests will be smaller. This is an application of the Processing versus Frequency Principle.

The next improvement addresses selectSeats. Often frequent flyers will select a flight that has good seats available, rather than sit in a middle seat on a packed flight. So, they may get all the way to the selectSeat step only to realize that they would prefer a different flight. We can address this improvement by putting a load factor (percent of occupied seats) on the selectSegments screen. It could even take into account the frequent flyer's elite status when reporting the number of seats available. They could then take this information into account when selecting the segments, and thus reduce the number of times the selectSeat step executes.

With these two revisions:
- The end-to-end time is reduced from 274 seconds to 112 seconds
- The time to selectSeats is still 61 seconds, but it is not in the find-Flights outer loop, so
- The time for the findFlights step is reduced from 259 seconds to 46 seconds to find the flight-fare combination plus 61 seconds to select the seats, for a total of 107 seconds

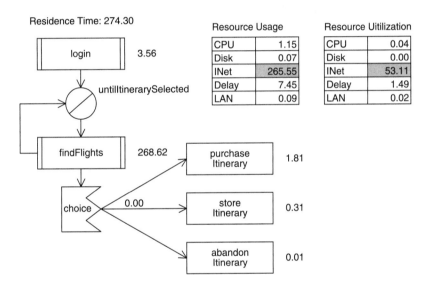

Figure 13-14: System Model Results

approximately 274 seconds, and thus the elapsed time for the individual steps is similar to the values in Figure 13-11. The reason for this is that the utilization of the shared devices, the CPU, Disks, and LAN, is below 4%. Thus, at this point in the project, the primary problem is the amount of data sent across the Internet.

Following the SPE process, the next step is to add performance scenarios based on other use cases and look for problems with the combination. Also, additional processing details should be included, such as a limit on the number of CGI processes that can be active, constraints on the connections to the mainframe, synchronization among processes, the number of threads for each process, and so on.

This model approximates the performance of the system by focusing on the scenario that executes on the WebServer, and estimating delays for interactions with other systems such as the Mainframe. This allows us to quickly build and solve both the software and system models for the WebServer.

Note: Later, we create a separate performance scenario for each process on each of the other processors in the system (e.g., those shown in Figure 13-2), specify resource requirements for their processing, and estimate the delay to interact with each of the other scenarios in the model. The model solutions are iterative—the solution of each independent performance scenario quantifies its processing time, which serves as the delay for system interactions in the subsequent model. Still later, we can connect each of the scenarios with an advanced system model to evaluate synchronization and communication among systems, and compute the delay directly.

13.4.8 Sensitivity and Scalability Analysis

To study sensitivity, you would use various values for resource requirements, and evaluate whether or not results change significantly. Given the low device utilization in this model, the primary sensitivity is the amount of data sent via the INet, and the delay for accessing the mainframe. If you are to meet the 8-second performance objective, you must reduce the size of the page and its data below a threshold. You can determine this threshold by solving models with various sizes until you find the size that meets your performance objective.

The scalability curve is introduced in Chapter 1.

Scalability is not an issue for this initial version of the model. Scalability will be more important once the additional details from the previous section are added to the model. To evaluate scalability, gradually increase the arrival rate of performance scenarios, and look for the knee of the scalability curve.

13.5 Typical Performance Problems

The Nachtfliegen.com case study illustrates many, but not all, of the typical performance problems with Web applications. This section discusses problems that we see regularly. They fall into these three main categories:

- Failure to control the architecture
- Failure to control the front-end interactions
- Failure to control the back-end interactions

Technical Architecture Selected Before the Software Requirements Are Complete It seems obvious that you do not want to constrain your environment before you determine what you are going to build, but many organizations do just that. Someone reads about the latest technology in a trade journal, learns that another organization has adopted it, or for a variety of other reasons, he or she decides to use it. We call this the "solution looking for a problem." Someone then implements a new system (the "problem" selected for the technical "solution"), and usually finds that many workarounds are needed when the "solution" is not a good match for the "problem."

Several years ago, we visited an organization that had been given the mandate that "all future systems shall use client/server technology" (rather than its traditional mainframe technology). The first "problem" for this "solution" was a disaster, because the data could not be partitioned to match the client's geographic locations. *All* interactions with geographically distributed clients had to be routed to a central-server database, whereupon large amounts of data were transferred back to the clients. This caused unnecessarily high network traffic between clients and servers, and thus long delays for simple tasks.

Performance problems are only one of the consequences of selecting technical architectures too early; many *functional* problems also occur. A better approach is to define your problem first, and then evaluate the suitability of a variety of solutions before selecting one.

Select the technical architecture after you have defined the performance, system, and software requirements.

Lack of a Software Architecture Many Web applications grow organically. Initially, the site displays only static HTML. Then, Web applications are added one at a time to the site. There is seldom time to step back and define a consistent overall strategy and software architecture for all Web applications. The result is that each application uses its own middleware for system interactions; some "home-grown" products are mixed with several other commercial products. This type of system is difficult to maintain and often has erratic performance, because it is extremely difficult to manage and provide consistent performance without a coherent architecture or design. A better approach is to define an extensible software architecture, using a notation that provides a consistent, uniform method for specifying the architecture and its behavior (such as the UML). Use the architecture specification as a baseline for new Web applications, and use SPE techniques to manage its evolutionary performance.

Note: We have found Kruchten's 4 + 1 View Model [Kruchten 1995] to be useful for describing the architectures of Web systems.

Define an extensible software architecture, using a notation that provides a consistent, uniform method for specifying the architecture and its behavior. Use the architecture specification as a baseline for new Web applications, and use SPE techniques to manage its evolutionary performance.

System Architecture Mimics the Organization This tends to be another common occurrence. As Conway's Law states:

> Organizations that design systems are constrained to produce designs that are copies of the communication structures of these organizations.
>
> —Melvin Conway

Typical performance consequences of this phenomenon are

- *Data coordination problems*: When independent systems perform a subset of the functions of a business task, coordinating the state of the data becomes problematic. The wasteBucks.com example in Chapter 6 had multiple systems for processing portions of an order: Order Entry, Customer Service, Warehouse, and Purchasing. In that system, the Customer Service system was created to track orders, maintain their state, and manage the progress through the various systems. We saw the performance penalty for the communication required for each item in the orders.

- *Data availability schedule*: Data may not be available when it is needed if, for example, the originating system encounters problems. The destination system must contrive workarounds to handle the situation when the data is requested but is not available.

One organization had this problem when reports were requested the first thing in the morning. If the data was not yet available, the reports contained old data. The workaround had convoluted logic to try to determine what the user wanted to see in the reports (whether they wanted the report now regardless of the status of the data, or if they wanted to wait until the updates arrived). When the data arrived late, it was difficult to meet deadlines for producing the reports in the time they were needed, and there were many re-runs required when the software made the wrong choice about what contents the users wanted.

The solutions to these problems are more difficult than others. Try evaluating your assumptions about the system. For example, we saw a distributed system that had one data center in "Metropolis" because the organization that provided the data was located there, and another data center in "Gotham City" because its developers were located there. The geographical differences caused long delays to transfer large amounts of data, and many of the problems mentioned earlier. The organization should re-evaluate its decisions about hardware and software locations, based on how the business tasks should flow, in order to find the best solution to the problem.

Question system and software assumptions that are based on organizational boundaries early in the development process.

Failure to Control Front-End Interactions This topic includes the size of pages, the amount of data, and the amount of code transmitted to and from browsers. Large page sizes result from too many graphics and too much page customization code. Large data sizes result from a failure to identify the data the user most likely needs, and to customize the result set to it. For example, if I want to view my financial account portfolio (with my current online brokerage service), I typically want to see a subset of the data available, such as symbols, number of shares, original cost, current value, change in value today and since purchase, purchase date, and available cash. My brokerage service has redesigned its user interface at least three times. The original implementation provided the best combination of information for my needs. The latest design does not provide either the purchase date or the available cash on the portfolio page, so I must request four pages to see the information I need most frequently. I have seen designs for other brokerage services that provide an excessive amount of data that still doesn't provide the information I would like to see combined.

Performance problems may occur if developers (of any kind of Web application) do not spend enough time refining the requirements, but instead send all available data. Performance problems also occur if data that is likely to be needed at the same time is not provided at the same time, because it must be retrieved from a different location. A better solution is to determine the subset of data that users are most likely to need together, and to send all of that data but no more.

> *Determine the subset of data that users are most likely to need together, and send all of that data but no more.*

You may have several types of users, each with his/her own view. If so, apply this guideline to create an appropriate subset of data for each type of user.

Failure to Control Back-End Interactions This problem includes the retrieval of information from other servers or a mainframe, and the middleware that supports the interactions among distributed systems. Problems occur when legacy systems must interface with Web applications, and the API of the legacy application is not well suited to the information requirements. The wasteBucks.com case study in Chapter 6 showed an example that required too many interactions with the Order Entry database to retrieve order details. We reduced the interactions by consolidating the items in an order, and returning information about the collection rather than individual details. Another alternative would be to pass order information along with the WorkAlert, so that processes would not have to make additional interactions to retrieve it.

Problems also occur when the middleware that supports the interaction is not well suited to the access patterns and workload volumes. For example, if you need guaranteed delivery of messages (and thus failure-recovery), your middleware should provide those functions without expensive workarounds. Similarly, if you need to support high traffic volumes, your middleware should be able to maintain open connections without security risks.

 Use SPE models to match back-end interactions to user needs and to find the best implementation alternatives to meet those needs.

13.6 Summary

This chapter demonstrated how to apply the SPE techniques we have covered to Web applications. It explained the importance of both responsiveness and scalability in Web applications. We saw how responsiveness is largely dependent on page and data size. Scalability, however, is affected by all the processing required by the Web application.

We use the SPE models early in development to evaluate the software architecture, the technical architecture, and the implementation choices for the Web application. The Nachtfliegen.com case study illustrated how to apply the distributed system modeling techniques introduced in Chapter 5 to Web applications. The case study used much of the data from the walkthrough in Chapter 7 to illustrate the data-gathering process. The combination of Chapter 7 and this chapter illustrates how to go from a very vague notion of what a system will do to having a quantitative model that lets you evaluate the performance of many alternatives.

This chapter focused on creating SPE models for early evaluation of alternatives. It did not address other important problems, such as forecasting the number of hits to a Web site or capacity planning to handle future loads. Menascé and Almeida discuss Web performance management and capacity planning [Menascé et al. 1998], [Menascé et al. 2000]. Their models are system execution models; however, they do not explicitly model the software architecture. Herzog and Rolia provide an overview of techniques appropriate for more detailed modeling and measurement studies of Web and other distributed systems [Herzog and Rolia 2001]. Gunther describes how to use statistical analysis techniques to predict capacity requirements for rapidly growing Web sites in [Gunther 2000].

Chapter 14

Embedded Real-Time Systems

I think there is a world market for maybe five computers.
> —Thomas Watson
> Chairman of IBM, 1943

In This Chapter:

- Overview of real-time and embedded systems
- Performance issues in embedded systems
- Performance problems and solutions
- Case study

14.1 Introduction

Thomas Watson's prophesy notwithstanding, computers are everywhere—and the machine on your desk is just the tip of the iceberg. Computers are in all kinds of consumer products, from microwave ovens to automobiles. They also control many of the processes that we take for granted in our daily lives, such as producing electric power, or routing airplanes from one city to another. The bulk of these computers are in real-time embedded systems.

Embedded real-time systems have several important differences from other software-intensive systems. The most important, from our perspective, is that performance is an explicit, measurable requirement in real-time systems. Also, much of the development is "close to the machine." It often involves interfaces to custom hardware and operating system capabilities that influence performance objectives.

Real-time embedded systems are often used to control processes that are safety critical. A safety-critical system is one whose failure could, in certain circumstances, lead to injury, the loss of life or health, economic loss, or environmental damage. Examples of safety-critical systems include aircraft flight management systems, nuclear power plant shutdown systems, and medical instruments. In safety-critical systems, performance is also a safety issue. Nancy Leveson provides an excellent discussion of safety issues related to software [Leveson 1995].

Note: Safety-critical systems do not need to be real-time embedded systems. For example, a medical database could be a safety-critical system since an erroneous response to a query could result in a dangerous treatment being prescribed.

This chapter describes an SPE approach to embedded real-time software. As with other types of software, we address issues of response time and resource utilization. We do not directly address issues such as schedulability in detail. However, we do illustrate how the results of SPE analysis provide the information required to resolve schedulability issues early in the development process, before the software has actually been implemented. For a detailed discussion of the development of embedded systems, see Douglass [Douglass 1999].

14.2 Embedded Real-Time Systems Background

This section discusses aspects of embedded real-time systems that are different from the traditional information systems that are the focus of many of our earlier SPE examples. An *embedded system* is a computer system that is part of a larger system whose primary purpose is not computation. Examples include air traffic control, telephony switching, industrial process control, and medical instrumentation. While we didn't analyze the performance of the Automated Teller Machine (ATM) itself, the ATM application introduced in Chapter 3 is an example of an embedded system.

A *real-time system* is one that has timing deadlines (performance constraints) on its execution. A deadline may be specified as a time interval, such as: "The system shall respond to a temperatureOverLimit event within 50 ms." or "The system shall archive data every 30 minutes." A deadline may also be specified as a particular point in time, for example: "The traffic controller shall enter nightMode at midnight each day." In a *hard real-time system*, the deadlines must be met each time they are encountered. Missing a deadline is considered a failure, equivalent to producing an erroneous result. In these systems, performance is a correctness issue. In a *soft real-time system*, occasionally missing a deadline is acceptable as long as it doesn't happen too often. "Too often" is defined as part of the requirements for the system. For example, in a telephony switch, it may be acceptable to delay providing a dial tone to the user if the number of call attempts exceeds a predetermined threshold. In a heart pacemaker, on the other hand, any delay in providing electrical stimulus to the heart may be unacceptable.

An embedded real-time system, therefore, is an embedded system that has deadlines on its execution. This covers a lot of ground—from the software that controls a microwave oven, to the control and safety systems for a nuclear power plant; from the software that controls the PBX (Private Branch Exchange—a sort of local telephony switch) in your office, to the satellite-based telephony system that manages global communications.

As Figure 14-1 shows, embedded systems typically connect to devices that monitor (sensors) or control (actuators) aspects of their external environment. Sensors provide information on variables monitored by the system, such as temperature or pressure in a process control application or engine thrust, altitude, and attitude in an aircraft flight control system. Actuators control external environment variables, such as heater status or valve position in a process control application, or aircraft control surface (e.g., aileron) position in a flight control system.

14.2.1 Timing Requirements

Due to the nature of their inputs and outputs, embedded systems may have several different types of timing constraints.

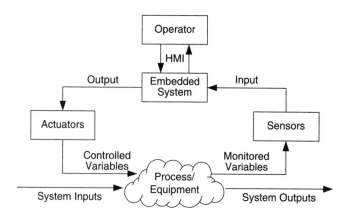

Figure 14-1: Embedded System

Sensors provide information needed to detect events that occur in the external environment. Because these events occur in the real world, they are seldom completely predictable. Events may be characterized as *periodic* or *aperiodic*. Periodic events occur with a fixed time interval, which may include a small variation known as *jitter*. Aperiodic events do not occur with a regular time interval—they are more or less random. Aperiodic events may be bounded in time (i.e., there is a known minimum time between events), or they may be unbounded (in which case their arrivals must be characterized using a statistical distribution). Aperiodic events may also exhibit "bursty" behavior, whereby sequences of events may occur in clusters.

As discussed above, timing constraints in real-time systems arise because of the nature of the external events to which they must respond. Timing constraints can also arise because of the nature of the devices that are attached to the system, and the semantics of the application. For example, an analog-to-digital converter is not ready for reading immediately after receiving an input. A certain amount of time must pass in order for the device to convert the analog signal to a digital value. Or, it may be that a push-button switch must be closed for a certain amount of time (e.g., 10 ms.) in order for a pressed event to be recognized.

Similarly, the semantics of the application may limit the rate at which the system responds to events or produces outputs. For example, in an industrial process control application, responding too rapidly to a change in a monitored quantity, such as temperature, can sometimes cause wide fluctuations in its value (a phenomenon known as hysteresis). You've probably experienced a similar phenomenon with the temperature control in a room. Someone turns up the heat, and when the room doesn't immediately warm up, turns it up some more. Then the room becomes too warm, so he/she turns down the heat. Then the room becomes too cool and the cycle repeats. In a heart pacemaker, there is a minimum amount of time that must pass between pacing pulses. If the pulses are too close together, it may cause the heart to beat in an uncontrolled way known as ventricular fibrillation which, if untreated, could lead to death.

Because of these phenomena, real-time embedded systems often have different types of timing constraints than other types of applications. Three types of timing constraints are typical [Dasarathy 1985]: maximum, minimum, and duration. All of these types of constraints can be specified using time expressions such as the following, written in the UML's Object Constraint Language (OCL):

1. *Maximum*: No more than t units of time may pass between the occurrence of one event and the occurrence of another.

   {event2.time() - event1.time() $\leq$ t}

2. *Minimum*: No less than t units of time may pass between the occurrence of two events.

   {event2.time() - event1.time() $\geq$ t}

3. *Duration*: A state must exist for t units of time.

   {state.endTime() - state.startTime() = t}

Note that any of the relational operators (=, $\leq$ and $\geq$) can be used in these expressions.

Booch et al. [Booch et al. 1999] provide examples of other time expressions that are useful for real-time systems. These include:

{every 1 ms.}	a periodic event that occurs every millisecond
{after 10 sec.}	the event occurs 10 seconds after some other event (such as entering a state)
{when 9:02am}	an absolute time

14.2.2 Hardware Constraints

The size of the processor used in a real-time application may be limited by several factors. Economic considerations may force the choice of a slower processor or smaller memory. This is especially true in consumer products where even a small per-unit saving on millions of units can have a significant impact on profitability. Consider, for example, the remote control unit for a videocassette recorder (VCR). A memory upgrade for the on-board processor may cost only $1.00 per unit but, if you produce a million units a year, this adds $1,000,000 to your annual production costs.

Environmental considerations, such as limits on power consumption, may also constrain the choice of processor. For example, the power consumption of the processor in a space probe may be constrained by the power output of the satellite's solar panels.

14.2.3 Real-Time Operating Systems

Real-time systems typically execute under the control of a real-time operating system (RTOS). The RTOS may be either a commercial or home-grown operating system designed specifically for real-time applications, or a general-purpose operating system that has been augmented with features that support real-time applications.

An RTOS provides many services similar to those provided by other types of operating systems, including memory management, device I/O service routines, multitasking, and interprocess communication. These services are different from those in a general-purpose operating system, however.

One of the biggest differences between a traditional UNIX operating system and an RTOS is the scheduling policy. In UNIX, for example, multitasking emphasizes fairness—all tasks have equal access to the CPU. This may be achieved by simply giving each task a turn to use the CPU, and relying on each task to be well behaved, or by using a preemptive scheduler that periodically interrupts the executing task and allows another process access to the CPU. An RTOS must be able to assign priorities to tasks, and interrupt the executing task to allow one with a higher priority to execute instead.

These context switches can be resource intensive, so an RTOS typically provides mechanisms for efficient context switches, as well as other mechanisms (e.g., locking a task in memory to avoid swapping it in from disk), to reduce the overhead required to switch from one task to another.

14.2.4 Distributed Systems

Many embedded real-time systems are distributed. Distribution may be used for a number of reasons. For example, multiple processors may be used to take advantage of some inherent parallelism in a computation to speed up the processing. Or, specialized processors (such as a digital signal processor, or DSP) may be used to perform specialized functions. Finally, multiple processors may be used to locate a controller close to the physical process it controls. An example would be a process control application in which there are several workstations on an automated assembly line, each with its own controller.

14.2.5 Database

Many real-time systems also interact with a database. For example, it may be necessary to log certain information (such as the occurrence of an event), or to use information from the database to determine how to respond to an event. The database may be in memory, on disk, or even on a remote node in the system.

The Spread-the-Load Principle is in Section 9.5. The Flex Time pattern is in Section 10.6.

It is not unusual to encounter an in-memory real-time database that is periodically written to an archival database on another processor. In these cases, the usual problems of simultaneous access to data (also known as database locking) must be overcome, while preserving performance. The database archive example explained with the Spread-the-Load Principle and the Flex Time pattern addressed these performance issues.

14.3 Performance Issues

The principal performance issues in embedded real-time systems are
*   *Response time*: the amount of time required to respond to an event

- *Throughput:* the number of events that can be processed in a given amount of time or, for database interaction, the amount of data that can be transferred in a given amount of time
- *Stability:* the quality whereby a symbol on a display should move smoothly across the screen and not jitter or dance around. To prevent jitter, the computation that sets its position each cycle must meet its deadline and must not finish *too* soon, and it must not have high variability in completion time.
- *Schedulability:* the ability to guarantee that certain critical deadlines will be met, even under conditions where the system is temporarily overloaded

14.3.1 Response Time and Throughput

For non-real-time software, we are primarily interested in average values for response time and throughput. For example, in a customer service department inquiryTransaction, it is sufficient to evaluate the predicted average response time. The average may vary during peak and non-peak hours. For real-time software, peak values are typically more interesting than averages. For example, a real-time stock quotation system must keep the price of every stock up-to-date, while processing tens of thousands of transactions per hour. Losing transactions during peak hours is not acceptable. In this case, we would evaluate the maximum response time and the peak throughput.

In other embedded real-time systems, it may be important to know what percent of responses meet their timing deadlines. For example, in a telephony switch, a performance objective might be to provide a dial tone within 0.5 second of a subscriber lifting the receiver to place a call 99% of the time.

Response times for events are typically stated as end-to-end requirements; that is, the amount of time from when the event is received until the response is complete. Typically, the response to such an event will involve collaboration among several objects. In these cases, it is useful to break the overall performance goal into components corresponding to individual operations or chains of related operations, and assign a "performance budget" to each component. Drawing a sequence diagram for the collaboration will help you assign performance budgets, and allow you to create software execution models to determine whether these budgets can be met.

In situations where the software is temporarily overloaded, it may not be possible to meet objectives for response time or throughput. Performance objectives should specify what should happen in these cases. For example, consider the telephony switch mentioned above. If the performance goal is to provide a dial tone within 0.5 second of a subscriber lifting the receiver to place a call, what happens if the switch is overloaded and cannot meet this deadline? One possibility is to put the request in a queue and apply the dial tone as soon as possible, whatever amount of time has passed. An alternative is to "drop" the request (providing no dial tone at all) and assume that the user will hang up and try again when the deadline can be met. Whichever alternative is selected, it should be documented as part of the performance specification.

Another way to deal with temporary overloads is to identify a critical set of tasks that must be performed under all conditions, and then ensure that their deadlines can, in fact, be met—even if other tasks are not performed. This is the issue addressed by schedulability analysis, which is discussed in the next section.

14.3.2 Schedulability

Schedulability is concerned with determining whether certain critical tasks in a multitasking system will meet their deadlines, even under conditions where the software is temporarily overloaded. A complete discussion of schedulability is beyond the scope of this book. However, this section provides an introduction to the topic and indicates how SPE can assist in performing the analysis.

While there are many techniques for scheduling tasks in real-time systems, the best known is *Rate Monotonic Analysis* (RMA). RMA is a set of techniques that you can use to determine whether a set of tasks is *schedulable*. A set of tasks is schedulable if all of its deadlines are met; that is, if every task in the set finishes processing before the end of its period.

Note: The term *task* is used here to indicate a unit of concurrency—either a process or a thread.

RMA is based on Rate Monotonic Scheduling theory [Liu and Layland 1973]. Rate monotonic scheduling provides an algorithm for scheduling a set of tasks that are periodic, are not synchronized with one another, do not suspend themselves during execution, and are capable of being preempted by higher-priority tasks.

According to the following theorem, such a set of tasks will always meet its deadlines if the following condition is met:

$$\frac{C_1}{T_1} + \frac{C_2}{T_2} + \ldots + \frac{C_n}{T_n} \le U(n)$$

where: C_i is the execution time for task i

T_i is the time between activations (the *period*) for task i

n is the number of tasks

$U(n)$ is the utilization bound for n tasks

and: $U(n) = n(2^{1/n} - 1)$

In addition, the task with the shortest period is assigned the highest priority, the task with the next shortest period is assigned the next highest priority, and so on. The quantity C_i/T_i, the ratio of the task's busy time to its period, is known as the utilization of task i. Note that the utilization bound for the set of tasks depends only on the number of tasks.

Note: The term "rate monotonic scheduling" derives from the fact that task priorities are a *monotonic* function of the *rate* of the periodic process.

Example 14-1 illustrates the calculation for a hypothetical set of tasks. The algorithm illustrated in Example 14-1 is pessimistic in that it considers the worst case. There may be sets of tasks whose utilization is greater than the bound, but which are still schedulable. This algorithm also requires that the very restrictive set of assumptions about the tasks described above holds true. Work at the Software Engineering Institute (SEI) has extended rate monotonic theory to include a comprehensive set of analytical methods for scheduling in real-time systems. This set of methods is known as Rate Monotonic Analysis. It provides techniques for dealing with more realistic situations as well as aperiodic tasks,

Example 14-1: Rate Monotonic Analysis

Consider the following three periodic tasks:

Task	Execution Time	Period	Deadline
1	18 ms.	90 ms.	90 ms.
2	35 ms.	125 ms.	125 ms.
3	86 ms.	300 ms.	300 ms.

Inserting the execution times and periods for these three tasks into the schedulability condition presented above gives:

$$\frac{18}{90} + \frac{35}{125} + \frac{100}{350} \leq U(3) = 3(2^{1/3} - 1)$$

The total utilization of these tasks is 0.767, and the utilization bound for three tasks is 0.779. Because the total utilization is less than the bound, the tasks are schedulable. That is, they will meet their deadlines if task 1 is given the highest priority, task 2 is given the next highest priority, and task 3 is given the lowest priority.

synchronization requirements, priority inversion, and other situations that arise in real-time systems. A detailed discussion of rate monotonic analysis appears in [Klein et al. 1993].

How does SPE relate to rate monotonic scheduling? Consider the calculation illustrated in Example 14-1. In order to use this algorithm, we need to know the execution time and the period for each task. The period for the task is usually determined by the frequency of the event to which it responds. If the event occurs every 90 ms., then the task must execute in less than 90 ms. if every event is to be handled.

We only have control over the execution time of a task; its period and deadline are fixed by the nature of the system we are constructing. The techniques described in this book allow you to estimate the execution time early in the process, before any code has been written. A software execution model is sufficient for these estimates, because the rate monotonic algorithm handles contention effects.

Best- and worst-case analysis is discussed in Chapter 1.

Using best- and worst-case analyses will bound the execution time for each task. If the worst-case estimate is within the bounds of the rate monotonic algorithm, you can proceed with confidence. The SPE techniques will help you manage performance throughout the development process to ensure that you meet your goals.

If the best-case estimate indicates that there are problems, you may need to refine your requirements. For example, you may be able to find a Fast Path that requires less processing for this event. Alternatively, you may be able to reduce the amount of processing required for another task, so that the entire set is schedulable.

Performance measurement is discussed in Chapter 8.

If the model analyses for one or more tasks are somewhere between the best and worst, those tasks represent a high performance risk. You may want to prototype or implement them early, and measure their performance to reduce that risk.

14.4 SPE Models for Embedded Real-Time Systems

The SPE process is described fully in Chapter 15.

As with other types of software, we follow the SPE process introduced in Chapter 2. We begin by identifying the critical use cases. Typically, these are the uses of the system that are most important to responsiveness as seen by users. For embedded real-time systems, however, we are typically more concerned with responding to external events than with processing end-user transactions. In many cases, a critical use case might not involve end-users at all. The external actors that participate in the use case may be devices or other systems rather than users.

Augmented sequence diagrams are described in Chapter 3.

Once the critical use cases have been identified, we select the key performance scenarios for these use cases. These are most likely to be the scenarios that are executed most frequently; that is, those that correspond to the most frequent events. In addition, there may be some critical events that don't occur frequently, but must be handled whenever they do occur. These key scenarios should be represented using augmented sequence diagrams.

The simple-model strategy is discussed in Chapter 1.

The approach to performance modeling for embedded real-time systems follows the simple-model strategy. At each step along the way, we construct and solve the simplest possible model that identifies problems with the software's architecture, design, or implementation plans. Thus, we begin by translating the key performance scenarios into one or more software execution models. Solving this model gives the end-to-end time required to respond to an event in the absence of contention delays. After fixing any problems identified by the software execution model, we proceed to solve the system execution model to evaluate the effects of contention delays and interaction among scenarios.

We start with deliberately simple models of the distributed environment. We begin by creating a software execution model for each process. Whenever the process interacts with another process, we estimate the delay required to receive the result from the remote process. Details of this simple-model approach for modeling distributed systems are in Chapter 5.

Thus far, most of our discussion of performance models has focused on using them to compute anticipated response time and CPU utilization. These quantities are also important for embedded real-time software.

14.5 Case Study: Telephony Switching

This case study illustrates an SPE study for a typical real-time embedded system: the software for a telephony switch. This is not a hard real-time system, but it does have some important performance objectives which are driven primarily by economic considerations: A telephony system should be able to handle as many calls per hour as possible.

The case study is based on information in [Schwartz 1988] and our own experience. It is not intended to be representative of any existing system. Some aspects of the call processing have been simplified so that we may focus on the basic performance issues and modeling techniques.

14.5.1 Overview

When a subscriber places a call, the local switch (the one that is connected to the caller's telephone) must perform a number of actions to set up and connect the call, and, when the call is completed, it must be cleared. For simplicity, we'll focus on the simplest type of call, often referred to as POTS (plain, ordinary telephone service). Figure 14-2 schematically illustrates the connection between the calling and called telephones. Note that switches A and B may be connected directly, or they may be connected by a route through the public switched telephone network (PSTN). It is also possible that the calling and called telephones are connected to the same local switch.

Figure 14-2: Telephony Network

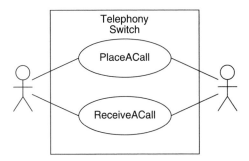

Figure 14-3: POTS Use Case Diagram

Figure 14-3 shows a use case diagram for the telephony switch. Since we're limiting ourselves to POTS calls, the only use cases are PlaceACall and ReceiveACall. In placing or receiving a call, the local switch interacts directly with only one other switch in the PSTN. There may, however, be several intermediary switches involved between the caller and the receiver of the call.

Figure 14-4 shows the sequence of events required to complete a call for a customer. For simplicity, we show only two switches in the PSTN.

The sequence of events follows:

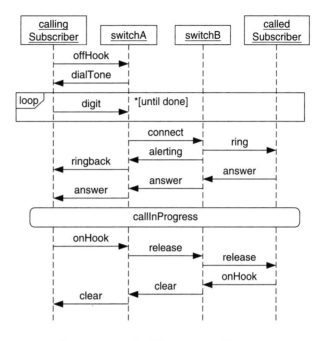

Figure 14-4: Call Sequence Diagram

1. The caller picks up the telephone handset, generating an offHook event to the switch. The switch responds by applying a dial tone to the telephone.

2. The caller then dials a number of digits. The number of digits dialed may depend on the type of call (local versus long distance).

3. The switch analyzes the dialed digits, determines which outgoing trunk to use, and transmits a connect message to the next switch. This message "seizes" or reserves the connection until the call is completed.

4. The destination switch applies a ring signal to the called telephone, and sends an alerting message back to the originating switch which, in turn, applies a ringback tone to the calling telephone.

5. When the called subscriber answers, the destination switch sends an answer message to the calling switch, which completes the connection to the caller's telephone. The call then proceeds until one of the parties hangs up.

6. When one of the parties hangs up, an onHook message is transmitted to his/her local switch. That switch then sends a release message to the other switch.

7. When the other party hangs up, a clear message is returned.

Our task is to provide the software that manages the processing of a call for an individual switch.

Note: The sequence diagram in Figure 14-4 shows one scenario from the PlaceACall use case. There are several other scenarios belonging to this use case. For example, some calls receive a busy signal, some are unanswered, sometimes the caller hangs up before the call can be answered, and so on. For this example, we focus on the scenario described by Figure 14-4. Later, we'll discuss how to include these other possibilities.

14.5.2 Architecture and Design

A telephony switch serves a number of lines for subscriber telephones and trunks, over which calls can be made to, or arrive from, other switches. To make it possible to easily field switches of different capacities, or upgrade an existing switch to handle more lines, it has been decided that the switch will be composed of a number of module processors. Each module processor serves a fixed number of lines or trunks. To increase the capacity of a particular switch, we simply add more module processors, up to the maximum capacity of the switch.

When a subscriber places a call, it is handled by the module processor that is connected to the user's telephone (the *calling* module processor). The calling module processor sets up the call and determines a path through the switch to a module processor (the *called* module processor) connected to the required outgoing line or trunk. The outgoing line may be attached to the called party's telephone, or it may be connected via an outgoing trunk to another switch in the PSTN. Figure 14-5 illustrates the interaction between modules.

Each module also has a line/trunk interface. This interface provides analog-to-digital and digital-to-analog conversion for analog telephone lines, as well as capabilities for communication with other switches via trunks. The line/trunk interface also provides a path for communication with other modules within the same switch.

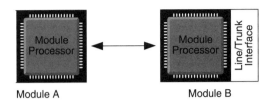

Figure 14-5: Module Interaction

With this architecture, each call is handled by two module processors within each switch: a calling module processor and a called module processor. Each module needs objects to manage its view of the call.

To accommodate the two views of a call, we use two active classes: an OriginatingCall and a TerminatingCall, as shown in Figure 14-6[1]. For each call, there is an instance of OriginatingCall in the calling module processor, and an instance of TerminatingCall in the called module processor. Each instance of OriginatingCall and TerminatingCall has a DigitAnalyzer object to analyze the dialed digits, and a (shared) Path object to establish and maintain the connection. These are passive objects that execute on the thread of control belonging to their respective call objects.

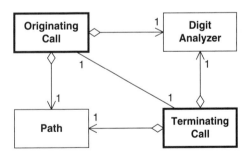

Figure 14-6: Class Diagram

When a subscriber goes "off hook," an OriginatingCall object is created to handle the call. The OriginatingCall object, in turn, creates instances of DigitAnalyzer and Path as needed. (The Path object maintains the

---

1. The active classes are indicated using the usual stereotype of a thick-bordered rectangle.

physical connection through the switch—it does not need to interact with other objects.) The refined sequence diagram for call origination is shown in Figure 14-7. There is a similar refined sequence diagram for call termination which is not shown here.

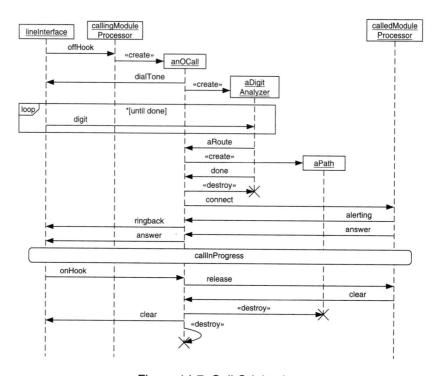

Figure 14-7: Call Origination

Note: We have already seen that creating a new call object for each call is an example of the Excessive Dynamic Allocation antipattern. This example illustrates how you would uncover and fix this problem using performance models.

The software model for call origination is straightforward; there is no looping or repetition. The only issue in constructing this model is how to handle the time between when the call is connected and when one of the parties hangs up. We could estimate an average call duration, and include it as a delay corresponding to the callInProgress step in the sequence diagram. This is awkward, however, and the long delay will hide more interesting aspects of the model solution.

It is much simpler to divide this scenario into two parts: one for initiating the call, and one for ending the call. Thus, we create a separate performance scenario for originating a call and for a hang-up. The hang-up scenario would have the same intensity (arrival rate) as call origination, because every call that is begun must also be ended.

We actually have four performance scenarios for each module processor: call origination (for calls that originate in that module), call termination (for calls that terminate in that module), calling-party hang-up (for when the calling party hangs up first), and called-party hang-up (for when the called party hangs up first).

Figure 14-8 shows the execution graph for call origination. Most of the nodes in this execution graph are expanded nodes that aggregate several steps in the sequence diagram of Figure 14-7. This graph shows the major steps in call origination. The graphs detailing the expanded nodes (see Figure 14-10 and Figure 14-11) contain primitive steps that correspond more directly to the messages in Figure 14-7.

Figure 14-9 shows the execution graph corresponding to the calling party ending the call.

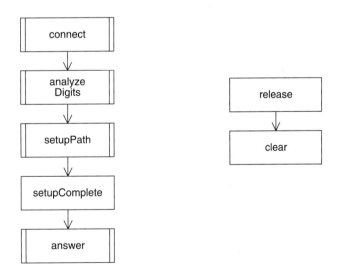

Figure 14-8: Call Origination
Execution Graph

Figure 14-9: Calling-Party Hang-Up
Execution Graph

To solve the models, we need workload intensities for these scenarios. We'll assume that a performance walkthrough has determined that a module should be able to set up three originating calls per second, and handle their setup within 0.5 second.

Note: The time to set up a call does not correspond directly to the end-to-end time for the execution graph of Figure 14-8. Call setup does not include the processing that occurs after the called party has answered (the last node in the graph). Thus, the time to set up the call is taken to be the time from when the user goes "off hook" until the setupComplete step is done (the first four nodes in Figure 14-8).

The arrival rate for the call origination scenario is 3 calls per second. For each originating call in one module, there must be a corresponding terminating call in some other module. Thus, on average, each module must also handle three termination calls per second.

To derive intensities for the hang-up scenarios, we'll assume that the probability of the calling party hanging up first is the same as the probability of the called party hanging up first. Then, the arrival rates for these scenarios are the same and, to keep a steady-state rate of calls, they must each also be 3 calls per second. Table 14-1 summarizes the workload intensities for the four scenarios.

Table 14-1: Workload Intensities

Scenario	Intensity
Call Origination	3 calls/sec
Call Termination	3 calls/sec
Calling Party Hang-Up	3 calls/sec
Called Party Hang-Up	3 calls/sec

We begin by solving the software model for call origination. This will tell us whether we can meet the goal of 3 calls per second in the best case—with no contention between scenarios.

Table 14-2 shows the overhead matrix for these scenarios. There are two devices of interest: the CPU and the line interface. CPU requirements are specified in units of K instructions.

Table 14-2: Overhead Matrix

Devices	CPU	Line I/F
Quantity	1	1
Service Units	K Instr	Visits

CPU	1	
Line I/F	100	1

Service Time	.000015	.005

Several processing steps require sending or receiving one or more messages via the line interface. We could explicitly model the sending or receiving of each message. However, this level of detail complicates the model and adds nothing to our understanding of the software's performance. Instead, we include the line interface as overhead, and specify the number of visits to the line interface to send or receive a message for each processing step. Each visit to the line interface requires 100K CPU instructions and a 5 ms. delay to enqueue or dequeue a message and perform the associated processing.

Figure 14-10 and Figure 14-11 show the expansion of the first two nodes in the call origination execution graph of Figure 14-8. The figures also show the resource requirements for each node. Again, these resource requirements are reasonable for this type of system, but are not representative of any particular telephony switch.

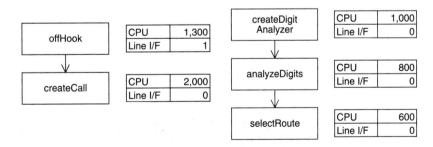

Figure 14-10: Expansion of
connect node

Figure 14-11: Expansion of
analyzeDigits node

The simple-model strategy is presented in Chapter 1.

For this example, we focus on the call origination scenario. We'll follow the simple-model strategy and begin with the software model. Figure 14-12 shows the solution for the software model (no contention) for this scenario. The overall response time is 0.2205 second. The time required to set up the call is 0.1955 second (0.2205 - 0.0250).

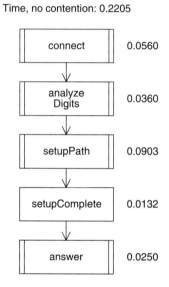

Figure 14-12: Software Model Solution

The response time indicated by the software model is well within our goal of 0.5 second, so we proceed to solve the system model to determine the effects of contention for this one scenario. The system model solution indicates a residence time of 0.3739 second for call setup. This is still within our required time limit. Table 14-3 shows the residence time, time for call setup, and CPU utilization for each of the four scenarios.

We now proceed to the next level of complexity in our modeling, constructing and solving the system execution model for all four scenarios. The solution to this model will show the effects of contention among the four scenarios for system resources. The solution indicates a residence time of 16.31 seconds for call setup. This is clearly well over our design goal of 0.5 second.

Table 14-3: Contention Results for Individual Scenarios with Object Creation

Scenario	Residence Time	Setup Time	CPU Utilization
Call Origination	0.4156 sec	0.3739 sec	0.53
Call Termination	0.2326 sec	0.2143 sec	0.38
Hang-Up (Called Party)	0.0492 sec		0.12
Hang-Up (Caller)	0.0661 sec		0.14

The reason for this high number can be found by examining the CPU utilization. With all four scenarios executing on the same processor, the CPU utilization is 1.00—the CPU is saturated. In fact, if you add the utilizations for the individual scenarios in Table 14-3, you find that they total more than 1.00!

Recall the formula for residence time at a device from Section 6.2:

$$RT = \frac{S}{1 - U}$$

As the CPU utilization gets closer to 1, the residence time goes to infinity. Our result of more than 16 seconds is an indication that the denominator in this formula is approaching zero.

To meet our design goal, we must reduce the CPU utilization. While no single scenario exceeds the limits, the combined demand on the CPU is enough to put us over the limit.

The Excessive Dynamic Allocation antipattern is discussed in Chapter 11.

If we pre-allocate a block of call objects instead of creating them dynamically, we can save this unnecessary overhead. This is an example of "recycling" objects—one of the recommended refactorings of the Excessive Dynamic Allocation antipattern. Each call object is used over and over again, rather than creating a new one for each offHook event.

Pre-allocating calls instead of creating them dynamically is a classic example of a time-space trade-off. Here, we're trading lower CPU utilization (and, therefore, faster response time) for the extra memory needed to hold the block of pre-allocated calls.

When this change is made, the software model result for call origination becomes 0.1280 second (call setup only), and the contention solution for this scenario is 0.1726 second. Table 14-4 shows the residence time, time for call setup, and CPU utilization for each of the four scenarios without dynamic object creation.

Table 14-4: Contention Results for Individual Scenarios without Object Creation

Scenario	Residence Time	Setup Time	CPU Utilization
Call Origination	0.2048 sec	0.1726 sec	0.32
Call Termination	0.1243 sec	0.1087 sec	0.22
Hangup (Called Party)	0.0224 sec		0.05
Hangup (Caller)	0.0376 sec		0.08

Solving the system execution model with all four revised scenarios shows a residence time for call origination of 0.3143 second, with an overall CPU utilization of 0.68, which is within our performance objective.

We have been following the simple-model strategy; at each step building the simplest possible model that will uncover any problems. We have modeled call processing assuming that all calls are actually completed. As we noted earlier, this is not the actual case. In fact, some calls receive a busy signal, some are unanswered, sometimes the caller hangs-up before the call can be answered, and so on. At this point, we might go back and include these other possibilities. We could then construct scenarios for these additional possibilities, and use either probabilities or arrival rates to reflect the percent of time that they occur.

We'll leave the construction and solution of these additional models as an exercise for the reader.

14.6 Typical Performance Problems

There are many types of performance problems that arise in embedded real-time systems. Many real-time systems are barely able to meet their performance objectives, and require the "special" techniques discussed in Chapter 12 to achieve their objectives. Those types of problems and solutions are not repeated here. This section focuses on problems that are generally introduced in early development stages, but not discovered until after implementation—particularly those problems that we see regularly.

Obsessive Optimization In real-time systems development, awareness of performance issues is seldom a problem. Developers are acutely aware that there are time limits on the computations that they code as well as constraints on the size of the processor and memory where that code will execute. Problems still arise, however, when specific performance objectives have not been established—"Make it as fast as possible"—or when the performance objectives are managed in an ad hoc way. In either case, it is easy to become obsessed with efficiency rather than taking a systematic approach to meeting performance objectives.

We call this problem obsessive optimization. Its symptoms are one or both of the following:
- Excessive optimization, or
- Premature optimization

Both excessive optimization and premature optimization consume project resources, delay release, and compromise the software design without directly improving performance. In fact, because they do not systematically address performance issues, they may result in poorer overall performance.

Excessive optimization occurs when developers become fixated on "efficiency." A common manifestation of this symptom is the belief that everything must be coded in assembly language if timing constraints are to be met. While it is true that meeting some very stringent performance objectives may require coding portions of the software in assembly language, it is rare that all of the coding must be done this way. Coding the entire application in assembly language is seldom necessary. Doing so does not address the fundamental performance issues, and it only increases development and maintenance costs. A better approach is to use the SPE models to identify performance risk areas, and use the model results to determine whether it might be better to code those portions of the application in assembly language.

Premature optimization is a related symptom. It occurs when a developer spends extra time optimizing the efficiency of a portion of the code, without knowing how often that code is called during important uses of the software. Thus, a significant effort might go into optimizing a piece of code that is called only once at system initialization. Again, it is better to model the software and determine how a section of code is used and what its performance constraints are before spending time trying to optimize its efficiency.

Model the software and determine how a section of code is used and what its performance constraints are before spending time trying to optimize its efficiency.

Over Parallelism This is one type of obsessive optimization, but one that occurs frequently. Because developers are trying to make software "as fast as possible," as well as achieve maximum scalability, they break software processing into many lightweight threads. The performance problem that results is excessive context switching, in order to schedule many small tasks. In the extreme, most of the CPU cycles are spent in context switching, and very few in doing real work. Traditional systems execute a large amount of I/O, and are thus able to effectively schedule other processes to use the CPU while the I/O is executing. Most real-time systems, however, tend to be CPU bound, so the number of parallel processes that may actually execute concurrently is limited by the number of processors in the system, not the idle time on a single CPU.

The Parallel Processing Principle is discussed in Chapter 9.

A better approach is to use early SPE models to evaluate the scalability properties of the architecture, and to identify the proper parallelism for the application. Recall that the Parallel Processing Principle suggests that you execute processing in parallel only when the processing speed-up offsets communication overhead and resource contention delays.

Model the software architecture to determine the amount of parallelism appropriate for the application in order to achieve performance and scalability objectives.

Polling *Polling* is any procedure that repeatedly checks whether a condition is true. Conditions are typically the arrival of data, availability of a lock, and readiness to accept input. One mechanism for controlling the interval between polls is a *busy wait,* generally a tight loop that repeatedly checks the condition. The other mechanism is to deactivate the task and activate it again at regular intervals to poll again. Busy waits cause problems if they prevent other work from executing. This phenomenon is covered later in this section. Polling itself can cause performance problems even if the processes are inactive between polls:

1. If the interval between polls is too long, the waiting process is unnecessarily delayed. It can't proceed until it is activated to poll again.

2. If the interval between polls is too short, there is excessive context switching overhead to check for the condition and then deactivate again, because the condition is (still) false.

The Thundering Herd is discussed in Section 12.3.

A better strategy may be to deactivate, and then be notified when the condition is true. It won't be better, though, if the actual delay is always shorter than the time it takes to deactivate/reactivate, or if you have a "Thundering Herd" of processes all awakened, only to discover that the condition is no longer true. The proper strategy depends on many factors such as the expected length of the wait, the mechanism for polling and its overhead, the mechanism for deactivation and waking, and so on. The SPE models can help to determine the proper strategy.

Notification is generally better than polling for real-time systems.

When you check a condition, you may not even know whether or not the call you make causes a busy wait—the mechanism may be hidden in the operation. The name of the operation that checks the condition may even be misleading—implying that you may sleep and be awakened later (e.g., an Object.nap operation with a busy wait inside).

Busy waits are sometimes appropriate when the duration of the wait is very short, and there are enough spare processors. A problem occurs, however, when the task executing the busy wait actually prevents the condition from becoming true.

We saw an interesting example in which several inputHandlers received input, processed it, and then synchronized with a single downstream process that accepted the input. The synchronization was actually a hidden busy wait, so if an inputHandler had data but the downstream process was unable to accept it, it would busy wait until the input could be accepted. The problem was that the busy wait prevented the downstream process from executing so that it could reach the "ready" condition. The inputHandler eventually timed out, but if another inputHandler was scheduled next (rather than the downstream process), it would begin another busy wait.

> *Don't use busy waits if they will prevent other, more important work from executing.*

Flow Balancing Filters in a pipe-and-filter architecture perform some processing and then pass the results, via a pipe, to a downstream filter for additional processing [Shaw and Garlan 1996]. Filters may then execute in parallel, and a filter may be multithreaded to increase its throughput. Pipe-and-filter architectures are particularly well suited to data acquisition applications. Problems can occur, however, when the processing rates of filters in a pipeline are imbalanced. Two problems are typical: imbalanced filter processing rates, and flow control between filters. Each is discussed below.

The first problem, imbalanced filter processing rates, occurs when one filter is considerably slower than the others in the pipeline. In this case, the overall throughput of the pipeline will be determined by the throughput of the slowest filter—the *dominant filter*. If there are many other filters that are much faster than the dominant one, the system spends unnecessary time in context switches. The overall throughput can be improved by combining the faster filters, if the cycles used in context switching can be reclaimed to speed up the dominant filter.

You can use the SPE models to compute the maximum processing time per filter given the overall throughput objective for the pipeline. This will allow you to identify filters that can be combined, and those that require reductions in processing time.

> *Balance the rate of pipelined processing stages.*

The second problem, flow control, occurs when the transfer of data between filters is not well balanced. For example, a filter may receive its input in "bursts," causing it to be idle for long periods, which are followed by short periods in which it is overloaded.

Locking mechanisms are discussed in Chapter 12.

The transfer of data between filters is typically managed by using a buffer to regulate the flow. Two buffer-handling issues affect the overall performance: the locking mechanism on the buffer, and the number of items inserted/removed at a time. Locking mechanisms are covered elsewhere, and polling for locks was addressed in the previous section. Thus, these topics are not discussed further here.

The Batching pattern is presented in Chapter 10.

The overhead for inserting or removing items is high when the buffer is in external storage, when the insertion or removal requires synchronization with another task, or when the buffer is on a different processor. In these cases, you can reduce the overhead with the Batching pattern. Rather than inserting or removing items one at a time, you collect them into batches, and insert or remove an entire batch at a time.

Batching is good for reducing overhead; however, it can adversely affect flow control in pipelined systems. If the batch size is too large, then the downstream process has "bursty arrivals," meaning that sometimes the downstream process has nothing to do, and then all at once it is inundated with too much work. Even worse, some of the work is old—it has been waiting for the batch to fill up.

An optimal batch size saves overhead and maintains a balanced pipelined processing rate. The SPE models help you determine the optimal batch size. If the processing rate is critical and may be variable, you will want an adaptive, self-regulating algorithm for adjusting batch sizes to accommodate variable arrivals.

> *Use a batch size for buffer insertion or removal that maintains a steady processing rate.*

We saw an example of using the batch size to balance the processing rates of two filters in the memory-archive example of Section 10.7. In that example, the original buffer size was the entire memory database; the revised buffer size was one-third of the data.

Another example occurs in applications that use a pipe-and-filter architecture to acquire and process stock market data, such as equity quotes or equity trades. The arrival rate of market data is extremely high, and the system throughput is sensitive to the buffer size. The overhead of insertion or removal of a single message at a time is unacceptable. However, a batch size that is too large causes unacceptable delay of messages, and prevents the system from achieving optimal throughput. Again, constructing and solving the SPE models will help you determine the optimum buffer size for a given situation.

14.7 Summary

Real-time embedded systems have several characteristics, such as limited CPU and memory size, stringent timing constraints, and the need to respond to external events rather than user actions, which distinguish them from traditional information systems. Despite these differences, the SPE techniques in this book apply to real-time embedded systems. Model results can be used to determine response time and throughput in real-time embedded systems, and to provide data for performing early schedulability analysis.

The simple-model strategy was introduced in Chapter 1.

The use of SPE models to evaluate real-time embedded systems follows the simple-model strategy. We begin by constructing and solving the software execution model for individual performance scenarios, to determine whether their performance is acceptable in the absence of contention effects. If the software execution model indicates that there is a problem, we fix it before proceeding.

If the software execution model does not indicate that there are problems, we proceed to construct and solve the system execution model. Initially, we look for problems due to contention for resources between multiple uses of the same scenario. Then we look for contention effects among different scenarios. The telephony switching case study follows this model progression, and illustrates the effects of contention among multiple scenarios.

This chapter focuses on the early life cycle steps. Real-time embedded systems typically require that performance be managed throughout the software development process. Techniques for managing performance during later life cycle phases are discussed in Chapter 12.

SPE models can also be used to manage additional concerns, such as the extent of parallelism, polling mechanisms, and pipelined processing rates. While the models are useful for many of these later life cycle issues, it usually is not necessary to model every one of them. The early high-level models identify the higher-risk areas, and then the later models can focus on those areas that have the greatest impact.

Use the early SPE models to identify parts of the system with the greatest performance risk, and then focus the later modeling studies on those parts with the greatest impact.

Part VI

Making SPE Happen

Chapter 15

The SPE Process

If you don't change the direction in which you're headed, you're likely to get to where you are going.

—Chinese Proverb

In This Chapter:

- Steps in the SPE process
- Late life cycle and post-deployment SPE activities
- SPE artifacts
- Integrating SPE into the software process

15.1 Introduction

An effective software development process provides a disciplined approach to producing quality software—on time and within budget. It defines what artifacts or deliverables are to be produced, who should produce them, and when they should be produced. As Grady Booch points out, a well-defined process has four roles [Booch 1996]:

- It provides guidance as to the order of a team's activities
- It specifies what artifacts are to be developed
- It directs the tasks of individual developers and the team as a whole
- It offers criteria for monitoring and measuring the project's products and activities

One purpose of a software process is to reduce the organization's reliance on individuals. There is a persistent myth in the software industry that you can hire talented people and they will intuitively be able to produce quality software without the need for a formal software process. The work on software process maturity by Watts Humphrey and others at the Software Engineering Institute shows how dangerous this myth can be [Humphrey 1989]. Even the best teams need the support of a disciplined software process.

SPE can become part of that process. To be effective, SPE should not be an "add-on;" it should be an integral part of the way in which you approach software development. Integrating SPE into the software process avoids two problems that we have seen repeatedly in our consulting practice. One is over-reliance on individuals. When you rely on individuals to perform certain tasks instead of making them part of the process, those tasks are frequently forgotten when those individuals move to a different project or leave the company. The other problem is that, if SPE is not part of the process, it is easy to omit the SPE evaluations when time is tight or the budget is limited.

    Make SPE an integral part of your software process.

Chapter 2 illustrated the SPE process, and various other chapters have provided examples of the steps in the process. This chapter consolidates those topics and adds information that you need to make SPE an integral part of your software process. It describes the SPE activities, the order in which they are performed, and the artifacts that are produced. It also includes a discussion of the SPE activities to conduct later in the life cycle, and after deployment.

15.2 The SPE Process

SPE begins as early as possible in the development process. It uses quantitative techniques to identify architectural and design alternatives that will meet performance objectives or, if this is not possible, assists in formulating revised performance objectives that are feasible. SPE relies on models to forecast the performance of the proposed software. The type of model used depends on the purpose of the analysis, the level of detail known about the software, and the precision of the input data.

The steps in the SPE process were introduced in Chapter 2.

The activity diagram in Figure 15-1 summarizes the SPE workflow. These steps are repeated throughout the SPE-inclusive development process. The following sections describe these steps.

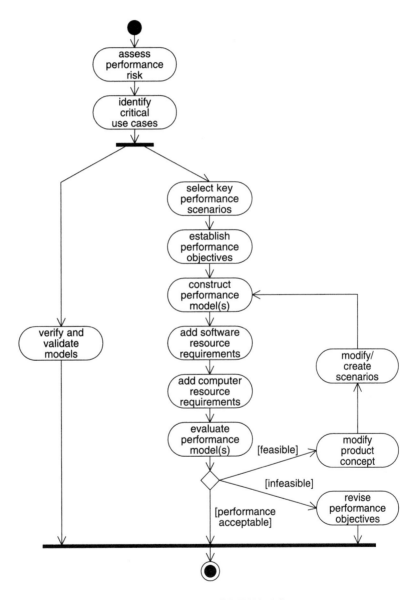

Figure 15-1: The SPE Workflow

15.2.1 Assess Performance Risk

A *risk* is anything that has the possibility of endangering the success of the project. Risks include: the use of new technologies, the ability of the architecture to accommodate changes or evolution, market factors, schedule, and others. If not meeting your performance goals would endanger the success of your project, you have a performance risk. Other types of risks are also possible in software projects. For example, there may be a risk that you will misunderstand the functional requirements and thus implement the wrong thing. These other risks, however, are beyond the scope of this book.

SPE is a risk-driven process. The level of risk determines the amount of effort that you put into SPE activities. If the level of risk is small, the SPE effort can be correspondingly small. If the risk is high, then a more significant SPE effort is needed. For a low-risk project, the amount of SPE effort required might be about 1% of the total project budget. For high-risk projects, the SPE effort might be as high as 10% of the project budget.

Match the level of SPE effort to the performance risk.

To assess the level of performance risk, begin by identifying potential risks.[1] For example,

- The Nachtfliegen Airlines Web site (Chapters 7 and 13) may not be capable of handling peak loads for itinerary planning
- During peak hours, our telephony switch (Chapter 14) might not be able to complete calls within the required time

Once you have identified potential risks, try to determine their impact. The impact of a risk has two components: its probability of happening, and the severity of the damage that would occur if it did. For example, if you were unable to complete calls within the required time, the damage to the project might be extreme. However, it may also be that the team has implemented several similar systems, so the probability of this happening might be very small. Thus, the impact of this risk might be classified as moderate. If there are multiple performance risks, ranking them according to their impact will help you address them systematically.

---

1. [Boehm 1991] provides an overview of software risk assessment and control.

15.2.2 Identify Critical Use Cases

Use cases and use case diagrams are discussed in Chapter 3.

A use case specifies a set of action sequences (scenarios) that describe the external behavior from the point of view of one or more actors. Use cases capture the user's view of what the system is supposed to do. They are identified as part of requirements definition. In UML, use cases are represented by use case diagrams. The complete set of use case diagrams is known as the use case model. The use case model specifies the functional requirements of the system you are developing.

If use cases have already been identified as part of requirements analysis, these will be your starting point. If not, you will need to begin by performing this activity yourself. Jacobson et al. [Jacobson et al. 1999] provide guidelines for identifying use cases. If you can get involved early in the use case identification process, so much the better. By assessing the performance implications of use cases early, you can avoid specifying unreasonable requirements.

Critical use cases are those that are important to responsiveness as seen by users, or those for which there is a performance risk. That is, critical use cases are those for which the system will fail, or be less than successful, if performance goals are not met.

The 80-20 rule was introduced in Section 7.2.

Not every use case will be critical to performance. For example, in the ATM, operator transactions are executed infrequently and are not seen by end-users. These would most likely not be included in the critical use cases. The 80-20 rule applies here: A small subset of the use cases (≤20%) accounts for most of the uses (≥80%) of the system. The performance of the system is dominated by these heavily used functions. Thus, these should be your first concern when assessing performance.

Don't overlook important functions that are used infrequently but must perform adequately when they are needed. An example of an infrequently used function whose performance is important is recovery after some failure or outage. The airline reservations success story in Example 1-2 illustrates such a critical use case.

Focus on use cases that are important to responsiveness as seen by users or on those for which there is a performance risk.

15.2.3 Select Key Performance Scenarios

Each use case consists of a set of scenarios that describe the sequence of actions required to execute the use case. Not all of these scenarios will be important from a performance perspective. For example, variants are unlikely to be executed frequently and, thus, will not contribute significantly to overall performance.

Additional information on selecting performance scenarios is in Section 7.2.

For each critical use case, focus on the scenarios that are executed frequently, and on those that are critical to the user's perception of performance. For embedded real-time systems, focus on the typical operating conditions, as well as on the worst-case situations that must be handled gracefully. For some systems, it may also be important to include scenarios that are not executed frequently, but whose performance is critical when they are executed. For example, recovery from a crash may not occur often, but it may be critical that it be done quickly.

> *For each critical use case, focus on the scenarios that are important to performance.*

Augmented sequence diagrams are discussed in Chapter 3.

UML sequence diagrams augmented with features from the message sequence chart (MSC) standard [ITU 1996] represent the performance scenarios. These additional features make it possible to represent hierarchical structure (instance decomposition and references), looping, alternation, and concurrency.

15.2.4 Establish Performance Objectives

Performance objectives are discussed in Section 7.2.

Each performance scenario should have at least one associated performance objective. Performance objectives specify quantitative criteria for evaluating the performance characteristics of each scenario. Performance objectives should be established early in the development process. Initially, these will be end-to-end requirements. Later, particularly for real-time systems, it may be desirable to break an end-to-end performance objective into sub-objectives that are assigned as performance budgets to each part of the processing for an event.

You can express performance objectives in several different ways, including response time, throughput, or constraints on resource usage. For information systems or Web applications, you will typically describe response time for a performance scenario from a user perspective, that is, the number of seconds required to respond to a user action or request, or the end-to-end time to accomplish a business task. For embedded real-time systems, response time is the amount of time required to respond to a particular external event. Throughput requirements specify the number of transactions or events to be processed per unit time. Constraints on resource usage may be limitations on the overall utilization of a resource, for example, "Total CPU utilization must be less than 65%." Constraints may also be limits on the amounts of various resources used by a given scenario or a portion of it.

The ATM example is introduced in Chapter 2 and continued in Chapter 4.

For each combination of scenario and performance objective, you should also specify the conditions under which the required performance is to be achieved. These conditions include the workload mix and intensity. The workload mix specifies the kinds of requests made for the scenario. For example, for the ATM, the workload mix might be 90% withdrawals, 4% balance requests, 1% deposit, and 5% other requests. The workload intensity specifies the level of usage for the scenario. The workload intensity might be 10 customers per ATM per hour.

Note: The following steps are repeated until there are no performance problems for the current phase of the development process.

15.2.5 Construct Performance Models

SPE is a model-based approach to software development and evaluation. By building and analyzing models of proposed software architectures and designs, we can evaluate their suitability for meeting the performance objectives for a given set of conditions.

The simple model strategy is introduced in Chapter 1. The software execution model is discussed in Chapter 4.

The construction and evaluation of performance models follows the simple-model strategy: You want the simplest model that identifies problems with the system architecture, design, or implementation plans. The simplest model is the software execution model. Performance models are derived from the performance scenarios. Each model should specify the processing steps for the selected scenario. Model specifications also include

- The number of times that the scenario executes in a given interval (e.g., 10/sec.) or the arrival rate of requests, and
- The amount of service needed for each of the software resources for each processing step in the model

Solving the software execution model provides a static analysis of the mean, best-case and worst-case response times. It characterizes the resource requirements of the proposed software alone, in the absence of other workloads, of multiple users, or of delays due to contention for resources. The lack of contention causes the software execution model solution to produce optimistic results. However, if the predicted performance of the software execution model without the additional contention delays is unsatisfactory, then there is no need to construct more sophisticated models—adding delays due to contention will only make matters worse.

The system execution model is discussed in Chapter 6.

Once any problems identified by the software model have been addressed, the results serve as input to the system execution model. The system execution model is a dynamic model; it characterizes the software's performance in the presence of factors that could cause contention for resources, such as other workloads or multiple users. This competition may arise due to multiple users of the same scenario, or due to the need to share the same computer resources among more than one scenario. Solving the system model provides additional information on the effects of resource contention, sensitivity of performance metrics to workload composition, and scalability. It also helps identify bottleneck resources. Solving the system execution model for different combinations of workloads and execution environments provides comparative data on options for improving performance via workload changes, software changes, hardware upgrades, and various combinations of each.

Initial models should be constructed as early as possible in the process. Model construction and analysis should be part of the requirements analysis process. While not many internal details of the software are known at this stage, simple calculations can help determine whether requirements are reasonable before committing to the project. Recall the following anecdote from Chapter 1:

> Performance engineers conducted a study of a new system early in the requirements analysis phase. Initial requirements called for events to be posted to an online relational database within three minutes of occurrence. The analysts estimated the size of the hardware required to support the requirement (assuming a streamlined software system) to be 20 mainframes!

 Early identification of unreasonable performance requirements makes change easier, and helps prevent a disaster.

As more is known about the system architecture and software design, the models should be updated based on the revised sequence diagrams.

15.2.6 Determine Software Resource Requirements

Software resource requirements capture computational needs that are meaningful from a software perspective. For example, we might specify the number of messages sent or number of database accesses required in a processing step.

Identifying software resources and estimating their values are discussed in Chapters 4 and 7.

Begin by determining the key types of software resources for your system. The types of resources that are important will depend on the type of application you are constructing, the execution environment, and the software with which you interface. Examples of software resource types include

- *WorkUnits*: the thousands of instructions executed (in this example)
- *DB*: the number of database accesses
- *Messages*: the number of messages of a specified size sent across a network.
- *Delay*: the estimated delay for remote processing

Then, for each step in the processing, specify the number of times each software resource is used.

15.2.7 Add Computer Resource Requirements

Computer resource requirements are discussed in Chapters 4 and 7.

Computer resource requirements map the software resource requirements from the previous step onto the amount of service they require from key devices in the execution environment. Each software resource specified in the previous step will require service from one or more of the devices in the execution environment. Computer resource requirements may be specified in an overhead matrix, such as the one in Table 15-1.

Table 15-1: Example Overhead Matrix

Devices	CPU	Disk	Delay		Network
Quantity	1	1	1		1
Service Units	KInstr	Visits	Visits		Msgs

	CPU	Disk	Delay		Network
WorkUnits	1				
DB	100	3			
Msgs	100				1
Delay			1		

	CPU	Disk	Delay		Network
Service Time	.000015	0.02	1		0.015

The contents of the overhead matrix and the derivation of values is discussed in Chapters 4 and 7.

The overhead matrix specifies the key devices in the execution environment and the amount of service that each software resource requests from each. For example, the row for DB indicates that each database access requires 100 K CPU instructions and 3 I/Os. The row for WorkUnits indicates that each WorkUnit executes on the processor specified in the CPU column (and requires no Disk, Delay or Network activity). The overhead matrix also specifies the service time for each device. For example, Table 15-1 specifies that executing 1K CPU instructions requires 0.000015 sec.

Note: The Network column is separated from the others because it is shared by scenarios executing on other processors, but the other devices are only shared by scenarios executing on this processor.

15.2.8 Evaluate the Models

The principal model results are the elapsed time for each scenario or event-response pair, and the overall computer resource utilization. Other information from solving the models, such as the maximum queue length, may help in establishing design parameters (e.g., buffer size).

Models should be constructed and solved for each combination of design alternative and execution environment being considered. A design change may improve some results and make others worse. By quantifying these changes, you will be able to evaluate trade-offs and choose the best alternative.

Sensitivity studies are performed by varying a model parameter and observing the effect on the results. A large change in a result, such as elapsed time, for a small change in a model parameter indicates that the model is sensitive to that quantity. Early in the development process, sensitivity studies are valuable for pinpointing areas where more data is needed. If a model is sensitive to the estimated value of a computer resource requirement, you need to obtain a precise estimate of that requirement. Later, sensitivity studies will tell you what to expect when resource requirements or processing loads vary from those expected.

If solving either the software execution model or the system execution model indicates that there are problems, you have two alternatives.

Performance principles are discussed in Chapter 9. Performance patterns are discussed in Chapter 10. Performance antipatterns are discussed in Chapter 11.

1. *Modify the product concept:* The first step is to look for feasible, cost-effective alternatives for achieving the stated performance objectives. Modifying the product concept means re-architecting or redesigning the software, or refactoring the existing design to improve its performance. The performance principles presented earlier are a good place to start. Performance patterns provide more guidance on how to realize some of the performance principles. Also, check the existing design to see if it contains a performance antipattern. If so, apply the suggested refactoring.

   If a feasible, cost-effective alternative is found, modify the corresponding scenario(s) or create new ones to represent the new software plans. We then solve the model(s) again to evaluate the effect of the changes on performance. This step is repeated until the performance is acceptable, or until no additional cost-effective improvements can be found.

2. *Revise performance objectives:* If no feasible, cost-effective alternative exists, then it is necessary to modify the performance objectives to reflect this new reality. While this is not the most desirable outcome, it's better to know it early and plan accordingly than it is to wait until the end of the project and discover that you have a problem.

   In an extreme case, you may decide that it is not worthwhile to proceed with revised performance objectives. Again, it's better to cancel the project early than to incur the cost of development, only to learn that the result is not usable.

15.2.9 Verify and Validate Models

Model verification and validation is an ongoing activity that proceeds in parallel with the construction and evaluation of the models. *Model verification* is aimed at determining whether the model predictions are an accurate reflection of the software's performance. It answers the question: "Are we building the model right?" For example, it determines if the resource requirements that we have estimated are reasonable.

Model validation is concerned with determining whether the model accurately reflects the execution characteristics of the software. It answers the question: "Are we building the right model?" We want to ensure that the model faithfully represents the evolving system. Any model will only contain what we think to include. Therefore, it is particularly important to detect any model omissions as soon as possible.

Chapter 8 describes measurement techniques that assist in model verification and validation.

Both verification and validation require measurement. In cases where performance is critical, it may be necessary to identify critical components, implement or prototype them early in the development process, and measure their performance characteristics. The model solutions help identify which components are critical by showing which ones have the highest resource usage.

While final demonstration that performance goals have been achieved only occurs when the system is installed, intermediate models must be validated and verified to prevent the need to "fix-it-later." It is necessary to demonstrate that performance models accurately reflect the performance of the emerging software. It is also necessary to conduct performance tests to determine how the software performs under heavy loading conditions.

Note: Be sure to test under conditions that exceed your requirements, in order to look for performance and scalability problems.

Chapter 8 describes how to collect the specific data needed for the verification and validation of models and software performance. It also describes how to design experiments to capture data representative of the software's operational environment. You verify and validate models by:

- Comparing the measured workload intensity and scenario mixes to the model parameters
- Comparing the measured resource requirements to those in the model
- Comparing the measured response time, throughput, and device utilization to the model results

You may need to calibrate the models so that they agree with the measurements, to a reasonable degree of accuracy, under a variety of workload intensities (low to high to extra high).

You verify that the actual software performance meets the performance objectives by measuring the software under the specified loading conditions, in the specified environment; and reporting the measured results. This is discussed later under performance testing.

15.3 Late Life Cycle SPE Activities

The steps in the SPE process and most of this book have focused on SPE techniques that are used during the early life cycle phases (e.g., inception and elaboration) to help prevent performance problems. Similar SPE activities are planned and conducted in later life cycle phases. We still construct and evaluate models for key performance scenarios and, if the models indicate that there are problems, modify our plans before continuing. The principal difference between SPE activities for late life cycle phases and those for earlier phases is that we know more about the detailed design and implementation of the software. Because we have more detailed information about the software:

- The models become more detailed. Many of the details (such as communication mechanisms) that were included at a very abstract level in the earlier models are later modeled explicitly.
- We use more precise data about the software's resource requirements. Because we know more about how the software will be implemented, we improve our estimates of resource usage and, when available, replace estimates with measured values.
- We begin software testing to verify that the performance will be as we expected. Performance testing also enables us to perform verification and validation on the models that we have been using.

- We capture baseline models and results to track and report performance evolution of the software. We also use them to conduct further investigation of earlier results.

These topics are discussed in the following sections.

15.3.1 More Detailed Models

At the later phases of the development process, our knowledge of the software's design and implementation is considerably more detailed than it was during the architectural and high-level design phases. At this point, it may be appropriate to add these details to our performance models. For example, if you model a CORBA application, and the early models of remote communication (using the approximations that we introduced in Chapter 5) show that the communication may significantly impact performance, you need to model the communication explicitly with more detailed models of the actual synchronization mechanisms.

Another related situation occurs in distributed system models: Early models explicitly represent the servers and/or the network, but represent the client processing as a delay. Later models add details of the client processing when it is determined that: the client processing is a significant portion of the end-to-end time, the client processing causes variability in response time, or you have client-platform selection questions. Similarly, early models capture processing steps and resource requirements, but may model multiple processes in one scenario. Later models might add details of how objects will be assigned to processes and threads, and study how many threads are needed.

The Batching pattern is discussed in Chapter 10.

Later models also provide timing details. For example, the Batching pattern calls for combining requests into batches to reduce the processing overhead. Early models represent the average behavior of batches, whereas later models study timing details caused by processing "bursts." Bursts result from receiving a batch of multiple requests at once, followed by a delay while waiting for the arrival of the next batch.

Note: You can predict the *average* behavior during bursts with the simple models. More advanced solution techniques are required to study details of "transient behavior."

Software execution models are discussed in Chapter 4. System execution models are presented in Chapter 6.

These more detailed models are typically more complex than those that we cover in this book. They are also more expensive and time-consuming to construct and solve than the simple software and system execution models. Building these models and interpreting their results also frequently requires specialized knowledge of both performance modeling and mathematical techniques. A discussion of these modeling techniques is beyond the scope of this book. If you want to learn more about this type of model, consult a performance expert or refer to the body of literature on performance modeling, such as: [Jain 1990], [L&S], [Menascé et al. 1994], [Mesquite], [SIGMETRICS], [SIGSIM], [Smith 1990].

15.3.2 More Precise Data

As software development progresses, more and more of the details of the software's design and implementation become fixed. As these details become known, it is possible to replace the rough estimates of resource usage with more detailed estimates, or even with measurements of actual usage.

Work units are discussed in Chapter 7.

Note: For example, when you constructed the software execution model, you may have used work units to estimate CPU requirements for individual processing steps. You may now know enough of the software's details to replace the crude estimations with reasonably precise estimates of the number of CPU instructions executed in each step, or with measurements of the actual amount of CPU time required.

Among other things, we used early models to identify when the performance results were sensitive to the values used for resource requirements. The later models need more precise data in *those sensitive portions of the models* to provide better predictions of the software's ultimate performance. It is counter-productive to add details for portions of the software that have little impact on performance, because the additional details only obscure the more important details.

 Create more precise models for portions of scenarios that are sensitive to model parameters.

15.3.3 Performance Testing

Performance testing is vital to confirm that the software's performance actually meets its performance objective, and that the models are representative of the software's behavior. Performance testing usually requires testing individual scenarios, as well as testing various loading conditions in the proper operational environment.

Performance testing includes test planning, execution, and reporting. Test planning should begin early in the development process. In many cases, performance scenarios can be used to define or develop scripts for performance tests.

Performance measurement is discussed in Chapter 8. Test reports are covered in Section 15.5.

Execution of performance tests can begin as soon as portions of the software are implemented. Performance testing is complete when the software is deployed and measurements of the operating environment are made. The techniques for conducting performance tests are those described for performance measurement.

15.3.4 Baseline Models

The models evolve throughout the life of the software with additional details and more precise data. Use these models to capture the performance characteristics of the software as the software evolves. When you reach milestones in the software development process, capture the current state of the models, including: development status, model input data, model assumptions, model results, predictions, measurements, findings, recommendations, and resulting actions.

You will likely find it useful to refer back to the baseline models to further investigate details of alternatives that you considered earlier. As you make implementation decisions and get more detailed information about the software, the feasibility of alternatives or the resource requirements may change, thus invalidating earlier results. If you have already modified the earlier models, it may be too difficult to revert to the earlier state to investigate alternatives. If you save baseline models at key milestones, it will be easier to revise earlier models.

Keep baseline models for tracking and reporting the performance evolution of the software, and for further investigation of earlier results.

15.4 Post-Deployment Performance Management

After deploying your new software system, there are some additional tasks required for managing the performance throughout the life of the software. The first task uses SPE techniques to manage the performance of evolutionary changes; the second addresses long-term capacity management of the hardware and software environment to support future demands.

15.4.1 Evolutionary Changes

Throughout the life of your software, you will likely make many modifications to it. Some will be minor changes to correct bugs, modify the way features work, and so on. Others will be major enhancements to add significant new functions, or to make extensive changes to the existing functions.

Major changes should use the steps of the SPE process to manage the evolving software performance, from assessing the performance risk of the changes through the modeling, measurement, and testing for performance-critical changes. If you have the SPE models developed during the software's creation, you can usually reuse them for the enhancements, by revising the affected portions of the model to reflect the expected performance behavior. Make sure the models are up to date before reusing them! If changes, such as bug corrections or revisions to functions, were made to the software without corresponding changes to the models, you need a relatively quick way to update the models. Consider this as you design software instrumentation, and the model updates will be much easier than if you need to start from scratch.

> *Make sure SPE models are up to date before reusing them. Design instrumentation to provide data for quickly and easily updating models after software deployment.*

15.4.2 Capacity Management

Capacity management is the process of characterizing future workloads, forecasting workload volumes and their computer and network resource requirements, planning the acquisition of computer resources to support the demand, and controlling the future resource requirements through

SPE. It is an established discipline—usually part of the computer system management organization.

Capacity planning uses quantitative methods—usually system execution models similar to those described in Chapter 6. The modeling process is as follows:

- Measure current resource usage
- Characterize homogeneous workloads (e.g., separate database queries from updates, etc.)
- Construct and calibrate the system execution model to match measurements
- Forecast demands of new software
- Forecast demands due to new requirements
- Update the models and explore sensitivity to forecast parameters and future demands

Performance drivers are discussed in section 15.5.

While it is possible to base capacity plans solely on system execution models constructed from measurements, by explicitly starting with the software execution models, you can correlate the capacity requirements to the performance drivers and their software processing requirements. This gives you the ability to control the capacity requirements by changing the software, rather than simply responding to limitations in the software that require excessive capacity.

Refer to [CMG] and [ICCM] for more information on capacity management.

15.5 SPE Artifacts

This section describes the artifacts that are produced during the SPE process. These artifacts are divided into four broad categories:

- *Plans*: These artifacts are targeted primarily at project management. They include technical plans for each development phase, as well as configuration management plans, policies, and procedures governing the production and maintenance of other SPE artifacts.
- *Performance objectives*: These artifacts include specifications for key performance scenarios, along with quantitative, measurable criteria for evaluating the performance of the system under

development. They also include specifications for the execution environment(s) to be evaluated.

- *Performance models and results:* This category includes the performance models for key scenarios and operating environments, along with the model solutions for comparison to performance objectives.

- *Performance validation, verification, and measurement reports (V&V):* This category includes documentation and measurement results that demonstrate that the models are truly representative of the software's performance, and that the software will meet performance requirements.

These artifacts may stand alone or be integrated with other development artifacts. The choice will depend on the particular life cycle model being followed, as well as specific organization and project considerations.

Adapt these artifacts to your organization.

Not every project will require all of these artifacts. For example, a small project being developed by a few individuals may not require extensive configuration management plans or detailed policies and procedures. Others may require extremely detailed documentation. Safety-critical systems, for example, are subject to intensive validation and verification procedures, and will require evidence that SPE (as well as other development activities) has been properly performed.

Table 15-2 summarizes the SPE artifacts and their contents. The amount of detail for each artifact depends on the life cycle stage in which it is produced. For example, the performance V&V reports in the inception stage will be based primarily on walkthroughs and preliminary model results, whereas in the transition phase they will be primarily based on measurement results.

The following sections describe these artifacts in more detail.

15.5.1 Performance Management Plans

An overall SPE management plan specifies how the SPE tasks will be managed, who is responsible, when each will be completed, and what budgeting and staffing allocations will be made. SPE technical task plans specify how the technical tasks (e.g., modeling, measurement, etc.) will

Table 15-2: SPE Life Cycle Artifacts

Artifact	Contents
Performance Management Plans	Description of the SPE tasks, responsibilities, completion dates, staffing, and SPE technical task plans
Performance V&V Plan	Description of procedures for ensuring that models are representative of the software's performance, and that performance objectives are met
SPE Configuration Management Plan	Plan for identifying, baselining, and controlling change in SPE artifacts
Performance Drivers	Key planning elements that determine system performance
Performance Scenarios	Key scenarios from critical use cases
Performance Objectives	Quantitative objectives for each performance scenario and the associated workload intensity
Execution Environment Specification	Hardware/software configuration, software resource template, and overhead
Performance Models	Description of processing steps and estimates of resource requirements for each performance scenario
Model Results	Model solutions for performance scenarios and operating environments, along with results for alternatives, sensitivity studies, and the computer capacity required to support the software
Performance Instrumentation	Design of performance instrumentation, documentation of API, and specifications for activation and use
Performance V&V Reports	Summaries of performance walkthroughs, performance design decisions, performance patterns used, and results of performance reviews
Performance Test Plan	Performance scenario mixes, workload intensities, execution environment parameter settings, and generation procedure. Test data: amount of data, size of test data base, and generation procedure. Measurement procedure: tools, start-stop procedures and coordination, metrics to be collected, and measurement interval.
Performance Test Results	Key performance metrics, source, and experimental observations

be accomplished, who will conduct each task, and, more specifically, what will be accomplished. The plans describe how the other SPE artifacts will be developed.

15.5.2 Performance V&V Plan

The performance validation and verification plan describes the procedures to be performed and measurements to be collected to demonstrate that the system meets its performance requirements.

It may be necessary to establish an infrastructure for demonstrating that performance objectives have been achieved. This includes the design and implementation of performance instrumentation, as well as the development of performance test plans.

It should be an SPE practice to begin formulating the performance test plan at this stage, and to augment it with additional specifications through the life cycle as the software evolves.

15.5.3 SPE Configuration Management Plan

Many of the SPE artifacts evolve with the software. For example, performance scenarios and the models that represent them will be augmented as the design evolves. Managing changes to these SPE artifacts is similar to the configuration management used to manage changes to designs or code. Configuration management also makes it possible to ensure that a particular version of a performance model is accurately matched to the version of the design that it represents. While it isn't essential for many systems to have a formal configuration management plan, safety-critical systems and others require both the plan and the control of SPE artifacts.

Baselines for scenarios and models are established following their initial validation and verification. Once an artifact has been baselined, it may only be changed using the established change control procedure.

The configuration management plan should specify how to identify an artifact (e.g., CustomerOrder software model v1.2), the criteria for establishing a baseline for an artifact, and the procedure to be used when making a change.

15.5.4 Performance Drivers

Performance drivers are discussed in Chapter 7.

The performance drivers are the subset of key planning elements that impact the performance of the system. Performance drivers document the key planning elements for determining system performance. Examples of performance drivers for the automated teller machine example include the number of ATMs, the number of bank customers, the number of bank accounts per customer, and so on.

In your organization, these key planning elements may be documented and forecast by business analysts. If so, you can use their projections for SPE modeling and analysis.

15.5.5 Performance Scenarios

Chapter 3 discusses how to represent performance scenarios.

You should document the selection of performance scenarios from the universe of use cases, the key scenarios that developers will follow through the life cycle, and the characteristics of the scenarios, such as their planned workload intensity, their processing steps, and the interactions among objects. Also, document the consensus of the team on the selection of the set of performance scenarios.

15.5.6 Performance Objectives

Performance objectives are discussed in Chapter 7.

Performance objectives describe the specific, measurable criteria that the system must meet; and specifications of performance scenario mixes, assumptions, and operating conditions to be evaluated. Specific criteria are usually associated with each performance scenario, and may be a combination of UML annotations, formal specifications (e.g., Z [Spivey 1988] or VDM [Pedersen and Klein 1988]), or specific forms developed for your organization. The mixes, assumptions, and operating conditions are defined external to the performance scenario, so there is currently no formal notation for them.

15.5.7 Execution Environment Specifications

Execution environment specifications are discussed in Chapter 7.

Execution environment specifications document the hardware and network configuration upon which the software will execute, together with other software, such as the operating system or a database, that provides services to the system you are developing. The hardware configuration defines the type and number of hardware devices, such as CPUs or disks, and their service times. The software services are defined with a software specification template; their computer resource requirements are defined in an overhead matrix.

15.5.8 Performance Models

The performance models are the set of software execution models for the performance scenarios, including their processing steps, resource requirements, and workload intensity, as well as the overhead matrix that defines the execution environment. This artifact includes all the specifications required to construct and evaluate the performance models.

15.5.9 Model Results

The principal performance results are the elapsed time for each scenario or event-response pair, and the overall computer resource utilization. Some systems may use throughput as a principal result. In either case, the results for each alternative evaluated should be included.

Sensitivity studies examine potential fluctuation in principal results if resource requirements or workload intensity vary from those specified. If these are performed, they should be documented as well.

For capacity planning models, the results should specify the computer devices (and their processing power) that will be required to handle the projected loads. The report should include results for the combinations of workload mixes and operating conditions defined in the performance requirements. Again, results may also be included for the various alternatives modeled.

15.5.10 Performance Instrumentation

Document the design of performance instrumentation, the API for calling instrumentation objects, and specifications for the activation and use of the instrumentation, particularly when features may be selectively enabled. UML notation may be used for the design documentation. A user manual may document the activation and use of the features.

15.5.11 Performance V&V Reports

Systems with critical performance objectives, such as life-critical applications or systems vital to the success of an organization, will supplement the other SPE artifacts with reviews of the SPE steps conducted as the system evolves. The documentation of these reviews should be sufficient for an independent auditor to clearly evaluate that the SPE tasks were conducted satisfactorily, and that the performance objectives will be attained.

Performance V&V artifacts consist of reports of reviews conducted to find errors in the other SPE artifacts. Early in the life cycle, reviewers should use performance walkthrough transcripts and other artifacts to:

- Examine how thoroughly critical topics were covered
- Determine which concerns are flagged for further investigation
- Identify which model estimates and assumptions must be confirmed later through measurement studies
- Confirm that adequate plans for software instrumentation and measurement are in place
- Look for model omissions
- Document measurements for each of the performance objectives to confirm performance compliance (later in the process)
- Confirm that acceptable performance-oriented coding was followed (using results of performance code reviews of critical classes in extreme cases)

15.5.12 Performance Test Plans

The performance test plans are specific procedures for conducting the performance tests specified in the Performance V&V plan. They may be a part of the project's overall test plans. They include the following:

- A definition of each experiment, including the collection of performance scenarios to be tested, the workload intensity of each, and the procedure for generating the requests for each performance scenario. For example, a "trace file" of user commands recorded from a previous peak hour may be replayed to generate requests for several key order-taking processes. Occasionally, execution environment parameter settings, such as the number of active data feeds, may need to be documented and set for the experiment.
- A definition of the test data to be used for the experiment, including the amount of data, the size of the test data base, and procedures for generating the test data. For example, you may make a copy of a live database at the start of the day when the "trace file" was collected, and copy it to the proper location before starting the experiment.

Measure-
ment steps
and plans are
discussed in
Section 8.3.

- A definition of the measurement steps, including the measurements to collect, the tools to run, the parameter settings that specify metrics to be collected, formats, and the procedures and time to start and stop each tool. When creating the start and stop time specifications, consider tools whose results must be coordinated and the desired measurement interval.

A key purpose of these plans is to provide enough details so that the measurement results could be reproduced by a third party.

15.5.13 Performance Test Results

Performance test results document the outcomes of the tests to determine whether performance objectives are met and whether the measurements match the model specifications. Therefore, for each experiment conducted, you need the specified versus modeled versus measured values for each performance objective.

You should also include supplemental information such as:
- Key performance metrics (CPU, I/O, network utilization, etc.)
- The source of each of the metrics
- Any observations made during the experiment that may affect the interpretation of the results, such as "queues backed up 10 minutes into the experiment and stayed backlogged for 20 minutes"

You may also want to preserve the log of the tests, their acceptance criteria, and the authentication of successful completion.

Note: Ideally, the person who created the model should participate in the measurement study. Changes or adjustments that may affect the model may be needed while the measurements are being run, and they may not be captured in the test reports. Unexpected measurement results may suggest the need for measurement variations that can be done quickly while the measurement configuration is up and available.

15.6 Integrating SPE Into Your Software Process

The value of a well-defined software process was first recognized in the late 1960s [Royce 1970]. Since then, many different models of the software process have been proposed. In general, a software process model provides a high-level overview of how a software artifact should be developed. It defines the basic steps in the process, and provides guidelines on their rationale and the ways in which they are connected.

Integrating SPE into the software development process is not difficult. It is mainly a matter of defining milestones and deliverables (artifacts) that are appropriate to the specific process. To illustrate how this might be done, we consider three different software process models: the waterfall model, the spiral model, and the Unified Software Development Process.

15.6.1 The Waterfall Model

The traditional process was the waterfall model [Royce 1970], [Humphrey 1989]. Many organizations are modernizing their use of this process; many others still use this one. The traditional waterfall model divides the software development process into a number of sequential phases that "cascade" into one another, much as the levels of a waterfall. While details vary from author to author, all waterfall models include the canonical phases of analysis, design, code (implementation), test, and operation and maintenance. These phases may be broken down into smaller steps, and additional steps may be included.

In the waterfall process, SPE begins during analysis to ensure that performance objectives are reasonable. As soon as the product concept is defined, a set of performance models should be constructed. These models are refined during design and implementation. Performance measurement can begin during the implementation phase, as soon as there is something running. The testing phase should include performance testing. During operation and maintenance, you monitor software under actual conditions of use to verify workload parameters and provide early warning of scalability problems.

The end of each phase typically marks a project milestone. The artifacts that are delivered at these milestones will depend on the organization, the project, and the level of SPE effort.

15.6.2 The Spiral Model

While the waterfall offers an orderly approach to software development, real projects seldom proceed in the sequential fashion required by this model. To cope with this problem, some authors have suggested allowing iteration between adjacent phases, or even over the entire process. The "spiral model" [Boehm 1988] is one such iterative model.

The spiral model describes the software process as an iteration over four phases of activity. Each iteration involves a progression through the same sequence of steps, which take each portion of the product through a series of levels of elaboration, from concept to code.

SPE fits naturally into the spiral model. Each iteration begins by establishing objectives for the coming cycle, alternatives for achieving those objectives, and constraints that affect choices among alternatives. Performance objectives may provide constraints that affect choices among alternatives. The next phase is concerned with identifying and resolving risks. Solving the SPE models helps identify performance risks, and provides the information needed to resolve them. Once the performance (and other) risks have been resolved, the next level of product is constructed. During this phase, performance measurements on the evolving product help verify and validate the models.

The end of each iteration corresponds to a project milestone.

15.6.3 SPE in the Unified Process

The Unified Software Development Process [Jacobson et al. 1999] brings together the work of Jacobson, Booch, and Rumbaugh, and incorporates the experience of many other organizations and individuals. The Unified Process supports object-oriented techniques, and uses the UML as its principal notation. It captures many current "best practices" in software development, and can be adapted to a wide variety of organizations and application domains. The Rational Unified Process (RUP) [Kruchten 1999] extends the Unified Process with additional project management workflows such as configuration management.

Because the Unified Process specifically supports object-oriented techniques and the UML, it provides an ideal way of integrating SPE into object-oriented software development.

Like the spiral model, the Unified Process is iterative and incremental. Each iteration is a mini-project in which developers perform the same sequence of activities to add incremental capabilities to the product.

The Unified Process is divided into the following four phases, each of which focuses on a different aspect of the development process:

1. The *inception* phase focuses on the vision of the end-product and the scope of the project

2. The *elaboration* phase focuses on project planning, feature specification, and architecture definition

3. The *construction* phase focuses on building the product

4. The *transition* phase focuses on delivering the software, along with supporting documents and services, to its users

One pass through these four phases constitutes a *cycle*, which results in a release of the product to its customers (internal or external). The product evolves over time by repeating these four phases in additional cycles.

The end of each phase is a major project milestone, so it is a perfect place to include SPE artifacts along with other development artifacts.

Each phase is broken down into a series of iterations. Each iteration is a pass over five core workflows (the RUP defines nine core workflows):

- *Requirements capture*: The system's requirements are captured as use cases
- *Analysis*: The requirements are refined in an analysis model, which is an object model that identifies classes and collaborations needed to realize the use cases
- *Design*: The analysis model is elaborated to produce a design model which defines the system's architecture and includes design classes; these classes are needed to implement the use cases
- *Implementation*: The design model is refined into an implementation (code), and unit testing is performed during this workflow
- *Test*: A test plan is produced, the results of the tests are evaluated, and any defects are fed back into other core workflows, such as design and implementation

Additional workflows, such as planning and assessment, may be added for some or all iterations.

Each iteration produces an internal "release;" each of which adds an increment. Early iterations focus on defining the project scope, establishing an architecture, and resolving critical risks. These iterations incrementally define the product. Then, later iterations implement parts of the product and produce increments of functionality.

Again, the SPE artifacts depend on the organization, the project, and the level of SPE effort. These artifacts are produced during the various workflows, as appropriate. The end of each iteration corresponds to an internal milestone, and it is likely that you will want to define some SPE deliverables for these milestones.

The Unified Process has three key attributes that make it easy to include SPE:

- The Unified Process is *architecture-centric*. The process focuses on early definition of a software architecture. SPE advocates early evaluation of the software architecture. This focus on architecture aids in performing early SPE analysis, and the results of the SPE models ensure that the selected architecture will meet performance objectives.
- The Unified Process is *use-case-driven*. Use cases are a means of understanding the system's requirements. Use cases and the scenarios that describe them also provide a basis for deriving the analysis and design models, as well as for testing the product. Early identification of use cases and scenarios makes it easy to identify performance scenarios and construct performance models. In a process that is not use-case-driven, identification of performance scenarios and construction of models is more difficult.
- The Unified Process is *risk-driven*. The activities within each iteration are chosen to reduce risks. Risks are prioritized and addressed based on their priority. The Unified Process and SPE are complementary because the SPE models help identify and quantify performance risks, and assessment of these risks determines the amount of SPE effort required at each iteration.

Integrating SPE into the Unified Process is straightforward. When beginning a new project, you assess performance risk by evaluating the extent of use of new technology, experience of developers, complexity of the new software and operating environment, scalability requirements for anticipated volumes of usage, and other factors. When planning another iteration, you evaluate the results of the previous iteration to determine if there is a performance risk. Feasibility models can quantify the achievability of performance goals. If there is a performance risk, you plan and execute the current iteration to reduce that risk.

Note: In cases where performance is critical and the risk is high, you might perform an iteration specifically to address performance concerns. This iteration might involve, for example, implementing, or prototyping a critical component to provide measured values for model input or to demonstrate that the component under consideration can be constructed to meet its performance objective.

In the inception and elaboration phases, your knowledge of the details of the system's architecture and design are sketchy. As a result, during these phases, you will focus on best- and worst-case analysis using upper and lower bounds for resources required in each processing step in the execution graph. Later, as your knowledge of the system's details improves, you can elaborate the model and refine your estimates.

15.7 Summary

It is important to provide a disciplined approach to conducting the SPE steps, and to integrate them with a formal SPE-inclusive software development process. This guides the steps to be conducted and their proper order, the artifacts to be developed, and the tasks of individuals and the team, and offers criteria for assessing the SPE and project artifacts. Such discipline is vital in reducing an organization's reliance on individuals, and in making SPE an integral part of the development of software, rather than an add-on that can be omitted when time is tight.

The steps in the SPE process for object-oriented systems include the following:

- Assess performance risk
- Identify critical use cases
- Select key performance scenarios
- Establish performance objectives
- Construct performance models
- Determine software resource requirements
- Add computer resource requirements

- Evaluate the models
- Verify and validate the models and the software performance

These steps are repeated throughout the life cycle of the software. The focus changes, depending on how much of the software has been implemented.

The SPE artifacts are

- Performance management plans
- A performance V&V plan
- An SPE configuration management plan
- Performance drivers
- Performance scenarios
- Performance objectives
- Execution environment specifications
- Performance models
- Model results
- Performance instrumentation
- Performance V&V reports
- A performance test plan
- Performance test results

SPE is relatively easy to integrate with software processes such as the waterfall, spiral, and Unified Process. We provided some guidelines for each of them. You will need to customize the artifacts to your particular organizational process. Many organizations are "modernizing" their process, so now is a good time to integrate the SPE process with the overall development process.

Chapter 16

Implementing SPE

Do, or do not. There is no "try."

—Yoda
The Empire Strikes Back

In This Chapter:

- Key aspects of implementing SPE
- Modeling tools
- Organizational considerations
- Costs, risks, and critical success factors
- The future of SPE

16.1 Introduction

If your interest in SPE is primarily for your own use, perhaps for evaluating design decisions on personal projects or on your portion of a larger project, you can start using the techniques described in this book right away.

Doing SPE on your own while you're working in a group has drawbacks, however. The SPE work that you do may be seen as non-essential, and you may not be allowed to take the time to do it. To avoid this dilemma, make the value of what you do clear. For example, if you find and fix a problem using SPE, point out the savings. Better yet, use your knowledge and experience to lobby to make SPE part of the development process, so that everyone can benefit.

If your interest is in making SPE part of your organization's overall approach to software development, your task is more challenging. As discussed in Chapter 15, SPE should be an integral part of your software process. As with any new software technology, achieving a high level of integration for SPE requires careful planning and management. There are several factors—technical, organizational, and managerial—that affect the success of adopting SPE.

This chapter discusses several key aspects of adopting SPE. These include: tools, pilot projects, organizational structure, costs, risks, and critical success factors.

16.2 Tools

SPE requires tool support for several different tasks: modeling, measurement, development, and reporting. Measurement and reporting tools were presented in Chapter 8. Here, we focus on modeling tools. We also discuss the relationship between development tools and SPE, as well as some issues in tool interoperability.

16.2.1 Modeling Tools

Modeling tools for SPE can be categorized as system modeling tools or software modeling tools.

System execution models are discussed in Chapter 6.

Capacity planning is described in Chapter 15.

System Modeling Tools Most system modeling tools support the queueing network model paradigm for system execution models presented earlier in this book. They are not particularly useful for early SPE studies, as we discuss later in this section. Most are intended for use in capacity planning. Some capacity planning tools provide spreadsheet-like interfaces for defining server characteristics and workload service requirements. They typically use analytic solutions to provide data for determining how many machines of what size will be needed and when. QSOLVER/1 [Menascé et al. 1994] is an example of the tools in this category.

For system modeling, it is often useful to have tools that have libraries of path lengths (such as the processing requirements for a particular type of SQL statement), or that automatically create models from system measurements. Tools in this category include: BEST/1 [BMC], ATHENE

[Grummitt 1991], [Metron] and DIGITAL Capacity Planner [Compaq]. Some of these tools also allow you to model multiple applications running on multiple nodes in a network, and the communication between them.

Other system modeling tools are aimed at studying complex performance issues, such as the scheduling of parallel tasks or memory management strategies in parallel processors. Representative tools in this category include SES/Workbench [Turner et al. 1992], [HyPerformix] and CSIM [Schwetman 1990], [Mesquite]. SES/Workbench provides a graphical user interface. Users draw models with icons for queue-servers and arcs showing the flow of processing among them, define the workload service requests for the queue-servers, and specify how workloads are routed between them. The notation is similar to that presented in Chapter 6. CSIM is a process-oriented modeling tool that was originally developed at the Microelectronics and Computer Technology Corporation (MCC) in Austin, Texas, and is now available from Mesquite Software [Mesquite]. Modelers define process activity using a C or C++ language interface with CSIM primitives to specify resource usage, interprocess communication, synchronization, and so on. Both of these tools use simulation solutions to produce performance predictions.

As we mentioned, system modeling tools are not particularly useful for SPE because they do not focus on the performance characteristics of the *software*. Thus, it is difficult to relate the results produced by the tool to the structure of the software, in order to identify architectural or design alternatives for solving problems. Using these tools effectively also typically requires a high level of performance modeling expertise. This makes it difficult for developers to use them to create simple models to quickly evaluate design alternatives. They are most useful in later stages of development when it is necessary to model lower-level details of the system, such as a communication protocol.

Software Modeling Tools There are only a few tools specifically oriented to SPE. Those that are available enable modelers to describe the processing steps of the proposed software along with the execution environment, and then evaluate the predicted performance. These tools are better suited to the SPE tasks than system modeling tools, and they do not require special performance modeling expertise for their use. As a result, developers often use them to evaluate their own software.

SPE▪ED was used for the examples in this book.

Tools in this category include *SPE▪ED* [Smith and Williams 1997], [Smith and Williams 1998], [L&S], and Strategizer [HyPerformix]. *SPE▪ED*'s focus is the software performance model. Users create execution graph models of proposed software processing, and provide specifications of the execution environment. Users can choose to solve either the software execution model or the automatically generated system execution model. The software model is solved analytically; system models may be solved either analytically or by simulation. Model results are presented both with numeric values and color coding, making it easy to identify problematic processing steps or devices.

Execution graphs are discussed in Chapter 4.

Strategizer also uses a graphical interface with processor and network icons for defining the execution environment. Software processing may be defined by specifying service requirements, or via a pseudocode-like application specification language. Models are solved using simulation.

Tools such as these simplify SPE evaluations and make it possible for developers to conduct their own studies without needing extensive modeling expertise or assistance from a performance specialist.

16.2.2 Development Tools

Ideally, SPE modeling tools and development tools would be tightly integrated so that you could describe a proposed design using a computer-aided software engineering (CASE) tool, and then automatically generate and solve the performance model to evaluate that design. This would make it possible to rapidly create and evaluate design alternatives to find one that meets performance and other quality requirements. Tight integration of CASE and SPE tools would also eliminate the duplication of effort required to enter software models into both the development tool and the performance modeling tool. The following paragraphs give our view of the current state of the practice in SPE-inclusive development tools, and how we can improve the situation in the future.

Note: There is limited integration of performance measurement tools and CASE tools [RAT]. This discussion focuses on SPE tools that provide quantitative performance data that can be used to make architecture and design trade-off decisions before code is written.

Development tools that include SPE modeling capabilities do not currently exist for several reasons:

- Software development methods and SPE methods evolved separately. Thus, the notations used for modeling software designs and modeling performance are very different
- Design notations, such as the UML, do not include provisions for capturing information, such as resource requirements or execution environment characteristics, which is necessary for automatically constructing and solving performance models.
- Traditionally, software designs were created by one team while their performance was analyzed by another. Thus, there was little incentive for tool developers to provide integration.

Several attempts at integrating CASE tools and performance modeling tools have been made, such as [Opdahl and Sølvberg 1992]. These attempts were not successful for several reasons. First, at the time, CASE tools were in their infancy and not considered useful by many developers. Second, to produce the models, these tools were often targeted at a particular development environment (e.g., the Ada language with a particular compiler and hardware platform) and were not widely applicable. Finally, the automated translation from the design to the performance model was naive. As a result, the product was little more than a performance model template that was overly complex and required extensive performance modeling expertise to complete and solve.

There is, however, no reason why current software development tools and SPE modeling tools cannot be more tightly integrated. The current trend is to have a suite of specialized tools that can interoperate to provide a complete, custom development environment. Examples include

- The interoperability of configuration management tools and design tools to allow version control and configuration management of design models as well as code, or
- The interoperability of requirements tracing tools with design tools to associate portions of a design model with individual requirements, and then perform analysis to determine whether all requirements have been included.

Interoperability requires that tools provide an API that allows them to interact with other tools and a mutually agreeable format for exchanging data. While a mutually agreeable interchange format is adequate if you only want to exchange data between two particular tools, you need a standard interchange format if you want to achieve interoperability between a variety of CASE and SPE tools. We have developed a definition of the information required for SPE that provides the basis for developing such a standard [Williams and Smith 1995].

16.3 SPE Adoption and Use

If your interest is in making SPE part of your organization's overall approach to software development, there are several factors—technical, organizational and managerial—that affect the success of adopting SPE.

16.3.1 Experience

We begin this section with some words of wisdom from successful performance managers and performance engineers. We contacted four experienced professionals and asked for their opinions and advice.

- Mary Hesselgrave, Lucent Technologies
- Thad Jennings, IBM
- Dan Petlon, Aprisma Management Technologies
- Bernie Wong, Yantra Corporation

We have grouped their comments into four categories: establishing an SPE practice, qualifications, advice, and observation. Many of these points have already been made in the book, and a few are repeated. We include them here to emphasize their importance.

Establishing an SPE Practice Mary Hesselgrave's experience in establishing a corporate-wide SPE organization at Lucent is typical. She began as the primary performance engineer on a 500-person project. Later, as part of an architecture team, she provided performance support to multiple development organizations. She now heads a performance management team that supports corporate-wide SPE modeling, measurement, and analysis activities. As her experience exemplifies, SPE often starts small, and, once the organization recognizes its value, it becomes an established part of the development process.

Mary says that obtaining commitment from the projects is important. Developers and most technical managers are usually supportive. The challenge is in obtaining buy-in from department managers who are under pressure to meet schedules, and thus are tempted to omit extra tasks.

Bernie Wong echoes Mary's comment about the importance of obtaining commitment, but notes that this is not always easy. He has practiced SPE at several companies and finds selling SPE to be a Catch-22 at every new company and for every new project. It's hard to get commitment until you can demonstrate success, and it's difficult to demonstrate success until you have applied SPE on the project. He recommends a champion at the executive or director level to obtain assistance and disseminate information across groups. However, it takes credibility and some success in order to get this support. He usually has support because he is a recognized expert, but he knows the importance of re-establishing credibility at the first meeting with a new group.

Bernie recommends that, if you are new to SPE, you should start small and build up a string of successes, as Mary did. Begin with one or two key systems to demonstrate the value of SPE. Demonstrate your ability to predict, measure, report, and possibly optimize performance. Show how the software will (or could) scale with full usage and future workload intensities.

Dan Petlon agrees that you need buy-in from both senior managers and developers to be successful. He advises that you "sell, sell, sell," and never pass up an opportunity to convince senior management or developers of the value of what you do.

Dan also advises that you not worry about skeptics, because you will never convince everyone. Instead, he says to build good relationships with those who *will* listen, and pay special attention to their projects. He described a situation in which one senior developer, a skeptic who insisted that he had the code as optimized as possible, left the company. Since his departure, the company has improved the throughput of its main product by more than 100%. More people listen now.

Dan described a "stealth" project done early on, in which the developers on his performance engineering team quietly built an application to replace a portion of the company's primary product. They did it in Java to prove that Java applications can perform well when well-designed. They learned a lot, built a great little application, and demonstrated the value of SPE to the organization.

He also recommends that you start with small projects. Concentrating on the new parts of applications as they evolve is good because developers are more interested in them. Although developers have used SPE on 10 million lines of code that spanned several projects, they did not attack something that big until they had some experience.

Qualifications Mary says that it's important for a performance manager to be more than just a "back-room modeler." He or she must also be someone who is a good communicator and is committed to resolving problems, especially when it requires escalating bad news. Ideally, this person would be a part of, or work closely with, the architecture team.

Bernie agrees that communication skills are important. A performance engineer should be someone who is able to present the results of performance studies objectively, recognizing both the emotions and politics of all of the participants. If you present results with the intent to show off your skills at the expense of the other parties, you may win some battles, but you will eventually lose the war. You have to accept that politics are inevitable, but not necessarily bad.

Dan advises building a team that includes both developers and performance engineers. He has two developers on a team of six. He says developers "speak the language" better, and their presence enables the team to build tools for instrumentation, data collection, and analysis, without adding work for project developers.

He also advises getting training for team members to increase their credibility on projects. He suggests offering training sessions to other groups as well, in order to explain what SPE can offer, measurement concepts, principles, patterns and antipatterns, and examples of successes.

Advice Bernie advises you to build and measure prototypes early in development, especially if you are using new technology. Use the measurements as parameters for the models. Measure the prototype under heavy loads to understand the behavior of the software and the technology.

He also advises that, if you are using new technology (such as a new COTS package), you ask the vendor to provide references to customers who have used it to build systems that are *larger* than yours. Contact the references to get early warning of risk areas and pitfalls, *before you purchase* the product. If there is no larger system, make sure the level of effort for performance engineering matches this enormous performance risk.

Dan advises developers and performance engineers:

- To start with the use cases for GUI-based applications, and design them from the user's perspective. He says that when you apply the centering principle (and the Fast Path pattern) to the critical use cases, it is hard to go wrong.
- To start getting performance goals early, especially from marketing, because it is like pulling teeth. Work with marketing so that the goals are reality-based.
- To do performance walkthroughs, which are sometimes all that is needed. His organization uses sequence diagrams in walkthroughs, and sometimes just the act of visualizing the processing steps can identify problems.

Thad Jennings advises performance engineers who are supporting developers in the modeling and analysis tasks to learn about the internal design of the software, by reading design and product documentation, and even source code for performance sensitive areas.

He also recommends that you:

- Reserve some time every month to try out and/or develop new tools for modeling, measurement, and analysis. "You are only as good as the tools you use."
- Don't be discouraged by your infinite to-do list. Prioritize your work to focus on the items with the most risk (First Things First).
- Publicize your successes; however, don't go overboard producing endless reams of data if it won't be used.
- Actively participate in professional societies, such as the Computer Measurement Group [CMG] (regional and national). Also, try to attend conferences such as the Workshop on Software and Performance (WOSP), and publish a paper occasionally. Publishing papers is a great way to build your credibility.

Observation Mary observed the evolution of performance engineering on one particular project for more than 20 years. Initially, performance problems led to an increase in performance engineering staff and a performance focus that lasted for several years. Later, as SPE efforts reduced performance problems, the project settled down and the people moved on. Then, without attention to performance, more problems arose, and the cycle repeated. She has seen four such cycles on this project. Avoiding cycles such as this requires that you continually justify the need for SPE, as discussed below.

16.3.2 Key Considerations

Several considerations are necessary for the adoption and continued use of SPE.

Economic Justification for SPE An economic justification quantifies the benefits of SPE in terms that are meaningful to management. Following are two areas in which savings may be realized:

- *Development costs*: savings due to a decreased need for tuning and/or redesign, such as the cost of performance specialists to diagnose problems (especially when consultants would be required), the cost of developers to implement changes (especially if a new release must be distributed to users), the cost of repeating performance tests, and so on
- *Deployment costs*: money saved through less expensive hardware, deferred equipment upgrades, or reduced operational costs

It is vital to quantify the benefits of SPE to justify adopting and using it, as well as to justify sustaining SPE efforts. This may seem counterintuitive—if you deliver high-performance software, that should be enough, right? Unfortunately, SPE success is the *absence* of problems and thus is somewhat invisible and difficult to appreciate. In fact, we have heard the question, "Why do we have performance engineers if we don't have performance problems?" The best way to counter this attitude is to compile economic data at each SPE milestone in order to document the results of the SPE efforts as they are attained, and then to produce a report on the value of SPE for each project.

SPE success is the absence of problems. This success will be invisible unless you compile an economic analysis of the SPE accomplishments.

Even worse, tuning efforts that correct performance problems that arise due to a failure to employ SPE during software development often masquerade as SPE "successes." While tuning those systems can produce noticeable improvements, the resulting performance is unlikely to equal the performance of a well-architected system. The best way to counter this difficulty is to expose tuning "success" for what it is, by comparing what was possible with tuning to what you could have achieved by using SPE effectively. For example, if a tuning project is constrained to use the existing architecture because of the extent of changes that would be required to modify the architecture, some simple SPE models could quantify the difference in performance achieved through tuning, versus the performance with an improved architecture. Include an estimate of the total testing and development time required for the tuning approach, versus the time to create models and build the software correctly from the outset.

Expose tuning "success" for what it is.

Responsibility for SPE It is important that you designate one or more individuals to be responsible for performance engineering. You are unlikely to be successful without a performance engineer (or a performance manager) who is responsible for:

- Tracking and communication of performance issues
- Establishing a process for identifying and responding to situations that jeopardize the attainment of the performance objectives
- Assisting team members with SPE tasks
- Formulating a risk management plan based on shortfall and activity costs
- Ensuring that SPE tasks are properly conducted

The responsible person should be high enough in the organization to cause changes when they are necessary. The performance engineering manager should report either to the project manager or to that person's manager.

Note: The level of effort required depends on your performance risks. For minor risk projects, one person may be able to support two projects. On high-risk projects you may need several performance engineers. The organizational placement of performance engineers is discussed later.

Finding the Right People Not everyone is cut out to be a performance engineer. Filling this role requires a special set of talents and interests. A performance engineer is someone who:

- Has diverse experience and interests. Someone who has experience with a variety of software types as well as a quantitative background will be able to pick up the SPE techniques more quickly. A natural curiosity is desirable because it is often necessary to investigate the cause of mysterious performance problems.

- Has good communication skills and a good rapport with others in the organization. A performance engineer needs to work closely with developers, project managers, and corporate leaders. He or she must be able to present results that may be unpopular in a way that fosters communication and cooperation among the various stakeholders to solve the problem.

- Is able to see the big picture. Early in development, SPE requires the ability to distinguish performance-critical areas from the less important parts of the software. A tendency to focus on details rather than on the big picture makes it more difficult to identify those areas.

- Doesn't mind talking to users—and is good at it. Users can provide the best information on how the future system will be used. This helps to identify the Fast Path, workload intensities, execution path probabilities, loop repetitions, and other performance parameters.

- Feels comfortable working with software. Sometimes, especially if you're beginning an SPE effort late in a project, it is necessary to extract details of the software's behavior from the code. It is also necessary to be able to identify viable alternative implementations when the original strategy has unsatisfactory performance.

Performance modeling skills are much easier to develop than these intangible qualities. We have seen several situations where someone who had performance modeling or measurement experience but lacked one or more of the above characteristics was designated as a performance engineer. In each case, there were shortcomings for both for the organization and the individual. For example, no amount of mathematical modeling skill can compensate for the inability to effectively communicate the results, or the inability to identify software alternatives.

Finally, the best candidate is the person who *wants* to do the job. Assigning an uninterested person to the task will result in mediocre SPE efforts. We saw one instance in which the designated person was "unavailable" for key meetings, left work early, and so on. The result was that the person understood only a fraction of what he needed to know, and was unable to adopt and use the SPE models that we had created for the organization.

Proper Organizational Placement The person responsible for performance engineering should be in the development organization rather than the operations organization. You will have problems if responsibility for SPE is in the operations organization because developers will likely put priority on meeting schedules over making changes to reduce operational costs.

Making SPE a function of the capacity planning group is also a mistake in most organizations, even though that group usually already employs individuals with performance modeling expertise. While some capacity planners have the performance engineering skills listed in the previous section, most are mathematical experts who are too far removed from the software issues to be effective.

16.3.3 Pilot Projects

A pilot project is a small-scale project that is conducted to test a process under realistic conditions. It is small scale to keep the costs low. The conditions should be realistic so that you can evaluate whether the process can be used on a full-scale project. A pilot project is often also valuable as a learning tool. Pilot projects are also safer and less expensive than full-scale development efforts for introducing new technologies such as SPE.

Pilot projects are an excellent way to introduce SPE (or any new technology) into your organization. A pilot project allows you to:

- Assess the SPE techniques under realistic, but non-critical, conditions
- Develop standards and refine procedures for use on other projects
- Train key personnel for "seeding" throughout the organization
- Demonstrate the value of SPE to management

Choose a pilot project that is:

- *Manageable*: A pilot project is just that; it should not be a full-scale development effort. The team should be small (no more than four to six individuals), and the duration of the project should be short (no more than six months).
- *Non-trivial*: The pilot project should produce results that are visible and clearly valuable to the organization. This means that you should not use a "toy" application. If the results are not clearly relevant to the types of software that you develop, it is too easy to ignore them. The project should also have non-trivial performance issues.
- *Non-critical:* While the project should be realistic, it should not be one that is critical to your organization's survival or one that is under extreme schedule pressure. If the project gets into trouble, it is too easy to blame the new technology and go back to the old way of doing things without giving it a fair evaluation.
- *Measurable:* It is important to know whether you've succeeded. While members of the pilot project team may have a good feeling about the project, this is not sufficient to demonstrate success. You should develop objective criteria for evaluating the project, such as: "Does the product meet its performance objectives upon initial completion?" "How precise were early performance model predictions?" "Did performance models identify performance problems that were corrected?" and so on.

16.3.4 Critical Success Factors for Adoption and Use

We have seen many organizations adopt and use SPE with varying degrees of success. The following factors are characteristic of the successful projects.

The successful adoption and use of all new technologies requires a strong, persistent advocate of the new technology. That person follows up and resolves problems in using the technology, and assists others in learning and applying it. When occasions arise that might lead others to abandon the new techniques, the advocate ensures that its use continues.

The most successful SPE endeavors have a strong advocate. Find an advocate to adopt and use SPE.

The successful adoption of SPE requires commitment at all levels of the organization. This is typically not a problem with developers. Developers are usually anxious to do whatever is needed to improve the quality of their software.

If there is a problem with commitment, it usually comes from middle managers who are constantly faced with satisfying many conflicting goals. They must continually weigh schedule and cost against quality of service benefits. Without a strong commitment from middle managers, these other concerns are likely to force SPE aside. Commitment from upper management is necessary to help middle managers resolve these conflicting goals.

Secure the commitment to SPE at all levels of the organization.

It is important that there be enough time available for conducting SPE studies and for implementing remedies, should they be necessary. In Chapter 1 we saw an example in which it was decided not to spend two weeks redesigning the software for better performance. The project was later cancelled (after spending a lot of time and a very large sum of money), because the desired performance could not be achieved.

Many projects fall behind schedule during development. Because performance problems are not always apparent, managers or developers may be tempted to omit SPE studies in favor of meeting milestones. If SPE milestones are defined and enforced, it is more difficult to omit them.

Integrate SPE with the development process and schedule.

As discussed in Section 16.2, tools are essential for SPE. Modeling tools expedite SPE studies and limit the mathematical background required for performance analysts to construct and solve the models. Measurement tools are vital for obtaining resource consumption data, evaluating performance against objectives, and verifying and validating results. However, simply acquiring a set of tools will not guarantee success. You must also have the expertise to know when and how to use them. It is also important to know when the result reported by a tool is unreasonable, so that problems with models or measurements can be detected and corrected.

Acquire or develop proper SPE tools and the expertise to use them effectively.

User representatives, managers, designers, and performance analysts should form a cooperative team working toward the common goal of developing a product that satisfies quality of service objectives. The purpose of SPE is not to solve models, to point out flaws in either designs or models, or to make predictions—it is to make sure that performance requirements are correctly specified and that they are achieved in the final product.

Secure cooperation and work to achieve performance goals.

Pilot projects are discussed in Section 16.3.3.

You may need to establish the viability of the SPE models to predict the performance of *your unique* software problems. You will need to establish that the early models are capable of predicting the software's ultimate performance and identifying problems. Doing this when you adopt SPE promotes acceptance of the new technology and establishes the credibility of the analysts and the models. Keeping a history of the models for the project will make this easier. This should be a one-time effort. After that, the normal verification and validation steps should be sufficient.

Conduct a final analysis of the predictive ability of the SPE models, in order to counter resistance to SPE adoption and use, and to establish the credibility of the models and the analysts.

As mentioned in Section 16.3.2, the economic justification for SPE is vital both for the initial SPE adoption, and for sustaining its place in the development process.

Compile economic data at each SPE milestone to document the results of the SPE efforts as they are attained, and then produce a report on the value of SPE for each project.

16.4 SPE Implementation Strategies

Once you overcome the hurdles to the adoption and use of SPE, you need to decide how it should be organized and budgeted, how to manage the risks, and how to apply SPE successfully.

16.4.1 Organizational Issues

One important aspect of integrating SPE into your organization is deciding whether you will have a central group from which performance engineers assist development projects on request, or you will have developers with performance engineering skills as part of each design team. There is no single answer that is applicable to all organizations.

Centralized SPE Group A centralized SPE group has the following advantages:

- Better opportunities to develop modeling expertise through broad experience and concentrated training
- Leveraged efforts because spare time can be used to develop tools that can be used across multiple projects
- Better objectivity—analysts who become deeply involved in design decisions may lose sight of the big picture or overlook other performance implications

The primary disadvantage of a centralized SPE group is that the separate group may end up having responsibility for performing SPE studies without also having the authority to act on the results. It can be extremely frustrating to watch disasters building, and be unable to remedy them. If performance engineers work from a central group, they must work closely with the design teams. Ideally, the performance engineers and designers would be co-located.

The performance studies may take longer with a separate performance group because the external analysts need to learn how the system will work before beginning the models. Timely formulation and presentation of results and recommendations is vital, especially when corrective action is likely to be required. If a significant amount of time elapses between when the information is needed and when it is provided, key architectural or design decisions may have already been made. If this happens, the required changes may be more difficult to make, or they may no longer be feasible.

Produce and present results quickly, especially when corrective action is likely to be required.

Another disadvantage of a centralized SPE group is one that applies to any matrix organization structure. That is, with a centralized group, a performance engineer reports to both his or her SPE manager and the manager(s) of the project(s) for which he or she is consulting. This situation can create conflicts between the managers, and uncertainty for the performance engineer. For example, which manager writes performance reviews and makes recommendations for promotions or salary increases?

Performance Engineers as Part of the Development Team Having one or more performance engineers on the development team has the following advantages:

- Their performance intuition can influence early design decisions
- They can provide feedback in a more timely fashion than is possible with a separate performance organization
- Their familiarity with the software allows them to offer viable alternatives when problems occur
- Their first-hand knowledge of the system expedites data collection
- They can develop the specifications for the software performance instrumentation
- They are an integral part of the team rather than performers of an external activity that is easily expendable in a crisis

The primary disadvantage of having performance engineers as part of the design team is a potential loss of objectivity. This may occur if the performance engineer(s) becomes "too close" to the problem, and can no longer see the big picture.

A variation on this strategy is to train developers extensively in performance modeling. Then the developers are also, in effect, the performance engineers. There are two principal disadvantages to this approach. The first is the same potential loss of objectivity as with a performance engineer on the design team. If anything, the risk of this is higher because the developers are the ones who create the design.

The second potential disadvantage is that, if there is no performance specialist available, the level of performance expertise required of the developers is high. This is an unreasonable expectation. It is simply too much to ask that developers simultaneously be experts in the development method and in performance analysis.

A Combined Approach A combination of these two approaches can provide the benefits of both, while overcoming many of the disadvantages. With this approach, members of the development team are trained in the basic SPE techniques presented in this book. In the early phases of a project, the developers can apply these techniques to construct simple models that support architectural and design decisions. This allows developers to get feedback on the performance characteristics of their architecture and design in a timely fashion. Later, as the models become more complex, someone from the performance engineering group can take them over to conduct more detailed studies using more sophisticated techniques.

The performance engineering group develops tools, builds performance expertise, and assists developers with modeling problems. A member of this group may also review the team's models to confirm that nothing important has been overlooked. The central group can also develop reusable models or reference models, as well as provide data on the overhead for the organization's hardware/software platforms. Finally, the performance group can provide assistance in conducting measurements.

This combined approach has the advantages of the first two without most of the disadvantages. In particular, it provides for timely feedback without requiring that developers undergo extensive training in performance analysis. It is, however, more costly.

16.4.2 Who Pays for SPE?

One of the key decisions you will have to make is whether SPE is an overhead function, is part of the development budget for each project, or both. Overhead functions are the first to go when funding is tight or costs must be reduced. On the other hand, managers of development projects are reluctant to allocate funds for tools that will serve many projects. A higher source of funding is usually necessary for SPE adoption. Thereafter, the costs of SPE for new applications should be covered by the development projects, and the recurring costs, such as maintenance costs for tools, should be covered by "taxing" each project.

16.4.3 Costs

It is difficult to predict the costs of SPE because these costs depend on the size and complexity of the system under development, the level of performance risk, the expertise and experience of the performance team, and many other factors. Because of this, it is difficult to extrapolate the costs of one project to another, unrelated one. Nevertheless, our experience shows that the costs for SPE are very low relative to the total project costs.

> *For simple projects with low to moderate performance risk, the cost of SPE is frequently less than one percent of the total project budget. For complex systems with high performance risk, SPE efforts may account for up to ten percent of the project budget.*

16.4.4 Risks

There are several risks in applying SPE. One is that the time or cost to conduct SPE may exceed the SPE budget. This is a problem with software development projects in general, and it is controlled by improved project management. As with predicting the amount of effort required to develop the software, your estimates will improve as you become more experienced with SPE in your environment.

Another risk is that the model predictions may be inaccurate. You may predict a performance problem where there is none, and possibly waste project resources correcting a non-existent deficiency. Worse, you may fail to predict a problem when there actually is one, necessitating extensive tuning or redesign at the end of the project. Both of these are dangerous risks! When the consequences of performance failures are high, you control them by validating resource specifications with benchmarks, and verifying model results with measurement studies or additional models (such as using simulation models to compare against analytical models).

These risks are minor compared to the risks of developing critical new systems without SPE. The risk of making a large expenditure for a strategic software project and failing to develop an acceptable product is much more significant. Chapter 1 cited many examples that demonstrate the increasing likelihood of this threat.

The risk of making a large expenditure for a strategic software project and failing to develop an acceptable product is much more significant than the risks in applying SPE.

The final risk is that your SPE efforts may be ineffective. That is, you may conduct the SPE activities, but (for any number of reasons) fail to act on the results of the evaluation. This risk is controlled with the critical success factors in the next section.

16.5 Critical Factors for Successful Projects

There are several factors that we have found to be critical to success in applying SPE. This section discusses some of these factors.

The Performance Objectives Principle is discussed in Chapter 9.

Unless performance objectives are clearly defined, it is unlikely that they will be met. In fact, establishing specific, quantitative, measurable performance objectives is so central to the SPE process that we have made it one of the performance principles. When a team is accountable for their system's performance, they are more likely to manage it effectively. If the team is only accountable for completion time and budget, there is no incentive to spend time or money for performance.

Establish performance objectives and hold managers and developers accountable for meeting them.

The project team must have confidence in both the predictive capabilities of the models, and the analyst's skill in using them. Without this confidence, it is easier to attribute performance problems predicted by the models to modeling errors, rather than to actual problems with the software. If the developers understand the models and how they were created, they are more likely to have confidence in them.

Produce credible model results and explain them to participants who may not understand.

*Dominant
workload
functions are
discussed in
Chapter 7.*

People are also more likely to have confidence in the model results if they agree that the scenarios used and workloads used to obtain the results are representative of those that are actually likely to occur. Otherwise, it is easy to rationalize that any poor performance predicted by the models is unlikely, because the performance scenarios chosen will not be the dominant workload functions.

Secure consensus on the set of performance scenarios, and base SPE studies on them.

Measurements substantiate model predictions, and confirm that key performance factors have not been omitted from the models. Occasionally, software execution characteristics are omitted from a model because their effects are thought to be negligible. Later, you may discover that they in fact have a significant impact on performance, as illustrated in the following anecdote:

> An early life cycle model specified a transaction with five database "Selects." During detailed design, "Order by" clauses were added to three of the "Selects." The developers viewed the additional clause as "insignificant" because only one to five records would be sorted for each "Select." Upon investigation, though, the performance analyst discovered that over 50,000 instructions were executed for each sort!

The way to detect these omissions is to measure critical components as early as possible and continue measuring them, to ensure that changes do not invalidate the models.

Measure critical components early and often to validate models and verify their predictions.

*Best- and
worst-case
analysis is
discussed in
Chapter 1.*

Best- and worst-case analysis identifies when performance is sensitive to the resource requirements of a few components, identifies those components, and permits assessment of the severity of problems as well as the likelihood that they will occur. When performance goals can never be met, best- and worst-case results also focus attention on potential design problems and solutions rather than on model assumptions. If you make all the best-case assumptions and the predicted performance is still not acceptable, it is hard to fault the assumptions.

Use best- and worst-case results to identify critical components and to focus attention on problems rather than on model assumptions.

People are usually more receptive to the news that there is a problem if you can also present alternatives for solving it. Quantitative data on the costs and benefits of alternatives will help the project team make the best choice from among the alternatives.

     Produce quantitative data for thorough evaluation of alternatives.

16.6 SPE Future

Throughout the history of computing, there has been a pervasive attitude that the next generation of hardware will offer significant cost-performance enhancements, and it will no longer be necessary to worry about performance. There was actually a time in the early 1970s when computing power exceeded demand in most environments. The cost of achieving performance objectives, with the tools and methods of that era, made SPE uneconomical for many batch systems—its cost exceeded its savings. That is no longer the case for today's systems, especially those with high visibility such as Web applications.

Will tomorrow's hardware solve all performance problems and make SPE obsolete? It has not happened yet. Hardware advances merely make new software solutions feasible, so software size and sophistication offset hardware improvements. There is nothing wrong with using more powerful hardware to meet performance objectives, but SPE suggests evaluating all options early, and selecting the most cost-effective one. Thus, hardware may be the solution, but it should be explicitly chosen early enough to enable orderly procurement. SPE plays a key role in the development of today's software systems and will continue to do so.

SPE today does have limitations. The key ones are:
- *Tools:* As mentioned earlier in this chapter, in an ideal world, SPE tools would be interoperable with development tools to eliminate duplication of effort and make exploring the performance characteristics of design alternatives faster and easier. Unfortunately, this level of integration has yet to be achieved.
- *Process:* Ideally, SPE would be tightly coupled with software development processes, and it would be easy to adopt a process with SPE already incorporated. While Chapter 15 discussed the

SPE process and ways in which you can integrate SPE with your development process, there is no off-the-shelf integrated process that you can simply adopt. You need to do it yourself.

- *Time:* Ideally, there would be adequate time in the development schedule allocated for SPE tasks, and to make modifications indicated by the results of SPE studies. In reality, however, time is always of the essence in software development projects. When an entire project is supposed to be completed in six weeks it is difficult to find any time for SPE, but without it, projects with critical performance requirements are likely to fail.

There are many future opportunities for expanding the scope of SPE. For example, many of the quantitative analysis techniques apply to the modeling of an organization's overall business processes. One problem that we have seen is that a software product meets its performance goals, but its use perturbs the overall business process unacceptably. For example, replacing a simple manual procedure with a complicated computer-based one may actually *increase* the time required for the process. Using SPE techniques to evaluate the overall business process will help ensure that we "build the right product," as well as "building the product right." Initial research in this area is reported in [Brataas 1996].

16.7 Summary

Modeling tools for SPE can be categorized as system modeling tools or software modeling tools. System modeling tools support the system execution models presented earlier in this book, as well as other modeling strategies. System modeling tools are not particularly useful for SPE because they do not focus on the software processing steps. Software modeling tools enable modelers to describe the processing steps of the proposed software along with the execution environment, and then evaluate the predicted performance. These tools are better suited to the SPE tasks than system modeling tools, and are easy enough to use that special performance modeling expertise is not needed. Tighter integration of development tools and SPE modeling tools would eliminate duplication of effort and make exploring the performance characteristics of design alternatives faster and easier. Unfortunately, this level of integration has yet to be achieved.

There are several key issues in adopting SPE. They include the following:

- *Economic justification for SPE:* It is vital to quantify the benefits of SPE in terms that are meaningful to management to justify adopting and using it.
- *Responsibility for SPE:* It is important that you designate one individual to be responsible for performance engineering.
- *Finding the right people:* Not everyone is cut out to be a performance engineer. Filling this role requires a special set of talents and interests.
- *Organizational placement:* The person responsible for performance engineering should be in the development organization rather than the operations or capacity planning organization.

Pilot projects are an excellent way to introduce SPE (or any new technology) into your organization. A pilot project allows you to:

- Assess the SPE techniques under realistic but non-critical conditions
- Develop standards and refine procedures for use on other projects
- Train key personnel for "seeding" throughout the organization
- Demonstrate the value of SPE to management

We have seen many organizations adopt and use SPE with varying degrees of success. The following factors are characteristic of the successful projects:

- A strong advocate for SPE
- Commitment to SPE at all levels of the organization
- Integration of SPE with the software development process
- SPE tools and the expertise to use them effectively
- Cooperation among user representatives, managers, designers, and performance analysts to achieve performance goals
- Establishing the viability of the SPE models to predict the performance of the organization's software
- Economic justification of the value of SPE

You need to decide whether you will have a central group from which performance engineers assist development projects on request, or you will have developers with performance engineering skills as part of each design team. There is no single answer that is applicable to all organizations. A combination of these two approaches can provide the benefits of both, while overcoming many of the disadvantages.

There are several factors that we have found to be critical to success in applying SPE. In order to maximize your chances of success, you should:

- Establish performance objectives and hold managers and developers accountable for meeting them
- Produce credible model results and explain them to participants who may not understand
- Secure consensus on the set of performance scenarios and base SPE studies on them
- Measure critical components early and often to validate models and verify their predictions
- Use best- and worst-case results to identify critical components and to focus attention on problems rather than model assumptions
- Produce quantitative data for thorough evaluation of alternatives

Will tomorrow's hardware solve all performance problems and make SPE obsolete? It is not likely. Despite advances in hardware capabilities, SPE is essential for today's software systems, and it will continue to be needed in the future.

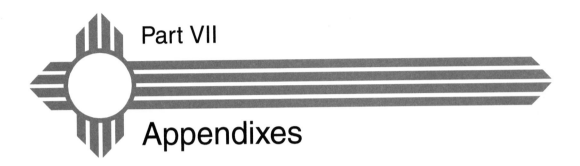

Part VII

Appendixes

UML Notation

This appendix summarizes the parts of the UML notation that are used in this book for capturing performance-related information. It is not a complete description of the UML notation. For a complete description, see Booch or Rumbaugh [Booch et al. 1999], [Rumbaugh et al. 1999].

A.1 Use Case Diagrams

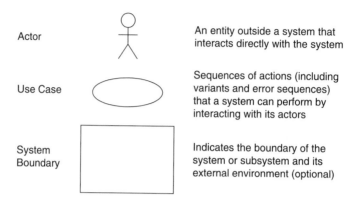

Actor		An entity outside a system that interacts directly with the system
Use Case		Sequences of actions (including variants and error sequences) that a system can perform by interacting with its actors
System Boundary		Indicates the boundary of the system or subsystem and its external environment (optional)

Figure A-1: Use Case Diagram Icons

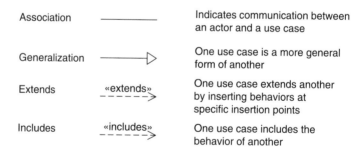

Association		Indicates communication between an actor and a use case
Generalization		One use case is a more general form of another
Extends	«extends»	One use case extends another by inserting behaviors at specific insertion points
Includes	«includes»	One use case includes the behavior of another

Figure A-2: Use Case Associations

A.2 Sequence Diagrams

A.2.1 Basic Sequence Diagrams

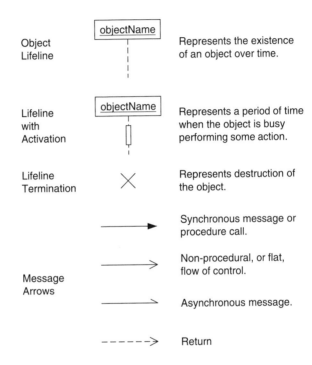

Figure A-3: Sequence Diagram Icons

A.2.2 Augmented Sequence Diagrams

Augmented sequence diagrams are introduced in Chapter 3.

Augmented sequence diagrams extend the UML notation with features from the message sequence chart (MSC) standard [ITU 1996]. These features make it possible to represent hierarchical structure (instance decomposition and references), looping, alternation, and concurrency.

Instance Decomposition Instance decomposition makes it possible to attach another sequence diagram to an object lifeline. This allows expansion of a high-level sequence diagram to show lower-level interactions. For the decomposition to be semantically meaningful, the order of messages on the decomposed instance must be preserved.

References References refer to another sequence diagram. They provide another way of hierarchically composing sequence diagrams.

Figure A-4: Reference

Inline Expressions Inline expressions denote iteration, alternative composition, optional regions, and parallel composition in sequence diagrams.

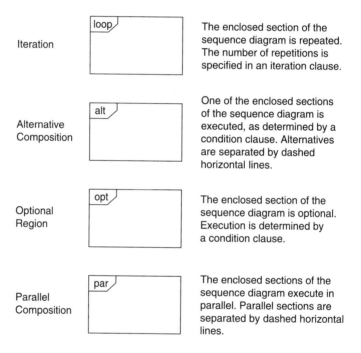

Figure A-5: Inline Expressions

Coregions Coregions allow an exception to the total ordering of messages. Messages within a coregion are unordered.

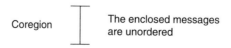

Figure A-6: Coregion

Synchronization You can show synchronous and asynchronous messages in the UML by using the different types of arrowheads shown in Figure A-3. It is also useful to model a situation similar to a synchronous interaction, in that the client sends a message to the server and expects a reply. In this case, however, the client sends the message and continues processing. Then, later, it requests the result. This type of interaction is shown using a dashed section of the activation bar to indicate that the client has a potential delay while the server finishes responding to the request.

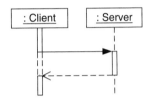

Figure A-7: Deferred Synchronous Communication

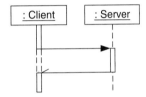

Figure A-8: Asynchronous Callback

Figure A-7 and Figure A-8 illustrate the use of this extension to model deferred synchronous communication and asynchronous callback, respectively.

A.3 Deployment Diagrams

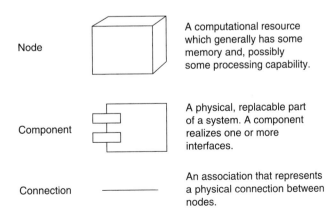

Node		A computational resource which generally has some memory and, possibly some processing capability.
Component		A physical, replacable part of a system. A component realizes one or more interfaces.
Connection		An association that represents a physical connection between nodes.

Figure A-9: Deployment Diagram Icons

A.4 Stereotypes, Tagged Values, and Constraints

A.4.1 Stereotypes

A stereotype allows you to create new model elements that are derived from existing UML elements but are specific to a particular problem domain. A stereotype is represented as a string enclosed in guillemets (« »), and it appears above the name of the element to which it applies. You can also define graphic elements or icons for stereotypes to give them a distinctive visual representation in a UML model. Figure A-10 and Figure A-11 illustrate these uses of stereotypes.

: Processor

Figure A-10: Stereotypes   Figure A-11: Stereotype Icon

A.4.2 Tagged Values

A tagged value is a pair of strings, consisting of a tag and a value, that holds information about a model element. The tag is the name of a property, such as processorSpeed, and the value is the value of that property for the model element to which the tagged value is attached. These strings are enclosed by braces ({ }) and are attached to a model element as illustrated in Figure A-12.

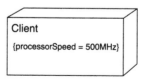

Figure A-12: Tagged Values

A.4.3 Constraints

A constraint is a condition or restriction that defines additional model semantics. A constraint may be attached to an individual model element or a collection of elements. The constraint is written as a string enclosed in braces ({ }). It is interpreted according to a language, which may be the UML Object Constraint Language; a programming language, such as C++; a formal notation, such as Z; or a natural language. The following examples illustrate constraints.

{b.sendTime() - a.receiveTime() < 10 msec}

{length = width}

{secure channel}

SPE Modeling Notations

Execution graphs are introduced in Chapter 4. Information processing graphs are first used in Chapter 6.

This appendix summarizes the elements of the execution graph and information processing graph notations used in this book. For a more detailed description of these notations, see [Smith 1990].

B.1 Execution Graph Notation

B.1.1 Basic Nodes

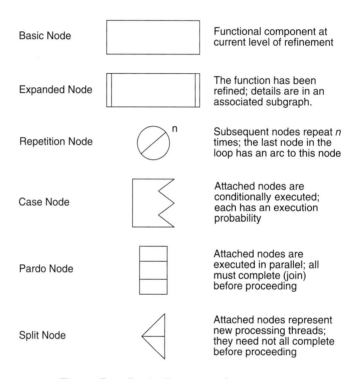

Basic Node		Functional component at current level of refinement
Expanded Node		The function has been refined; details are in an associated subgraph.
Repetition Node		Subsequent nodes repeat n times; the last node in the loop has an arc to this node
Case Node		Attached nodes are conditionally executed; each has an execution probability
Pardo Node		Attached nodes are executed in parallel; all must complete (join) before proceeding
Split Node		Attached nodes represent new processing threads; they need not all complete before proceeding

Figure B-1: Basic Execution Graph Nodes

B.1.2 Synchronization Nodes

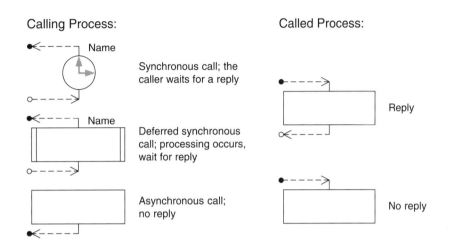

Calling Process:

Name — Synchronous call; the caller waits for a reply

Name — Deferred synchronous call; processing occurs, wait for reply

Asynchronous call; no reply

Called Process:

Reply

No reply

Figure B-2: Synchronization Nodes

Note: The appropriate node from the left column of Figure B-2 is inserted in the execution graph for the calling scenario. The called scenario represents the synchronization point with one of the nodes from the right column, depending on whether it sends a reply.

B.2 Information Processing Graph Notation

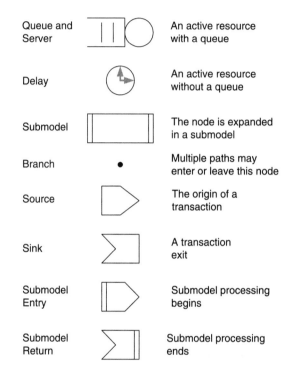

Queue and Server		An active resource with a queue
Delay		An active resource without a queue
Submodel		The node is expanded in a submodel
Branch	•	Multiple paths may enter or leave this node
Source		The origin of a transaction
Sink		A transaction exit
Submodel Entry		Submodel processing begins
Submodel Return		Submodel processing ends

Figure B-3: Basic Information Processing Graph Nodes

Bibliography

[Alexander 1979] C. Alexander, *The Timeless Way of Building*, New York, NY, Oxford University Press, 1979.

[Alexander et al. 1977] C. Alexander, S. Ishikawa, M. Silverstein, M. Jacobson, I. Fiksdahl-King, and S. Angel, *A Pattern Language*, New York, NY, Oxford University Press, 1977.

[Alexander and Bensley 2000] R. Alexander and G. Bensley, *C++ Footprint and Performance Optimization*, Indianapolis, IN, SAMS, 2000.

[ARM] *Application Resource Measurement Working Group*, www.cmg.org (Use the site list to locate ARM information).

[Auer and Beck 1996] K. Auer and K. Beck, "Lazy Optimization: Patterns for Efficient Smalltalk Programming," *Pattern Languages of Program Design, Volume 2*, J. Vlissides, J. Coplien, and N. Kerth, ed., Addison-Wesley, 1996.

[Bentley 1982] J. L. Bentley, *Writing Efficient Programs*, Englewood Cliffs, NJ, Prentice-Hall, 1982.

[BMC] *BMC Software*, 2101 City West Boulevard, Houston, TX 77042, (713) 918-8800, www.bmc.com.

[Boehm 1991] B. W. Boehm, "Software Risk Management: Principles and Practice," *IEEE Software*, vol. 8, no. 1, pp. 32-41, 1991.

[Boehm 1988] B. W. Boehm, "A Spiral Model of Software Development and Enhancement," *IEEE Computer*, vol. 21, no. 5, pp. 61-72, 1988.

[Boehm 1984] B. W. Boehm, "Verifying and Validating Software Requirements and Design Specifications," *IEEE Software*, vol. 1, no. 1, pp. 75-88, 1984.

[Bogda and Holzle 1999] J. Bogda and U. Holzle, "Removing Unnecessary Synchronization, Java," *Technical Report No. TRCS99-10*, Department of Computer Science, University of California, Santa Barbara, CA, 1999.

 [Booch et al. 1999] G. Booch, J. Rumbaugh, and I. Jacobson, *The Unified Modeling Language User Guide*, Reading, MA, Addison-Wesley, 1999.

[Booch 1996] G. Booch, *Object Solutions: Managing the Object-Oriented Project*, Menlo Park, CA, Addison-Wesley, 1996.

[Brataas 1996] Gunnar Brataas, "Performance Engineering Method for Workflow Systems: An Integrated View of Human and Computerised Work Processes," Norwegian University of Science and Technology, 1996.

[Brown et al. 1998] W. J. Brown, R. C. Malveau, H. W. McCormick III, and T. J. Mowbray, *AntiPatterns: Refactoring Software, Architectures, and Projects in Crisis*, New York, NY, John Wiley & Sons, Inc., 1998.

[Bulka 2000] D. Bulka, *Java Performance and Scalability, Volume 1: Server-Side Programming Techniques*, Boston, MA, Addison-Wesley, 2000.

[Bulka and Mayhew 2000] D. Bulka and D. Mayhew, *Efficient C++: Performance Programming Techniques*, Boston, MA, Addison-Wesley, 2000.

[Campbell et al. 1991] M. Campbell, R. Barton, J. Browning, D. Cervenka, B. Curry, T. Davis, T. Edmonds, R. Holt, J. Slice, T. Smith, and R. Wescott, "The Parallelization of UNIX System V Release 4.0," Proceedings, Winter 1991 USENIX Conference, January 1991.

[CA] *Computer Associates International, Inc.*, One Computer Associates Plaza, Islandia, NY 11788, (516) 342-5224, www.cai.com.

[CAND] *Candle Corporation*, 2425 Olympic Boulevard, Santa Monica, CA 90404, (310) 582-4864, www.candle.com.

[Clark et al. 1999] R. Clark, E. D. Jensen, A. Kanevsky, J. Maurer, P. Wallace, T. Wheeler, Y. Zhang, D. Wells, T. Lawrence, and P. Hurley, "An Adaptive, Distributed Airborne Tracking System," *Proceedings, International Workshop on Parallel and Distributed Real-Time Systems*, April 1999.

[Clements 1996] P. C. Clements, "Coming Attractions in Software Architecture," *Technical Report No. CMU/SEI-96-TR-008*, Software Engineering Institute, Carnegie Mellon University, Pittsburgh, PA, 1996.

[Clements and Northrup 1996] P. C. Clements and L. M. Northrup, "Software Architecture: An Executive Overview," *Technical Report No. CMU/SEI-96-TR-003*, Software Engineering Institute, Carnegie Mellon University, Pittsburgh, PA, 1996.

[CMG] *Computer Measurement Group*, P.O. Box 1124, Turnersville, NJ 08012, (800) 436-7264, www.cmg.org.

[CMG 1991] Computer Measurement Group, Software Performance Engineering Panel, moderator C. U. Smith, Computer Measurement Group, December, 1991.

[Compaq] *Compaq Computer Corporation*, 110 Split Brook Road, Nashua, NH 03063, (603) 884-0133, www.compaq.com.

[COMP] *Compuware Corporation*, 31440 Northwestern Highway, Farmington Hills, MI 48334, (248) 737-7300, www.compuware.com.

[Conallen 2000] J. Conallen, *Building Web Applications with UML*, Boston, MA, Addison-Wesley, 2000.

[Dasarathy 1985] B. Dasarathy, "Timing Constraints of Real-Time Systems: Constructs for Expressing Them," *IEEE Transactions on Software Engineering*, vol. SE-11, no. 1, pp. 80-86, 1985.

[DEMA] *Demand Technology*, 1020 8th Avenue S., Suite 6, Naples, FL 34102, (941) 261-8945, www.demandtech.com.

[Dimpsey et al. 2000] R. Dimpsey, R. Arora, and K. Kuiper, "Java Server Performance: A Case Study of Building Efficient, Scalable JVMs," *IBM Systems Journal*, vol. 39, no. 1, pp. 151-174, 2000.

[Domanski 2001] B. Domanski, "NT Benchmarking Techniques—An Update," *Journal of Computer Resource Management*, No. 101, CMG, Winter 2001.

[Douglass 1999] B. P. Douglass, *Doing Hard Time: Developing Real-Time Systems with UML, Objects, Frameworks, and Patterns*, Reading, MA, Addison-Wesley, 1999.

[Fowler 1999] M. Fowler, *Refactoring: Improving the Design of Existing Code*, Reading, MA, Addison-Wesley, 1999.

[Gamma et al. 1995] E. Gamma, R. Helm, R. Johnson, and J. Vlissides, *Design Patterns: Elements of Reusable Object-Oriented Software*, Reading, MA, Addison-Wesley, 1995.

[Goetz 2001] B. Goetz, "Double-Checked Locking: Clever, but Broken," JavaWorld, February, 2001.

[Grummitt 1991] A. Grummitt, "A Performance Engineer's View of Systems Development and Trials," *Proceedings, Computer Measurement Group Conference*, Nashville, TN, pp. 455-463, 1991.

[Gunther 2000] N. Gunther, "E-Ticket Capacity Planning: Riding the E-Commerce Growth Curve," *Proceedings, Computer Measurement Group*, Orlando, FL, 2000.

[Gunther 1998] N. Gunther, *The Practical Performance Analyst: Performance-By-Design Techniques for Distributed Systems*, www.perfdynamics.com, 1998.

[Harreld 1998a] H. Harreld, "NASA Delays Satellite Launch After Finding Bugs in Software Program," *Federal Computer Week*, April 20, 1998.

[Harreld 1998b] H. Harreld, "Panel Slams EOSDIS," *Federal Computer Week*, September 14, 1998.

[Herzog and Rolia 2001] U. Herzog and J. A. Rolia, "Performance Validation Tools for Software/Hardware Systems," *Performance Evaluation*, to appear 2001.

[Howes and Weaver 1989] N. R. Howes and A. C. Weaver, "Measurements of Ada Overhead in OSI-Style Communications Systems," *IEEE Transactions on Software Engineering*, vol. 15, no. 12, pp. 1507-1517, 1989.

[Howes 1990] N. R. Howes, "Toward a Real-Time Ada Design Methodology," *Proceedings, Tri-Ada 90*, Baltimore, MD, 1990.

[HP] *Hewlett-Packard*, 3000 Hanover Street, Palo Alto, CA 94304, (650) 857-1501, www.hp.com.

[Humphrey 1989] W. S. Humphrey, *Managing the Software Process*, Reading, MA, Addison-Wesley, 1989.

[HyPerformix] *HyPerformix, Inc.*, 4301 West Bank Drive, Building A, Austin, TX 78746, (512) 328-5544, www.hyperformix.com.

[ICCM] *Institute of Computer Capacity Management*, 1020 Eighth Avenue S., Suite 6, Naples, FL 34102, (941) 261-89445, www.iccmforum.com.

[INTU] *Intuitive Systems, Inc.*, 21020 Homestead Road, Suite 3, Cupertino, CA 95014, (888) 655-0055, www.optimizeit.com.

[ISM] *Information Systems Manager, Inc.*, One Bethlehem Plaza, Bethlehem, PA 18018, (610) 865-0300, www.perfman.com.

[ITU 1996] International Telecommunication Union, "Criteria for the Use and Applicability of Formal Description Techniques, Message Sequence Chart (MSC)," 1996.

[Jacobson et al. 1999] I. Jacobson, G. Booch, and J. Rumbaugh, *The Unified Software Development Process*, Reading, MA, Addison-Wesley, 1999.

[Jain 1990] R. Jain, *Art of Computer Systems Performance Analysis*, New York, NY, John Wiley & Sons, New York, NY, 1990.

[Johnson 1999] M. W. Johnson, "ARM 3.0—Enabling Wider Use of ARM in the Enterprise," *Proceedings, Computer Measurement Group*, Reno, NV, December 1999.

[Kazman et al. 1998] R. Kazman, M. Klein, M. Barbacci, T. Longstaff, H. Lipson, and J. Carriere, "The Architecture Tradeoff Analysis Method," *Proceedings, Fourth International Conference on Engineering of Complex Computer Systems (ICECCS98)*, August 1998.

[Kelvin] W. T. Kelvin, "Popular Lectures and Addresses, 1891–1894," Quoted by M. L. Shooman in the Introduction to *Proceedings, IEEE Workshop on Quantitative Software Models for Reliability, Complexity, and Cost*, 1980.

[Kernighan and Plaugher 1978] B. W. Kernighan and P. J. Plaugher, *The Elements of Programming Style*, New York, NY, McGraw-Hill, 1978.

[Killelea 1998] P. Killelea, *Web Performance Tuning*, Sebastopol, CA, O'Reilly, 1998.

[Klein et al. 1993] M. H. Klein, T. Ralya, B. Pollak, R. Obenza, and M. G. Harbour, *A Practitioner's Handbook for Real-Time Analysis*, Boston, MA, Kluwer Academic Publishers, 1993.

[Knuth 1971] D. E. Knuth, "An Empirical Study of FORTRAN Programs," *Software Practice & Experience*, vol. 1, no. 2, pp. 105-133, 1971.

[Knuth 1997] D. E. Knuth, *The Art of Computer Programming, Vol. 1: Fundamental Algorithms, Third Edition*, Reading, MA, Addison-Wesley, 1997.

[Knuth 1998] D. E. Knuth, *The Art of Computer Programming, Vol. 3: Sorting and Searching, Second Edition*, Reading, MA, Addison-Wesley, 1998.

[Kruchten 1995] P. B. Kruchten, "The 4+1 View Model of Architecture," *IEEE Software*, vol. 12, no. 6, pp. 42-50, 1995.

[Kruchten 1999] P. Kruchten, *The Rational Unified Process: An Introduction*, Reading, MA, Addison-Wesley, 1999.

[LAND] *Landmark Systems Corp.*, 8000 Towers Crescent Drive, Vienna, VA 22182, (703) 902-8000, www.landmark.com.

[Larman 2000] C. Larman, "Aggregate Entity Pattern," *Software Development*, vol. 8, no. 4, pp. 46-52, 2000.

[Larman and Guthrie 2000] C. Larman and R. Guthrie, *Java 2 Performance and Idiom Guide*, Upper Saddle River, NJ, Prentice Hall, 2000.

[Lea 1997] D. Lea, Concurrent Programming in Java: Design Principles and Patterns, Reading, MA, Addison-Wesley, 1997.

[Leveson 1995] N. G. Leveson, *Safeware: System Safety and Computers*, Reading, MA, Addison-Wesley, 1995.

[Little 1961] J. D. C. Little, "A Proof of the Queueing Formula L = λW," *Operations Research*, vol. 9, 1961.

[Liu and Layland 1973] C. L. Liu and J. W. Layland, "Scheduling Algorithms for Multi-Programming in a Hard Real-Time Environment," *Journal of the Association for Computing Machinery*, vol. 20, no. 1, pp. 40-61, 1973.

[L&S] *L&S Computer Technology, Inc.*, *Performance Engineering Services Division*, #110, P. O. Box 9802, Austin, TX 78766, (505) 988-3811, www.perfeng.com.

[Manhardt 1998] D. Manhardt, "Applications Optimization Methodology—An Approach," *Proceedings, First International Workshop on Software and Performance*, Santa Fe, NM, pp. 93-100, October 1998.

[Menascé et al. 1994] D. A. Menascé, V. A. F. Almeida, and L. W. Dowdy, *Capacity Planning and Performance Modeling*, Englewood Cliffs, NJ, PTR Prentice Hall, 1994.

[Menascé et al. 1998] D. A. Menascé and V. A. F. Almeida, *Capacity Planning for Web Performance: Metrics, Models and Methods,* Englewood Cliffs, NJ, Prentice Hall, 1998.

[Menascé et al. 2000] D. A. Menascé and V. A. F. Almeida, *Scaling for E-Business: Technologies, Models, Performance, and Capacity Planning*, Englewood Cliffs, NJ, Prentice Hall, 2000.

[MERR] *Merrill Consultants*, 10717 Cromwell Drive, Dallas, TX 75229, (214) 351-1966, www.mxg.com.

[Mesquite] *Mesquite Software, Inc.*, 8920 Business Park Drive, Austin, TX 78759, (512) 338-9153, www.mesquite.com.

[Metron] *Metron Technology Limited*, Osbourne House, Trull Road, Taunton, Somerset, TA1 4PX United Kingdom, +44-1823-259-231, www.metron.co.uk.

[MICR] *Microsoft Corporation*, One Microsoft Way, Redmond, WA 98052-6399, (425) 882-8080, www.microsoft.com.

[Neuse and Browne 1983] D. M. Neuse and J. C. Browne, "Graphical Tools for Software System Performance Engineering," *Proceedings, Computer Measurement Group Conference XIV*, Washington, DC, pp. 353-355, December 1983.

[NUME] *NuMega Technologies*, 9 Townsend West, Nashua, NH 03063, (603) 578-8400, www.numega.com.

[Opdahl and Sølvberg 1992] A. Opdahl and A. Sølvberg, "Conceptual Integration of Information System and Performance Modeling," *Proceedings Working Conference on Information System Concepts: Improving the Understanding*, 1992.

[Pedersen and Klein 1988] J. S. Pedersen and M. H. Klein, "Using the Vienna Development Method (VDM) to Formalize a Communication Protocol," *Technical Report No. CMU/SEI-88-TR-26*, Software Engineering Institute, Carnegie-Mellon University, Pittsburgh, PA, November 1988.

[Peterson 1975] J. L. Peterson, "A Programming Methodology," Unpublished Technical Report, University of Texas, Austin, TX, 1975.

[RAT] *Rational Software Corporation*, 18880 Homestead Road, Cupertino, CA 95014, (408) 863-9900, www.rational.com.

[Riel 1996] A. J. Riel, *Object-Oriented Design Heuristics*, Reading, MA, Addison-Wesley, 1996.

[Royce 1970] W. W. Royce, "Managing the Development of Large Software Systems," *Proceedings, WESCON*, 1970.

[Rumbaugh et al. 1999] J. Rumbaugh, I. Jacobson, and G. Booch, *The Unified Modeling Language Reference Manual*, Reading, MA, Addison-Wesley, 1999.

[SAS] *SAS Institute, Inc.*, SAS Campus Drive, Cary, NC 27513, (919) 677-8000, www.sas.com.

[Schmidt and Harrison 1996] D. C. Schmidt and T. Harrison, "Double-Checked Locking: An Optimization Pattern for Efficiently Initializing and Accessing Thread-safe Objects," *Proceedings, Third Annual Pattern Languages of Programming Conference*, Allerton Park, Illinois, September 1996.

[Schneider and Winters 1998] G. Schneider and J. P. Winters, *Applying Use Cases: A Practical Guide*, Reading, MA, Addison-Wesley, 1998.

[Schwartz 1988] M. Schwartz, *Telecommunications Networks: Protocols, Modeling, and Analysis*, Reading, MA, Addison-Wesley, 1988.

[Schwetman 1990] H. Schwetman, "Introduction to Process-Oriented Simulation and CSIM," *Proceedings, Winter Simulation Conference*, December 1990.

[Sedgewick and Flajolet 1996] R. Sedgewick and P. Flajolet, *An Introduction to the Analysis of Algorithms*, Reading, MA, Addison-Wesley, 1996.

[SGI] *Silicon Graphics, Inc.*, 1600 Amphitheatre Parkway, Mountain View, CA 94043, (650) 960-1980, www.sgi.com.

[Sharble and Cohen 1993] R. C. Sharble and S. S. Cohen, "The Object-Oriented Brewery: A Comparison of Two Object-Oriented Development Methods," *Software Engineering Notes*, vol. 18, no. 2, pp. 60-73, 1993.

[Shaw and Garlan 1996] M. Shaw and D. Garlan, *Software Architecture: Perspectives on an Emerging Discipline*, Upper Saddle River, NJ, Prentice Hall, 1996.

[Shirazi 2000] J. Shirazi, *Java Performance Tuning*, Sebastopol, CA, O'Reilly, 2000.

[SIGMETRICS] ACM-SIGMETRICS, "Proceedings Sigmetrics Conference on Measurement and Evaluation of Computer Systems," ACM Press, 1974 +.

[SIGSIM] ACM-SIGSIM, "Proceedings Winter and Summer Simulation Conferences," ACM Press, 1970 +.

[SITR] *Sitraka Software*, 260 King Street East, Toronto, Ontario, Canada M5A 4L5, (800) 663-4723, www.sitraka.com.

[Smith 1990] C. U. Smith, *Performance Engineering of Software Systems*, Reading, MA, Addison-Wesley, 1990.

[Smith and Williams 1997] C. U. Smith and L. G. Williams, "Performance Engineering of Object-Oriented Systems with SPE•ED," *Lecture Notes in Computer Science 1245: Computer Performance Evaluation*, R. Marie et al., ed., Berlin, Germany, Springer, pp. 135-154, 1997.

[Smith and Williams 1998] C. U. Smith and L. G. Williams, "Performance Engineering Evaluation of CORBA-Based Distributed Systems with SPE•ED," in *Lecture Notes in Computer Science*, R. Puigjaner, ed., Berlin, Germany, Springer, 1998.

[SPEC] *Standard Performance Evaluation Corporation*, 6585 Merchant Place, Suite 100, Warrenton, VA 20187, (540) 349-7878, www.spec.org.

[Spivey 1988] J. M. Spivey, *Understanding Z: A Specification Language and Its Formal Semantics*, Cambridge, MA, Cambridge University Press, 1988.

[SPSS] *SPSS Inc.*, 233 S. Wacker Drive, 11th Floor, Chicago, IL 60606, www.spss.com.

[SUN] *Sun Microsystems, Inc.*, 901 San Antonio Road, Palo Alto, CA 94303, www.sun.com.

[TIVO] *Tivoli Systems*, 9442 Capitol of Texas Highway N, Austin, TX 78759, (512) 436-8000, www.tivoli.com.

[TOG 1998] Open Group Technical Standard, C807, No. ISBN 1-85912-211-6, July, 1998.

[Trott 1999] B. Trott, "Victoria's Secret for Webcasts Is IP Multicasting," *InfoWorld*, August 16, 1999.

[Turner et al. 1992] M. Turner, D. Neuse, and R. Goldgar, "Simulating Optimizes Move to Client/Server Applications," *Proceedings, Computer Measurement Group Conference*, Reno, NV, pp. 805-814, December 1992.

[Waldo et al. 1994] J. Waldo, G. Wyant, A. Wollrath, and S. Kendall, "A Note on Distributed Computing," *Technical Report No. SMLI TR-94-29*, Sun Microsystems Laboratories, Inc., Mountain View, CA, November 1994.

[Weiss 1999] M. A. Weiss, *Data Structures and Algorithm Analysis in Java*, Reading, MA, Addison-Wesley, 1999.

[Weiss 2001] M. A. Weiss, *Data Structures and Algorithm Analysis in C++*, Boston, MA, Addison-Wesley, 2001.

[WHAM] *WHAM Engineering and Software, Inc.*, 9390 Research Blvd., Kaleido II, Suite 400, Austin, TX 78759, (512) 345-9925, www.wham.com.

[Wheeler et al. 1998] T. Wheeler, E. D. Jensen, A. Kanevsky, J. Maurer, P. Wallace, D. Wells, R. Clark, Y. Zhang, T. Lawrence, and P. Hurley, "Application of QoS-Driven Adaptive Computing," IEEE Real-Time Systems Symposium, Madrid, Spain, December, 1998.

[Williams and Smith 1995] L. G. Williams and C. U. Smith, "Information Requirements for Software Performance Engineering," *Quantitative Evaluation of Computing and Communication Systems, Lecture Notes in Computer Science*, vol. 977, H. Beilner and F. Bause, ed., Heidelberg, Germany, Springer-Verlag, pp. 86-101, 1995.

[Wilson and Kesselman 2000] S. Wilson and J. Kesselman, *Java Platform Performance*, Boston, MA, Addison-Wesley, 2000.

Index

Symbols

λ, system arrival rate, 143
N, queue length, 144–145
RT, residence time, 144–145
S, mean service time, 143, 145
U, utilization, 143, 145
V, number of visits, 143
X, throughput, 143, 145

Numerics

80-20 rule, 171, 245, 311, 314–316, 411

A

Action, 88
Activation, 54, 170
Active class, 62
Active object, 62
ActiveX Control, 344
Activity diagram, 52, 58, 73, 89
Actor, 50
Adapter pattern, 344
   Circuitous Treasure Hunt and, 301
Adapt-to-precision strategy, 19–20
Adopting and using SPE, 444–455
   advice, 446–447
   advocate, need for, 445, 453
   commitment, 453
   commitment, obtaining, 445–446
   credibility, 445, 459
   credibility, building, 447, 454
   economic justification, 448–449
   experience, 444–448
   funding, 457–458

   justification, 448
   key considerations, 448
   organizational issues, 444–446, 451,
      455–457
   pilot projects and, 451–452
   risks, 458–459
   savings, 448
   skeptics, 445
   success factors, 440, 452–455, 459–
      461
   success, credibility and, 445, 447, 459
   teamwork, 446, 454
   training, 446
Advanced system model, 151–152, 346,
   421
Alexander, C., 262
Alexander, R., 315
Algorithm and data structure choices,
   322–323
Algorithm, random selection, 278
Almeida, V. A. F., 371
alt, 56, 65, 470
Alternate Routes pattern, 276–279
   benefits, 278–279
   consequences, 279
   database, 276–277
   One-Lane Bridge and, 305
   problem, 276–277
   solution, 277–278
Alternation See alt
Analytic solution
   See System execution model

Antipattern, 287–288
Antipattern, performance
    See Performance antipattern
Aperiodic event, 376
Approximate solution technique, 152
Architecture, 40–43
    alternatives, 346
    antipatterns and, 288
    multiprocessing, 318–319
    multi-tier, 106
    performance and, 9, 11, 17
    performance improvements and, 309,
        311
    pipe-and-filter, 400
    software, 344, 367–368
    SPE and, 47, 111, 435
    SPE models and, 72, 115, 121
    system, 368–369
    technical, 344, 367
    tuning and, 449
Architecture evaluation, 89–102, 343–
        345, 366–371
ARM (Application Resource
        Measurement), 233–236
    API, 234–236
    purpose, 233
    system development kit (SDK), 234
    use of, 236
ARM Working Group, 234
Arrival rate
    distribution, 139
    specifying, 139, 171
    specifying units, 149
    workload and, 147
ASP (Active Server Pages), 344
Assembly language, efficiency and, 397
Asynchronous callback, 66, 118, 160,
        471
Asynchronous communication, 65, 117
ATM (automated teller machine)
    case study, 32–39
    Fast Path, 246–247, 264, 266–267
    measurement, 227
    measuring resource requirements, 208

performance failure, 8
use case diagram, 50
Auer, K., 10
Average value, 152, 380

B
Basic node, 73, 77, 476
Batch job, 255
Batching pattern, 272–276
    average versus transient behavior, 420
    Batching rule and, 325
    benefits, 275
    consequences, 275–276
    database, 273
    flow balancing and, 401
    problem, 272–274
    receiver-side Batching, 274
    sender-side Batching, 274
    solution, 274–275
    versus individual items, 273
Batching rule, 325
Beck, K., 10
Benchmark
    See Performance benchmark,
        Measurements for SPE
Bensley, G., 315
Bentley, J., 323–326
Best- and worst-case
    analysis, 41, 384
    estimate, 30, 102, 197
    importance, 460
    model strategy, 164
    response time, 72
    results, 39
    strategy, 19
    Unified Process and, 436
Blob
    See god Class antipattern
Booch, G., 265, 407, 433, 467
Bottleneck, 5, 151, 165, 314, 414
Brown, W. J., 288
Bulka, D., 327, 332
Busy wait, 398–400

C

C++
  collections, 322
  constraint specification, 49, 473
  inlining, 331–332
  multithreading, 332
  object creation, 329
  sharing strategy, 320
C++ solutions, 331–332
Caching rule, 324–325
Call processing example, 8, 294–296
  Excessive Dynamic Allocation
    antipattern, 294
Capacity management, 423–424
Capacity planning, 20, 109, 429
  modeling and, 424
  SPE and, 451
  tools, 440
CASE (Computer-Aided Software
    Engineering), 179
  integration with SPE tools, 442–444
Case node, 75, 77, 476
Centering Principle, 245–247
  application, 246–247
  Caching rule and, 325
  definition, 245–246
  example, Web application, 362
  Fast Path speed-up and, 316
  patterns and, 263, 266, 269, 272, 283
  performance antipatterns and, 306
  summary, 259
  using, 257, 447
CGI (Common Gateway Interface), 344,
    354
Circuitous Treasure Hunt antipattern,
    250, 296–301
  Adapter pattern and, 301
  ICAD case study and, 297
  performance gain from refactoring,
    299
  problem, 297–299
  refactoring, potential disadvantages,
    300
  solution, 299–301
Class diagram, 30

Clements, P. C., 9–10, 115
Client/server application, 341
Clock, operating system, 219–220
CMG (Computer Measurement Group),
    222, 424, 447
Cohen, S. S., 291–292
Collaboration, 265
Collaboration diagram, 50, 52
Collections, 322–323
COM (Component Object Model), 110
COM+, 111
Common mistakes
  See Performance antipatterns
Communication, 115, 271
Communication overhead, 254
Communication protocol, 319–320
Compiler optimization, profile-based,
    317
Component, stereotype, 91
Computer device usage, 85
Computer resource requirement, 176–
    178
  database, 221
  example, 87, 126
  example, Web application, 358
  explanation, 176–178
  measurement, 226
  obtaining, 201
  overview, 30
  specification, 37–39, 86
  types, 176
  use of, 415–416
  walkthrough information, 192
Concurrency, 62–67, 254
Condition clause, 57
Conditional path probability, 76
Configuration management plan
  specification, 427
Constraint, 472–473
  hardware utilization, 173
  resource usage, 173, 413
  SPE and, 43
  UML, 49–50
Constructor overhead, 97–98

Contention, resource
  definition, 134
  Parallel Processing Principle and, 254
  reducing, 253, 256
  sources, 135
  Spread-the-Load Principle and, 256
  system execution model and, 150–151
Context switch, overhead, 319
CORBA (Common Object Request
    Broker Architecture), 16, 66, 110,
    120, 301, 320, 342, 420
Coregion, 63–64, 470
COTS (commercial off-the-shelf
    software), 8, 109, 344, 447
Coupling pattern, 269–272
  benefits, 272
  consequences, 272
  distributed systems, 270
  legacy application and, 344
  multi-tier architecture, 270
  problem, 270–271
  solution, 271–272
  Web applications, 270
CPU (central processing unit)
  instructions, estimating, 175, 421
  software resource, 175
  time, 84, 421
  usage, estimating, 175
Critical component
  model sensitivity and, 103, 460
  performance principles and, 257
  verification and validation and, 32,
    418, 460
Critical resource
  model sensitivity to, 103, 460
Critical use case
  Centering Principle and, 246
  definition, 51
  identifying, 29, 411
Cyclic function, 282

D
Data gathering
  See also Measurements for SPE
  approximations, 178
  estimates, 178
  issues, 178–179
  strategy, 178
  technique, 222–224
  tips for success, 193–195
Data Structure Augmentation rule, 325
Database
  example
    Alternate Routes pattern, 276
    Batching pattern, 273
    Coupling pattern, 270
    One Lane Bridge antipattern, 302–
      303
  measurements, 221, 224–225
  scenario, example, 129
DCOM (Distributed Component
    Object Model), 301
Deferred synchronous communication,
    66, 117, 160, 471
Delay
  See also Contention, resource
  estimating, 348–349
  example, 127
  network, 347
  software resource, 175
  specification, 38
  synchronization estimate, 122
  system interactions and, 348
Delay node, 145
  See also QNM
Demand, 39, 142, 148
Deployment diagram, 30, 48, 63, 471
Design, 40–43
  alternatives, 97
  antipatterns and, 288
  object location, 114
  performance and, 9, 17
  performance improvements and, 311
  SPE and, 47, 111
  SPE models and, 72, 115, 121
Design model, 118
Design pattern See Pattern
Device service time
  See Service time
Device, computer, 38, 148, 178

Dimpsey, R., 334
Distributed system, 105–132, 301
  case study, 153–164
  early versus late models, 420
  example, Coupling pattern, 270
  Instrumentation Principle and, 245
  performance success, 13
  SPE and, 16
Dominant workload function, 245, 460
DOT (Distributed Object Technology),
    109–114
  effective use, 114
  limitations, 111–114
  middleware, 120
Double-Checked Locking pattern, 321
Douglass, B. P., 374
DrawMod
  See also ICAD case study
  Circuitous Treasure Hunt antipattern,
    297–301
  execution graph, 92
  measurement example, 212–214
  processing overhead, 94
  scenario, refactored, 300
  sequence diagram, 92, 298
  software resource requirements, 93–94
Driver *See* Performance driver

E
e-commerce application, 123–130
Efficiency versus performance objectives,
    397–398
EJB (Enterprise JavaBeans), 16, 271,
    320, 344
Elapsed time, 84
Embedded real-time system, 373–403
  assembly language and, 397
  database, 379
  distributed, 379
  efficiency, 397–398
  example, First Things First pattern,
    267
  hardware constraints, 378
  overview, 374–375
  performance issues, 379–384

performance objective, 413
performance scenarios, 412
response time, 380–381
schedulability, 381–384
SPE models, 384–385
throughput, 380–381
timing requirements, 375–377
typical performance problems, 396–
    402
  flow balancing, 400–402
  obsessive optimization, 397–398
  over parallelism, 398
  polling, 398–400
Embedded system
  See also Embedded real-time system
  definition, 374
  performance problems, 313
Event, 376
Excessive Dynamic Allocation
    antipattern, 293–296
  call objects, 395
  cost, 295
  example, 294
  Flyweight pattern and, 296
  ICAD case study and, 296
  multithreading and, 336
  problem, 293–295
  Processing Versus Frequency Principle
    and, 296
  recycling objects, 296
  sharing objects, 296
  solution, 295–296
  solutions, language-independent and,
    327
Executable component, 63
Execution environment, 30, 174, 190,
    415, 428
Execution graph, 30, 72–83
  additional types of nodes, 77
  basic node, 73, 77, 476
  case node, 75, 77, 476
  choice, 35
  communication node, 119, 477
  computed time, 80
  expanded node, 74, 77, 476

Execution graph, *continued*
    expansion, 35
    flowchart and, 79
    initial node, 78
    measurement data for, 228
    notation, 77, 119
    notation summary, 475–477
    parallel execution, 76
    pardo node, 76–77, 476
    reduction algorithm, 80–82
    repetition node, 35, 75, 77, 476
    restriction, 77–79
    sequence diagram, deriving from, 35,
        88–89
    solution algorithm, 80–83
    split node, 76–77, 476
    subgraph, 35, 74
    synchronization node, 77, 119, 477
    tools for analysis, 73
Expanded node, 74, 77, 476

F
Facility, computer, 38, 85, 121
Failure *See* Performance failure
Fast Path pattern, 246, 263–267
    benefits, 266
    consequences, 266–267
    Fast Path speed-up and, 316
    inlining and, 332
    problem, 264
    schedulability and, 384
    solution, 264–266
    using, 447
Fast Path speed-up, 327, 330
First Things First pattern, 267–269
    benefits, 269
    consequences, 269
    problem, 267–268
    solution, 268–269
Fixing, 247
Fixing-Point Principle, 247–249
    applications, 248
    Caching rule and, 325
    Data Structure Augmentation and,
        325
    definition, 247–248
    example, Web application, 362
    patterns and, 266
    Store Precomputed Results rule and,
        324
    summary, 259
    using, 257
Fix-it-later strategy, 9–10, 15, 107, 418
Flex Time pattern, 279–281
    benefits, 281
    consequences, 281
    One-Lane Bridge and, 305
    problem, 279–280
    solution, 280–281
Flexibility, 247, 318
Flexibility versus performance, 247
Flow balancing, 400–402
Flyweight pattern, 96, 296
Focus of control *See* Activation

G
Gamma, E., 262–263, 319
Garbage collection
    memory leak and, 334
    overhead, 333–335
god Class, 250
god Class antipattern, 288–293
    behavioral versus data forms, 291
    example, 289–290
    excessive message traffic, 291
    performance gain from refactoring,
        293
    problem, 289–292
    refactoring, 290
    solution, 292–293
Graph reduction algorithm, 80–82
Gunther, N., 371
Guthrie, R., 315, 319, 333

H
Hardware configuration, 428
Hardware utilization constraint, 173
Hardware/software platform
    dependencies, 326
Harrison, T., 321

Heavy hitter, 171, 314
Helm, R., 262
Herzog, U., 371
Hesselgrave, M., 444–446
Holding time, 253
HotSpot dynamic compiler, 333–334, 336
HTTP Accept example, 317
HTTP request, 324
Humphrey, W. S., 408
Hybrid solution
    See System execution model

I
I/O device
    modeling strategy, 152
    specification, 176
I/O estimation techniques, 197
I/O, software resource, 175
ICAD case study, 89–102, 255
    architecture 1, 90–96
    architecture 2, 96–98
    architecture 3, 98–102
    DrawMod scenario
        See DrawMod
    example
        Circuitous Treasure Hunt
            antipattern, 297
        Excessive Dynamic Allocation
            antipattern, 296
    Flyweight pattern and, 96
    software resource requirements, 93
    use cases, 89
Implementation decisions, 310
Implementation solutions, 309–338
    See also Performance solutions
Independent principles, 242, 245–252
Information Processing Graph, 141
    notation summary, 478
    See also QNM
Inline expression, 56, 64, 470
Inlining, 330–331
    C++, 331–332
    Java, 333
    profile-based, 332

Instance decomposition, 55, 469
Instrumentation, 227–233
    data reporting, 233
    design considerations, 228, 230–231
    documenting, 429
    dynamic selection, 231
    example, 230
    granularity, 230
    implementation alternatives, 231–233
    implementation example, 232
    model updates and, 423
    selective recording, 231
    use of, 225, 227–229
Instrumenting Principle, 217, 227, 243–245
    applications, 244–245
    definition, 243–244
    example, Web application, 362
    patterns and, 267
    summary, 259
Interaction diagram, 50, 52
Interoperability of tools, 443–444
Interpreter rule, 326
Iteration *See* loop

J
J2EE (Java 2 Enterprise Edition), 110, 342
Jacobson, I., 10, 411, 433
Java
    collections, 322
    garbage collection, 333–335
    inlining, 331, 333
    language specification deficiency, 322
    measurement results and garbage collection, 334
    multithreading, 336
    notify, 321
    object creation, 329
    performance, 446
    serialization, 335
    sharing strategy, 320
    thread creation-destruction, 336
Java solutions, 333–337
JDK (Java Development Kit), 336

Jennings, T., 444, 447
JIT (Just-In-Time) compiler, 333
Jitter, 376
Job flow balance, 139
Job, definition, 136
Johnson, R., 262
JVM (Java Virtual Machine), 271

K

Kazman, R., 345
Kelvin, W. T., 244
Kernighan, B. W., 325
Kesselman, J., 334
Killelea, P., 109
Knuth, D., 315

L

LAN (local area network), modeling,
   348–349
Larman, C., 271, 315, 319, 333
Late life cycle activities, 43, 419–422
Lazy Evaluation rule, 325
Legacy systems, 39, 107, 109
Leveson, N., 374
Little, J. D. C., 140
Little's Formula, 140, 146
Local versus distributed objects, 112–
   114
Locality, 225–226, 249
Locality Principle, 249–251
   applications, 250–251
   Data Structure Augmentation and,
      325
   definition, 249–250
   example, Web application, 362
   patterns and, 266, 272
   performance antipatterns and, 293
   summary, 259
   using, 257
Location, specification, 63
loop, 56–57, 65, 470
Loop, repetitions, 226
Looping *See* loop

M

Maintainability, tuning and, 311
Mayhew, D., 327, 332
Measurement tools
   event recorders, 216–217, 224
   load drivers, 209, 214, 221
   monitors, 215–216
   profilers, 203, 314–315
   program monitors, 222–223
   system monitors, 222
   use of, 447
   value of, 453–454
Measurements for SPE, 203–238
   See also Instrumentation,
      Instrumenting Principle,
      Measurement tools
   average versus peak loads, 220
   benchmark, 210
   capture ratio, 219
   clock, operating system, 219
   computer resource requirement, 226
   computer resource usage, 208–225,
      227
   coordinating tools, 211
   cost effectiveness, 214
   data analysis, 218
   data characteristics, 205, 207, 226
   data collection technique, 222–224
   database SELECT, 221
   deriving specifications, 34
   designing and conducting, 210–214
   dynamic selection, 231
   events, 215–217, 219, 230–231
   example, 212–214, 230
   granularity, 217, 225, 230
   instrumentation, 227–233
   internal versus external, 217
   Java, garbage collection and, 334
   locality, 225–226
   measurement environment, 209
   middleware overhead, 121
   model precision and, 421
   model updates, 423
   overhead, 211, 218–219
   path characteristics, 205, 207, 226

performance models and, 460
performance test, 430–431
perturbation, 218–219
problems, 211
processing overhead, 205, 207–208, 226
purpose, 204
repetition count, 226
reports, 218, 233
representative, 208, 220
reproducible, 208, 220–221
resource usage, 206
scenario response time, 205
scenario throughput, 205
software resource usage, 205, 207–208, 226
start-up conditions, 221
states, 215–216, 219
static versus dynamic, 214
synthetic programs, 209
system overhead, 219
test plan, 208, 211–212, 214, 312–313
time period, 220
timing, 219
tool identification, 211
traces, 315
tuning, 312–313
types of data, 205
typical behavior, 221
use of, 195–196, 206, 214, 218–221, 446
verification and validation, 32, 39, 214, 418
what to measure, 204–208
workload data, 205, 207, 225–226
workload generation, 221
workload planning, 208–209
Memory allocator cost, 328
Memory leak, 333
Memory leak, garbage collection and, 334
Menascé, D. A., 371
Message, 170
  asynchronous, 53, 65, 471

interleaving, 64
notation, 53
parallel composition, 64–65
representing in sequence diagrams, 52
specification, 38, 86, 175
synchronous, 53, 65, 471
time-ordering, 52
unordered, 63
Method invocation, 330–331
Middleware, 110–111, 120–121, 175, 320, 342
Model omission, 32, 39, 418, 460
Modeling hints, 102–103, 130–131, 165
  abstraction, 102
  average versus peak performance, 165
  best- and worst-case estimate, 102
  bottlenecks, 165
  early synchronization models, 130
  multiple users and workloads, 165
  performance scenarios, 130
  sensitivity and scalability analysis, 102, 165
  synchronous versus asynchronous, 131
Modeling strategy
  adapt-to-precision, 19–20
  best- and worst-case, 19, 83, 164
  simple-model, 18–19, 83, 134, 152, 164, 413
Modeling tools, 440–442
  use of, 447
  value of, 453
MQSeries, 342
MSC (message sequence chart), 55, 412, 469
Multithreading
  C++, 332
  Java, 336
Multithreading strategy, 163
Multi-tier architecture, 106
  example, Coupling pattern, 270

N
Nachtfliegen Airlines Web site, 183
Nachtfliegen.com, 349–366
  computer resource requirements, 192

Nachtfliegen.com, *continued*
   execution environment, 190
   hardware/software environment, 356–358
   measurement, 230
   overview, 184–185
   performance drivers, 188
   performance improvements, 362–365
   performance objective, 190, 350
   performance principles and, 362
   plan itinerary scenario, 350–355
   processing overhead, 356–358
   refactored solution, 363
   requirements, 186–188
   resource requirements, 358–360
   scenarios, 188
   sensitivity and scalability analysis, 366
   sequence diagram, 189
   software execution model, 356–361
   software execution model solution, 360–361
   software resource requirements, 191, 357–360
   system execution model, 363–366
   system execution model results, 365
   use cases, 186
   workload intensity, 190, 351
NASA (National Aeronautics and Space Administration), 6
Network
   messages, estimating, 200
   modeling strategy, 152
   specification, 38, 86, 174
Network of queues, 141–146
   See also QNM
New software, effect on performance, 151
No contention solution, 39, 133, 414
Notification versus polling, 399
Number of users
   See Users, number of
Number of visits
   See Visits, number of

O
Object
   concurrency, 113–114
   creation and destruction, 55, 327–330
   hidden creation, 329
   inline, 330–331
   latency, 112
   lifeline, 52, 55
   local versus distributed, 112–114
   location, 114
   memory allocator cost, 328
   partial failure, 113
   pointer versus object reference, 113
   recycling, 296
   sharing, 296
   String, elimination of temporary String, 329
   temporary, elimination, 329
Object Adaptor, 120
Object Constraint Language, 49, 377, 473
Object-oriented systems
   SPE for, 21–24
   special problems, 21
ObjectSpace Voyager, 320
One-Lane Bridge antipattern, 276, 280, 301–304
   Alternate Routes and, 305
   example, 302
   Flex Time and, 305
   performance improvement from refactoring, 303–304
   problem, 301–302
   Shared Resources Principle and, 304
   solution, 302–304
   Traffic Jam and, 304–305
opt, 56, 65, 470
Optimization, excessive, 397
Optimization, premature, 397–398
ORB (Object Request Broker), 120–121
Overhead
   communication, 254
   communication, patterns and, 272
   constructor, 97–98
   context switch, 319

garbage collection, 333–335
Java serialization, 335
locking, 321
method invocation, 330–331
middleware, 121
object creation and destruction, 328
resource contention, 254
system, 219
Overhead matrix
example, 38, 94, 126–127, 156, 416
example, call processing, 392–393
example, Web application, 356–358
explanation, 85, 176–178
use of, 415

P

Packing rule, 326
par, 65, 470
Parallel composition, 64–65, 354
Parallel Processing Principle, 254–255
applications, 255
definition, 254–255
embedded real-time systems and, 398
summary, 259
Pardo node, 76–77, 476
Passive resources, 152
Pattern, 42, 261–263
Adapter, 301, 344
Double-Checked Locking, 321
Flyweight, 96, 296
performance patterns and, 263
Proxy, 262–263, 265
Proxy, Caching rule and, 324
Proxy, Fast Path and, 265
Singleton, locking and, 322
Pattern, performance
See Performance pattern
Performance, 3–6
architecture and, 9, 11
concerns, 108
constraint, 29, 412
definition, 4
flexibility and, 247
global, 257
importance, 6–14

improvement
See Performance solutions
intuition, 16
myth, 10–12
portability and, 250
problems, 313
reality, 10–12
Performance antipattern, 287–308
Centering Principle and, 306
Circuitous Treasure Hunt, 296–301
Excessive Dynamic Allocation, 293–296
god Class, 288–293
One-Lane Bridge, 301–304
overview, 42–43
performance pattern and, 287
performance principles violated, summary, 306–307
role in SPE process, 42
summary, 306–307
Traffic Jam, 304–306
tuning and, 316
using, 417
Performance benchmark, 121, 210
Performance budget, 380
Performance control principles, 242–245
Performance driver, 181, 188, 424, 428
Performance engineer
characteristics, 450–451
manager, 444, 446, 449
modeling skills and, 451
qualifications, 446
responsibilities, 449
Performance failure, 6–12
accounting system, 7
ATM, 8
call processing, 8
causes, 9
consequences, 9
COTS, 8
distributed order management, 7
electronic trading, 8
NASA, 6
risk, 16, 458
Victoria's Secret, 7

Performance failure, *continued*
  Web applications, 107
Performance management, 12, 14–18
  See also SPE artifacts, SPE process
  effort, 11
  manager, performance, 444, 446, 449
  performance V&V plan, 427
  plans, 425
  post-deployment, 423–424
  proactive, 15–16
  reactive, 14–15
  responsibility, 449
Performance metrics, 136, 138–139
Performance model
  See also Software execution model,
    System execution model, Software
    resource requirement, Computer
    resource requirement
  assumptions, 460
  baseline, 422, 427
  calibration, 419
  confidence in, 459
  configuration management, 427
  constructing, 35, 413–415
  contention, 414
  credibility, 454, 459
  data gathering, 170–183, 446
  data gathering tips, 193–201
  details added, 420–421
  distributed system interaction, 115–
    123
  early versus late, 420
  embedded real-time system, 384–385
  evaluation, 31, 39, 416–417
  evolution, 422
  identification of problems, 42
  measurement and, 446, 460
  omission, 32, 39, 418, 460
  overview, 20
  precision, 39, 421
  purpose, 30
  resource estimation techniques, 195–
    201
  reuse, 423
  SPE artifact, 429

  timing details, 420
  use of, 114, 343–345
  verification and validation, 204, 418–
    419
  Web application, 345–349
Performance objective, 172–174
  accountability, 459
  benefits, 172
  efficiency and, 397
  essential characteristics, 173
  example, 35, 190, 380
  example, call processing, 392
  example, Web application, 350
  importance, 41, 397, 459
  information systems, 173
  meeting, 41, 43
  obtaining, 174, 447
  principles and, 42, 257
  real-time systems, 173
  response time, 173
  revising, 31, 417
  SPE artifact, 428
  specification, 29, 50, 62, 172–173,
    412–413, 428
  throughput, 173
  well-defined, 243
  workload intensity, 413
Performance Objectives Principle, 242–
  243
  applications, 243
  definition, 242–243
  example, Web application, 362
  summary, 259
Performance pattern, 262–285
  See also individual patterns
  Alternate Routes, 276–279
  Batching, 272–276
  Coupling, 269–272
  design patterns and, 263
  Fast Path, 263–267
  First Things First, 267–269
  Flex Time, 279–281
  overview, 42
  role in SPE process, 41
  Slender Cyclic Functions, 282–284

summary, 284
using, 417
Performance principle, 242–260
See also individual principles
Centering Principle, 245–247
effective use, 248
Fixing-Point Principle, 247–249
Independent principles, 245–252
Instrumenting Principle, 243–245
Locality Principle, 249–251
overview, 42
Parallel Processing Principle, 254–255
Performance control principles, 242–245
Processing Versus Frequency Principle, 251–252
purpose, 241
quantifying improvement, 259
role in SPE process, 41
Shared Resources Principle, 253–254
Spread-the-Load Principle, 256–257
summary, 259
synergistic principles, 252–257
time for space trade-offs and, 326
tuning and, 316
using, 257–258, 417
Performance risk, 410, 447
assessment, 29, 33, 410
controlling, 11, 43, 384, 433, 458
definition, 410
examples, 410
SPE omission, 459
Unified Process and, 41, 436
Web applications, 107
Performance scenario, 33, 39, 170–171, 345, 412
baseline, 427
definition, 50
distributed system, 121
documenting, 428
end-to-end, 345
execution graph and, 35, 73
importance of, 460
selecting, 412
use case and, 29, 33

verification and validation, 39
Web application, 121
Performance solutions, 41–44, 326–338
algorithm and data structure choices, 322–323
alternatives, 31, 417, 461
Batching rule, 325
C++, 331–332
Caching rule, 324–325
capacity requirements, controlling, 424
collections, 322–323
communication protocol, 319–320
cost-effective, 417
Data Structure Augmentation rule, 325
dynamic allocation, 320
example, 157–158
example, Web application, 362–365
Fast Path speed-up, 316–318, 327, 330
feasible, 417
flexibility and, 318
garbage collection overhead reduction, 333–335
general, 316–327
hardware/software platform, 326, 461
HTTP Accept example, 317
inline called method, 330–331
inline, C++, 331–332
inline, Java, 333
Java, 333–337
Java synchronization, 336
Java thread creation-destruction, 336
language-independent solutions, 327–331
late life cycle, 42
Lazy Evaluation rule, 325
locking strategy, 321–322
method invocation overhead, 330–331
middleware, 320
multiprocessing architecture, 318–319
multithreading C++, 332
multithreading, Java, 336

Performance solutions, *continued*
object creation and destruction, 327–330
object creation, hidden, 329
Packing rule, 326
profile-based inlining, 332
quantitative data, 151
resource pools and, 320
reusability and, 318
scalability, 318–322
serialization, Java, 335
sharing strategy, 320–321
sockets and, 319
space for time trade-off, 323–325
Store Precomputed Results rule, 323–324
temporary object creation-destruction, 329
thread contention, 320
time for space trade-off, 326
trade-offs, quantifying alternatives, 151, 242, 416, 461
tuning options, 315–316
Web applications, 366–371
Performance specialist, 23, 153, 241
Performance success, 12–14
airline reservation recovery, 13
airline reservation system, 12
data acquisition and reporting, 13
distributed data, 13
event update, 12
Web application, 12
Performance testing, 421–422
planning, 422, 430–431
reporting results, 431
specifying, 430
stress testing, 418
use of, 421
verification and validation and, 419
Performance tuning
See Tuning
Performance walkthrough, 179–195
example, 183–195
frequency, 183
iterating steps, 183

missing items, 187
participants, 180–181
purpose, 179, 181
roles, 180–181
tips for success, 193–195
topics, 180
using, 447
when to conduct, 182–183
Periodic event, 376
Periodic function, 282
Petlon, D., 444–447
Pilot project, 451–452
Pipe-and-filter architecture, 400
Plaugher, P. J., 325
Polling, 398–400
Polling versus notification, 399
Polymorphism, 323
Portability versus performance, 250
Principle
See Performance principle
Priority and First Things First, 268
Proactive performance management, 15–16
Probability, specification, 37, 58, 75–76, 207
Process, 62, 268, 318–320, 381
definition, 135
Process, software
antipatterns and, 288
effective, 407
iterative and incremental, 22
model, 431–432
purpose, 408
roles, 407
SPE in, 22–23, 40–41, 408, 431–436, 440, 453, 461
spiral model, 40, 432–433
Unified Process, 40, 433–436
waterfall, 40, 432
Processing overhead, 85, 156, 176, 226
Processing step, 39, 73, 346, 413
See also Software execution model
definition, 50
Processing Versus Frequency Principle, 251–252

applications, 251–252
Caching rule and, 325
definition, 251
example, Web application, 362
Lazy Evaluation and, 325
object creation-destruction and, 328
patterns and, 266, 272, 275, 281
performance antipatterns and, 296
summary, 259
using, 257
Product concept, modifying, 417
Profiler
    See Measurement tools, Tuning
Prototype, 39, 418, 446
Proxy pattern, 262–263
    Caching rule and, 324
    Fast Path and, 265
PTL (Portable Thread Library), 332

Q
QNM (queueing network model), 141–146
    closed, 145–146
    delay node, 145
    example, 149, 159
    example solution, 144–145
    open, 142–145
    open versus closed, 147
    sink node, 145
    solution, 143–145
    source node, 145
QoS (Quality of service), 345
Quality attributes, trade-offs, 345
Queue
    See also QNM
    definition, 135
    length, 137, 140
    model solution, 139–141
    queue length, 137, 140
    residence time, 136–137
    server, 135
    service time, 136
    throughput, 137
    utilization, 137
    wait time, 136

Queue scheduling discipline, 147, 152

R
Random selection algorithm, 278
Rate Monotonic Analysis, 381–384
    example, 383
    First Things First and, 269
    SPE and, 383–384
Rate Monotonic Scheduling, 153, 382–384
Reactive performance management, 14–15
Real-time operating system, 378–379
Real-time system
    See also Embedded real-time system
    definition, 375
    hard, 375
    soft, 375
Recycling objects, 296
Refactoring, 288, 316, 417
Reference, 56, 88, 470
Reliability specification, 51
Repetition, 56
    specification, 37, 58
Repetition factor, 75
Repetition node, 75, 77, 476
Requirements analysis, SPE models and, 414
Residence time, 136–137
Resource estimation techniques, 195–201
    best-worst case estimates, 197
    computer resource requirements, 201
    I/O requirements, 197
    network messages, 200
    study measurements, 196
    use a mentor, 196
    use measurements, 195
    what to estimate, 197
Resource pools, 320
Resource requirement
    See Computer resource requirement,
        Software resource requirement
Resource usage constraint, 173, 413

Response time
  average value, 380
  best- and worst-case, 72
  definition, 3
  embedded real-time system, 380–381
  end-to-end, 35, 39, 173, 380, 413
  mean, 72
  objective, 29, 412
  specification, 50
  Web application, 350
Responsiveness, 4–5, 310
  business tasks, 35
  definition, 4
  distributed systems, 106
  user-perceived, 343, 412
  Web applications, 107, 343
Reusability, 318
  tuning and, 311
Riel, A. J., 288, 293
Risk
  See also Performance risk
  definition, 410
  examples, 410
  impact, 410
  new technologies, 410
  SPE and, 435
  SPE models and, 433
Rolia, J. A., 371
Rumbaugh, J., 433, 467
RUP (Rational Unified Process), 433

S
Safety
  performance and, 374
  specification, 51
Safety-critical system, 425
Scalability, 5–6
  analysis, 151, 165, 366
  architecture and, 309
  communication protocol and, 319–320
  context switches and, 319
  Coupling and, 270
  definition, 5
  distributed systems, 106

  dynamic allocation and, 320
  improving, 318–322
  locking strategy, 321–322
  middleware and, 320
  monolithic architecture and, 318
  multiprocessing architecture, 318–319
  parallel architecture and, 318
  performance patterns and, 42
  resource pools and, 320
  risk, 41
  scalability curve, 5
  Shared Resources Principle and, 320–321
  sharing strategy, 320–321
  sockets and, 319
  spin locks and, 321
  Spread-the-Load Principle and, 320
  thread contention, 320
  Thundering Herd and, 321
  Web applications, 6, 106–107, 343
Scenario
  See also Performance scenario
  definition, 52
  end-to-end, 345
  example, 188
  link to SPE, 21
  optional portion, 56
  probability, 34
  selecting performance scenarios, 171, 460
  use of, 27
Schedulability, 153, 381–384
  definition, 381
Scheduling time, 253
Schmidt, D., 321
Security, specification, 51
SEI (Software Engineering Institute), 382
Sensitivity, 39, 151, 165, 366, 417, 421, 429, 460
Sensitivity study
  performing, 417
  SPE artifact, 429
Sequence diagram, 469
  alternation, 56, 470

augmented, 412
coregion, 63–64, 470
elaboration, 55
example, 34, 100, 124, 153, 189
example, call processing, 387, 390
example, Web application, 351–355
execution graph and, 35, 88–89
extension, 55–59, 63–66, 88, 469–471
hierarchical composition, 58
inline expression, 56, 64, 470
instance decomposition, 55, 469
iteration, 56, 470
looping, 56, 470
measurement studies and, 313
notation, 53, 55–58, 60–67
optional region, 56, 470
parallel composition, 64–65, 470
performance scenarios and, 412
reference, 56, 88, 470
scenario description, 50, 52
software model from, 88–89
specifying location, 63
synchronization, 65–67, 471
time in, 60
translation to software execution model, 30
use of, 380, 384
versus collaboration diagram, 52
Serialization, Java, 335
Server
    See also Queue, QNM
    definition, 135
    residence time, 136–137
    service time, 136
    throughput, 137
    utilization, 137
    wait time, 136
Service time, 38
    calculating, 148
    definition, 136
    determining, 139
    mean, 142
    QNM and, 139, 142
    specifying units, 149

Sharble, R. C., 291–292
Shared Resources Principle, 253–256
    applications, 253–254
    definition, 253
    One-Lane Bridge and, 304
    patterns and, 281, 283
    performance antipatterns and, 304
    scalability and, 320–321
    summary, 259
Sharing objects, 296
Simple-model strategy, 18–19, 71, 134, 152, 164, 346, 385, 394, 396, 413
Simulation solution, 152
Simulation tool, 150
Singleton pattern, locking and, 322
Sink node, 145
    See also QNM
Slender Cyclic Functions pattern, 282–284
    benefits, 283
    consequences, 284
    problem, 282–283
    solution, 283
Software architecture
    See Architecture, software
Software evolution, SPE and, 423
Software execution model, 71–104
    See also Performance model, System execution model
    activity diagram and, 83
    advanced solution techniques, 83
    analysis procedure, 83–88
    data, example, 356–360
    distributed system interaction, 115
    example, 124, 129, 155, 356–361
    example solution, 157–158
    example solution, call processing, 394
    example solution, Web application, 360–361
    example, embedded real-time systems, 390–394
    parameters, input, 72, 219
    processing step, 39
    purpose, 79
    sequence diagram and, 83

Software execution model, *continued*
  sequence diagram, deriving from, 88–89
  solution, 39
  solution algorithm, 80–83
  solution example, 95, 98, 100, 128
  solution, approximate, 121–123
  SPE process and, 413
  spreadsheets and, 80
  synchronization example, 160–162
  synchronization solution, 121–123
  tools, 80, 97
  use of, 67, 72, 79, 131, 133, 164, 414
  Web applications, 346
Software modeling tool, 441–442
Software process
  See Process, software
Software resource requirement, 174–176
  capacity planning and, 424
  computer device usage and, 85
  database, 225
  example, 36, 93–94, 126, 155, 191
  example, call processing, 393
  example, Web application, 357–360
  execution environment specifications, 428
  explanation, 174–176
  measurement, 207, 226
  overview, 30
  specification, 36, 38, 84, 175, 415
  SQL, 175
  types, 175, 415
  use of, 415
  value, 84
Solution algorithm
  execution graph, 80–83
  open QNM, 143–144
Solution methods, advanced system models, 152–153
Solutions
  See Performance solutions, 309
Source node, 145
  See also QNM
Space for time trade-off, 323–325
SPE (software performance engineering)

See also Performance management, SPE process
adoption and use
  See Adopting and using SPE
advocate, 445
audit activities, 430
benefits, 18, 448
communication, 446
cost, 22–23, 458
credibility, 445, 459
data requirements, 170–179
definition, 16
early versus late life cycle, 309
economic justification, 448–449, 454
effort, 29, 410, 447
failure to use, 459
future, 461–462
implementation decisions, 310
implementation solutions, 309–338
implementation strategies, 455–459
integration into software process, 22, 408, 431–436, 440, 453, 461
integration into Unified Process, 41
justification, 448
late life cycle activities, 419–422
limitations, 461–462
management commitment, 23, 445–446, 453
model-based approach, 10, 16–18, 413
modeling strategy, 18–20
organization, 23, 451, 455
overview, 16–24
performance balance, 17
post-deployment, 423–424
proactive approach, 15
process, 384
Rate Monotonic Scheduling, and, 153
reasons for non-use, 10–12
risks in applying, 458–459
safety-critical systems, 425
savings, 448
schedule, 453
skills, essential, 23, 446, 450–451
small projects, 425

software evolution, 423
software-oriented approach, 17
spiral model and, 433
success, 445, 447–448
sustaining efforts, 448
time, 453, 462
tool support, 146, 440–444, 453, 461
Unified Process and, 435–436
use of, 439–440
waterfall process and, 432
what you need, 23, 444, 448–455
workflow, 409
SPE artifacts
    See also SPE process
    adapting to your organization, 425
    audit, 430
    categories, 424
    configuration management plan, 427
    execution environment specifications,
        428
    model results, 429
    performance drivers, 428
    performance instrumentation, 429
    performance management plan, 425
    performance models, 422, 429
    performance objectives, 428
    performance scenarios, 428
    performance test plans, 430
    performance test results, 431
    performance V&V plan, 427
    performance V&V reports, 429–430
    summary, 425–426
    summary table, 426
    Unified Process and, 435
SPE process, 408–419
    See also SPE artifacts
    overview, 27–32
    quantitative techniques and, 408
    software evolution and, 423
    steps, 409–419
    workflow, 409
SPE•ED, 146–147, 150, 159, 162, 363,
    442
SPEC (Standard Performance Evaluation
    Corporation), 210

Spin locks, 321
Spiral model, 432–433
Split node, 76–77, 476
Spreadsheet, 80
Spread-the-Load Principle, 256–257
    applications, 256–257
    definition, 256
    patterns and, 278, 281
    scalability and, 320
    summary, 259
SQL
    See Software resource requirement,
        Database
Stakeholder, 31
Static analysis, 72, 414
Stereotype, 48, 58, 91, 472
Store Precomputed Results rule, 323–
    324
String object, 329
Subgraph, 74
Success
    See Performance success
Synchronization model
    advanced model results, 162
    example, 160–164
    solution example, 162
    strategy, 155, 162
Synchronization node, 77, 160–161
Synchronous communication, 65, 115–
    117, 127
Synergistic principles, 242, 252–257
System execution model, 134–166
    See also Performance model, Software
        execution model
    analytic solution, 152
    approximate solution technique, 152
    basics, 135
    example, 158
    example results, 365
    example solution, 159
    example solution, Web application,
        348
    example, Web application, 347
    hybrid solution, 152
    interpreting results, 163

System execution model, *continued*
  multiple scenarios, 150
  simulation solution, 152
  solution algorithm, 143–144
  solution methods, 152–153
  SPE process and, 31, 414
  tools, 135, 143, 440–441
  use of, 72, 132, 134, 414
  workload, 225–226
  workload intensity, 139, 207
System measurement tool limitations,
    244
System model parameter
  example calculation, 148–150
  from software model results, 146
System modeling tool, 146, 440–441
  limitations for early SPE studies, 440–
    441

T
Tagged value, 49, 65, 472
Task, 381
TCP/IP, 319–320
Technical architecture, 344, 367
Telephony switching case study, 385–
    396
  architecture and design, 388–396
  overview, 385–388
  performance improvement, 395–396
  performance objective, 392
  performance scenarios, 391
  processing overhead, 392–393
  software execution model, 390–394
  system execution model, 394–396
  workload intensity, 392
Think time, 147
Thread, 62, 268, 318–320, 332, 336,
    381
  definition, 135
Throughput, 137
  definition, 3
  embedded real-time system, 380–381
  objective, 29, 412
  specification, 50
Thundering Herd, 321, 399

Time
  See also Service time, Response time
  CPU, 84, 421
  elapsed, 84
  end-to-end, 173
  holding, 253
  in sequence diagrams, 60
  in the box, 35
  residence, 136–137
  scheduling, 253
  service, 136
  wait, 136
Time expression, 60, 377
Time versus space trade-offs, 323–326
Timeout, 61
Timing constraint, 60–61
Timing diagram, communication, 116–
    118
Timing mark, 60
Timing requirement, specification, 59
Tool interoperability, 443–444
Tools
  See Measurement tools, Modeling
      tools, Software modeling tools,
      System modeling tools
Traffic Jam antipattern, 276, 280, 304–
    306
  One-Lane Bridge and, 304–305
  problem, 305
  solution, 305–306
Tuning, 311–316
  definition, 311
  heavy hitters, 314
  hot spot, 314
  impact, 314
  improvement options
    See Performance solutions
  limitations, 311
  maintainability, and, 311
  measurement overhead, 315
  object location, 111
  performance antipatterns and, 316
  performance principles and, 316
  performance solutions, 315
  process, 44, 312–316

profiling, 314–315
reasons for, 310
refactoring and, 316
reusability, and, 311
steps, 312–316
steps, summary, 312
system versus software tuning, 314
traces, 315
versus SPE, 449

U

UDP (User Datagram Protocol), 320
UML (Unified Modeling Language),
    47–68
  collaboration, 265
  constraint, 49–50, 472–473
  extension, 55–59, 63–66, 469–471
  notation summary, 467–473
  Object Constraint Language, 49, 377,
      473
  performance objectives and, 428
  sequence diagram, 412
  stereotype, 48, 472
  tagged value, 49, 65, 472
  time expression, 60, 377
Unified Process, 433–436
  core workflows, 434
  iteration, 41, 433, 435
  iteration for performance, 436
  phases, 40, 434
  SPE in, 27, 40–41, 435–436
Usage patterns, principles and, 248
Use case
  annotations, 51
  critical, 29, 33, 246, 345, 411
  critical, definition, 51
  definition, 50
  designing from, 447
  example, 89, 186
  requirements definition, 21, 27
  scenarios, 313
  SPE and, 435
  system specifications and, 51
Use case diagram, 33, 50, 411, 468
Use case model, 411

Users, number of, 147, 171
Utilization, 137
  residence time and, 395

V

Value specification, 84
VDM (Vienna Development Method),
    428
Verification and validation, 31, 39, 204,
    418–419
  critical components and, 418, 460
  measurement and, 418
  model omission, 418, 460
  performance models, 418–419
  performance testing and, 419
  plan, 427
  reports, 429–430
  risk mitigation, 458
  SPE and, 31, 39
Victoria's Secret, 7
Visits, number of, 142, 148
Vlissides, R., 262

W

Wait time, 136
Walkthrough, 179
  See Performance walkthrough
wasteBucks.com case study, 153–164
  example, Batching pattern, 273–274
Waterfall process, 432
Web application, 105–132, 341–371
  e-commerce case study, 123–130
  example
    coregions, 64
    Coupling pattern, 270
    Fast Path pattern, 264–265
    success, 12
  execution environment, 174
  generic class diagram, 108
  implementation options, 344
  performance objectives, 412
  responsiveness, 107, 343
  scalability, 6, 107, 343
  software architecture, 344
  SPE techniques, 345

Web application, *continued*
  static versus dynamic content, 341–343
  system execution model, 347
  technical architecture, 344
  typical performance problems, 366–371
    back-end interactions, 370–371
    front-end interactions, 369–370
    software architecture, 367–368
    system architecture, 368–369
    technical architecture, 367
Web environment, overview, 341
Web-page bitmaps, 324
Wilson, S., 334
Wong, B., 444–446
Work unit, 84, 86, 156, 175, 356, 421
Workload, 27
  data, 225–226
  dominant, 264, 460

  mix, 413
  representative, 460
Workload intensity
  arrival rate, 171
  characterizing, 313
  definition, 139
  example, 190, 351
  example, call processing, 392
  forecasting, 423
  number of users, 146, 171
  peak, 313
  performance objective and, 29, 413
  specification, 33, 142, 147, 171, 413
  think time, 146
  verification and validation, 39
WOSP (Workshop on Software and Performance), 447

Z
Z, 49, 428, 473

Also Available from Addison-Wesley

Software Project Management
A Unified Framework
By Walker Royce
The Addison-Wesley Object Technology Series

This book presents a new management framework uniquely suited to the complexities of modern software development. Walker Royce's pragmatic perspective exposes the shortcomings of many well-accepted management priorities and equips software professionals with state-of-the-art knowledge derived from his twenty years of successful from-the-trenches management experience. In short, the book provides the software industry with field-proven benchmarks for making tactical decisions and strategic choices that will enhance an organization's probability of success.

0-201-30958-0 • Hardcover • 448 pages • ©1998

Building Web Applications with UML
By Jim Conallen
The Addison-Wesley Object Technology Series

Building Web Applications with UML is a guide to building robust, scalable, and feature-rich Web applications using proven object-oriented techniques. Written for the project manager, architect, analyst, designer, and programmer of Web applications, this book examines the unique aspects of modeling Web applications with the Web Application Extension (WAE) for the Unified Modeling Language (UML).

0-201-61577-0 • Paperback • 320 pages • ©2000

UML for Database Design
By Eric J. Naiburg and Robert A. Maksimchuk
The Addison-Wesley Object Technology Series

This pragmatic guide introduces you to the UML—the standard graphical notation for modeling business and software application needs—and leads you through the process of UML-based database modeling and design. It proves that when used as a common modeling language for system development, the UML can serve as a unifying framework that facilitates the integration of database models with the rest of a system design.

0-201-72163-5 • Paperback • 320 pages • ©2002

Doing Hard Time
Developing Real-Time Systems with UML, Objects, Frameworks, and Patterns
By Bruce Powel Douglass
The Addison-Wesley Object Technology Series

In this book, Bruce Douglass offers ideas that are up-to-date with the latest concepts and trends in programming to facilitate the daunting process of developing real-time systems. It presents an embedded systems programming methodology that has been proven successful in practice. The process outlined in this book allows application developers to apply practical techniques—garnered from the mainstream areas of object-oriented software development—to meet the demanding qualifications of real-time programming.

0-201-49837-5 • Hardback • 800 pages • ©1999